Data Communications
From Basics to Broadband

Fourth Edition

William J. Beyda
University of California Extension, Berkeley
Siemens Information and Communication Networks, Inc.

PEARSON
Prentice
Hall

Upper Saddle River, New Jersey 07458

Library of Congress Cataloging-in-Publication Data

Beyda, William J.
   Data communications : from basics to broadband / William J. Beyda. -- 4th ed.
      p. cm.
   Includes index.
   ISBN 0-13-145692-X
      1. Data transmission systems. I. Title

TK5105.B48 2004
004.6--dc22   2004044650

Vice President and Editorial Director, ECS: *Marcia J. Horton*
Senior Acquisitions Editor: *Kate Hargett*
Editorial Assistant: *Michael Giacobbe*
Vice President and Director of Production and Manufacturing, ESM: *David W. Riccardi*
Executive Managing Editor: *Vince O'Brien*
Managing Editor: *Camille Trentacoste*
Production Editor: *Lakshmi Balasubramanian*
Director of Creative Services: *Paul Belfanti*
Creative Director: *Carole Anson*
Art Director and Cover Manager: *Jayne Conte*
Managing Editor, AV Management and Production: *Patricia Burns*
Art Editor: *Gregory Dulles*
Manufacturing Manager: *Trudy Pisciotti*
Manufacturing Buyer: *Lisa McDowell*
Marketing Manager: *Pamela Shaffer*
Marketing Assistant: *Barrie Reinhold*

© 2005 Pearson Education, Inc.
Pearson Prentice Hall
Pearson Education, Inc.
Upper Saddle River, NJ 07458

The author and publisher of this book have used their best efforts in preparing this book. These efforts include the development, research, and testing of the theories and programs to determine their effectiveness. The author and publisher make no warranty of any kind, expressed or implied, with regard to these programs or the documentation contained in this book. The author and publisher shall not be liable in any event for incidental or consequential damages in connection with, or arising out of, the furnishing, performance, or use of these programs.

Printed in the United States of America

10 9 8 7 6 5 4 3 2 1

ISBN: 0-13-145692X

Pearson Education Ltd., *London*
Pearson Education Australia Pty. Ltd., *Sydney*
Pearson Education Singapore, Pte. Ltd.
Pearson Education North Asia Ltd., *Hong Kong*
Pearson Education Canada, Inc., *Toronto*
Pearson Educación de Mexico, S.A. de C.V.
Pearson Education—Japan, *Tokyo*
Pearson Education Malaysia, Pte. Ltd.
Pearson Education, Inc., *Upper Saddle River, New Jersey*

To Cathy, Joey, and Rachel

Contents

Preface

The prior editions of this book were more successful than I had originally hoped. The third edition of this book has been adopted at universities around the world. But this industry changes quickly, and with the many advances in data communications, a fourth edition was required to update certain topics and add new ones as networks become a part of everything we do.

The goals of the fourth edition remain the same as those of the first three. After years of teaching data communications classes, I was still not satisfied with the scope, clarity, and readability of other available textbooks. Some textbooks were aimed at advanced electrical engineering students, while others covered only the business aspects of data communications. I sought to create a text that would be accessible to the novice and at the same time challenging to the engineer or technical professional. Those readers who desire a broad overview can simply follow the body of this text, while more advanced readers can examine concepts in detail inside the special shaded boxes.

Simply stated, I have tried to demystify data communications. I draw on practical examples to explain all technical concepts, as I have found this technique very successful in my teaching experience. This text introduces the language of data communications. It provides a practical understanding of all the relevant terminology, concepts, hardware, software, protocols, architectures, and other information necessary to make the reader literate in data communications. Current and future product offerings are discussed. After finishing the book, the reader should be able to make intelligent decisions on the appropriate design, purchase, integration, and use of data communications equipment and systems.

The text begins with a thorough introduction to telecommunications, an understanding of which is essential in order to appreciate data communications hardware and software designs. The book then progresses logically from the basic concepts of data communications to transmission and interface standards and then to data integrity and security. At that point, it is appropriate to discuss architectures and protocols in order to tie the components together, which leads to a thorough presentation of different networks. The text concludes with a discussion of the convergence of voice and data communications and an in-depth examination of standards currently being developed.

At the end of each chapter, I have provided a summary, as well as a list of newly introduced terms. Exercises are also included to help the reader review the material. A thorough glossary of more than 1,350 terms and acronyms, an improved index, and a topical bibliography will ensure this book's usefulness to the reader as a reference tool long after any courses are completed.

The impact of continuously evolving technologies in this vital industry must not be overlooked. I have therefore focused on both fundamental concepts and practical applications so that the reader can understand data communications today and also be prepared to understand future advances in technology, products, and standards. The key in developing such a text is not only what to include, but also what to leave out. Many thicker books on data communications are available. Unlike these other texts, this book boils it down to the essentials.

I believe that I have succeeded in providing a clear, well-balanced, and practical approach to data communications.

WHAT'S NEW IN THE FOURTH EDITION

The entire book has been revised with the increasing importance of the Internet and client/server computing in mind. For example, the fourth edition does the following:

- Provides enhanced coverage of the Internet, search engines, Web servers, load balancing, Web storage, chat, instant messaging, browsing, Web backup, streaming media, and access technologies
- Describes the latest corporate and home LAN environments, including Fast Ethernet, Gigabit Ethernet, and 10-Gigabit Ethernet
- Covers the latest IEEE 802.11 a/b/g Wi-Fi wireless LAN standards and hot spots
- Includes expanded coverage of protocols: TCP/IP, SMTP, MIME, HTTP, Telnet, FTP, UDP, SNMP, SLIP, PPP, ARP, ICMP, DNS, DHCP, MPLS, POP3, IMAP4, Mobile IP, SSL, IPSec, PPTP, SIP, and many others
- Offers an in-depth security discussion of network threats, defense mechanisms, and encryption technology
- Explains changes in the telecommunications industry and Voice Over IP
- Describes the latest high-speed interface and transmission technologies
- Provides enhanced coverage of cellular 1G/2G/2.5G/3G technologies

The following organizational changes have been made since the third edition:

- Data interfaces and transmission have now been split into two chapters.
- The chapter on improving data communications efficiency has been removed. The discussion of multiplexers is now found in the data transmission chapter, while the discussion of front ends and related legacy equipment has been moved to Appendix B for those who are interested.
- The chapter on architectures and protocols now focuses almost entirely on open, standard approaches. Proprietary protocols are mentioned briefly as examples

only where appropriate, and SNA coverage has been moved to Appendix C for those who are interested.

- The last chapter has been broadened to cover the convergence of voice and data communications, and it includes comparisons of the different technologies, as well as a section on future prospects.

Finally, definitions of more than 250 new terms and acronyms within the new material have been added to the glossary. A companion website for students, as well as a dedicated instructor's website with numerous instructional resources, can be found at `http://www.prenhall.com/beyda` .

ACKNOWLEDGMENTS

The efforts of a few and the inspiration of many were instrumental to the successful completion of this book. My father, Joseph D. Beyda, was a constant source of suggestions and moral support while I wrote the first edition, though he did not live to see the later editions. My mother, Barbara M. Beyda, once again applied her considerable editorial skills to ensure the readability of this text. My son, Joey, assisted with some logistical tasks associated with manuscript preparation, and my daughter, Rachel, applied her creative talents to the cover design. My wife, Cathy, helped with the wording of some of the marketing materials, and even our dog Polly got into the act, sitting by my side as I wrote late into the night.

Though I left Stanford University with a strong academic and technical foundation, along with a B.S. in electrical engineering and an M.S. in engineering management, it was only upon entering the communications industry that I acquired more practical knowledge. I have been privileged to work with some of the sharpest minds in the industry at Siemens, where we learn from each other every day.

For the last 20 years, I have been teaching introductory classes on data communications at U.C. Berkeley Extension. My students have given me a new perspective on the field, and I am grateful for their insights. Their comments and questions planted the seed for this work. I would also like to thank Joan Shao, Chair of the Department of Business and Technology at U.C. Berkeley Extension, for her support of my academic endeavors. Dr. Richard Tsina, now Director of Campus Relations at U.C. Berkeley Extension and founder of the communications and networking program, encouraged me to write the first edition of this work.

The technical reviewers, namely Bill Allen, David Auer, Bruce Hartpence, Samuel Kohn, and Dave Whitmore, contributed significantly to the accuracy and readability of this text. As they are active instructors in the field, their perspective has been invaluable. The editorial and production staff at Prentice Hall has been very helpful as well.

Finally, to the readers of this book, thank you for your feedback over the years and for your interest in this field.

C H A P T E R   1

Overview
and Introduction

In order to understand data communications, we should start with a few basic definitions. *Communication* is often defined as the exchange of information between two individuals using a common set of symbols, signs, or behavior. More specifically, telecommunications usually involves a significant distance between the individuals and some electronic equipment for transmission and reception of the information. Finally, data communications requires that the communicating individuals or devices exchange data in the form of ones and zeroes. Typically, computers and related devices communicate in this manner.

Today, in the so-called information age, more and more functions in our lives are performed by or with the help of computers. For example, most authors wouldn't even attempt to write a book today using just a typewriter. We have already become accustomed to computerized billings, automated teller machines, and even cars that remember when they're due for their next tune-up. It is only logical that with more and more of society's information stored on computers, we certainly will want to access much of this information and link all of our computers.

The term *data communications* often conjures up images of complex systems. For example, one vendor's perfectly sound equipment is often unable to communicate with equally expensive counterparts from another vendor because of seemingly insurmountable compatibility problems. However, data communications need not be such a mystifying topic. After all, data communications really is nothing more than the transmission of ones and zeroes from one place to another. The complexity arises from the various means we use to transmit and receive those ones and zeroes and what we do with them at the destination.

This book attempts to demystify data communications. In fact, half the battle in understanding data communications is getting through all of the jargon and acronyms. Therefore, this book introduces the language of data communications and provides a basic understanding of all the relevant terminology, concepts, hardware, software, protocols, architectures, and other information necessary to allow the reader to achieve literacy in data communications.

The book introduces and explains more than 1,350 terms and acronyms. Many of these terms are generic in nature. For example, thousands of routers are on the market, and one manufacturer's "router" may be called a "gateway" by another manufacturer. There is a wide variety of terminology in the data communications industry, just as in the auto industry, where, for example, there's no clear-cut definition of a "sports car." Throughout this book, we use definitions and examples that represent common usage and practice in the industry.

The information presented here should help put current and future product offerings of the industry in context. By providing a comprehensive overview of many topics, the book prepares the reader for further study of more specific areas, such as local area networks. Finally, the goal is for the reader to be able to make intelligent decisions on the appropriate design, purchase, integration, and use of data communications equipment and systems.

A LOGICAL PROGRESSION

This book presents topics in a logical order. The following description of the book's chapters may include terminology unfamiliar to some readers; however, all terms are explained in the respective chapters.

Chapter 2, Understanding Telecommunications, includes an overview of telecommunications, which is required to put data communications in the appropriate context. A basic understanding of telecommunications should help the reader appreciate the purpose and suitability of the different data communications hardware and software discussed in the rest of the book.

Different network topologies, the public network, signaling, divestiture, regulation, and call routing are all presented. Communications service options are compared, including common carrier services and customer-premises equipment. Wireless voice communications, including analog and digital cellular, is discussed in detail. Various cellular standards such as AMPS, USDC, CDMA, TDMA, and GSM are discussed. The various categories of these technologies, including 1G, 2G, 2.5G, and 3G, are also explained.

Chapter 3, Basic Data Communications Concepts, lays the foundation upon which the rest of the book is built. Host computers and terminals, as well as clients and servers, are used to illustrate basic principles.

Common character codes are presented and compared. The differences between parallel and serial transmission, between asynchronous and synchronous transmission, and between simplex, half duplex, and full duplex transmission are all analyzed.

Chapter 4, Data Interfaces, discusses data interface standards. The ANSI, IEEE, EIA, ECSA, IETF, ISO, ITU (CCITT), and NIST standards organizations are described. The chapter analyzes in detail the methods used to connect devices using common serial interfaces. RS-232-C is used as an example to illustrate the functions needed for serial communication. The use of signals for handshaking is explained, and the speed and distance limitations are discussed. Clocking of signals using separate data and clock pins is also explained, and various connector schemes are introduced.

The RS-232-C, RS-449, RS-422-A, and RS-423-A standards are compared to illustrate the similarities between all serial standards. The Universal Serial Bus, including the USB and USB2 versions, is introduced and explained. Firewire and its various versions known as IEEE 1394/1394A/1394B are also presented.

Chapter 5, Data Transmission, introduces digital and analog bandwidth and examines different transmission media. Common cabling schemes, including the various categories of unshielded twisted-pair wiring, are also presented. Various fiber optic technologies are discussed as well. Baseband transmission and broadband transmission are presented, and various modulation methods are illustrated. Modem standards are explained and compared, and facsimiles and fax modems are also discussed.

Different multiplexing methods are presented. Time division multiplexing, in both its pure and statistical forms, is analyzed and explained. Frequency division multiplexing is also presented. Data compression devices and their uses are explained.

Chapter 6, Data Integrity and Security, discusses means for preventing errors and protecting data. In any data communications network, there is the possibility of errors occurring during transmission. The prevention or correction of such errors is often referred to as maintaining data integrity. Error detection and correction methods, such as echo checking, parity checking, cyclical parity, the Hamming code, various checksums, and the cyclical redundancy check, are all explained.

As computers take on a larger and larger share of business transactions, the need for data security becomes evident. In this chapter, security goals and measures are explained, including historical and statistical logs, closed user groups, firewalls, callback techniques, and encryption methods. Intrusions by hackers into networks are discussed. Various security threats, including viruses, worms, and denial-of-service attacks, are assessed, and preventative measures are explained. Security for wireless networks is examined, including the WEP, WPA, and IEEE 802.11i approaches.

Chapter 7, Architectures and Protocols, explains how communications architectures and protocols enable all devices to communicate in an orderly manner by defining precise rules and methods for communications.

This chapter introduces the OSI model, along with examples of widely used protocols and architectures. We explain polling and selecting and compare ARQ methods. BSC and SDLC are presented as examples of byte-oriented and bit-oriented protocols, respectively. Similarities between SDLC, HDLC, LAP-B, and PPP are explored and discussed. TCP/IP and related protocols are discussed, including SMTP, MIME, Telnet, FTP, HTTP, UDP, and SNMP. The TCP header and IP headers are also presented in detail, along with a discussion of the difference between IPv4 and IPv6.

Chapter 8, Data Transport Networks, describes wide area and local area networks. Data transport networks connect a wide variety of devices located in the same building or across the world, providing the means for transmitting and receiving data.

Packet switching network nodes, IXCs, and PADs are explained. The difference between packet and circuit switching is explained. Packet routing and services are also described. Frame relay networks are introduced as well. The Internet is described in detail, including discussions of email, browsers, web servers, load balancing, and instant messaging. Protocols that make the Internet more convenient, like DNS, DHCP, ARP and NAT, among others, are introduced.

Local area network topologies are compared, along with the various access methods. Ethernet and token ring networks are presented, and the IEEE 802 standards are explained. Emphasis is placed on the various versions of Ethernet, including Fast Ethernet (100 Mbps), Gigabit Ethernet, and 10-Gigabit Ethernet. Internetworking applications involving repeaters, bridges, routers, and gateways are described. The client/server model of computing is expanded upon, as are thin clients, network computers, intranets and extranets.

An extensive discussion of wireless networking is presented. Fixed wireless and standards like WiMax, IEEE 802.16, and LMDS are discussed. Wireless LANs based on the various IEEE 802.11 standards, including 802.11a/b/g, are presented and compared.

Chapter 9, Network Management, describes how harmony in a network can be maintained, ensuring consistent reliability and availability of the network, as well as timely transmission and routing of data.

This chapter introduces network management concepts, as well as specific network management tools. The key functions of network management are presented, and measures of availability, reliability, response time, and throughput are described. Various network management approaches and protocols like SNMP are considered, along with MIBs and RMON. Finally, several diagnostic methods and the role of specialized test equipment are analyzed.

Chapter 10, The Convergence of Voice and Data Communications, concludes the book with a discussion of the latest communications technologies and the impact of their possible future implementation. Several years into the 21st century, telecommunications and data communications are converging. Digital technology is now being used in almost all types of communications equipment.

This chapter introduces digital PBXs, pulse code modulation, and the T-1 standard. The ISDN standards are explained, including the differences between European and North American implementations. Equipment classifications and reference points are described, and ISDN services and video transmission are examined. Digital subscriber line services and the infrastructure behind residential DSL, including DSLAMs, splitters, and filters, are presented. Cable-modem systems are discussed as well. Broadband ISDN and ATM are explained in detail. Voice over IP, or VOIP, is presented, along with a comparison of the SIP and H.323 protocols. The chapter also includes discussions about the impact of convergence on the future of data communications.

USING THIS BOOK

This book should be accessible to all readers. Readers who have had some exposure to computers, either through regular use, introductory computer science classes, or other technical training, should be able to follow the body of the text. Throughout the book, many specific topics are examined in detail for the advanced or interested reader; these discussions are placed in special shaded boxes.

In addition, there is a summary at the end of each chapter to help readers review key ideas and concepts. Terms and acronyms are usually italicized the first time they are introduced or used in a new context, and a list of these terms is provided for review at the end of each chapter. Finally, exercises are provided to help readers review the material further.

Those who have had no prior exposure to computers may need to consult Appendix A, which explains the binary number system. Appendix B covers mainframe-related equipment that is not typically installed any more, but that is still in use in many businesses, including front-end processors, port-sharing devices, line splitters, and remote intelligent controllers. Appendix C describes IBM's Systems Network Architecture, which may be of interest to readers if their organizations still have SNA networks installed.

For the reader's convenience, a glossary of more than 1,350 terms and acronyms can be found at the end of the book. A bibliography of useful reference books and publications, sorted by chapter, is also included. Finally, a companion website for students, as well as a dedicated instructor's website with numerous instructional resources, can be found at `www.prenhall.com/beyda`.

C H A P T E R   2

Understanding Telecommunications

THE IMPORTANCE OF TELECOMMUNICATIONS

The invention of the telephone by Alexander Graham Bell in 1876 has forever altered the way we communicate. It is hard to imagine life without telecommunications. *Telecommunications* is defined as the exchange of information, usually over a significant distance and using electronic equipment for transmission. Our businesses and social lives are highly dependent on the telephone.

We now demand that the telephone network carry more than just our voice conversations. The cost of data communications is the fastest growing segment of most companies' telecommunications budgets. Even though most of this book focuses on data communications, we begin with a discussion of today's telecommunications network.

A basic understanding of telecommunications is necessary to place data communications in the appropriate context. Since almost all data communications networks include or connect to the public telephone network at some point, we start by introducing that aspect of telecommunications.

THE PUBLIC NETWORK

The *public network*, also referred to as the *direct distance dial network*, or *DDD network*, is very familiar to all of us. Each time we pick up our home telephone, we are accessing the *public network*, also known as the *public switched telephone network*, or *PSTN*.

A *network* is simply a group of interconnected devices communicating with each other. These devices can be telephones, as is the case with the public network, or computers, as described in Chapter 3. The word *network* is commonly used today to describe a group of people communicating. In some circles, it is used as a verb: "I networked with a lot of interesting people at that party."

Although the public network allows us to communicate with almost any location on the globe, simple telephone conversations do not require complex equipment. In fact, when Bell invented the phone, he simply had two makeshift telephone instruments (a microphone and a speaker), two wires, and a battery.

Today's analog telephones require a negative 48-volt DC power source. Think of this as 32 "D" batteries attached end to end. Figure 2-1 shows the connection of two telephones. If we have phone conversations only with our neighbor, we could connect our phone to his or hers with two wires, attach a 48-volt power source, and converse forever.

Eventually, we decide that it would be convenient to be able to talk to any of our six neighbors via telephone. We start by running wires to each of the other six houses in our neighborhood. The neighbors could each run wires to their neighbors' houses as well. For neighbors to communicate, the party on each end attaches the correct wires to his or her phone, and one of the parties attaches a power source. Figure 2-2 illustrates this network without power sources. We call this configuration a *mesh network* because wires are running from each user to all of the other users.

If our neighborhood gets any more populated, there will soon be wires everywhere. In fact, with hundreds of millions of telephone customers in the United States alone, it becomes clear that the mesh network is not an effective solution.

Instead, today's telephone network resembles a *star network*, as shown in Fig. 2-3. In a star network, each user is connected to the central point. In the telephone network, this central point is responsible for providing the power needed for the telephones, as well as for routing the calls to the proper parties.

Central Offices and Local Loops

The *central office* is the term used to describe the hub of our city's telephone network. Each central office is the center of a star network in a particular area. A large city might have several central offices, with each central office handling a portion of the telephone lines. Smaller cities might share a central office with other cities. Our local phone company operates the equipment at our central office. Other names for the central office are the *end office* and the *local exchange.*

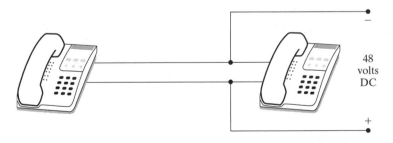

48 volts DC

FIGURE 2-1

Basic telephone connection.

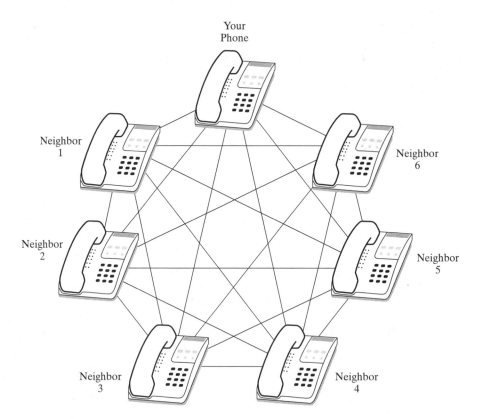

FIGURE 2-2

Mesh network.

The pair of wires that runs from the central office into our home or business is known as the *local loop*. Many homes actually have two pairs of wires running from the central office, just in case we decide to install a second telephone line. If we have only a single telephone number, the extra pair of wires remains unconnected at the central office.

The central office provides power for our telephones, routes our calls, and bills us accordingly. The piece of equipment that performs all of this work is known as the *central office switch*. The term *switch* is used often in telecommunications when referring to a device that routes communications to different parties. Originally, these devices were made up of a series of mechanical switches. Today, most central office switches are electronic, or even digital, with no moving parts involved. Digital central offices are more reliable than electromechanical switches, and because they are computer controlled, they are able to offer many special features, such as call forwarding or three-way calling.

Signaling on a Voice Network

In the process of routing our calls, the central office performs various *signaling* functions. We first signal the central office when we pick up our phone. This action is known

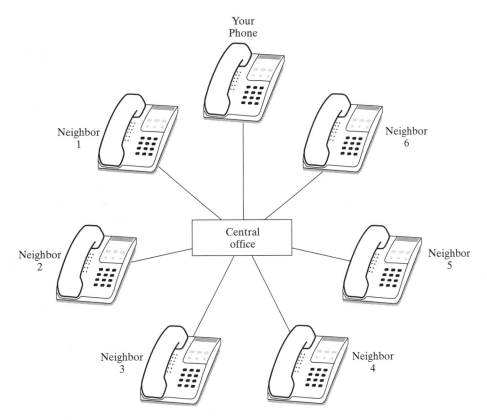

FIGURE 2-3

Star network.

as the *off-hook signal* and tells the central office that we would like to dial. The central office then signals us with a *dial tone*, indicating that we can dial a number.

Another example of a signal that the central office provides us is the *ringing* of our telephone when we are receiving a call. While ringing our telephone, the central office provides the *ringback signal* to the party calling us. Other signals that the central office provides are the *busy signal*, which we get when we call someone who is already using the phone, and the *howler signal*, which is that irritating tone that sounds when we leave our phone off the hook. Some common central office and telephone user signals are listed in Fig. 2-4.

When we dial a number on our phone, we are signaling to the central office our desire to be connected to that phone number. Phone numbers are dialed using *rotary dialing*, also known as *pulse dialing*, or by *touch-tone dialing*, also known as *dual tone multifrequency (DTMF) dialing*.

Rotary, or pulse, dialing requires the alternate opening and closing of a switch at the end of the local loop at a fixed rate of speed. When we dial the number 8 on a rotary phone, the dial mechanism returns at a fixed rate of speed as we release the dial, causing the switch to open and close 8 times, one-tenth of a second apart. Special

Signal name	From:	To:	Function
Off-hook	User	Central office	Informs central office that user wants to place a call
Dial tone	Central office	User	Informs user that central office is ready to accept dialing
Touch-tones or rotary pulses	User	Central office	Informs central office of call destination
Ringback tone	Central office	User	Informs user that the destination phone is ringing
Ringing voltage	Central office	User	Special voltage sent by central office to cause a phone's bell to ring
Busy signal	Central office	User	Informs user that destination phone is already in use
On-hook	User	Central office	Informs central office that user wishes to disconnect call
Call waiting tone	Central office	User	Informs user that another call is waiting on the line
Flash	User	Central office	A combination of the on-hook and off-hook signals—the user quickly depresses the switch-hook and releases it; often used to pick up a waiting call
Howler tone	Central office	User	Alerts user the phone is off the hook

FIGURE 2-4

Central office and telephone user signals.

equipment in the central office, often known as a *rotary register*, can detect this switch opening and closing by monitoring the electric current in the local loop. The same opening and closing of the switch can be accomplished by alternately hanging up and picking up our telephone. If we can briefly depress our switch hook eight times, one-tenth of a second apart, without pausing, we will dial the number 8. Most of us aren't this accurate, however, causing us to pause too long and to dial a 5 and then a 3, for example, instead of an 8.

Touch-tone, or DTMF, dialing works very differently. Each row and column on the DTMF pad has a different tone associated with it. Imagine three different high-pitched tones for the columns and four different low-pitched tones for the rows. A picture of the DTMF pad is shown in Fig. 2-5, along with the frequencies of the associated tones. We explain frequencies in detail in Chapter 5, but for now just think of frequency as a measure of how high or low a tone's pitch is; the higher the frequency, the higher the pitch. The number 8 on our DTMF pad is in row 3 and column 2. When we push the number 8 on our DTMF pad, our phone produces two tones simultaneously: the row 3 tone and the column 2 tone. It sounds like one tone to our ear, but two separate tones are actually played together in harmony. At the central office, a piece of equipment, often known as a *DTMF register*, listens to those tones and then determines that we sent a row 3 tone and a column 2 tone and, therefore, dialed the number 8.

	Column 1 (1209 Hz)	Column 2 (1336 Hz)	Column 3 (1477 Hz)
Row 1 (697 Hz)	1	ABC 2	DEF 3
Row 2 (770 Hz)	GHI 4	JKL 5	MNO 6
Row 3 (852 Hz)	PRS 7	TUV 8	WXY 9
Row 4 (941 Hz)	*	OPER 0	#

FIGURE 2-5

Dual tone multifrequency dialing.

By now, the name *dual tone multifrequency* should make sense. We send two tones at the same time (dual tone), and each can be one of several pitches (multifrequency). Since the name *dual tone multifrequency* is so cumbersome, the simpler name *touch-tone* has caught on instead. Interestingly enough, the DTMF standard actually provides for a fourth column, allowing 16 different combinations of row and column tones. This 16-number keypad, however, is used only in special applications, and most applications today use the abbreviated 12-key pad (the numbers 1, 2, 3, 4, 5, 6, 7, 8, 9, and 0, as well as the * and # symbols).

We are so accustomed to hearing the dial tone almost instantly when we pick up the phone that we hardly think of it as a signal to dial; in fact, some people don't even listen for it. But if every telephone user attached to our central office picks up the phone at the same time, not all users will receive the dial tone immediately. Most central offices are not able to provide a dial tone to everyone at once because a dial tone is an indication that a piece of equipment in the central office is ready to listen to our pulse or DTMF digits. The phone companies don't expect everyone to pick up the phone at the same time, so they usually don't install enough DTMF and rotary registers to listen to everyone dial at once. If we pick up the phone on Mother's Day and notice a delay in getting a dial tone, that's because so many people are already dialing their phones that no rotary or DTMF registers are available at the central office to listen to us dial. As soon as a register is available, it is connected electronically to our line, and we hear a dial tone.

DIVESTITURE

The methods used for routing calls throughout the telephone network today are largely a result of the U.S. government's antitrust case against *American Telephone & Telegraph*, or *AT&T*. We briefly examine the results of this case as it relates to telephone call routing because its impacts are still felt today.

A local phone company, known as a *local exchange carrier*, or *LEC*, operates the central office. These local phone companies include companies formerly controlled by AT&T, known as the *Bell Operating Companies*, or *BOC*s, as well as many *Independent Telephone Companies*, or *ITC*s.

In 1974, the U.S. Department of Justice filed an antitrust law suit against AT&T. At that time, AT&T owned a controlling share of 22 of the 24 BOCs and carried a large majority of America's long-distance traffic; together, these two components were referred to as the *Bell System*. The domination of both the regulated local and long-distance service by AT&T was deemed an unfair monopoly by the U.S. Department of Justice.

AT&T eventually reached a settlement with the government, described in a document known as the *Modified Final Judgment*, or *MFJ*. The MFJ required AT&T to divest itself of the BOCs on January 1, 1984. This *divestiture* is commonly referred to as the *breakup* of the Bell System. AT&T accomplished the divestiture by exchanging its old stock for shares of stock in the new AT&T and the newly formed holding companies we discuss later. The MFJ allowed AT&T to continue to provide long-distance service. AT&T could enter other businesses, but could not initially provide local telephone service. In addition to relinquishing control of the local phone service, AT&T was forced to compete on an equal basis with other long-distance carriers, known as *interexchange carriers*, or *IEC*s.

The newly divested BOCs had to provide *equal access* to all long-distance phone companies, and AT&T had no special priority with its newly divested BOCs. AT&T kept some of the *Bell Labs* research facility and the *Western Electric* manufacturing facility, which produced central office switches, private branch exchanges (PBXs), and other telephone equipment. A new company, known as *Bell Communications Research*, or *Bellcore*, was formed to act as a research and administrative services company for the newly formed BOCs. Bellcore is now known as *Telcordia*, and Western Electric and Bell Labs eventually became part of *Lucent Technologies*.

As a result of divestiture, AT&T, often referred to as Ma Bell, was split into many so-called Baby Bells. To allow the newly divested BOCs to remain efficient and achieve economies of scale, they were allowed to group together to form *Regional Holding Companies* (*RHC*s) or *Regional Bell Operating Companies* (*RBOC*s). Figure 2-6 presents a chart of the newly formed BOCs and RBOCs just after divestiture, as well as their current status after mergers in the ensuing years. The RBOCs, in addition to owning their BOCs, could not originally enter other businesses. They were also initially prohibited from manufacturing equipment or providing long-distance service. The original seven RBOCs are now down to only four after mergers: BellSouth, SBC, Qwest, and Verizon.

As part of the divestiture settlement, each BOC divided itself into several *local access and transport areas*, or *LATAs*. The BOC is responsible for providing customers with access to the public network, and it may also transport calls placed inside the LATA. When a call's destination is outside the LATA, the BOC might only transport the call to the *point of presence*, or *POP*, of a long-distance carrier. This POP is located inside the LATA, and it is the long-distance carrier's responsibility to transport the call to its destination in another LATA. Hence, the BOC's two main functions within its LATA are local access and local transport.

Original RBOC	Original BOC	States	Current Company
Ameritech	Illinois Bell Telephone	Illinois	SBC
	Indiana Bell Telephone	Indiana	
	Michigan Bell Telephone	Michigan	
	Ohio Bell Telephone	Ohio	
	Wisconsin Bell	Wisconsin	
Bell Atlantic	Bell Telephone of Pennsylvania	Pennsylvania	Verizon
	Chesapeake & Potomac	Maryland	
		Virginia	
		Washington, D.C.	
		West Virginia	
	Diamond State Telephone	Delaware	
	New Jersey Bell Telephone	New Jersey	
BellSouth	South Central Bell Telephone	Alabama	BellSouth
		Kentucky	
		Louisiana	
		Mississippi	
		Tennessee	
	Southern Bell Telephone	Florida	
		Georgia	
		North Carolina	
		South Carolina	
NYNEX	New England Telephone	Connecticut	Verizon
		Maine	
		Massachusetts	
		New Hampshire	
		Rhode Island	
		Vermont	
	New York Telephone	New York	
Pacific Telesis	Nevada Bell	Nevada	SBC
	Pacific Bell	California	
Southwestern Bell	Southwestern Bell Telephone	Arkansas	SBC
		Kansas	
		Missouri	
		Oklahoma	
		Texas	
U S WEST	Mountain Bell	Arizona	Qwest
		Colorado	
		Idaho	
		Montana	
		New Mexico	
		Utah	
		Wyoming	
	Northwestern Bell	Iowa	
		Minnesota	
		Nebraska	
		North Dakota	
		South Dakota	
	Pacific Northwest Bell	Oregon	
		Washington	

FIGURE 2-6

RBOCS and BOCS.

A LATA is usually centered around a major metropolitan area. For example, there is a LATA for the entire San Francisco Bay Area, including the cities of San Francisco, Oakland, and San Jose. This area spans many different area codes, including 415, 650, 510, 707, 408, and others. Most of this LATA is served by SBC, an RBOC.

INTRA-LATA CALL ROUTING

If a customer in San Jose places a call within his or her own central office, the call routing is fairly simple. As shown in Fig. 2-7, parties 1 and 2 are both connected to the same central office. Party 1 picks up the phone, waits for the dial tone, and then dials party 2's phone number. The central office looks at the first three digits of the phone number and determines that the called party is in this central office. The central office then checks to see if party 2 is already on the phone. If party 2 is already on the phone, the central office sends party 1 a busy signal. If party 2 is not on the phone, the central office sends party 1 a ringing tone and sends a special voltage to party 2's phone, causing it to ring. This call is placed entirely through SBC lines and offices.

The central office knows that party 2 is one of its customers because it knows which *office codes* are in its territory. As an example, in the phone number 555-1234, 555 is the *office code*, or *prefix*, and 1234 pinpoints the particular customer in that office code. A central office may have several office codes for its customers.

Returning to Fig. 2-7, suppose that party 1 calls party 3. Party 3 lives in Santa Clara, another city in the 408 area code and within party 1's LATA, but in a different central office. In this case, the San Jose central office recognizes that the call is destined for the Santa Clara central office by examining the office code. The San Jose central office routes the call to the Santa Clara central office over an *interoffice trunk*, or *IOT*. A *trunk* is another name for a line connecting two switches; an interoffice trunk connects two central office switches in a local area. In this case, the call is routed over party 1's local loop, through one central office, over an interoffice trunk, to another central office, and finally to party 3's local loop. This call is placed entirely through SBC lines and offices.

Area codes, which were in use long before divestiture and before the concept of LATAs existed, have nothing to do with whether a call is local or long distance. Instead, they represent a certain geographical area, usually determined by the population in that area. Sometimes an area code covers an entire state, as in Wyoming (307). In the case of a large city, multiple area codes are sometimes required, as in New York City (212, 718, and others).

The proliferation of area codes in North America is partly due to the increase in use of cellular phones, pagers, fax machines, and modems, all of which require additional numbers that use up the capacity in a given area code. In addition, with the advent of increased competition among local carriers, large blocks of numbers are assigned to each carrier. A carrier with only a handful of customers might use thousands of phone numbers, because limitations in the existing installed carrier equipment require the allocation of numbers to carriers in large blocks, no matter how few customers a carrier may have. The creation of new area codes is expected to continue in North America for many years, until extra digits will need to be added to the current 10-digit numbering

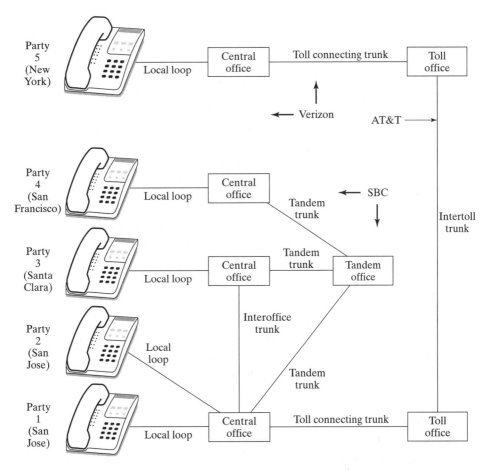

FIGURE 2-7

Call routing.

scheme to allow for the addition of new numbers. When new area codes are added, in some cases existing area codes are split geographically, with customers in some locations assigned to new area codes and customers in other locations retaining their old area codes. In other cases, an *overlay* area code is created. In this case, the same geographic area is covered by multiple area codes. Existing customers retain the old area code, but new phone lines on the same block, or even in the same house, may receive a number in the new area code. Although this method has the advantage of minimizing the changes in existing phone numbers, it may require people to dial 10 or more digits to reach a number across the street.

Even though area codes affect the numbers we need to dial to reach a particular party, they do not alter the routing process. A call is routed based on whether it is in the LATA or outside the LATA, regardless of area code. Suppose that party 1 in San Jose, within the 408 area code, calls party 4 in San Francisco, as illustrated in Fig. 2-7. This call is to the 415 area code, but it is still within the San Francisco Bay Area LATA. Party 1 dials the number, and the San Jose central office examines the area code and office code and determines that the destination is a SBC central office in San Francisco in the same LATA. Instead of running trunks from every central office in a LATA to every other central office, the local phone company can run *tandem trunks* from all of the central offices into a *tandem office*, as shown in Fig. 2-7. In this case, party 1's call is routed over his or her local loop, through the San Jose central office, through a SBC tandem office, through the San Francisco central office, and over party 4's local loop. Once again, all of this call routing is done over SBC equipment and lines in a fraction of a second, and SBC will bill the customer for the call.

Calls inside a LATA, or intra-LATA calls, are not necessarily what we think of as local calls. The local phone company may label some intra-LATA calls covering great distances as *toll calls*, but they are not true long-distance calls because they are still intra-LATA. Initially, after divestiture, all intra-LATA calls were routed entirely over the local phone company's equipment and were billed to the customer by the local phone company without involving any long-distance carriers. Today, multiple carriers can handle intra-LATA calls in some LATAs.

One constant source of confusion is the fact that not all LATAs are served entirely by one local phone company. For example, in the LATA we have been describing, a group of customers in the town of Los Gatos is served by Verizon, while most of the rest of the San Francisco Bay Area LATA is served by SBC. In cases like these, the different local phone companies cooperate to ensure that customers receive the same service that a single company would provide.

INTER-LATA CALL ROUTING

What happens when party 1 wants to call a number outside his or her LATA? Such a call is an *inter-LATA*, or *long-distance, call*, and a long-distance carrier must enter the call-routing process. Before divestiture, the call usually would have been placed over AT&T lines. Since divestiture and the advent of equal access, customers are free to choose their long-distance carriers. Figure 2-8 lists some of the long-distance carriers that entered the market for inter-LATA calls after divestiture.

Telephone customers with equal access choose a particular carrier to be their standard, or *default*, long-distance company through a process known as *presubscription*. Whenever the customer dials an inter-LATA call, the call will be automatically routed over the presubscribed carrier unless the customer dials a special code.

In most areas, a customer must dial a 1 before placing calls to another area code. The presence or absence of this requirement does not affect equal access. Dialing a 1 plus the phone number still routes the call over the presubscribed carrier. Dialing a special code, in the format 10*xxxxx*, where *xxxxx* is the carrier code, routes the call over an alternative carrier. A list of some carrier codes is also provided in Fig. 2-8. While these codes were initially five digits long, they were later lengthened to seven digits to accommodate additional carriers.

A central office is connected to a long-distance carrier's office, known as a *toll office*, by a *toll connecting trunk*, or *TCT*. A long-distance carrier connects its toll offices

Carrier	Access code
AT&T	1010288
MCI	1010222
Sprint	1010333
Telecom* USA (MCI)	1010321
Note: Not all carriers serve all areas, and access codes may vary.	

FIGURE 2-8

A sampling of long-distance carriers after divestiture.

all around the country with *intertoll trunks*, in much the same way that the local phone companies connect their central offices with interoffice trunks. Intertoll trunks are also often called *IXCs*, or *interexchange circuits*. Intertoll trunks that can carry many conversations simultaneously are known as *high-usage intertoll trunks*.

We will assume for our example that party 1 has presubscribed to AT&T for his or her long-distance service. Referring to Fig. 2-7, party 1, in San Jose, California, is calling party 5 in New York. This call is clearly outside the San Francisco Bay Area LATA. The call is routed over party 1's local loop, to the San Jose SBC central office, over a toll connecting trunk, and to an AT&T toll office in California. It is then routed across the country on an AT&T intertoll trunk, to an AT&T toll office in New York, over a toll connecting trunk, to a Verizon central office, and out over party 5's local loop. It will be the New York central office's responsibility to provide a busy signal or ringing tone, depending on whether or not party 5 is on the line.

This call routing involves three separate companies: two BOCs and one long-distance carrier. This call routing is possible because very clear standards dictate the signaling that must take place between the different offices handling a call. These standards apply to all central offices and all long-distance carriers.

The SBC central office informs the AT&T toll office of the call originator and the call destination through special signaling. The long-distance company has the choice of billing the customer directly, billing through a third party, such as SBC, or even billing the customer's credit card. All of this call routing and signaling takes place in a few seconds. Long-distance calls take longer to place than local calls because these signals have to be passed through many different offices and switches.

Though our example assumes an intertoll trunk between San Jose and New York, this is not necessarily the case. The long-distance carrier is free to route the call to New York through whichever cities it wishes, just as an airline may require passengers traveling between those cities to change planes in Chicago. The long-distance carrier might run all of its trunks into Chicago, routing all calls through a national switching center there. Typically, this routing is done regionally, with several switching centers spread out all over the country. There is an entire hierarchy involving regional and area toll offices, but we won't consider it here because it does not directly affect the customer. In our example, SBC routes the call to AT&T, and it becomes AT&T's responsibility to get the call to New York using any route it wishes.

REGULATION

Companies that provide voice and data communications transmission services to the general public are known as *common carriers*, which include the local phone companies and the long-distance companies. These common carriers must file *tariffs* for all services they offer with the appropriate regulating bodies. A tariff describes a particular service in detail, along with the rate charged for that service. In some cases, the regulating body may reject a particular tariff (e.g., if it feels that the rates are too high).

The *FCC*, or *Federal Communications Commission*, is responsible for regulating all interstate communications in the United States. Thus, the FCC regulates calls that are inter-LATA and interstate, as well as the few calls that are intra-LATA and interstate (where LATAs cross state lines).

Each state has a *PUC*, or *public utilities commission*, responsible for regulating all intrastate phone service. The PUCs regulate all local phone service, all intra-LATA/intrastate calls, and all inter-LATA/intrastate calls.

Each regulating agency reviews and approves tariffs filed for services in its jurisdiction. Since the local phone companies have a basic monopoly on providing phone service within their communities, PUCs are likely to scrutinize rate increases very carefully. The FCC, on the other hand, may allow the long-distance carriers more leeway in pricing new and innovative services, since consumers have equal access to all carriers and can choose the services they prefer.

National issues affecting all of the RBOCs are typically addressed by the FCC. In the postdivestiture environment, the FCC started to require that the RBOCs implement an *Open Network Architecture*, or *ONA*. With an ONA, the public network services are divided into *basic service elements*, or *BSEs*; customers can subscribe to any combination of the BSEs. For example, one BSE might be the ability to forward calls, while another might be conference calling. The customer could select either or both of these BSEs, but would not be forced to take both together as a package. By separating all of the public network's services into BSEs, an *enhanced service provider*, or *ESP*, would be guaranteed access to network services needed to perform special functions. For example, an answering service company is an ESP that would use the call forwarding BSE, combined with its staff of operators or answering machines, to provide a special, or enhanced, service to the customer.

Many countries have their own equivalent of the FCC, often known as a *PTT*, or *postal, telephone, and telegraph administration*. In some countries, the PTT regulates and runs the public network. This system would be the equivalent of the FCC owning, operating, and regulating the predivestiture AT&T, with all of its BOCs.

INCREASED COMPETITION

Divestiture was one of the most sweeping, dramatic changes in American telecommunications history. It unleashed competition in the long-distance industry, and within a decade it became clear that the formula had worked. Long-distance rates had plummeted to less than 50% of what they had been during AT&T's domination of the market.

Unfortunately, consumers also became increasingly confused about the rich variety of carriers and service options. This confusion may have slowed the continuing deregulation of the industry, but a new impetus came from the cable television market.

Due to the increased penetration of cable television in the U.S. marketplace, customers became reliant on certain information sources, such as news and sports networks. Over time, some cable channels became an integral part of American society, and as cable rates increased, angry consumers pressured their government for rate reduction. The FCC, faced with the compelling evidence in the long-distance market, began to encourage competition in the cable industry and actively supported rate reductions.

New switching technologies that make it possible to deliver voice and video on the same network, combined with a trend toward deregulation, are laying the framework for competition between cable television and telecommunications companies. The *convergence* of these voice and data technologies into a universal network is described in more detail in Chapter 10.

While the FCC and PUCs can generally set the pace for deregulation, the courts and the legislative branch can speed up this process. If traditional regulations continue to be discarded, there is nothing to prevent cable television companies and telecommunications companies from competing on an equal footing. Even within the telecommunications industry, the postdivestiture long-distance companies are offering local service in some areas, and some local carriers now offer long-distance service. The *Telecommunications Act of 1996* started a new era in regulation, with specific restrictions imposed on phone companies and cable companies alike. Today, increased competition has resulted in several choices of local service for businesses in metropolitan areas. However, business customers outside of major service areas, as well as many residential customers, still have no choice when selecting a local carrier. In some cases customers can choose a different local provider, who in turn resells the service of the original BOC to them. The customer receives a bill from this third-party local "provider," but the service is actually delivered over the lines of the original BOC. This is not true competition, but instead is a step toward opening up the market. Most of the BOCs are now able to offer long-distance service if they meet certain requirements for opening up competition in their local market.

Though the pace of deregulation may vary over the years, it appears unstoppable. Certain regulations will probably remain to guarantee availability and quality of service as well as appropriate standards to protect consumers in terms of fair billing and business practices. Mergers among the original RBOCs, like that between Pacific Telesis, Ameritech, and Southwest Bell and between NYNEX and Bell Atlantic, are some examples of consolidation in the industry. While the Telecommunications Act of 1996 placed firm restrictions on mergers between cable companies and local telephone companies, cable companies are free to merge with long-distance carriers. It is unlikely that the separation of the cable television and telecommunications industries will still be so well defined in the coming years, and the new combined industry should be dramatically less regulated than in the past.

VOICE COMMUNICATIONS SERVICE OFFERINGS

Many different communications services are available, particularly to the business community, which has large volumes of telephone traffic. One of these services is *WATS*, or *wide area telecommunications services*. WATS is a bulk-rate, long-distance service for users with high call volumes. Traditionally, WATS pricing was done in bands: The United

States was divided into several bands, or zones, and the customers paid a per-hour cost for calls to each zone. A California business that placed a lot of calls to the West Coast but very few to the East could subscribe to WATS only for the West Coast bands. Since divestiture, many long-distance carriers offer services labeled as WATS with different characteristics. Some simply offer volume discounts regardless of zone; others are more complex, offering discounts to certain area codes and office codes at certain times. The only safe generalization that can be made about a postdivestiture WATS line is that it offers some discounts for volume long-distance users.

A type of WATS service, *inward-WATS*, is known to most of us as a *toll-free number*, or an *800 number* or *888 number*. The customer agrees to pay for all incoming long-distance calls from certain areas, but at the reduced WATS rates. Another service, known as a *foreign exchange*, is used by a business that wants a phone number in a city other than the one where its offices are located. The business pays a fixed rate for the service, in addition to a mileage charge to the distant area. Calls to and from its customers in that area can then be made at local call rates.

Another way for businesses to save on communications costs is to use *leased lines* to locations they call frequently. A leased line is a permanent connection from one point to another provided by common carriers. In a sense, it is a phone call that never hangs up. The carrier only has to route the call once; after that, all the customer is really renting is a pair of wires from one point to another, along with some amplifying equipment and power. Leased-line services are generally priced by the mile. Whether the line is used frequently or not at all, the monthly price is still the same because that line has been reserved for the exclusive use of the customer.

For example, a corporation with offices in Santa Clara, California, and Austin, Texas, may discover that it is making many long-distance calls between the two facilities. Rather than continue to pay per-minute rates on the dial-up network, or even per-hour rates through WATS, the customer can opt to lease lines. Leasing lines becomes economical surprisingly fast, often after a few dozen hours of use per month. If the business has an advanced phone system that ensures that the leased lines are used wherever appropriate, the economic benefit is almost guaranteed.

When we pick up our home phone and dial a number, we are accessing the dial-up network. It's up to the common carriers to route our call to the appropriate destination, but we have no control over what route the call takes. Furthermore, every time we place a call to the same number, it may take a slightly different route, depending on what facilities the carriers have available at that instant. This system explains why sometimes we get a good connection and other times we don't. This problem is more likely to be encountered when calling parts of the world with less-developed telecommunications infrastructures.

One of the key attributes of the dial-up network is that the flexible routing of calls allows for very high reliability in making connections. For example, a call from San Jose to New York might normally go over a transcontinental intertoll trunk, but if that line is currently out of service, the call could be routed through Chicago. However, with this high reliability in making connections comes the uncertainty of whether or not our next connection will be of high quality.

Leased lines, however, can consistently ensure high-quality connections. When a leased line is installed, it must meet a certain specification, such as *voice grade*, suitable for voice communications and most data communications. The customer can even demand a special leased line suitable for high-speed data transmission, known as a *conditioned* leased line. There is an extra charge for the hardware required to meet this improved specification.

A leased-line customer, however, is vulnerable to a service outage on that line's particular wire and hardware. If the line is down, the telephone network will not automatically reroute the call. Either the line must be repaired, another line must be installed, or a backup call must be placed on the dial-up network.

The choice boils down to the high reliability and sometimes questionable quality of the dial-up network versus the questionable reliability and high quality of a leased line. Of course, the application and priorities of each customer determine which solution is appropriate.

There are many ways to provide leased-line services in higher volumes and at lower costs. These methods include T-1 carrier, satellite, microwave, and fiber optics. We consider these high-volume transmission options in Chapter 5.

ECHO SUPPRESSORS AND CANCELLERS

The dial-up telephone network is equipped with a variety of devices to help stop echoes during normal conversation. The nature of telephone transmission causes some signals to bounce back from the receiving telephone, just as our voices bounce off a canyon's walls and return to our ears.

On a local call, we don't even notice the echo because the party we are talking to is within a few miles of us, and our voice travels at the speed of electricity (almost 300 million meters per second). Our echo returns to our earpiece so quickly that it doesn't even seem to be an echo; instead, it sounds as if the telephone is simply amplifying our voice in the earpiece.

However, long-distance connections can span many thousands of miles. It may take an echo a half second to complete its round-trip back to your telephone. An echo a half second after we have said something is very disconcerting. Several different devices are in use today to help eliminate echoes, including *echo suppressors* and *echo cancellers*.

Echo suppressors work by allowing only a one-way communications path. As soon as we start talking, the path from the other person to us is cut off. If our voice echoes back, it is not transmitted. If the other person begins speaking louder than we do, he or she gets control of the line. This system works well for normal conversation; when we stop talking and the other person begins, his or her voice takes over. If the other person interrupts us midsentence, he or she probably is speaking louder than we are, so we hear him or her. The echo suppressor hears the volume difference and gives the other person the line. Since echoes are going to be softer than the original voice, an echo on the rebound never takes control of the line. Echo suppressors are shown at work in Fig. 2-9. Echo cancellers are more sophisticated devices. They allow a continuous two-way conversation, but are able to remove your own echo before it returns to your telephone. Echo cancellers are a sophisticated version of acoustical ceiling tiles used to absorb noise. The difference is that echo cancellers are able to detect the difference between true conversation and an echo and selectively absorb only the echo.

Most long-distance carriers install either echo suppressors or cancellers at the end of their equipment. This equipment can be disabled on a particular call by using a special tone. This capability is useful for certain data communications transmissions, which we will review later.

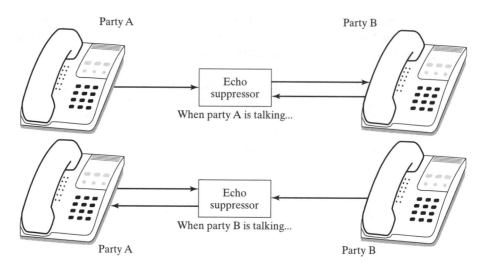

FIGURE 2-9

Echo suppressors.

TASI VS. VOICE CALL MULTIPLEXING

Long-distance carriers often combine several calls on the same intertoll trunk using one of two methods. The first method, known as *TASI*, or *time assignment speech interpolation*, allocates a communications path a few milliseconds after the caller begins to speak. This time lapse is not noticed during voice transmission, but is often damaging to data transmission, where a few lost milliseconds can result in the loss of precious data. The preferred method, known as *voice call multiplexing*, combines conversations without risking any loss of voice or data. Fortunately, most carriers today use the latter technique.

LEASING SERVICES VS. BUYING CUSTOMER-PREMISES EQUIPMENT

Regardless of the size of a business or the diversity of its telecommunications require-ments, there is always the option of leasing services from others or owning them out-right. Equipment used at the customer's site is known as *customer-premises equipment*, or *CPE*. Many of us already own our own CPE: our home telephones.

Centrex

Some businesses choose to let the local phone company handle all of their external and internal calls in the central office. This service is called *Centrex*, because the central of-fice is acting as the customer's exchange, or switch. A local loop connects every exten-sion to the central office. The central office interprets the numbers dialed in a special way for the Centrex customer. For example, if employee A in Fig. 2-10 dials the four-digit extension of employee B, the central office recognizes this call as an internal one

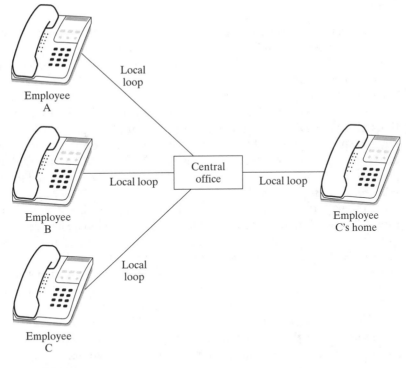

FIGURE 2-10

Centrex service.

and routes it back to the appropriate desk. If employee C dials a 9 and then his or her home phone number, the central office recognizes the call as an external one and grants the employee an outside dial tone, without any operator intervention.

Centrex gives a business the appearance of having its own phone system. Employees dial internal calls just by dialing the last few digits of the phone number and don't usually realize that their call is going through the phone company's central office. Centrex is usually very dependable, because central office switches are highly reliable, with a full-time maintenance and troubleshooting staff. However, the customer must pay a fee for each Centrex line each month, in addition to per-call charges, just as we do for our home telephone service. With Centrex, the customer usually has the option of purchasing or renting the phone instruments.

Today's Centrex services can be tailored to offer some of the same advanced features previously found only in customer-owned systems. However, Centrex is by its nature technically inefficient, since a call destined for a colleague's desk only 10 feet away must take a 2-mile round-trip to the central office. In addition, the user relies on the phone company to perform most changes, such as moving telephone locations or changing extensions. Some customers, however, prefer Centrex because they don't have to purchase and maintain a phone system. They are willing to pay higher monthly fees to avoid the initial capital outlay required to purchase a phone system.

Key Systems

For some small businesses, *key systems* may provide a suitable telecommunications solution. Early key systems were merely a collection of multiline phones connected with special wiring. These early key systems provided intercom functions, allowing customers to communicate internally over intercom lines. Any external calls were made over local loops.

Early key systems had little or no intelligence, and the user performed all functions manually by pushing the appropriate buttons. To place an external call on early key systems, the user pushed an external-line button on the phone. Similarly, internal conversations were initiated by pressing an intercom button. In addition, calls could be placed on hold using a hold button. Early key systems were limited to only a handful of telephone lines.

Today's key systems are more sophisticated, providing special features such as call forwarding and call transfer. Some of today's key systems can handle up to 150 users. Key systems are usually compact and use standard electrical power. In addition, they can often be repaired by the customer. Key systems, and the phones attached to them, are usually purchased by the customer, though they can be leased. Key systems eliminate the inefficiency of Centrex, since an internal call does not go to the central office. A key-system customer does not need a local loop for each telephone, only one for each outside line.

However, most key systems cannot provide many advanced features and are severely limited in their ability to grow beyond 150 lines. For these reasons, medium-sized to large businesses usually do not choose key systems. There is, however, another alternative to Centrex for these customers.

Private Branch Exchange

The *PBX*, or *private branch exchange*, is the most advanced customer-premises equipment telecommunications solution. A PBX acts as a mini central office, dedicated not to an entire community or town, but to the customer that owns it. The lines running from the PBX to employees' phones are known as PBX *station lines* and are owned by the customer, not the phone company. A PBX can often accommodate thousands of phones, enough to satisfy the needs of even the largest customers.

All internal calls are routed through the PBX and never go to the central office. If an employee places an external call, the PBX routes the call off the premises to the central office. For example, in Fig. 2-11, assume that employee A dials employee B. The PBX connects the two parties, and the entire connection is inside the customer's private network. Hence, there are no charges from the central office for this call. In fact, the local phone company doesn't know, or care, that the call took place, because its facilities were not used.

What about external calls? One advantage of a PBX is that a company does not need a local loop for each employee, because only a small percentage of employees make external calls at any given moment. In typical companies, one outside line for every 10 extensions might be sufficient. Special situations require more outside lines. For example, at an airline reservations center, employees spend a majority of their time answering incoming calls from outside lines. Every business has different requirements; the fewer outside lines needed, the more a PBX saves the customer in local-loop costs.

FIGURE 2-11

PBX call routing.

We have already mentioned that two switches are connected using a special type of line known as a trunk. PBXs, therefore, are connected to the central office using trunks. Several different types of PBX trunks are illustrated in Fig. 2-11. An employee gains access to those trunks by dialing a special code, like 9. The PBX can then select the appropriate trunk, based on the call's destination.

The *central office trunk* is the standard trunk used for all external intra-LATA calls and for calls that the central office routes to a long-distance carrier. Incoming calls over a central office trunk must be answered by the customer's *operator*, or *attendant*.

Customers that want incoming calls automatically routed to their employees' desks without going through an operator must rent *direct inward dial trunks*, or *DID trunks*, from the central office. On a DID trunk, the central office actually signals to the PBX which extension an incoming call is destined for, allowing the PBX to route it properly.

An *outward-WATS trunk* is a connection to a discounted long-distance service that we have already mentioned. An *inward-WATS trunk* is the PBX's connection for a *toll-free number*.

Finally, a *tie trunk* is used to connect two PBXs. These PBXs can be at the same or at different locations. An employee on one PBX can place a call to an employee on the other PBX, and the call can be automatically routed over these tie trunks. Calls over the tie trunks incur no per-call cost, since these lines are leased on a monthly basis.

Early PBXs provided a cost savings simply by reducing the number of local loops. Today's advanced PBXs are loaded with features, which are generally divided into two basic categories: system features and station features.

System features are functions performed and controlled for the entire system, such as voice messaging. A table of popular PBX system features is presented in Fig. 2-12. *Station features* are functions performed for and controlled by each individual user, such as call forwarding. A table of popular PBX station features is shown in Fig. 2-13. Although not all PBXs have all of these features, the system and station features presented in the figures are a representative sample of features provided by most advanced PBXs.

Feature name	Function
Automatic call distribution (ACD)	Allows callers to be routed to a group of agents, with calls distributed evenly among all of them. Statistics are available on each agent, including the number of calls, duration, etc. Often used for customer service departments, airline reservationists, etc.
Call detail recording (CDR)	Provides records on each call placed out of the PBX, including information about the caller, the called party, the duration, the time of day, etc. Allows a company to track its telephone costs by department or even by user. Further enhancements allow special account codes to be entered when placing a call to bill it to a particular client or project.
Class of service distinction (COS)	Allows users to be combined into different groups, each with access to different features and each with different external calling capabilities.
Data switching	Allows for switched digital pathways. Available only on digital PBXs, data switching provides for sharing of resources, including computers or modems, among many different terminal devices. Personal computers can also communicate with each other through data switching.
Direct inward dial (DID)	Allows callers from outside the company to dial directly to employees' desks or station lines.
Direct inward system access (DISA)	Allows a user who is away from the office to dial the PBX, enter a special code, and then use the PBX to place internal and external calls, exactly as if the person were at his or her desk.
Direct outward dial	Allows users to dial external calls directly without going through the PBX operator.
Distinctive ringing	Allows different ring patterns to be provided for different calls. For example, internal calls can be indicated by a single ring; external calls, by two quick rings; etc.

FIGURE 2-12

Popular PBX system features.

Feature name	Function
Hunt groups	Allows phones in a department to be assigned to a special group. People calling the departmental number are routed to the first available person in the department's hunt group.
Intercom lines	Allows abbreviated dialing within a department, making it seem that each department has its own system.
Least-cost routing	Automatically routes all external calls over the cheapest route, including WATS lines, tie trunks, foreign exchanges, etc.
Music on hold	Provides a PBX connection to a music source so that callers placed on hold will know they are still connected.
Paging	Provides a PBX connection to a loudspeaker so that users can page someone by dialing a special code and speaking into the telephone.
Remote polling	Allows the computers of the PBX manufacturer's service organization to telephone the PBX on a regular basis and check the PBX's diagnostic information for any irregularities. A service technician can then be dispatched, if necessary, often before the customer is even aware of any problem. In addition, call detail recording information can be collected from the PBX for further analysis.
Route optimization	Provides the same functionality as least-cost routing.
System speed dial	Allows a set of telephone numbers to be programmed into the system. Any system user can then automatically dial one of these numbers by entering a brief code.
Trunk queuing	Queues users placing an external call (puts them in line) for a trunk when all trunks are busy. With some systems, the user can hang up, and the system will call back when a trunk is available.
Voice messaging	Provides automated call answering for phones left unattended or phones that are busy. Calls are usually answered by an attached voice messaging system that plays a greeting in the call receiver's own voice and then offers several options. The caller can leave a message, which is stored in the system and can be retrieved by the user. Users are usually notified of messages through message-waiting lights on their phones, through an interrupted dial tone, known as stutter, or broken, dial tone. Messages can usually be forwarded to other users.

FIGURE 2-12

(Continued)

Many advanced PBXs are able to send calls over the least expensive route. This system feature, known as *least-cost routing*, or *route optimization*, has become increasingly sophisticated with the advent of equal access. An advanced PBX can be programmed with the rates of all of the long-distance carriers and can select the cheapest carrier for each call, based on the rate tables and the time of day. This feature can provide considerable cost savings and is often the main reason for purchasing a PBX instead of using Centrex services.

Almost all of today's advanced PBXs are *digital PBXs*. The ROLM CBX, or Computerized Branch Exchange, first installed in 1975, was the first computer-based digital PBX. Digital PBXs are actually computers that treat the telephones and trunks as specialized input and output devices.

One advantage of digital PBXs is their ability to provide a myriad of sophisticated features. In addition, these digital PBXs can use special digital telephones that allow the transmission of voice and data over a single telephone line. Some digital PBXs

Feature name	Function
Account codes	Allows users to key in a special code for each call, ensuring that each call is billed to it particular account. Accounts often represent clients or projects.
Buzz	Allows users to buzz each other as they would on an intercom system.
Camp-on	When a user encounters a busy signal on an internal call, he can camp-on. This is an automated version of waiting for the line to be free. With some systems, the user can hang-up and the system will call back when the called party is free.
Conference calls	Allows users to create telephone conferences, adding multiple users to each conversation.
Do not disturb	Allows users to block incoming calls. Callers receive a busy signal.
Executive override	Allows a high-priority user to interrupt the conversations of others in case of emergency or for urgent messages.
Forwarding	Allows users to forward their incoming calls to another user, or to voice messaging systems.
Hold	Allows users to place calls on hold.
Mute	Allows users to listen to callers without callers hearing them.
Park	Allows users to put calls in progress on hold at another person's extension. For example, a call answered at your desk can be parked at your colleague's desk. You can then go to your colleague's office, get some information, and pick up his phone, continuing your conversation.
Pick	Allows users to answer their phone from another person's desk.
Station speed dial	Allows users to program in their own set of frequently dialed phone numbers, which can later be dialed using a short code. This is similar to system speed numbers, but system speed numbers are preprogrammed for the entire system.
Transfer	Allows users to transfer a call to other users.

FIGURE 2-13

Popular PBX station features.

even have integrated terminals and telephones in a single unit. Further advantages of digital communications are discussed later in the book, along with the alternative of sending voice over data networks instead of using a PBX. This technique, known as voice over IP, or VOIP, is discussed in Chapter 10.

WIRELESS COMMUNICATIONS

The use of telephones and related equipment without cabling is often referred to as *wireless communications*. The simplest type of wireless communications exists in a conventional *cordless* telephone. These single-user devices use a handset that is a miniature radio, communicating with a base station connected to the telephone line. Certain radio frequencies, or channels, have been reserved for these devices. Most conventional cordless phones in use today can select from one of several channels to ensure clear communications. New frequencies have been added as the use of these devices has increased. The transmission power is relatively low, so they are typically limited to only a few hundred feet in range and are very susceptible to noise.

Wireless communications are also used in the business environment, sometimes in conjunction with a PBX. A good example of this application is a large warehouse, where many employees are somewhere inside a specific building, but none stay in any specific office. If each employee were to carry a simple cordless phone, there might be insufficient range, and the phones would constantly interfere with each other due to the small number of available channels. One approach to solving this problem involves setting up a series of intelligent base stations, each to cover a particular zone, or *cell*, inside the building. These base stations, and the special handsets that communicate with them, are very intelligent and can switch frequencies during conversations as needed to maintain a clear connection. The base stations are networked to each other, and often to a PBX, and the calls are switched from one base station to the next without the user's intervention. For example, a user can start a conversation through one base station, but as the user walks through the building, another base station senses that the user is nearby. This second base station communicates with the original base station and requests control of the call. The appropriate commands are sent between the two base stations and the handset to coordinate the almost instantaneous switching of the call to the new channel on the new base station. A user walking around the building is unaware of this switch of base stations, even though the connection may switch many times. In this way, users are guaranteed the best possible transmission at any point, because the system automatically switches them to the closest base station with an available channel.

In this example, a building is divided into several cells to create a private wireless communications system. Because these cells are small, this system is often called a *microcellular* phone system. When this technique is employed over a wider area by a commercial carrier and made available to the public, it is called a *cellular* phone system. In this case, the base stations are attached to antennas that may be several stories high, and the cells may cover several miles. The cellular service provider maintains the antennas and transmitters and links the cellular calls with the land-based telephone network. Some of the frequencies set aside for use in commercial cellular systems are assigned to each cell. Neighboring cells are assigned differing frequencies to avoid interfering with each other. Occasionally, users cannot place calls because no channels are available in the cell they are in. When this scenario begins to occur often, carriers usually add another transmitter with additional frequencies in that area, thereby dividing the original cell into two smaller cells.

There are two key factors in providing adequate wireless coverage in a particular region. First, there must be a sufficient number of base stations to ensure that all areas can send and receive sufficiently strong wireless radio signals. Buildings, mountains, and other geographic features can reduce signal strength and require a larger number of base stations to adequately cover an area. Second, the number of users being served by a given base station is limited by the number of simultaneous conversations it can support. Even if there are enough base stations to ensure sufficient signal strength throughout a region, the limit on the number of simultaneous users per base station may cause a lack of service in one area. Densely populated areas may require additional base stations to provide additional coverage. It is not uncommon in major metropolitan areas to have several base stations on a single city block, while in the suburbs the base stations may be miles apart.

Commercial cellular networks must interconnect with a central office of the *public switched telephone network* (*PSTN*) in order to allow cellular users to reach noncellular users or *landline* users. Each base station can be interconnected with the PSTN, or a cellular carrier can connect all of its base stations to a central point in an area and then connect that point to the PSTN. This second configuration is shown in Fig. 2-14, where the dotted lines represent the cellular carrier's internal network of base stations, and the solid lines show the connection to the central office and the PSTN. Notice that some areas have more base stations than others, either to improve signal strength in those areas or to serve additional users.

In all of our wireless examples, we have assumed that a single frequency, or channel, can serve only one user. However, there are techniques available today for sharing a single channel among many users. The principles of wireless operation remains the same, but additional users can be handled by sharing channels.

Cellular phones, whether portable or vehicle mounted, are of much higher power than the microcellular phones described in the private warehouse application. Unfortunately, the added variables of terrain, weather conditions, large buildings, and other transmission sources all increase the noise on cellular connections. Traditional *analog cellular* phone systems cannot always solve these noise problems, and the noise decreases only if the user moves away from the noise source or is switched to another channel when approaching the next antenna. The two most popular analog cellular standards in use today are *AMPS* and *ETACS*. The *Advanced Mobile Phone Service*, or *AMPS*, was developed by Bell Labs in the 1970s and was first introduced in the U.S. market in 1983. It is still very popular in the United States, South America, Australia, and China. The *European Total Access Communication System*, or *ETACS*, was developed in the mid-1980s and is used throughout Europe. It is similar to AMPS, though there are some differences to accommodate the European phone numbering plan, as well as differences in the radio channels used for transmission.

These analog cellular systems were known as *first generation*, or *1G*, systems. The *second generation*, or *2G*, systems now being used are also known as *digital cellular*.

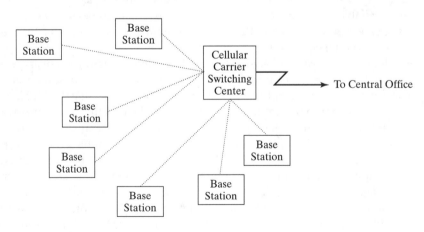

FIGURE 2-14

A cellular carrier's network.

Digital cellular solves the noise problems of analog and has other advantages of digital transmission that are covered in Chapter 5. The large investment in the installed analog cellular networks probably ensures their continued use in parallel with the newer digital networks for many years.

In the United States, *the United States Digital Cellular* standard, or *USDC*, was deployed in the 1990s to allow support of either AMPS or USDC transmission over the same radio channel range. Equipping the base stations with both standards allowed for a gradual migration of customers from analog to digital. USDC is based on a technology known as *Time Division Multiple Access*, or *TDMA*, where several conversations use a single channel by sharing transmission time on the channel. Its operation is similar in principle to time division multiplexing, which is explained in detail in Chapter 5. In addition to voice transmission, data transmission is possible at rates up to 9.6 kbps.

Another U.S. digital cellular standard that also uses the same channels as the AMPS system is known as *Code Division Multiple Access*, or *CDMA*. In CDMA, voice signals are spread across many different channels, using a technology known as *spread spectrum*. It supports data rates up to 14.4 kbps.

While major metropolitan areas are equipped with both AMPS and TDMA or CDMA equipment, rural areas still rely on AMPS alone. *Dual-mode* cellular telephones have become popular. These phones first try to connect using the better digital standard (TDMA or CDMA), but fall back to the analog standard if no digital base station can be reached.

Meanwhile, the *Global System for Mobile*, or *GSM*, standard was first introduced in Europe during the 1990s. It does not try to reuse existing AMPS/ETACS channels; rather, it is an entirely new standard based solely on digital transmission and signaling. It has many advanced signaling features, including a feature that allows the subscriber to insert a *Subscriber Identity Module*, or *SIM*, into any GSM phone. This module identifies the customer to the network, and all GSM calls for this customer are then routed to this handset. The SIM is often provided on a *smart card*, a credit-card-sized device programmed with unique identification and authentication information. A customer could insert this SIM into a hotel phone, a car phone, or a handheld phone, and incoming calls would automatically be routed to the correct location. In addition, outgoing calls from any of these locations would automatically be billed to the customer's account with his or her regular GSM carrier. These convenient features have led GSM to be deployed in much of the world. GSM supports data rates up to 9.6 kbps. USDC, TDMA, CDMA, and GSM are all 2G standards.

An intermediate generation, known as *2.5G*, provides even higher data rates. *General Packet Radio Service*, or *GPRS*, is an enhancement to GSM that provides data rates up to 170 kbps. A CDMA enhancement known as *Code Division Multiple Access 2000.1X*, or *CDMA 2000.1X*, allows for data rates up to 144 kbps.

All of these technologies provide significant improvements, but they are not as fast as the *third generation*, or *3G* technologies. Existing GSM and TDMA systems will likely use the newer *Wideband Code Division Multiple Access*, or *WCDMA* standards, also known in Europe as *Universal Mobile Telecommunications System*, or *UMTS*. Existing CDMA systems will probably migrate to the *Code Division Multiple Access 2000, or CDMA 2000*, standard. Both of these systems offer data rates up to 2.4 Mbps. *Enhanced Data rates for Global Evolution*, or *EDGE*, provides data rates up to

384 kbps on GSM or TDMA networks. Its speed is on the borderline between 2.5G and 3G and is sometimes categorized as either 2.5G or 3G. Unfortunately, the 2G, 2.5G, and 3G implementations differ in various regions (e.g., North America and Europe), so a universal standard is not yet on the horizon.

Few applications require the speed of 3G, so it is not clear when, if ever, it will be widely accepted. Deployment of a competing technology, known as wireless fidelity (Wi-Fi) hot spots, discussed in Chapter 8, is also slowing 3G's progress. Wi-Fi hot spots don't cover an entire region like cellular technologies, but instead only provide coverage in small zones in and around public buildings. Wi-Fi hot spots could be a significant competitor to 3G because most mobile workers already have Wi-Fi interfaces in their laptops and don't require data access in all areas. The cost of providing hot spots is much less than the cost of covering an entire region.

Most wide area digital services today consist of special-purpose applications, such as delivery tracking or remote access to email and calendars. These special-purpose applications usually operate with one of the public cellular services discussed above. Email messages and calendars can be received on a *personal digital assistant*, or *PDA*. These PDAs come in numerous shapes and sizes and can contain everything you would find in a typical desktop *PC* information-management program. Calendars, reminders, task lists, and email can be synchronized between a user's PDA and corporate or *personal computers*, or *PCs*. PDAs can often be synchronized through a public wireless network, as discussed above, or through the wireless local area networks discussed in Chapter 8.

Some satellite-based wireless telephone systems have also been launched that allow practically universal coverage with a single network. These systems tend to be more costly than the land-based cellular systems described here. More details on satellite-based systems are found in Chapter 5. Data from mobile sources, such as laptop computers, can be routed over any of these cellular telephone networks. There are other considerations when trying to transmit data over a wireless network, as well as some special networks designed for data transmission alone. These wireless data transmission issues are discussed further in Chapter 8.

SUMMARY

Understanding the basics of telecommunications is the first step in studying data communications. There are many different network topologies, including mesh and star. The public network, or direct distance dial network, is a series of interconnected star networks. At the center of each star network is a central office, which is connected to the users by local loops. Users signal the central office of call destinations using rotary pulses or touch-tones. The central office provides the user with other signals, including a dial tone, a ringback tone, and the busy and howler signals.

The divestiture of AT&T resulted in the formation of the Bell Operating Companies and Regional Bell Operating Companies, many of which have merged in the intervening years. Also, many long-distance carriers are now competing for customers' business, and all have equal access to the customer. The BOCs have divided their territory into local access and transport areas; the routing of inter-LATA calls involves interexchange carriers. Many different trunks are used to connect the various central offices and toll offices in the public network. The Federal Communications Commission regulates interstate calls, and the PUCs regulate intrastate calls. Internationally, many countries are regulated by PTTs. Increased competition and further deregulation appear inevitable.

Many voice service options are available to businesses, including outward-WATS, inward-WATS, and leased lines. Some businesses choose to lease basic telephone services by using their phone company's Centrex service. Key systems and private branch exchanges are both examples of customer-premises equipment that can be purchased. Many PBXs can handle thousands of lines and provide a variety of sophisticated features. A PBX can also help reduce a company's telecommunications costs by using the most efficient route. Today's digital PBXs will handle not only voice traffic, but data traffic as well.

Wireless communications is an increasingly popular option. From a simple cordless phone to vast cellular phone systems, there are a variety of wireless options to meet users' needs. Several analog and digital cellular systems are in use throughout the world today. The original analog systems are known as 1G, and the more modern digital systems are known as 2G, 2.5G, and 3G.

TERMS FOR REVIEW

1G
2G
2.5G
3G
800 number
888 number
Advanced Mobile Phone Service
American Telephone & Telegraph
AMPS
Analog cellular
Area code
AT&T
Attendant
Basic service element
Bell Communications Research
Bell Labs
Bell Operating Company
Bell System
Bellcore
BOC
Breakup
BSE
Busy signal
CDMA

CDMA 2000
CDMA 2000.X
Cell
Cellular
Central office
Central office switch
Central office trunk
Centrex
Code Division Multiple Access
Code Division Multiple Access 2000
Code Division Multiple Access 2000.1X
Common carrier
Conditioned line
Convergence
Cordless
CPE
Customer-premises equipment
DDD network
Default
Dial tone
DID trunk
Digital cellular
Digital PBX
Direct distance dial network

Direct inward dial trunk
Divestiture
DTMF
DTMF register
Dual tone multifrequency dialing
Dual-mode
Echo canceller
Echo suppressor
EDGE
End office
Enhanced Data rates for Global Evolution
Enhanced service provider
Equal access
ESP
ETACS
*European Total Access Communications
 System*
FCC
Federal Communications Commission
First generation
Foreign exchange
General Packet Radio Service
Global System for Mobile
GPRS
GSM
High-usage intertoll trunk
Howler signal
IEC
Independent Telephone Company
Interexchange carrier
Interexchange circuit
Inter-LATA call
Interoffice trunk
Intertoll trunk
Inward-WATS trunk
IOT
ITC
IXC
Key system
Landline
LATA
Leased line
Least-cost routing
LEC
Local access and transport area
Local exchange

Local exchange carrier
Local loop
Long-distance call
Lucent Technologies
Mesh network
MFJ
Microcellular
Modified Final Judgment
Network
Off-hook signal
Office code
ONA
On-hook signal
Open Network Architecture
Operator
Outward-WATS trunk
Overlay
PBX
PC
PDA
Personal computer
Personal digital assistant
Point of presence
POP
*Postal, telephone, and telegraph
 administration*
Prefix
Presubscription
Private branch exchange
PSTN
PTT
Public network
Public switched telephone network
Public utilities commission
PUC
Pulse dialing
RBOC
Regional Bell Operating Company
Regional Holding Company
RHC
Ringback signal
Ringing signal
Rotary dialing
Rotary register
Route optimization
Second generation

Signaling	*Time assignment speech interpolation*
SIM	*Time Division Multiple Access*
Smart card	*Toll call*
Spread spectrum	*Toll connecting trunk*
Star network	*Toll office*
Station feature	*Toll-free number*
Station line	*Touch-tone dialing*
Subscriber Identity Module	*Trunk*
Switch	*UMTS*
System feature	*United States Digital Cellular*
Tandem office	*Universal Mobile Telecommunications*
Tandem trunk	*System*
Tariff	*USDC*
TASI	*Voice call multiplexing*
TCT	*Voice-grade circuit*
TDMA	*WATS*
Telcordia	*WCDMA*
Telecommunications	*Western Electric*
Telecommunications Act of 1996	*Wide area telecommunications services*
Third generation	*Wideband Code Division Multiple Access*
Tie trunk	*Wireless communications*

EXERCISES

2-1. Why is the public telephone network a star network rather than a mesh network?

2-2. What functions does a central office perform?

2-3. What are the common signals between the central office and the user during a typical telephone call?

2-4. Explain the differences between rotary and DTMF dialing methods.

2-5. What are the roles of the local exchange carriers and the interexchange carriers, respectively, in inter-LATA calls?

2-6. What is a tariff? What is the difference between the FCC and the PUCs? Which agencies review which tariffs?

2-7. Compare WATS service to leased lines. Which is more useful for a customer who always calls between the same two locations? What about for a customer who calls between many different locations, but not often to any one location?

2-8. What are some ways for a business to enable an out-of-town customer to reach it via telephone at reduced cost or no cost? What about for calls from its own out-of-town factory?

2-9. What are the advantages and disadvantages of using the dial-up network versus leased lines?

2-10. Which equipment does the customer provide with Centrex service? What does the local exchange carrier provide?

2-11. What makes Centrex service inherently inefficient?

2-12. How does a PBX's method of handling internal calls differ from that of the Centrex service? How does this difference affect the customer's central office charges?

2-13. Compare the different types of PBX trunks.

2-14. What is the difference between PBX system features and PBX station features?

2-15. What is the main advantage of the route-optimization feature found in advanced PBXs?

2-16. How does a conventional cordless phone differ from a cellular phone?

2-17. What standard is typically used for analog cellular phones in North America? In Europe?

2-18. What standards are typically associated with 2G cellular service? 2.5G? 3G?

CHAPTER 3

Basic Data Communications Concepts

DEFINING DATA COMMUNICATIONS

Data communications is usually defined as the exchange of digital information between two devices using an electronic transmission system. *Digital* information is another name for ones and zeroes. Therefore, a less formal definition of *data communications* is the art of sending ones and zeroes from one point to another.

To help illustrate basic data communications concepts, we begin by examining the relationships between host computers, terminals, clients, and servers.

HOST COMPUTERS AND TERMINALS

A *host computer*, or *central processing unit* (*CPU*), can perform numerical calculations, store and retrieve data, and perform a variety of tasks known as *applications*. Examples of host computer *applications software* include word-processing programs, spreadsheets, accounting programs, and payroll programs.

There are many different types of host computers. *Mainframes* are host computers usually serving a large company. *Minicomputers* are host computers usually dedicated to a smaller set of users, perhaps a department or a division. *Microcomputers*, or *personal computers*, usually serve only one user. A *supercomputer* is an extremely fast mainframe dedicated to extensive mathematical calculations.

Many data communications networks allow host computers to exchange information with other locally or remotely located devices. One of these devices is known as a *terminal*. Other names for a terminal include *cathode ray tube* (*CRT*), *video display terminal* (*VDT*), and *display station*. Regardless of the name used, a terminal's basic function is to allow a user to communicate with a host computer. Terminals include a *keyboard* for entering information to be transmitted to the host computer and a *screen* for displaying information received from the host computer.

While some modern computer networks do not even contain terminals today, the simple connection between a terminal and a host computer serves as an ideal starting point for any discussion of basic data-communications concepts. More advanced networks build on these concepts, so any material presented in the early chapters that refers to these terminals will be applicable to the more advanced networks discussed in the later chapters.

Terminals are often classified in one of three ways: dumb, smart, or intelligent. A *dumb terminal* simply receives data from a host computer and displays it on its screen; it is unable to modify or change the data it receives. Similarly, any data typed using the keyboard is sent directly to the host computer, without any major modifications being made by the terminal.

A *smart terminal* usually sends extra information to a host computer, in addition to the data the user types. This additional information can include the terminal's address, or location, as well as special information to prevent errors from occurring. The host computer also sends similar information to the smart terminal, including specific instructions regarding when the terminal can send data. The smart terminal is smart enough to interpret these instructions and pass on any actual data to the user. We discuss the rules for smart-terminal communications in detail in Chapter 7.

The difference between an *intelligent terminal* and a smart terminal is very subtle. Intelligent terminals are just like smart terminals, but their behavior can be modified or programmed. After a smart terminal leaves the factory, it never changes its behavior and can never learn to perform new functions. An intelligent terminal can be programmed to perform new functions by many means, including special tapes, cartridges, diskettes, or keyboard commands, depending on the manufacturer.

In recent years, the terms *client* and *server* are often used instead of *terminal* and *host computer*. While a client usually has some local processing power, like a personal computer or *PC,* the server is simply another name for a host computer. While typical servers are physically much smaller than the old mainframes, they are still host computers and can be just as powerful. When we use PCs as clients to connect to servers in order to run programs and retrieve data, we are temporarily turning our sophisticated PCs into terminals.

BITS AND BYTES

Almost all computers and terminals, from the 100-dollar terminal to the multimillion-dollar supercomputer, communicate by sending a series of ones and zeroes to each other. We call each one or zero a *bit*, and we call a group of several (usually eight) ones and zeroes a *byte*. We use the *binary number system* to represent digital information. Readers who have not been exposed to the binary number system before or who simply need a quick review should refer to Appendix A.

While it is not likely that the device on an office desktop today is a terminal, terminals are still used widely in many dedicated applications, such as cash registers and other simple applications. The simple operation of a dumb terminal makes it an ideal tool for introducing some basic topics. The dumb terminal shown in Fig. 3-1 is connected to a host computer. Each time the user hits a key on the keyboard, a series of bits is

FIGURE 3-1

Terminal   Host computer   Terminal and host computer.

transmitted to the host computer. The host computer receives those bits and then determines which *character* they represent. Characters include letters of the alphabet, numbers, all punctuation marks, and special keys, such as Delete, used by different terminals.

CHARACTER CODES

Each time a user strikes a particular key on the dumb terminal, the terminal must translate that key into a series of bits, and the host computer must always recognize that series of bits as representing the same character. There are many ways to represent characters, and these different representations are known as *character codes*.

Several different character codes are in use today. We now examine in detail some of the more popular ones in the order of their evolution: Morse, Baudot, EBCDIC, and ASCII.

Morse Code

Morse code was one of the first character codes developed. It is a crude, but effective, code for transmitting characters over a telegraph circuit. Morse code was designed with a telegraph operator in mind; the operator sent combinations of a short beep, known as a *dot*, and a long beep, known as a *dash*, to transmit characters. The characters used most frequently need the fewest dots and dashes for transmission. A table of Morse code is shown in Fig. 3-2.

A	• —	N	— •	1	• — — — —
B	— • • •	O	— — —	2	• • — — —
C	— • — •	P	• — — •	3	• • • — —
D	— • •	Q	— — • —	4	• • • • —
E	•	R	• — •	5	• • • • •
F	• • — •	S	• • •	6	— • • • •
G	— — •	T	—	7	— — • • •
H	• • • •	U	• • —	8	— — — • •
I	• •	V	• • • —	9	— — — — •
J	• — — —	W	• — —	0	— — — — —
K	— • —	X	— • • —	.	• — • — • —
L	• — • •	Y	— • — —	,	— — • • — —
M	— —	Z	— — • •	?	• • — — • •

FIGURE 3-2

Morse code.

Notice in Fig. 3-2 that the letter "A" consists of a dot and a dash, or a short beep followed by a long beep. Every time a telegraph operator sent "dot-dash," the receiving operator knew that the letter "A" was being transmitted. Notice that the letter "R" starts out just like the letter "A", but then adds an extra dot at the end. How would operators distinguish between the letter "A" (dot-dash) followed by the letter "E" (dot) and the letter "R" alone (dot-dash-dot)? Morse code handled this problem by requiring the operator to pause for a short time between letters. "AE" became "dot-dash-pause-dot," thus distinguishing "AE" from the letter "R," "dot-dash-dot."

One of the features that makes Morse code unsuitable for computer communications is the extra time required between transmission of characters. Why waste the time of an expensive computer by pausing between characters? The small number of different characters that can be transmitted in Morse code is also severely limiting. Clearly, other character codes needed to be developed for computer communications.

Baudot Code

Baudot code was one of the first character codes developed with machines, not humans, in mind. Baudot code uses ones and zeroes, rather than dots and dashes, to represent characters.

Baudot code addressed the shortcomings of Morse code by using five bits of information for each character. The Baudot code table is presented in Fig. 3-3. As shown in the table, the bits in the Baudot character code are numbered with the bit on the far left as bit 5 and with the bit on the far right as bit 1.

Let's begin by examining the *Lower Case* column in this table. If a user types the letter "A" on a terminal that communicates using Baudot code, the terminal sends five bits, 00011, as shown on the first line of the chart. Assuming that the host computer receiving 00011 also uses Baudot code, it will then recognize 00011 as the letter "A". Similarly, if the user types the letter "B", 11001 will be transmitted. If the user types the letter "C", 01110 will be transmitted, and so on, as shown in the Baudot table.

What if the user types the number "3"? Notice that the number "3" is in the *Upper Case* column of our chart. The Baudot terminal must now switch to Upper Case to send the number "3". Much as one would hit the Shift Lock key on a typewriter, the terminal sends a special code to the host computer, 11011, to instruct it to switch to Upper Case. This code, known as the *Figures code*, instructs the host computer that all further transmissions will be from the Upper Case column of the chart. In this instance, Upper Case doesn't refer to capital letters, but instead, it translates to a whole new set of characters. Once the host computer has been alerted that future characters will be from the Upper Case column, the terminal can send the number "3" by sending 00001.

When the user later strikes a key from the Lower Case column, the terminal will send the *Letters code*, 11111, which instructs the host computer that future transmissions will be from the Lower Case column. This code is equivalent to releasing the Shift Lock key on a typewriter.

In addition to the Letters and Figures characters, there are two additional special characters: the *line feed* and *carriage return* characters. A line feed, when sent to a terminal, causes the terminal to advance one line, and a carriage return moves the print head (or cursor) back to the left margin.

Character		Data bits				
Lower Case	Upper Case	5	4	3	2	1
A	_	0	0	0	1	1
B	?	1	1	0	0	1
C	:	0	1	1	1	0
D	$	0	1	0	0	1
E	3	0	0	0	0	1
F	!	0	1	1	0	1
G	&	1	1	0	1	0
H	#	1	0	1	0	0
I	8	0	0	1	1	0
J	'	0	1	0	1	1
K	(	0	1	1	1	1
L	)	1	0	0	1	0
M	.	1	1	1	0	0
N	,	0	1	1	0	0
O	9	1	1	0	0	0
P	0	1	0	1	1	0
Q	1	1	0	1	1	1
R	4	0	1	0	1	0
S	BELL	0	0	1	0	1
T	5	1	0	0	0	0
U	7	0	0	1	1	1
V	;	1	1	1	1	0
W	2	1	0	0	1	1
X	/	1	1	1	0	1
Y	6	1	0	1	0	1
Z	"	1	0	0	0	1
Letters (shift to Lower Case column)		1	1	1	1	1
Figures (shift to Upper Case column)		1	1	0	1	1
Space		0	0	1	0	0
Carriage return		0	1	0	0	0
Line feed		0	0	0	1	0
Blank		0	0	0	0	0

FIGURE 3-3

Baudot code.

Baudot code was used for many years on telex equipment, and some teletype machines still use this code. In fact, the punched tape so familiar to teletype users is a direct representation of Baudot code. There are five positions across the punch tape; a hole in the tape represents a one, and no hole represents a zero.

Occasionally, a bit is changed during data transmission. We call this a *bit error*. In Baudot code, there is no way in which the receiving device can tell that a bit error occurred during transmission. The need for *error detection* led to an improvement on the Baudot code known as *International Baudot*. International Baudot adds a sixth bit, known as a *parity bit*, to check for errors. We explain in detail how parity bits work in Chapter 6. Simply stated, a parity bit is an extra bit transmitted in addition to the character-code bits. It allows the data to be checked for errors at the receiving end.

The five information bits of Baudot code yield 32 different combinations of ones and zeroes. To represent more than 32 characters, the Letters and Figures characters shift the user into different transmission and reception modes (Upper and Lower Case). Switching back and forth between Upper and Lower Case wastes a computer's time. For this reason, Baudot code is not often used for high-speed data communications. Later character codes remedied this problem.

Extended Binary Coded Decimal Interchange Code

Extended Binary Coded Decimal Interchange Code, known as *EBCDIC*, is an eight-bit character code developed by IBM. EBCDIC is a descendant of several older codes, including *Binary Coded Decimal*, or *BCD*, an early code used by computers to represent information internally. BCD led to the development of *Extended Binary Coded Decimal*, or *EBCD*, and finally to EBCDIC.

The eight bits of EBCDIC offer 256 different possible combinations of ones and zeroes. Most EBCDIC implementations, however, do not use all of the possible combinations. One EBCDIC implementation is presented in Fig. 3-4. Empty spaces in the chart can be used for other characters and functions needed for other implementations, including foreign language and graphics characters. The bits in EBCDIC are numbered with the bit on the far left as bit 0 and with the bit on the far right as bit 7. To read the EBCDIC chart, simply find a particular character; bits 0, 1, 2, and 3 are found on the left end of the row, and bits 4, 5, 6, and 7 are found at the top of the column.

If a user types the letter "A" on an EBCDIC terminal, the bits 11000001 are transmitted, as shown in Fig. 3-4. Similarly, typing the letter "B" causes 11000010 to be transmitted, typing the letter "C" causes 11000011 to be transmitted, and so on, as shown in the EBCDIC table. There are many special characters in EBCDIC; the abbreviations of those characters that are relevant to our discussion are also explained in Fig. 3-4. Certain characters, such as the line feed character, simply control printers and terminals. Others, such as the Start of Header (SOH) character, are used extensively in special communications protocols. These special characters are discussed in detail in Chapter 7.

In most cases, EBCDIC is used without parity bits. Usually, groups of EBCDIC characters are sent together, in blocks, and an entire block of characters is checked for errors at once. This technique is explained in detail in Chapter 6. Some variations of EBCDIC do add a ninth bit for parity checking, though in most cases this bit is removed before transmission.

American National Standard Code for Information Interchange

American National Standard Code for Information Interchange, known as *ASCII*, is a seven-bit data code with a single additional parity bit. ASCII (pronounced as-key) was developed by the *American National Standards Institute*, or *ANSI*, as a general-purpose character code. The ASCII table is presented in Fig. 3-5. The seven data bits of ASCII offer 128 different possible combinations of ones and zeroes. The bits in ASCII are numbered with the bit on the far left as bit 8 and with the bit on the far right as bit 1. Bit 8 is the parity bit, and bits 1 through 7 are the data bits.

If a user types the letter "A" on an ASCII terminal, the seven data bits transmitted are 1000001, as shown in Fig. 3-5. Similarly, typing the letter "B" causes 1000010 to

4	0	0	0	0	0	0	0	0	1	1	1	1	1	1	1	1
5	0	0	0	0	1	1	1	1	0	0	0	0	1	1	1	1
Bit 6	0	0	1	1	0	0	1	1	0	0	1	1	0	0	1	1
7	0	1	0	1	0	1	0	1	0	1	0	1	0	1	0	1
0123																
0000	NUL	SOH	STX	ETX	PF	HT	LC	DEL				VT	FF	CR	SO	SI
0001	DLE	DC1	DC2	DC3	RES	NL	BS	IL	CAN	EM			IFS	IGS	IRS	IUS
0010			FS		BYP	LF	EOB	PRE			SM			ENQ	ACK	BEL
0011			SYN		PN	RS	UC	EOT					DC4	NAK		SUB
0100	SP										¢	.	<	(	+	|
0101	&										!	$	*	)	;	¬
0110	-	/									¦	,	%	_	>	?
0111										\	:	#	@	'	=	"
1000		a	b	c	d	e	f	g	h	i						
1001		j	k	l	m	n	o	p	q	r						
1010		~	s	t	u	v	w	x	y	z						
1011																
1100	{	A	B	C	D	E	F	G	H	I						
1101	}	J	K	L	M	N	O	P	Q	R						
1110		S	T	U	V	W	X	Y	Z							
1111	0	1	2	3	4	5	6	7	8	9						□

Note: To read this chart, simply find the character on the chart, then look to the left side of the row for bits 0, 1, 2, and 3, and to the top of the column for bits 4, 5, 6, and 7. This is only one of many possible implementations of EBCDIC.

EBCDIC special characters

ACK	Acknowledgment	EOT	End of Transmission	PF	Punch Off
BEL	Bell	ETX	End of Text	PN	Punch On
BS	Backspace	FF	Form Feed	PRE	Prefix
BYP	Bypass	FS	File Separator	RES	Restore
CAN	Cancel	HT	Horizontal Tab	RS	Reader Stop
CR	Carriage Return	IFS	Information File Separator	SI	Shift In
DC1	Device Control 1	IGS	Information Group Separator	SM	Start Message
DC2	Device Control 2	IL	Idle	SO	Shift Out
DC3	Device Control 3	IRS	Information Record Separator	SOH	Start of Header
DC4	Device Control 4	IUS	Information Unit Separator	SP	Space
DEL	Delete	LC	Lower Case	STX	Start of Text
DLE	Data Link Escape	LF	Line Feed	SUB	Substitute
EM	End of Medium	NAK	Negative Acknowledgment	SYN	Synchronous Idle
ENQ	Enquiry	NL	New Line	UC	Upper Case
EOB	End of Block	NUL	Null	VT	Vertical Tab

FIGURE 3-4

EBCDIC code.

be transmitted, typing the letter "C" causes 1000011 to be transmitted, and so on, as shown in the ASCII table. In addition to these seven data bits, a parity bit usually is transmitted.

There are several *control characters* in ASCII, similar to those used in EBCDIC, and their abbreviations are also explained in Fig. 3-5. Some of these characters, known as *format effectors* (*FE*), perform special display functions on printers and terminals. Other characters, known as *information separators* (*IS*), are used by host computers in storing and retrieving data. Finally, another group of characters, known as *control codes* (*CC*), are used in protocols that we examine in detail in Chapter 7.

Some vendors have chosen to use their own modified versions of ASCII. Such versions, often known as *extended ASCII*, replace the parity bit with an eighth data bit.

Bits	Character	Bits	Character	Bits	Character	Bits	Character
7654321		7654321		7654321		7654321	
0000000	NUL	0100000	SP	1000000	@	1100000	`
0000001	SOH	0100001	!	1000001	A	1100001	a
0000010	STX	0100010	"	1000010	B	1100010	b
0000011	ETX	0100011	#	1000011	C	1100011	c
0000100	EOT	0100100	$	1000100	D	1100100	d
0000101	ENQ	0100101	%	1000101	E	1100101	e
0000110	ACK	0100110	&	1000110	F	1100110	f
0000111	BEL	0100111	'	1000111	G	1100111	g
0001000	BS	0101000	(	1001000	H	1101000	h
0001001	HT	0101001	)	1001001	I	1101001	i
0001010	LF	0101010	*	1001010	J	1101010	j
0001011	VT	0101011	+	1001011	K	1101011	k
0001100	FF	0101100	,	1001100	L	1101100	l
0001101	CR	0101101	–	1001101	M	1101101	m
0001110	SO	0101110	.	1001110	N	1101110	n
0001111	SI	0101111	/	1001111	O	1101111	o
0010000	DLE	0110000	0	1010000	P	1110000	p
0010001	DC1	0110001	1	1010001	Q	1110001	q
0010010	DC2	0110010	2	1010010	R	1110010	r
0010011	DC3	0110011	3	1010011	S	1110011	s
0010100	DC4	0110100	4	1010100	T	1110100	t
0010101	NAK	0110101	5	1010101	U	1110101	u
0010110	SYN	0110110	6	1010110	V	1110110	v
0010111	ETB	0110111	7	1010111	W	1110111	w
0011000	CAN	0111000	8	1011000	X	1111000	x
0011001	EM	0111001	9	1011001	Y	1111001	y
0011010	SUB	0111010	:	1011010	Z	1111010	z
0011011	ESC	0111011	;	1011011	[	1111011	{
0011100	FS	0111100	<	1011100	\	1111100	|
0011101	GS	0111101	=	1011101	]	1111101	}
0011110	RS	0111110	>	1011110	^	1111110	~
0011111	US	0111111	?	1011111	—	1111111	DEL

FIGURE 3-5

ASCII code.

ASCII control characters			
BEL	Bell	EM	End of Medium
CAN	Cancel	ESC	Escape
DC1	Device Control 1	NUL	Null
DC2	Device Control 2	SI	Shift In
DC3	Device Control 3	SO	Shift Out
DC4	Device Control 4	SUB	Substitute
DEL	Delete		
Control codes			
ACK	Acknowledge	ETX	End of Text
DLE	Data Link Escape	NAK	Negative Acknowledge
ENQ	Enquiry	SOH	Start of Heading
EOT	End of Transmission	STX	Start of Text
ETB	End of Transmission Block	SYN	Synchronous Idle
Format effectors			
BS	Backspace	HT	Horizontal Tabulation
CR	Carriage Return	LF	Line Feed
FF	Form Feed	VT	Vertical Tabulation
Information separators			
FS	File Separator	RS	Record Separator
GS	Group Separator	US	Unit Separator

FIGURE 3-5

(Continued)

This substitution allows for 256 combinations of ones and zeroes, doubling the number of characters that can be represented. Such an extension of the character set allows unusual characters, including foreign language characters, accent marks, and graphic or scientific characters, to be represented in the second set of 128 characters. These extra characters come at the expense of the parity bit and its error-detection capabilities, which we consider in Chapter 6.

Equipment Compatibility and Character-Code Comparisons

We have introduced several different character codes with different bit lengths. Clearly, terminals using a particular character code are designed to connect to computers using that same code. But what if a terminal uses ASCII code and a host computer uses EBCDIC code? *Code conversion* is required to connect devices that use dissimilar character codes, and *protocol conversion* may be necessary as well. Various protocols are reviewed in detail in Chapter 7.

Figure 3-6 shows the bit-position differences among the various character codes. In most implementations, the lower numbered bit (usually 0 or 1) is transmitted first, followed by the other bits. Remember that the bit-numbering schemes used in the

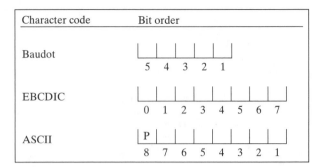

FIGURE 3-6

Bit position differences among various character codes.

different codes are simply conventions followed in the industry to ensure that transmitting and receiving devices send and receive the bits in identical order. The "P" shown in bit 8 of the ASCII code represents the parity bit.

Some typical data-bit and parity-bit combinations in the different character codes are compared in Fig. 3-7. Notice that there are variations in parity-bit implementations even within a single character code. The most common implementation is presented first in each case. Some manufacturers may choose different parity schemes from those shown. Doing so, however, can render their proprietary versions of the character codes incompatible with the versions used by the rest of the industry.

To the user, it is not really important which character code a terminal is using, as long as the host computer is able to understand the terminal. Character codes merely define exactly which sets of ones and zeroes are transmitted for each character. We now turn to other important data-transmission issues.

CHARACTER-CODE DESIGN AND TERMINAL IMPLEMENTATION

The most advanced character codes we discussed, ASCII and EBCDIC, both include uppercase and lowercase letters. In the ASCII code chart in Fig. 3-5, notice that the letter "A" is represented by 1000001, while the letter "a" is represented by 1100001. Similarly, the letter "B" is represented by 1000010, and the letter "b" by 1100010. Throughout the alphabet, the only difference between an ASCII letter in lowercase and an ASCII letter in uppercase is in bit number 6. Uppercase letters have a 0 in bit 6, and lowercase letters have a 1 in bit 6.

This system simplifies the character-code implementation on a terminal. Typically, a terminal user will press the Shift key to send an uppercase character. Pressing the Shift key on an ASCII terminal simply causes bit 6 to be sent as a 0 when another alphabetic key is struck. If the Shift key is released, the terminal sends a 1 for bit 6 when another alphabetic key is struck. If the terminal has a Shift Lock or Caps Lock feature, using that feature sets bit 6 to be a 0 all the time.

Similarly, in EBCDIC, as shown in Fig. 3-4, the only difference between the letter "A" and the letter "a" is in bit 1. Uppercase letters in EBCDIC use a 1 in bit 1, and lowercase letters use a 0 in bit 1.

Many ASCII terminal users are familiar with a key known as the *Control key*. Users can press the Control key and then hit another alphabetic key to perform a special function. Pressing the Control key causes bit 7 and bit 6 both to be 0.

One special character on the ASCII chart is the BEL character. Most ASCII terminals will sound a short beep when they receive this character. An ASCII terminal user who presses the Control key and the "G" key simultaneously will send the BEL character. "G" is normally represented by 1000111, but the control key changes bits 6 and 7 to 0, resulting in 0000111, or the BEL character. Similarly, pressing the Control key and the "g" key simultaneously will also send a BEL.

One common function often performed on ASCII terminals with control characters is *XON/XOFF*. In this case, an ASCII terminal can ask the host computer to stop transmitting data by sending the XOFF character, usually the DC3 character. Notice on the ASCII chart that an "S" is usually 1010011. Pressing the Control key and the "S" key simultaneously results in 0010011, or the DC3 character. Transmission can be resumed by sending the XON character, usually a DC1. The DC1 character can be sent by pressing the Control key and the "Q" key simultaneously.

From this discussion, we can see how character-code designers have allowed keyboards to use each key for several functions. Rather than needing hundreds of different keys, special keys like the Shift key and the Control key allow the size and cost of terminals to be minimized.

PARALLEL VS. SERIAL TRANSMISSION

Though a character code determines which bits need to be transmitted to represent a particular character, it does not define how these bits are to be sent. There are two common methods of data transmission: parallel and serial.

Assume that we have eight bits of information to send from point A to point B. For our example, assume that the eight bits are 01000001. This sequence happens to be the ASCII representation of the letter "A", with a 0 used for the parity bit. How do we send these ones and zeroes?

One method is to send all eight bits at once. This method is known as *parallel transmission*, as illustrated in Fig. 3-8. This method requires at least eight wires for transmission, one wire for each bit sent. It also requires other wires for functions examined in Chapter 4.

An analogy for parallel transmission can be drawn using cars and highways. If eight cars need to travel between point A and point B, the fastest way to get them to point B is with an eight-lane highway. Assuming that the cars travel at the same speed, all eight cars arrive at their destination at the same time.

The main advantage of parallel transmission is that the entire byte is received at once, since all eight ones and zeroes are sent at the same time. The main disadvantage is the number of wires (or lanes on the data highway) required for transmission.

Character code	Data bits	Parity bits	Total bits
Baudot	5	0	5
International Baudot	5	1	6
ASCII	7	1	8
	8	0	8
	8	1	9
EBCDIC	8	0	8
	8	1	9

Note: This chart contains the most commonly used parity/data bit combinations. There are other possible variations.

FIGURE 3-7

Typical data and parity combinations for various character codes.

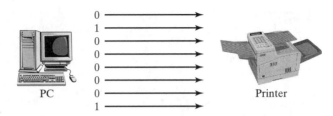

FIGURE 3-8

Parallel data transmission.

PC

Printer

Another method is to send the eight bits one after another, thus requiring only one wire for transmission. This method is known as *serial transmission*, as illustrated in Fig. 3-9.

An analogy for serial transmission is a one-lane road, with the eight cars traveling one behind the other. No matter how fast the cars travel, the first car in the line always arrives at the destination before the others. Of course, it is less expensive to build a one-lane highway than an eight-lane highway.

The main advantage of serial transmission lies in minimizing the number of wires (or lanes on the data highway) that are necessary for data transmission. However, some time is wasted because the byte must be disassembled, sent one bit at a time, and reassembled at the other end.

Both parallel and serial transmission have their places in data communications applications. For example, many personal computers communicate with their printers using parallel transmission. Since printers are usually located within 10 or 20 feet of the personal computers, the extra wires required for parallel transmission are short, and the slight extra cost is more than offset by the added speed.

A user connecting his or her device to another two buildings away, however, will most likely use serial transmission. In this case, the additional distance involved makes the cost of parallel transmission prohibitive, and speed is sacrificed for the economical advantage of serial transmission. Only one wire, or channel, is needed to send data in each direction, thereby lowering the transmission cost.

Since manufacturers expect most clients or terminals to be located some distance from servers or host computers, we almost always communicate using serial transmission. In fact, almost all data communications equipment we consider in the next few chapters uses serial transmission. Parallel transmission can be thought of as a special case, or an exception, suitable for short-distance transmission.

Now that we have established that most data communications activities are accomplished with serial transmission, we can examine the timing of the bit transmission.

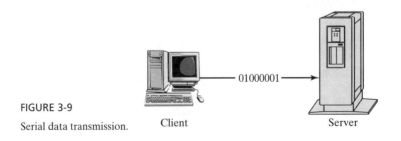

FIGURE 3-9

Serial data transmission.

Client

Server

ASYNCHRONOUS VS. SYNCHRONOUS TRANSMISSION

There are two common methods in use today for timing serial data transmission: asynchronous and synchronous.

Asynchronous transmission is commonly used by the dumb terminals we mentioned earlier, as well as on the serial ports on our PCs. For our discussion, we assume that our characters are represented by eight bits, including any parity bit. With asynchronous transmission, each device must be set to transmit and receive data at a given speed, known as the *data rate*. The data rate is often measured in *bits per second*, or *bps*. When an asynchronous device sends a byte, it begins by sending a *start bit*, which is always a 0, followed by each of the eight bits in the byte, and then followed by a *stop bit*, which is always a 1. These bits add up to form a 10-bit package for transmission. Some asynchronous devices send more than one stop bit, which simply lengthens the number of bits required to send a character.

The asynchronous transmission of the letter "A", followed by the letter "B", from a dumb terminal to a host computer using ASCII code is shown in Fig. 3-10. The terminal user types the letter "A" on the keyboard, and the terminal converts the letter "A" to the bit sequence 01000001, with a 0 used as the parity bit. If we assume that the terminal is set to transmit at one bit per second, then the terminal can send each bit one second apart. The terminal begins by sending the start bit, a 0, for the first second. It then sends the first data bit, a 1, during the next second, followed by the next bit, a 0, and so on. This transmission continues until the start bit, seven data bits, one parity bit, and the stop bit have been sent. The host computer, upon receiving the start bit, is thereby notified that it should expect seven data bits, one parity bit, and one stop bit. Each of these bits is sent 1 second apart. The start bit actually starts the host computer's internal stopwatch or clock, and the host then expects to receive the next nine bits 1 second apart. The stop bit is used to halt the host computer's internal stopwatch. Later, it can be started again by another start bit that is sent with the next character. In Fig. 3-10, the next character sent is the letter "B".

To visualize the process of asynchronous transmission, we can pretend that we are using a tennis-ball machine that throws balls to us every 5 seconds. We'll use orange balls to represent zeroes and yellow balls to represent ones. A friend loads 10 balls into

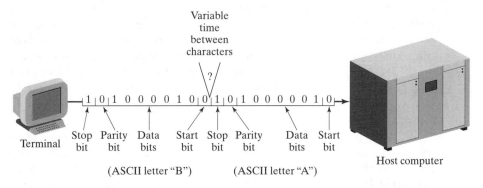

FIGURE 3-10

Asynchronous data transmission.

the machine; the first ball is an orange one, and the last ball is a yellow one. We set the machine to start as soon as it is filled with 10 balls. Once it is filled, it throws the first ball (an orange ball), or the start ball. After that, we expect a ball (any color) 5 seconds from now, another ball 10 seconds from now, and so on, until we finally receive the 10th ball, or stop ball (a yellow one), 45 seconds from now. If we don't receive one ball every 5 seconds and a yellow ball (the stop ball) in 45 seconds, we know that either the machine is not functioning or one of the balls fell out of the machine.

Similarly, in asynchronous transmission, the only way to know when the next bit is to arrive is to time how long it has been since the start bit was received. If fewer than 10 bits are received or if the stop bit isn't received when expected, either the transmitter is malfunctioning or one of the bits was lost in transmission.

Asynchronous transmission, often known as *start–stop transmission* because of the start and stop bits, is an excellent means for transmitting characters from terminals to host computers. As soon as the user strikes a key, the terminal decides which byte to send for that character and adds the start and stop bits; all 10 bits thus can be immediately transmitted. As shown in Fig. 3-10, there is a variable time between when the letter "A" and the letter "B" are transmitted. If the user strikes the keys one after another, the characters are transmitted one after the other. If the user types only the letter "A" and then takes a coffee break before typing the letter "B", the terminal remains idle and does nothing but wait during that coffee break. The user at the keyboard is like our friend loading the tennis-ball machine. We never know when our friend will load the machine, but when the machine has its 10 balls, it will start firing them at us at a fixed rate of speed. Similarly, we don't know when the user will strike a key, but as soon as the user hits a key on the keyboard, the terminal has the 10 bits it needs and will start sending them at a fixed rate.

We've been using data rates of one bit each second, or one every 5 seconds, to make our examples easier to understand. Actual data rates are more likely to be 110 bps, 300 bps, 1200 bps, 2400 bps, 4800 bps, 9600 bps, 19200 bps, and so on, all the way up to millions of bits per second. Of course, it is essential that the transmitting and receiving devices both be set at the same speed.

Besides asynchronous transmission, the other commonly used form of data transmission is *synchronous transmission*. Here, start and stop bits are not used. There is no pause between characters in synchronous data transmission, as shown in Fig. 3-11, and the letters "A" and "B" are sent one after the other. Instead of using start and stop bits, timing is supplied in two ways. The two methods, using sync characters or clock signals, can be used independently, though they are often used in conjunction with each other.

First, synchronous data transmission usually involves large blocks of characters, and special *sync characters* can be sent at the beginning of these data blocks. These sync characters are a special series of bits the receiving device can use to adjust to the transmitter's exact rate of speed.

The second method of timing used in synchronous transmission is *transmit clocks* and *receive clocks*. In this case, separate wires or channels are typically used to send information about the timing of the data being transmitted. The devices transmitting data often send their own timing information on a separate wire from the data, or the clock can be combined with the data using special techniques. The clock signals are a way of saying, "Here comes a bit right now."

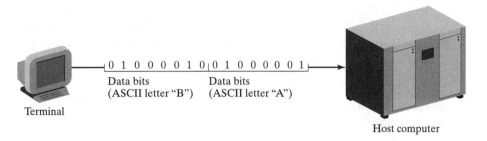

Data bits
(ASCII letter "B")

Data bits
(ASCII letter "A")

Terminal

Host computer

FIGURE 3-11

Synchronous data transmission.

We can compare clock signals and sync characters using our tennis-ball example. First, to better simulate synchronous data blocks, we will load the machine not with just 10 balls, but with a few hundred. Clock signals are the equivalent of setting the tennis-ball machine to operate with an audible signal. Just before the machine throws each ball, it sounds a beep. The beep is a clock signal that lets us know when to expect a ball to be thrown. Similarly, in synchronous data transmission, the transmit clock tells a terminal when to end a bit, and the receive clock warns a terminal when to expect to receive a bit.

Sync characters can be simulated in our tennis-ball machine if the first eight balls are always thrown in the same pattern (e.g., yellow–orange–orange–orange–orange–orange–orange–yellow). When we receive this pattern of balls, we "sync up," getting used to the pace. We begin our real practice with the ninth ball. Similarly, a sync character is a known pattern of bits. After receiving a certain number of sync characters, a device expects to receive real data.

Nothing prevents us from using both a set pattern of eight tennis balls at the beginning of each session and an audible signal. Similarly, many synchronous devices use sync characters initially to "sync up" to the transmission speed and then use clock signals to keep their internal stopwatch in line with the transmitter's stopwatch.

In addition, synchronous transmission is usually governed by protocols, which we explain in detail in Chapter 7. A major feature of these protocols is that data is usually sent in *blocks*, or groups, of characters, not one byte at a time. Most synchronous terminals are smart or intelligent terminals and most have an ENTER or XMIT key. As the user types information, the terminal holds all of the data until the user hits the ENTER or XMIT key. Then the terminal places special characters at the beginning and end of the data, according to the protocol, and sends the entire block of characters.

Asynchronous vs. Synchronous Transmission Efficiency

Synchronous transmission has an obvious advantage when large blocks of data must be sent: Time is not wasted sending a start and stop bit for each character. For example, as shown in Fig. 3-12, if a block of data contains 1000 characters and 10 special characters need to be used by the synchronous protocol at the beginning and end of the block, 1010 characters need to be sent. If we assume eight-bit characters, 8000 bits out of the

Asynchronous transmission efficiency

ABCDEFGHIJKLMNOPQRSTUVWXYZ, etc., ABCDEFGHIJKLMNOPQRSTUVWXYZ
Each character = 8 data bits, 1 start bit, 1 stop bit = 10 total bits

If we need to send 1000 characters,
   then 10,000 total bits are sent,
   of which 8000 are data bits   → 80% efficiency
If we need to send 40 characters,
   then 400 total bits are sent,
   of which 320 are data bits   → 80% efficiency
If we need to send 20 characters,
   then 200 total bits are sent,
   of which 160 are data bits   → 80% efficiency

Synchronous transmission efficiency

*****ABCDEFGHIJKLMNOPQRSTUVWXYZ, etc., ABCDEFGHIJKLMNOPQRSTUVWXYZ*****
Assume that each block of data needs 10 special characters (shown as *)
Each character = 8 data bits
If we need to send 1000 characters,
   we add the 10 special characters,
   for a total of 1010 characters,
   so we send 8080 total bits,
   of which 8000 are data bits   → 99.1% efficiency
If we need to send 40 characters,
   we add the 10 special characters,
   for a total of 50 characters,
   so we send 400 total bits,
   of which 320 are data bits   → 80% efficiency
If we need to send 20 characters,
   we add the 10 special characters,
   for a total of 30 characters,
   so we send 240 total bits,
   of which 160 are data bits   → 66.7% efficiency

FIGURE 3-12

Synchronous and asynchronous transmission efficiency.

8080 we are sending are actual data bits. This procedure is roughly 99.1% efficient. We consider the special characters, which make up the extra 80 bits, as *overhead* necessary for successful data transmission.

In asynchronous transmission of the same 1000 characters, as shown in Fig. 3-12, we must send 10,000 bits, since each character requires eight bits plus one start and one stop bit. Therefore, since 8000 of the 10,000 bits are data bits and 2000 bits are overhead, asynchronous transmission proves to be only 80% efficient for eight-bit characters.

Note that no matter how many eight-bit characters are sent, asynchronous transmission remains 80% efficient. Synchronous transmission efficiency, on the other hand, depends on the size of the block of characters being sent. The larger the block, the more efficient synchronous transmission becomes. Synchronous transmission of small blocks of data is relatively inefficient. For example, if the user types only one character before hitting the ENTER key, the same 10 special characters may be needed before and after the one data character, leaving an efficiency of eight data bits in 88 transmitted bits, or an efficiency of only 9.1%.

In our example, we chose one start bit and one stop bit for asynchronous transmission, and we assumed that 10 special characters were necessary in synchronous transmission. For this example, synchronous transmission becomes more efficient than asynchronous transmission for data blocks larger than 40 characters. This number is less than the number of characters in a line of a typewritten page. Synchronous terminals are usually smart or intelligent terminals. They are more expensive to build because they must be able to differentiate between actual data and the special synchronous characters, as well as follow special protocols that we explain in Chapter 7.

Asynchronous and synchronous transmission are two ways of timing bit transmission once a communications path is available. We must still consider the different types of paths used for communications.

SIMPLEX, HALF DUPLEX, AND FULL DUPLEX COMMUNICATIONS

There are three different types of communications paths for data transmission: simplex, half duplex, and full duplex.

Simplex communications is a one-way transmission path. One device transmits data, and the other device receives data. A student taught by an old-fashioned professor who does not permit any questions to be asked is part of a simplex communications path. The professor talks to the student, but the student does not have the opportunity to speak and ask questions.

Another example of a simplex path is a one-way street. Cars can pass in only one direction on a one-way street; in simplex data communications, ones and zeroes can be transmitted in only one direction.

An example of simplex data communications can be found at most airports. There is usually a central server that tracks all of an airline's arrivals and departures. Video-monitor clients are placed throughout the airport to display this arrival and departure information. The server sends the information to the client, but the clients do not send any data back to the server. This one-way, or simplex, communications path is illustrated in Fig. 3-13.

Half duplex communications is an alternating transmission path that goes in two ways but only one direction at a time. For example, a professor often conducts class in half duplex fashion. First, the professor lectures for a few minutes and then pauses for a second and waits for students to ask questions. One student asks a question, and then the professor answers; another student asks a question, and then the professor answers; and so on. Only one person, either the professor or a student, is talking at any one time. Most human conversations are conducted in half duplex fashion; first one person speaks, then the other.

Another example of a half duplex path is the reversible commuter lane that is becoming popular in many metropolitan areas, particularly on bridges or in tunnels. In the morning rush hour, cars are permitted to travel into the city in the reversible

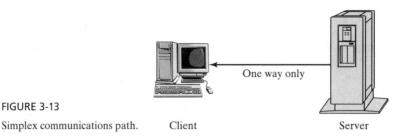

FIGURE 3-13

Simplex communications path.   Client   Server

commuter lane. At some point in the afternoon, the lane is closed for a few minutes to allow it to be cleared. Then the lane is reversed, and cars are allowed to travel out of the city in this reversible commuter lane. This is a half duplex path: first one direction, a short pause, and then the other direction.

An example of half duplex data communications can be found in certain clients and servers. First, the user types some information and hits a special key that sends the entire screen to the server. The server then responds by sending a screen of information back to the client. Only one device, either the client or the server, transmits data at any given time. Typically, a short pause occurs between completion of one device's transmission and the next device's reply. This half duplex communications path is illustrated in Fig. 3-14.

Half duplex transmission is often called *two-wire communications*, because originally one pair of wires was used for half duplex transmission. Since early equipment was unable to both transmit and receive over one pair of wires at the same time, it was necessary for the devices to share the line by alternating.

Full duplex communications is a two-way communications path. Some professors, for example, prefer to be interrupted in midsentence if their students have questions. In this case, the professors and students participate in a full duplex communications path.

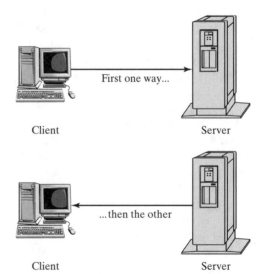

FIGURE 3-14

Half duplex communications path.   Client   Server

The professor may be talking, but a student may begin speaking at any time. Another example of such a full duplex communications path might be the classic husband–wife argument, where both parties are speaking simultaneously. Each party hears what the other is saying, but both refuse to stop talking.

Another analogy for a full duplex path is a two-way street, with one lane in each direction. Cars can proceed in both directions at the same time, and traffic on one side of the street is unaffected by traffic on the other side of the street.

An example of full duplex data communications can be found in certain clients and servers that have the ability to transmit and receive data at the same time. The client does not need to wait for the server to stop transmitting before the client itself transmits. The same is true for the server. This full duplex communications path is illustrated in Fig. 3-15.

Full duplex communications is often referred to as *four-wire communications*, because originally two pairs of wires were needed for full duplex communications. Early equipment transmitted data over one pair of wires in one direction and received data on the other pair.

Today's equipment is more sophisticated than its predecessors, and full duplex communications is now possible over only one pair of wires. Therefore, simply counting the number of wires leaving a device does not help the user determine whether the equipment is half duplex or full duplex. Unfortunately, the terminology has already caught on, and the terms "two-wire" and "four-wire" are sometimes used today to refer to half duplex and full duplex communications, respectively, regardless of the number of wires actually used for transmission.

Which method is the best: simplex, half duplex, or full duplex? It depends on the application. In the airport example we used earlier, a simplex communications path is perfect for the job of sending information to a video monitor. However, when a client is communicating with a server, either half duplex or full duplex communications are necessary, since a two-way communications path is essential.

Half duplex transmission is by nature slower than full duplex transmission. Only one device can transmit at any one time, and the clients and servers must often wait before they transmit to ensure that the other device has finished transmitting. Clearly, there is an advantage to having a full duplex connection, since either device is able to transmit data all the time. However, it is sometimes easier or cheaper to provide a half duplex communications path, and in most communications only one party transmits at one time anyway. As a result, some half duplex devices are still in use today.

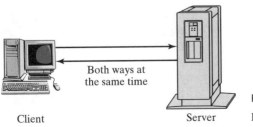

Client   Server

FIGURE 3-15

Full duplex communications path.

SUMMARY

Data communications is the exchange of digital information, or ones and zeroes, between two devices. Host computers and terminals, sometimes called clients and servers, usually communicate using groups of eight bits, or bytes. Character codes are different methods used by devices to represent information. The two most common character codes, ASCII and EBCDIC, use ones and zeroes to represent characters.

Code and protocol conversion are sometimes required to connect different manufacturers' devices. Even within a character code, some manufacturers may vary their use of parity bits, making some equipment incompatible.

A byte of data can be sent with parallel transmission, all at once, with one bit sent on each of eight separate wires. Serial transmission, however, requires only one wire, and the bits are sent one after another. Serial transmission is more widely used in data communications because the single wire is less expensive.

Asynchronous transmission uses start and stop bits to time serial transmission. Synchronous transmission, on the other hand, uses sync characters and clock signals for timing. Synchronous transmission is more efficient than asynchronous transmission for large blocks of data. Asynchronous transmission, however, is usually less expensive to implement.

Simplex communication provides a one-way communications path. Half duplex communication uses an alternating transmission path; it goes two ways, but only one direction at a time. Full duplex communication uses a two-way communications path. The terms *two-wire* and *four-wire* are often used to describe half and full duplex communications, respectively, even though four wires are no longer required for full duplex communications.

TERMS FOR REVIEW

*American National Standard Code for
  Information Interchange*
American National Standards Institute
ANSI
Applications software
ASCII
Asynchronous transmission
Baudot code
BCD
Binary Coded Decimal
Binary number system
Bit
Bit error
Bits per second
Block
Bps
Byte

Carriage return
Cathode ray tube
CC
Central processing unit
Character
Character code
Client
Code conversion
Control character
Control code
Control key
CPU
CRT
Dash
Data communications
Data rate
Digital

Display station
Dot
Dumb terminal
EBCD
EBCDIC
Error detection
Extended ASCII
Extended Binary Coded Decimal
Extended Binary Coded Decimal
   Interchange Code
FE
Figures code
Format effector
Four-wire communications
Full duplex communications
Half duplex communications
Host computer
Information separator
Intelligent terminal
International Baudot
IS
Keyboard
Letters code
Line feed
Lower Case
Mainframe
Microcomputer

Minicomputer
Morse code
Overhead
Parallel transmission
Parity bit
PC
Personal computer
Protocol conversion
Receive clock
Screen
Serial transmission
Server
Simplex communications
Smart terminal
Start bit
Start–stop transmission
Stop bit
Supercomputer
Sync character
Synchronous transmission
Terminal
Transmit clock
Two-wire communications
Upper Case
VDT
Video display terminal
XON/XOFF

EXERCISES

3-1. What is data communications?

3-2. How do the different types of host computers differ?

3-3. Describe the different types of terminals.

3-4. What is the difference between a bit and a byte?

3-5. What is the major drawback of Morse code?

3-6. What technique does Baudot code use to practically double the number of characters represented with five bits? What is the disadvantage of using this method?

3-7. How does the order of bit transmission in ASCII and EBCDIC codes differ?

3-8. What are the functions of the XON and XOFF characters?

3-9. What is the difference between parallel and serial transmission? Which is used more frequently in data communications, and why?

3-10. How do asynchronous and synchronous transmission differ? Which is better suited to large blocks of characters, and why?

3-11. Describe the difference between simplex, half duplex, and full duplex communications.

C H A P T E R   4

Data Interfaces

There are many different ways to connect clients to servers. We have already discussed basic data communications concepts, such as full and half duplex communications and asynchronous and synchronous transmission. The simplest connection, the serial port, is present on almost every client or server. Before we begin examining serial connections, we will review some of the organizations that create the common standards.

STANDARDS ORGANIZATIONS

Computer manufacturers usually conform to certain recognized standards to connect their equipment. Some standards introduced and promoted by one manufacturer are so successful that they become the industry standard. Other standards are formed by *standards organizations*. These organizations are generally chartered to devise standards for a particular industry within certain countries.

Typically, standards are developed by committees with representatives from leading companies in an industry. Certain standards organizations, particularly those covering military products, also have government representation. We now briefly examine the organizations that have the most impact on data communications.

The *American National Standards Institute*, or *ANSI*, is an umbrella organization for all of the standards organizations in the United States. ANSI accredits various organizations, which can then submit their standards to ANSI for acceptance as a national standard.

The *Institute of Electrical and Electronics Engineers*, or *IEEE*, is a professional organization of engineers. IEEE consists of many specialized societies whose committees prepare standards in their areas of specialty.

The *Electronic Industries Association*, or *EIA*, is an organization representing many manufacturers in the U.S. electronics industry. The EIA's standards have traditionally been titled *Recommended Standards*, or *RS*, followed by the number of a particular committee. In the last several years, the EIA, seeking to ensure the clear identification of its standards, has started using the EIA name instead of "RS" at the beginning of each standard, as in *EIA-232-E*. The RS designation, as in *RS-232-C*, is still used by most people in the industry to refer to standards that were issued before EIA began using the new designation. To avoid confusion, we refer to the more widely used RS designation for these previously issued standards.

The *Exchange Carriers Standards Association*, or *ECSA*, consists of telephone equipment manufacturing companies. ECSA was formed after the AT&T divestiture to continue work on standards previously developed by the Bell System.

The *National Institute of Standards and Technology*, or *NIST*, is a federal organization responsible for producing *Federal Information Processing Standards*, or *FIPS*. Meeting these FIPS is a requirement for many government suppliers. NIST was formerly known as the *National Bureau of Standards*, or *NBS*.

In the United States, most of the standards are only recommendations. With the exception of certain standards regarding interference and safety, the FCC does not regulate the internal workings of equipment; instead, it regulates only the manner in which it attaches to the public network. Internationally, telecommunications is regulated in most countries by a PTT. PTTs often impose strict requirements on all aspects of communications equipment used in a given country. The PTTs usually represent their countries on international standards organizations. There are two major international standards organizations. The *Consultative Committee on International Telephone and Telegraph*, or *CCITT*, is an international telecommunications standards organization. Its members include the regulating bodies from member countries and leading companies in the field, as well as representatives from other organizations. The CCITT is a committee of a larger organization known as the *International Telecommunications Union*, or *ITU*. Recently issued CCITT standards are now labeled *ITU-Telecommunications Standardization Sector, ITU-T*, or even simply *ITU*. Most of the standards already in existence are known by the widely used CCITT designation. To avoid confusion, we will refer to all of the standards of this organization with the label ITU(CCITT).

In the *International Standards Organization*, or *ISO*, each member country is represented by its own national standards organization. ISO and ITU(CCITT) cooperate on certain standards, but they often develop completely different standards for the same technical areas. Membership in both ISO and ITU(CCITT) is possible and often occurs.

The *Internet Engineering Task Force*, or *IETF*, is an international organization open to any individual interested in furthering the development of the Internet architecture. Working groups prepare recommendations and proposals for items important to the operation and evolution of the Internet, which is discussed in more detail in Chapter 8.

These domestic and international standards organizations prepare standards on many topics. We now examine some of those standards used for data communications.

SERIAL INTERFACE STANDARDS

The point at which one device connects to another is known as an *interface*. An interface standard defines exactly which electronic signals are required for communication between two devices. Some interface standards also define the physical connector to be used. We will defer any discussion of interfaces to local area networks (LANs) to Chapter 8, where they are covered in great detail, along with other LAN topics.

The RS-232-C Standard

One of the most common interface standards for data communications in use today is EIA's *Recommended Standard 232C*, or *RS-232-C*. RS-232-C defines exactly how ones and zeroes are to be electronically transmitted, including the voltage levels needed and the other electronic signals necessary for computer communication.

The ITU(CCITT) has standards similar to EIA's RS-232-C, known as *V.24* and *V.28*. The V.24 standard defines all of the signals described in RS-232-C, and the V.28 standard defines the same voltage levels described in RS-232-C.

RS-232-C voltage levels.   What does it mean when we transmit a 1 or a 0? In RS-232-C, ones and zeroes are transmitted using positive and negative voltages. Those readers unfamiliar with the concept of positive and negative voltages should not be concerned; devices can be built that can both send and recognize these different signals.

RS-232-C defines the process of sending a 1, known as a *mark*, as an electronic signal between −3 and −15 volts. It defines the process of sending a 0, known as a *space*, as an electronic signal between +3 and +15 volts. Signals outside these ranges are considered undefined—neither a one nor a zero—and are ignored by the receiver. This signal definition is illustrated in Fig. 4-1.

A client communicating according to RS-232-C must therefore be able to send and receive voltages in the range of −15 to +15 volts. For example, to send the ASCII letter "A", with a 0 as the parity bit, or 01000001, an asynchronous RS-232-C device must first send (starting from the left) the start bit, a 0, or +15 volts; followed by a 1, or −15 volts; followed by five 0s, or five +15-volt pulses; followed by another 1, or a −15-volt pulse; followed by a 0, or a +15 volt pulse; and finally followed by the stop bit,

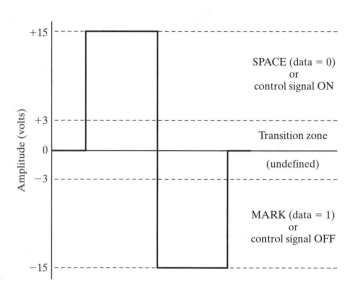

FIGURE 4-1
RS-232-C voltage levels.

or −15 volts. If we assume a transmission rate of one bit per second, then Fig. 4-2 shows the ASCII transmission of the letter "A". If the letter "A" were to be sent at a faster rate, the time periods shown in Fig. 4-2 would be shorter. For example, at 1200 bits per second, each of the time periods would be 833 microseconds (1/1200 second) long. Remember that these pulses don't have to be exactly +15 or −15 volts; instead, all voltages in the range of +3 to +15 or in the range of −3 to −15 are acceptable. After sending the stop bit, the transmitter remains at the negative voltage until the next character, which begins with a start bit (a positive voltage).

DTEs and DCEs in RS-232-C. In addition to defining how ones and zeroes are transmitted, RS-232-C also defines other electronic signals useful for communications. RS-232-C assumes that there are two types of interfaces. The first, known as *data terminal equipment*, or *DTE*, is the interface most often found on terminals, clients, host computers, servers, and printers. The second, known as *data circuit-terminating equipment*, or *DCE*, is the interface usually used on devices known as modems and on some multiplexers. DCE is often also referred to as "data communications equipment." Even though RS-232-C defines only the type of interface, we often describe an entire device by referring to its interface. For example, clients are often called DTEs, and modems are often called DCEs.

The usual purpose of DCEs is to allow DTEs to be located remotely from each other. The DTEs are the data communications equivalent of the people in a telephone conversation. The DCEs are the equivalent of the phones in the conversation; DCEs are simply instruments used to allow DTEs to communicate. This comparison is presented

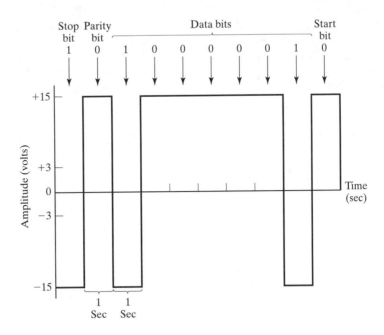

FIGURE 4-2

RS-232-C transmission of the ASCII character "A".

FIGURE 4-3

DTEs and DCEs.

in Fig. 4-3. Notice that a client (DTE) can be connected to a remote server (DTE) using a pair of DCEs and the public telephone network. RS-232-C defines how DTEs communicate with DCEs, but not how DCEs communicate with each other. We examine the methods DCEs use to communicate with each other in Chapter 5.

RS-232-C specifies the signals exchanged between DTEs and DCEs, but not the exact type of physical connector to be used. For many applications, the *DB25* connector, defined in *ISO standard number 2110* and illustrated in Fig. 4-4, has become widely accepted. There are two versions of the DB25 connector, male and female. The male connector contains 25 pins, and the female connector contains 25 small receptacles or sockets for these pins. For applications where fewer signals are needed, the nine-pin *DB9* connector, also shown in Fig. 4-4, is used.

For example, consider the standard electrical outlet in our homes. These outlets accept two-prong or three-prong plugs, depending on whether or not the circuit uses

FIGURE 4-4

The DB25 and DB9 connectors.

the third grounding prong. A DB25 connector takes this concept one step further, with 25 separate pins. In a standard electrical outlet, there is a specific size for each plug, as well as a specific distance between the prongs. Similarly, the ISO 2110 standard defines the exact size and shape of the DB25 connectors.

Each of the pins and their corresponding sockets are numbered from 1 to 25 on the DB25 connector and from 1 to 9 on the DB9 connector. These connector pin numbers for the DB9 and DB25 connectors, the commonly used signal names, and the common abbreviations, which we explain in the upcoming sections, are shown in Fig. 4-5. The discussion of pin assignments in the rest of the text refers to the DB25 connector, but the reader can easily refer to Fig. 4-5 for the DB9 pin assignments. The EIA and ITU(CCITT) have their own signal abbreviations; although not as commonly used, they are provided in the chart for reference.

There is no technical reason to place certain signals on any particular pin. Instead, these conventions are usually followed to allow for compatibility among different vendors' equipment. Figure 4-5 also describes the device, a DTE or DCE, that generates each of the signals.

DB25 Pin No.	DB9 Pin No.	Common Abbreviation	Name	Direction	EIA abbreviation	CCITT abbreviation
1		GND	Protective Ground	Both ways	AA	101
2	3	TD	Transmitted Data	DTE to DCE	BA	103
3	2	RD	Received Data	DCE to DTE	BB	104
4	7	RTS	Request to Send	DTE to DCE	CA	105
5	8	CTS	Clear to Send	DCE to DTE	CB	106
6	6	DSR	Data Set Ready	DCE to DTE	CC	107
7	5	SG	Signal Ground	Both ways	AB	102
8	1	DCD	Data Carrier Detect	DCE to DTE	CF	109
9			Positive Test Voltage	DCE to DTE		
10			Negative Test Voltage	DCE to DTE		
11			Unassigned			
12		SDCD	Secondary Data Carrier Detect	DCE to DTE	SCF	122
13		SCTS	Secondary Clear to Send	DCE to DTE	SCB	121
14		STD	Secondary Transmitted Data	DTE to DCE	SBA	118
15		TC	Transmit Clock	DCE to DTE	DB	114
16		SRD	Secondary Received Data	DCE to DTE	SBB	119
17		RC	Receive Clock	DCE to DTE	DD	115
18			Unassigned			
19		SRTS	Secondary Request to Send	DTE to DCE	SCA	120
20	4	DTR	Data Terminal Ready	DTE to DCE	CD	108.2
21		SQ	Signal Quality Detect	DCE to DTE	CG	110
22	9	RI	Ring Indicator	DCE to DTE	CE	125
23		DRS	Data Rate Select	Either way	CH/CI	111/112
24		XTC	External Transmit Clock	DTE to DCE	DA	113
25			Unassigned			

FIGURE 4-5

RS-232-C signals.

Typically, a cable coming from a DTE device has a male DB25 connector on its end. DCE devices usually have a female DB25 connector to accept the cable from the DTE. RS-232-C limits the maximum length of the cable from a DTE to a DCE to 50 feet. In addition, RS-232-C limits data-transmission rates to a maximum of 20,000 bits per second (20 kilobits per second, or 20 kbps). The distance and speed limitation is often exceeded by users without causing operational difficulties, though doing so technically violates the RS-232-C standard. Manufacturers may refuse to support or service installations that do not comply with the standard.

RS-232-C data-signal definitions.   We have already examined how data is transmitted and received using positive and negative voltages. In RS-232-C, the DTE sends data on the *TD*, or *Transmitted Data*, pin. In other words, the DTE can provide a positive (+3 to +15 volt) electronic signal on the TD pin to send a 0 (space), or the DTE can provide a negative (−3 to −15 volt) electronic signal on the TD pin to send a 1 (mark). TD is usually found on pin number 2 of the DB25 connector.

Similarly, a DTE receives data on the *RD*, or *Received Data*, pin. Notice that the pins are named with respect to the DTE. The DCE receives data from the DTE on the TD pin and sends data to the DTE on the RD pin. Also, regardless of whether a device is a DCE or DTE, we almost always refer to pin numbers rather than sockets, since the signal is named with respect to the DTE and the DTE usually uses the male connector with pins. Therefore, even though RD is a signal produced by the DCE, we state that RD is usually found on pin number 3 of the DB25 connector, because that's the corresponding pin number on the DTE's male connector.

RS-232-C ground-signal definitions.   Another function needed to ensure proper data transmission is fulfilled by the *Signal Ground*, or *SG*, pin. This signal acts as a zero-volt reference for all of the other signals. An analogy of a reference voltage can be drawn by looking at the sky on a clear day. A philosophy professor asks, "Is the sky light blue or dark blue today?" Half of the class thinks it's light blue, and the other half thinks it's dark blue. Their answers vary because every person has a different idea of what light and dark really mean. If the professor is wearing a navy blazer jacket and asks the class, "Is the sky a darker blue or lighter blue than my jacket?", the entire class will reply, "The sky is a lighter blue." They all give the same answer because the entire class used the same reference point: the professor's jacket.

The Signal Ground in RS-232-C is a zero-volt reference. Signals can be compared to the SG pin; those with higher voltages than the SG pin are positive voltages, and those with lower voltages than the SG pin are negative voltages. When a DTE sends a signal on the TD pin, the DCE compares this voltage to the SG pin to determine whether the data sent was a 1 or a 0. SG is usually found on pin number 7 of the DB25 connector.

There is another ground signal, known as *chassis ground, protective ground*, or *frame ground*. This signal, sometimes simply abbreviated as *GND*, is not necessary for data transmission, but it can be used to prevent certain errors. Special shielded cable, designed to reduce interference and electronic noise, can attach its shield to the GND pin. Interference and electronic noise can be generated by large electrical motors, such as those found in elevators or factories, or by ordinary fluorescent lights. With shielded cable, the noise never makes it to the data wires because it runs on the shield, through the GND pin, and through the DTE's or DCE's own electrical ground. This shield should be connected to the GND pin only on one side of the cable; otherwise, it could pose a potential electrical hazard (if the attached equipment is faulty) and violate the *National Electrical Code*. GND is usually found on pin number 1 of the DB25 connector.

RS-232-C timing signal definitions.   In asynchronous transmission, no timing signals are needed. For synchronous transmission, however, clock signals are provided in RS-232-C. These clock signals are a series of positive and negative pulses, from +15 to −15 volts, that repeat indefinitely and are known as a *square wave*. If the data is being transmitted at 1200 bits per second, there are 1200 complete square waves each second. This process allows the device receiving the clock signal to "sync up" to the data rate of the other device. It is a process of continuous calibration, in which the device receiving the clock signal is constantly adjusting its speed, if necessary, to match that of the other device. An example of using a square wave as a clock signal to time data transmission is shown in Fig. 4-6.

The *TC*, or *Transmit Clock*, signal is used by the DCE to time the data sent by the DTE on the TD pin in synchronous data transmission. Some DTEs allow the DCE to provide this clock signal. TC is usually found on pin number 15 of the DB25 connector.

The *XTC*, or *External Transmit Clock*, signal is used by the DTE to time the data it sends on the TD pin in synchronous data transmission. Some DTEs insist on providing this clock signal themselves. XTC is usually found on pin number 24 of the DB25 connector.

The *RC*, or *Receive Clock*, signal is used by the DCE to time the data it sends to the DTE on the RD pin in synchronous data transmission. RC is usually found on pin number 17 of the DB25 connector.

RS-232-C control-signal definitions.   Using the TD, RD, and SG pins, data could be transmitted asynchronously between DTEs and DCEs. Synchronous transmission would also require use of the TC, RC, and XTC pins. However, other functions are usually performed before data is transmitted.

The *control signals* of RS-232-C are used to indicate the status of a given connection. A control signal is said to be *ON*, or *raised*, or *asserted*, or *true* when it is set to between +3 and +15 volts. Similarly, a control signal is said to be *OFF*, or *low*, or *false* when it is set to between −3 and −15 volts. By raising and lowering the control-signal voltages, the DTE and DCE can communicate information about the status of a given call and about both devices' readiness to communicate. We begin by describing the most common control signals used in RS-232-C.

When a DTE device is powered on and placed online, it asserts the *DTR*, or *Data Terminal Ready*, signal. This signal announces to the DCE that a DTE is attached and ready to begin communications. DTR is usually found on pin number 20 of the DB25 connector.

The *DSR*, or *Data Set Ready*, signal is asserted by the DCE and indicates that the DCE is powered on and is ready to begin communications. DSR is usually found on pin number 6 of the DB25 connector.

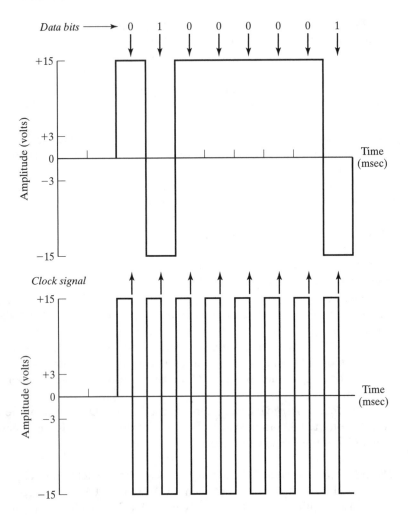

FIGURE 4-6

Using clock signals to time data transmission.

The *RTS*, or *Request to Send*, signal is asserted by the DTE to ask permission to send data. In full duplex, the DTE asserts this signal immediately, because a full duplex device wants a continuous two-way communications path. In half-duplex devices, the DTE asserts this signal only when it actually has data to send (e.g., when the Enter key has been hit on a device). RTS is usually found on pin number 4 of the DB25 connector.

The *CTS*, or *Clear to Send*, signal is asserted by the DCE in response to RTS when the DCE is able to accept data from the DTE. CTS is usually found on pin number 5 of the DB25 connector.

The *DCD*, or *Data Carrier Detect*, signal is asserted by the DCE to alert the DTE to expect to receive data at any time. In full duplex devices, DCD remains continuously asserted since it is a continuous two-way path and since data can arrive at any time. In half duplex devices, DCD is asserted only when data is being sent to the DTE. This signal is often abbreviated as *CD* or *CX*. DCD is usually found on pin number 8 of the DB25 connector.

The *RI*, or *Ring Indicator*, signal is asserted by the DCE to alert the DTE that a remote device wants to initiate communications. RI is usually found on pin number 22 of the DB25 connector.

The control signals we have just analyzed are the most commonly used control signals. There are several less frequently used signals in RS-232-C as well.

The *SQ*, or *Signal Quality Detect*, signal is asserted by the DCE when it believes that transmissions are of high quality and that there are no errors occurring. The DCE drops this signal when it determines that the transmission quality has degraded and an error may have occurred. SQ is usually found on pin number 21 of the DB25 connector.

The *DRS*, or *Data Rate Select*, signal can be asserted by either the DTE or the DCE to change the other device's speed under special conditions. Data Rate Select is usually found on pin number 23 of the DB25 connector.

RS-232-C secondary signals.   There are also several secondary signals: *Secondary Transmitted Data* (STD, pin 14), *Secondary Received Data* (SRD, pin 16), *Secondary Request to Send* (SRTS, pin 19), *Secondary Clear to Send* (SCTS, pin 13), and *Secondary Data Carrier Detect* (SDCD, pin 12). These signals are equivalent to their primary counterparts, which we have already considered, but they are rarely used by most DTEs and DCEs. Together, these signals provide a second data channel on which data can be transmitted and received independently of the primary channel.

Other RS-232-C signals.   Two other signals described in RS-232-C as "Reserved for Data Set Testing," pins 9 and 10, are usually defined as positive and negative test voltages, respectively. These signals are often useful for troubleshooting.

The remaining three pins, numbered 11, 18, and 25, were left unassigned by the RS-232-C standard. Many manufacturers have used these pins for their own purposes.

In most cases, when signals are not being used by a manufacturer, such as the clocking pins in asynchronous transmission, these pins are simply omitted from the connector to cut manufacturing costs. Some manufacturers who need only a few of the signals described here actually use the DB9 connector rather than the DB25 to economize and save space. Other manufacturers have invented their own functions for the unassigned pins, which can make it difficult to connect two different vendors' equipment.

EIA-232-D and EIA-232-E vs. RS-232-C.   *EIA-232-D* and *EIA-232-E* are revisions of the RS-232-C standard that make some minor improvements. The use of connectors and the grounding shield are better defined, and some of the lesser used signals are eliminated. Further, additional test and loopback signals are provided on previously unassigned pins. Though these improvements make EIA-232-D and EIA-232-E technically superior to RS-232-C, there are so many RS-232-C devices already installed that the new features are seldom used. While the EIA-232-D and EIA-232-E devices can communicate with RS-232-C devices, the new diagnostic features can only be used between the newer devices. In fact, since most RS-232-C devices use nine or fewer signals, these improvements are having little effect on the marketplace.

RS-232-C HANDSHAKING

Now that we are familiar with the basic RS-232-C signals, let's see how they're used in asynchronous communications. The interaction of the RS-232-C signals we have already described is known as RS-232-C *handshaking*.

Assume that we have a client (DTE) connected to a DCE, which we refer to as the local DCE, as illustrated in Fig. 4-7. This DCE communicates with another DCE, known as the remote DCE, which is in turn connected to a server (DTE).

The client is powered up and immediately asserts the DTR signal. The local DCE responds by asserting the DSR signal, thereby establishing communications with the remote DCE. The remote DCE temporarily asserts the RI signal to alert the server that another party would like to communicate with it. The server, if powered on and ready, then asserts the DTR signal. The remote DCE responds by dropping the RI signal and asserting the DSR signal, completing the connection between the client and the server.

If the client and server are communicating using a full duplex connection, they would have asserted the RTS signals almost immediately after receiving the DSR signal from the DCE. The purpose of the RTS signal is to request a transmission path. The DCEs would then respond with the CTS and DCD signals as soon as communications are established (between the DCEs). The CTS signal confirms that a transmission path is available for the DTE to send data to the DCE. The DCD signal confirms that a transmission path is established in the other direction, from the DCE to the DTE. For devices using a full duplex connection, whenever a transmission path is available, it is available in both directions; therefore, the CTS and DCD signals are asserted by both DCEs. Data transmission can now occur between the client and server, in both directions simultaneously, through the DCEs.

To summarize, in a full duplex connection the DTEs assert the DTR and RTS signals, and the DCEs assert the DSR, CTS, and DCD signals. Once the connection is established, these signals do not change. Typically, a DTE ends the connection by dropping its DTR and RTS signals.

Server

Client

DTE

RS-232-C
Interface

Local
DCE

Remote
DCE

RS-232-C
Interface

DTE

FIGURE 4-7

Connecting DTEs and DCEs with RS-232-C.

An interesting function is performed by the DCEs during the connection. The client transmits data on the TD pin to the local DCE, which sends the data to the remote DCE using methods we introduce in Chapter 5. The remote DCE sends this data to the server on the RD pin. Notice that the DCEs have performed a *crossover* of the data signal, much as telephones do for us. When we talk into our telephone mouthpiece (the equivalent of TD), our voice is received in the other party's earpiece (the equivalent of RD). Similarly, the server transmits data on TD to the remote DCE, but this data is sent to the client by the local DCE on the RD pin.

Half duplex communications differ slightly from full duplex communications. Although the DTR and DSR signaling is the same, half duplex communications require an alternating transmission path (first one direction and then the other), which is accomplished by the use of the RTS, CTS, and DCD signals.

After the DTR/DSR signal interchange at both the client and server, one of the DTEs will then want to transmit data—we'll assume it's the client. The client asserts its RTS signal, and the local DCE informs the remote DCE that data will be arriving shortly. The remote DCE then asserts DCD to the server to inform it that data will be arriving shortly. Meanwhile, the local DCE has asserted the CTS signal, indicating that the client can now send data. A one-way transmission path has now been established from the client to the computer. The computer will not try to send data because it is receiving the DCD signal, thus implying that data is already on its way. When the client finishes sending data, it drops the RTS signal; the local DCE drops the CTS signal and informs the remote DCE that the transmission is complete. The remote DCE then drops DCD to the server. The server is now free to assert its RTS signal and start the process all over again in the other direction. This process will repeat indefinitely, first in one direction and then in the other, as long as there is still data to transmit.

We have been discussing asynchronous transmission here. Synchronous transmission functions identically, with the addition of the clock signals (TC, RC, XTC) mentioned previously.

CONNECTING A DTE TO ANOTHER DTE IN RS-232-C

While RS-232-C is intended to connect a DTE to a DCE, it is possible to connect two DTEs together using a special cable known as a *null modem cable*. This cable simulates the behavior of the two DCEs and the network between them, which are usually found in RS-232-C connections. An example of an asynchronous null modem cable is shown in Fig. 4-8.

A signal ground is connected between the two DTEs to provide a reference voltage. DTR and DSR are crossed so that when each DTE raises DTR to indicate that it is online, the other DTE sees DSR, indicating that its partner is online. When a DTE raises RTS, it sees CTS, giving it permission to send, and the other DTE sees DCD, indicating that data may arrive at any time. Finally, TD and RD are crossed, so when either DTE transmits, the other DTE receives the data.

FIGURE 4-8

An asynchronous null modem cable.

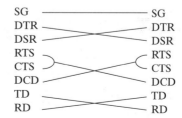

There are many other variations of null modem cables that will work in different situations. With certain vendors' equipment, it may also be necessary to connect RI to DTR if one of the DTEs is expecting to see an incoming call. When synchronous transmission is used, appropriate clock signals must be connected between the DTEs to provide the timing needed by these devices. The reason for using any type of null modem cable is to convince the attached DTEs that a pair of DCEs and a network are between them so that the DTEs can play their intended role.

RS-449, RS-422-A, and RS-423-A

The main complaints from the user community about RS-232-C focused on its speed limitation (20 kbps), its distance limitation (50 feet), and the lack of standardization on both a particular connector type and pin locations. Realizing the deficiencies of RS-232-C, the EIA later introduced a set of three new standards, known as *RS-449, RS-422-A*, and *RS-423-A*.

These new standards share the same basic goal as RS-232-C or any other interface standard. All define a standard method for connecting two devices, one known as a DTE and the other known as a DCE. Regardless of the shape of the connector, the number of pins used, or the speed of transmission, a similar set of functions must be provided by all interface standards. For example, "Data Terminal Ready," or the equivalent function with a slightly different name, is found in almost any interface standard.

RS-449 can be thought of as the parent standard, and it describes the mechanical and functional characteristics of the DTE/DCE interface. *RS-422-A* and *RS-423-A* address the specific details of two different electrical signal characteristics. Together, these three standards were intended as replacements for RS-232-C. However, they are still only in limited use, and RS-232-C devices far outnumber RS-449 devices today.

The RS-449 standard, unlike RS-232-C, defines the exact connector to be used, the *DB37* connector, as presented in Fig. 4-9. The DB37 connector is similar to the DB25, though it is somewhat larger and has 37 pins. In addition, the RS-449 standard developers realized that the secondary channel of RS-232-C was seldom used, so they opted to place those signals on a separate DB9 connector, previously shown in Fig. 4-4. This 9-pin connector is optional, and if the secondary channel is not needed, it can be completely omitted. RS-449 therefore defines a total of 46 pins, many more than those in RS-232-C; the extra pins allow for added functions and higher data rates, which we explain in the text that follows. The 37-pin and 9-pin connectors are also defined in the *ISO Standard 4902*.

DB37 male connector   DB37 female connector

FIGURE 4-9

DB37 connectors.

DB9 Connector pin no.	DB37 Connector pin nos.	RS-449 Circuit	RS-449 Description	Category	RS-232-C Equivalent
1	1		Shield		GND
5	19	SG	Signal Ground		SG
9	37	SC	Send Common	II	
6	20	RC	Receive Common	II	
	4,22	SD	Send Data	I	TD
	6,24	RD	Receive Data	I	RD
	7,25	RS	Request to Send	I	RTS
	9,27	CS	Clear to Send	I	CTS
	11,29	DM	Data Mode	I	DSR
	12,30	TR	Terminal Ready	I	DTR
	15	IC	Incoming Call	II	RI
	13,31	RR	Receiver Ready	I	DCD
	33	SQ	Signal Quality	II	SQ
	16	SR	Signaling Rate Selector	II	DRS (DTE)
	2	SI	Signaling Rate Indicator	II	DRS (DCE)
	17,35	TT	Terminal Timing	I	XTC
	5,23	ST	Send Timing	I	TC
	8,26	RT	Receive Timing	I	RC
3		SSD	Secondary Send Data	II	STD
4		SRD	Secondary Receive Data	II	SRD
7		SRS	Secondary Request to Send	II	SRTS
8		SCS	Secondary Clear to Send	II	SCTS
2		SRR	Secondary Receiver Ready	II	SDCD
	10	LL	Local Loopback	II	None
	14	RL	Remote Loopback	II	None
	18	TM	Test Mode	II	None
	32	SS	Select Standby	II	None
	36	SB	Standby Indicator	II	None
	16	SF	Select Frequency	II	None
	28	IS	Terminal in Service	II	None
	34	NS	New Signal	II	None
	3		Undefined		
	21		Undefined		

FIGURE 4-10

RS-232-C and RS-449 signal equivalents.

The functions performed by the RS-449 signals are similar to those used in RS-232-C. The RS-449 signals and their RS-232-C equivalents are compared in Fig. 4-10. Notice that some of the RS-232-C functions are also found in RS-449, though they have slightly different names. For example, Transmitted Data in RS-232-C is the equivalent of Send Data in RS-449. RS-449 also includes additional signals that are not present in RS-232-C. Most of these new signals are used for testing and diagnostic purposes; others are necessary for RS-422-A and RS-423-A transmission.

Notice that some of the signals in RS-449 use two pins. These signals are known as *Category I* signals, and the second pin allows for RS-422-A transmission, which we present below. The other signals on the RS-449 interface, which use only one pin, are known as *Category II* signals.

The real technical advantage of the RS-449 standard is found in its methods of electrical transmission of signals, as described in the RS-422-A and RS-423-A standards. These standards can surpass the RS-232-C speed and distance limits, while allowing for compatibility with older RS-232-C devices.

RS-422-A describes a method of *balanced transmission* that can be used for the RS-449 Category I signals. Balanced transmission requires two wires to send data or a control signal, allowing for high data rates and high reliability. Therefore, each of the Category I signals requires two pins. RS-422-A allows a variable transmission rate, according to the distance involved, as shown in Fig. 4-11. The maximum distance varies from 40 feet to 4000 feet, and the maximum speed can reach 10 million bits per second, or 10 *Mbps*.

RS-423-A describes a method of *unbalanced transmission* used for all of the RS-449 Category II signals. Unbalanced transmission sends the signal over one wire, and all signals share a *common return*. There are two of these returns, *Send Common* and *Receive Common*, one for each direction. RS-423-A also allows a variable transmission rate, according to the distance involved, as illustrated in Fig. 4-11. The maximum distance varies from 40 feet to 4000 feet, and the maximum speed can reach 100 kbps.

RS-449 devices can use RS-422-A for their Category I circuits if the added performance is needed. Of course, the extra wires and circuitry costs required for balanced transmission make RS-422-A more expensive than RS-423-A. Therefore, many applications of RS-449 use RS-423-A for their Category I circuits. The balanced transmission has the additional advantage of being less susceptible to noise and interference errors than unbalanced transmission.

Category II circuits, for which performance is generally not an issue, always use RS-423-A. In addition, RS-423-A devices can be attached to RS-232-C devices using a special wiring adapter, since the unbalanced transmission is similar. Of course, then both devices are limited by the RS-232-C distance and speed limitations. RS-449 handshaking is so similar to that used in RS-232-C that we do not elaborate further on the specific RS-449 signals here.

FIGURE 4-11

RS-422-A and RS-423-A speed and distance limitations.

ITU(CCITT) has a set of equivalent standards for RS-449, RS-422-A, and RS-423-A. The functional signals that are shared by RS-232-C and RS-449 are described by the ITU(CCITT) V.24 standard already mentioned. The RS-422-A and RS-423-A transmission standards are similar to the ITU(CCITT) *V.11* and *V.10* standards, respectively. A similar ITU standard, known as *V.35*, combines V.11 balanced transmission of the higher speed signals with unbalanced transmission of the control signals. The V.35 standard is typically used to interconnect a company's premises data networking equipment with its digital phone lines, as discussed in detail in Chapter 10.

High-Speed Desktop Serial Interfaces

Several high-speed serial interfaces are used in short-distance applications, typically for attaching devices on a desktop to a personal computer. These desktop standards offer speeds much higher than that offered by traditional data communications interfaces like RS-232-C.

One such standard is the *Universal Serial Bus*, or *USB*. The first version, *USB 1.0* or *Low-Speed USB*, commonly operates at 1.5 Mbps. *USB 1.1*, known as *Full-Speed USB*, operates at 12 Mbps. The newest version, *USB 2.0* or simply *USB2*, known as *Hi-Speed USB*, operates at speeds of up to 480 Mbps. It is backward compatible with the original USB and USB 1.1, so a USB2 port can accept an older device at a slower speed.

In addition, all types of USB ports can provide low levels of power to the attached devices, making it an extremely convenient interface. For desktop computers, USB ports can reduce the number of power supplies needed for small accessory devices; for laptop computers, the accessories can feed off the laptop's batteries. The power available through the interface is not enough to power a laser printer, but it would be sufficient for an external memory device or a mouse. USB ports are now as common as an RS-232-C port on a desktop computer and may someday supplant them altogether. A *USB Hub* can be plugged into a USB port, allowing it to accept multiple devices.

There are two styles of USB connector, type A and type B, as shown in Fig. 4-12. The computer generally has a type A connector, and the peripheral device generally has a type B connector. USB cables are widely available with appropriate connectors on each end to allow these ports to be connected. Virtually all PCs today are delivered with at least one USB port.

FIGURE 4-12

USB connectors.

Another high-speed standard is *IEEE 1394*, also known as *High Performance Serial Bus* or *Firewire*. Its first version, *IEEE 1394A* operates at speeds up to 400 Mbps, while IEEE *1394B* can achieve a speed of 3200 Mbps. Multimedia applications often use this high-end standard. Video recorded on a digital camcorder can be quickly transferred to a computer through an IEEE 1394 port for editing, storage, or retransmission. These ports are also commonly used to attach peripherals like DVD drives.

Like USB, IEEE 1394 ports can also supply power to attached devices. If data and power connections are needed, a six-pin connector is required, while data-only connections require only a four-pin connector. To save space, some consumer electronics devices (e.g., a camcorder) are equipped with an IEEE 1394 port that has the smaller four-pin connector. The desktop computer interface often uses the six-pin connector, requiring the use of a converter cable between the two. The two most widely used Firewire connector types are shown in Fig. 4-13.

Wireless Serial Interfaces

While we will discuss wireless local area networks further in Chapter 8, there are some short-distance wireless interfaces used to connect devices in close proximity to each other.

Vendors have presented the *Bluetooth* standard as an all-purpose solution to the multiple devices used by today's mobile workforce. The Bluetooth standard operates at up to 1 Mbps and was originally intended to cover a distance of 30 feet. Handheld organizers, also known as *personal digital assistants*, or *PDAs*, as well as cellular phones, desktop or laptop PCs, headsets, and peripherals, can all be equipped with these ports. The idea of universal wireless connectivity in your workspace, or in your car, is appealing. While simple combinations, like a wireless headset and a cellular phone, are already in wide use, more complicated cases are proving troublesome. For example, the wireless headset user may want to switch between connectivity to the cell phone and

FIGURE 4-13

Firewire connectors.

connectivity to the PC. The software for automating and simplifying these connections is not widely available today. For now, Bluetooth holds much promise in the office environment, but it is not yet a unifying technology seamlessly connecting all devices. It also has some unforeseen applications in factories as an inexpensive method to connect sensors to control equipment.

The *Infrared Data Association*, or *IrDA* standard, is widely available on laptop computers, PDAs, and some printers. It sends infrared signals up to 4 Mbps for a short distance (up to 3 feet) and relies on an unblocked "line of sight" between the devices. These parameters have limited its usefulness, and software compatibility issues have made even simple applications, like printing from a laptop, a difficult chore.

SUMMARY

There are numerous ways to connect clients to servers. Many standards organizations, including ANSI, IEEE, EIA, ECSA, IETF, NIST, ITU(CCITT), and ISO, develop specifications for both domestic and international use.

One commonly used digital interface standard is EIA's RS-232-C. RS-232-C defines the voltage levels and necessary signals for computer communication between DTE and DCE interfaces. There are data, ground, timing, and control signals in RS-232-C. Many of these functions are replicated in the seldom-used secondary channel of RS-232-C. The interaction of RS-232-C control signals between the DTE and the DCE is referred to as handshaking. RS-232-C is limited to a distance of 50 feet and a maximum speed of 20 kbps. A null modem cable can be used to connect two DTEs. EIA-232-D and EIA-232-E offer some minor improvements over RS-232-C, but neither standard is having a significant impact.

RS-449 is a more recent standard that describes DTE-to-DCE communications. It specifies the interface connector, the necessary signals, and two possible transmission methods. RS-422-A is a method of balanced transmission, with a maximum distance of up to 4000 feet and a maximum speed of 10 Mbps. RS-423-A uses unbalanced transmission, with a maximum distance of 4000 feet and a maximum speed of 100 kbps.

Several high-speed desktop serial interfaces are available, including USB and IEEE 1394. The various USB versions offer speeds that vary between 1.5 and 480 Mbps. Various versions of Firewire, or IEEE 1394, provide speeds up to 3200 Mbps. Wireless serial interfaces, including IrDA and Bluetooth, cover short distances and operate at 1 and 4 Mbps, respectively.

TERMS FOR REVIEW

American National Standards Institute   *CCITT*
ANSI   *CD*
Asserted   *Chassis ground*
Balanced transmission   *Clear to Send*
Bluetooth   *Common return*
Category I   *Consultative Committee on International*
Category II   *Telephone and Telegraph*

Control signal
Crossover
CTS
CX
Data Carrier Detect
Data circuit-terminating equipment
Data Rate Select
Data Set Ready
Data terminal equipment
Data Terminal Ready
DB9
DB25
DB37
DCD
DCE
DRS
DSR
DTE
DTR
ECSA
EIA
EIA-232-D
EIA-232-E
Electronic Industries Association
Exchange Carriers Standards Association
External Transmit Clock
False
Federal Information Processing Standards
FIPS
Firewire
Frame ground
Full-Speed USB
Gbps
Gigabits per second
GND
Handshaking
High Performance Serial Bus
Hi-Speed USB
IEEE
IEEE 1394
IEEE 1394A
IEEE 1394B
IETF
Infrared Data Association
Institute of Electrical and Electronics
    Engineers

Interface
International Standards Organization
International Telecommunications Union
Internet
Internet Engineering Task Force
IrDA
ISO
ISO Standard 2110
ISO Standard 4902
ITU
ITU-T
ITU-Telecommunications Sector
Leased
Low
Low-Speed USB
Mark
Mbps
National Bureau of Standards
National Electrical Code
National Institute of Standards and
    Technology
NBS
NIST
Null modem cable
OFF
ON
PDA
Personal digital assistant
Protective ground
Raised
RC
RD
Receive Clock
Receive Common
Received Data
Recommended Standard
Recommended Standard 232C
Request to Send
RI
Ring Indicator
RS
RS-232-C
RS-422-A
RS-423-A
RS-449
RTS

SCTS	*TD*
SDCD	*Transmit Clock*
Secondary Clear to Send	*Transmitted Data*
Secondary Data Carrier Detect	*True*
Secondary Received Data	*Unbalanced transmission*
Secondary Request to Send	*Universal Serial Bus*
Secondary Transmitted Data	*USB*
Send Common	*USB 1.0*
SG	*USB 1.1*
Signal Ground	*USB 2.0*
Signal Quality Detect	*USB Hub*
Space	*USB2*
SQ	*V.10*
Square wave	*V.11*
SRD	*V.21*
SRTS	*V.24*
Standards organization	*V.28*
STD	*V.35*
TC	*XTC*

EXERCISES

4-1. How does the role of standards in the United States differ from the role of standards in the rest of the world?

4-2. In the RS-232-C standard, how are ones and zeroes transmitted? How are control signals represented?

4-3. What are the two types of RS-232-C interfaces? Which devices typically fit into each category?

4-4. What is the purpose of the signal ground in RS-232-C? Why is it important?

4-5. Which RS-232-C signals are used only in synchronous transmission? Which of these signals are generated by the DTE, and which by the DCE? What is the purpose of these signals?

4-6. What is the purpose of the control signals in RS-232-C? When is a null modem cable used?

4-7. What does RS-449 define that RS-232-C leaves undefined?

4-8. What are the main differences between the RS-422-A and RS-423-A standards?

4-9. What is USB? What are the differences between USB 1.0, 1.1, and 2.0?

4-10. What is Firewire? What are the differences between IEEE 1394A and 1394B?

C H A P T E R   5

Data Transmission

All of the interface standards we mentioned in the prior chapter are intended for transmission on a user's premises, over a relatively short distance. The user generally owns all of the wiring or cabling between the devices.

But what about clients who access servers across town, across the country, or across an ocean? Our public telephone network's standard voice communications circuits are not well suited to the *digital transmission* we have been discussing. These square waves, however, can be sent over special *digital circuits* provided by the common carriers, or they can be sent through other *transmission media*. Alternatively, the signals can be *modulated* and sent in analog form over standard phone lines, using *modems*. We will discuss all of these options, beginning with digital phone circuits.

REMOTE DIGITAL TRANSMISSION

When digital phone circuits are available, the client, or server, typically communicates using one of the standard DTE interfaces we have already examined, such as RS-232-C. The DTE is then connected to a special device known as a *digital service unit*, or *DSU*. This DSU uses a DCE interface to communicate with the client or server and then transmits the data in a special format over the common carrier's digital circuits. Typical use of a DSU is depicted in Fig. 5-1.

Usually, the voltage levels required for transmission of data between the DSUs are different from those used by a short-distance interface, such as RS-232-C. The DSU is able to convert the signals from the voltage levels used by the client to those needed by the digital circuit. Even if RS-232-C is used to connect the client to the DSU, the 50-foot limitation applies only to the distance between the DSU and the client, not to the distance between the local DSU and the remote DSU.

A *channel service unit*, or *CSU*, is sometimes required at the end of the common carrier's circuit. The trend today, however, is to incorporate the functions of the CSU into the DSU. Since a separate CSU is not always used, it is shown with dashed lines in Fig. 5-1.

FIGURE 5-1

Typical use of DSUs and CSUs.

The "digital circuit" portion of Fig. 5-1 can span several miles, or several thousand miles, depending on the locations of the server and client. Special equipment, known as *repeaters*, is placed at regular intervals in the digital circuits to maintain the data-signal strength over these long distances and to ensure that the receiving DSU/CSU can understand the signal.

An analogy for the repeater function can be found in the classic firefighter's bucket line. Rather than one firefighter taking a bucket of water up a hill, the firefighter instead hands the bucket to another firefighter, who hands it to the next firefighter, etc. Eventually, the bucket reaches the top of the hill. The effort, then was shared by many firefighters.

A digital repeater simply receives a digital signal (a square wave) and sends it on to the next repeater. In the firefighter's bucket line, some water may spill as the bucket is passed from one firefighter to the next. Similarly, as data is transmitted, it becomes weaker as it gets farther from the repeater. It is the function of the repeater to rejuvenate or regenerate the signal before sending it on. (Imagine each firefighter keeping a spare glass of water in order to "top off" the bucket, if necessary, before passing it on).

Fig. 5-2 illustrates a repeater's function, using a square wave between −10 and +10 volts as the digital signal. The signal deteriorates as it gets farther from the DSU. Before the signal enters the repeater, the highest portion of the signal is barely +9 volts, and it is far from square. The repeater regenerates the signal and sends out a clean square wave at the full 10 volts. The key to using repeaters is that they must be placed close enough to each other so that the signal is still recognizable when it enters the repeater. Without repeaters, the signal would simply fade out, much as a person's voice becomes unintelligible as we walk farther and farther away from that person. These digital repeaters can be separate devices or can be incorporated into the common carrier's switching equipment.

We have already considered the general functions of digital transmission. Several specific digital-transmission options are available from common carriers for digital circuits.

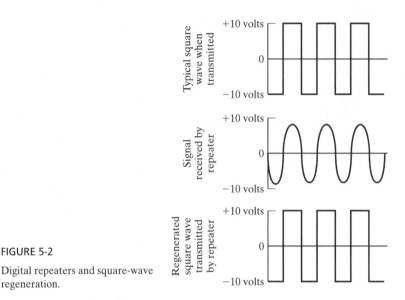

FIGURE 5-2

Digital repeaters and square-wave regeneration.

T-1 and ISDN

T-1 carrier service, available from almost all of the common carriers, is a 1.544-Mbps digital path. For users with lower data rates but with many devices at each location, the T-1 carrier can be divided into 24 separate channels. Since some of the 1.544 Mbps is used for signaling information, the 24 channels can each carry either roughly 64 kbps of digitized voice or 56 kbps of data. T-1 is nothing more than a high-speed method of digital communications between DSUs. We discuss the use of the T-1 carrier and of higher speed digital circuits more extensively in Chapter 10. In Europe and other areas, a 2.048-Mbps service known as *E-1* is also popular. Lower speeds than those offered by T-1 are also available in some areas.

The *Integrated Services Digital Network*, or *ISDN*, is a standard for digital voice and data communications. The data-circuit portion of ISDN includes data rates from 16 kbps to 64 kbps for the individual user and typically up to 1.544 Mbps for high-volume transmission. Even higher bandwidth is possible with *Broadband ISDN*. We present ISDN more extensively in Chapter 10.

Wide Area Data Networks

Another method of long-distance data transmission is through the use of packet-data networks, including *packet switching* and *frame relay networks*. These networks allow clients and servers to connect to other servers anywhere on the network, which can span thousands of miles. The user can either connect to the same server all of the time or choose a different computer with each connection, much as we do on the public telephone network. The *Internet* is another packet-data network that can transport data around the globe. We examine these and other networks in detail in Chapter 8.

Digital access to wide area networks can also be provided by *digital subscriber line (DSL)* services. These services offer digital connections at various speeds to the central office, where the data can then be passed to any network. Another option for local access is provided by *cable modems*. In this case, data is carried by the cable television company to a data network. The Internet is the data network most people connect to with these services. DSL and cable modems will be discussed in more detail in Chapter 10.

In some areas, data can be transmitted to homes or businesses using special signaling on electrical power lines. While the power companies have the advantage that they already own cabling to these locations, the technology is not yet widely deployed.

Digital and Analog Bandwidth

A common measure of the usefulness of a communications circuit is its *bandwidth*, or carrying capacity. In the digital circuits we have been discussing, bandwidth is simply the capacity or speed, in bits per second, that can be transmitted.

However, not all communications circuits are digital. In digital transmission, only ones and zeroes are sent and received. Normal telephone lines, like those found in our homes, are designed to carry the wide range of pitches that make up human speech, not ones and zeroes. We call these different pitches *frequencies*. A high-pitched tone is therefore also a high-frequency tone, and a low-pitched tone is a low-frequency tone. Human speech, music, and the noise made by a car's engine are all a series of unpredictable sounds, each with its own constantly varying pitch and volume. This type of signal is called an *analog* signal. Whereas digital information is a predictable 0 or 1 (and nothing in between), analog information can vary infinitely over a given range. A comparison between a digital signal and an analog signal can be found in Fig. 5-3.

There is no way to predict what a person will say on the telephone. We can, however, predict what the average human voice sounds like and what type of equipment will be needed to transmit and receive those sounds. The analog bandwidth of a communications circuit is the range of frequencies that can be transmitted.

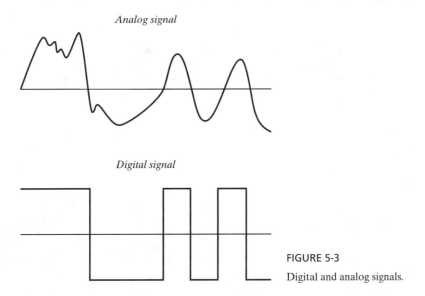

FIGURE 5-3

Digital and analog signals.

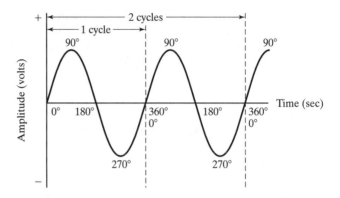

FIGURE 5-4

Sine wave.

How do we determine the frequency of a signal? A perfect tone that maintains its pitch and volume indefinitely looks like a *sine wave* when it is converted to electrical energy. Notice that a sine wave, as illustrated in Fig. 5-4, repeats itself again and again; each repetition is known as a *cycle*. Each cycle contains a peak and a valley, and the height of each peak (and the depth of each valley) doesn't vary in a perfect sine wave. The height of each peak is known as the *amplitude* of the sine wave; this amplitude is also equal to the depth of each valley. In addition, the time for each complete cycle is also constant and is known as the *period* of the sine wave. The number of cycles of a sine wave per second is known as its *frequency*. The frequency of a sine wave is therefore measured in *cycles per second*; the term *hertz*, abbreviated *Hz*, is equivalent to cycles per second and is commonly used today.

For the sake of convenience, each cycle of a sine wave can be divided into 360 degrees, just like a circle, as shown in Fig. 5-4. Regardless of the frequency or amplitude of a sine wave, the wave crosses the axis at 0, 180, and 360 degrees (360 is the same as 0, since the sine wave repeats forever). The peak is always at 90 degrees, and the valley is always at 270 degrees. For example, a sine wave of one cycle per second would reach its peak a quarter of a second into its cycle, or at 90 degrees; a sine wave of two cycles per second would reach its peak an eighth of a second into its cycle, also at 90 degrees.

A standard telephone line adequately transmits tones between 300 Hz and 3300 Hz. As illustrated in Fig. 5-5, the tones near the center of these frequencies are transmitted the best. Most human speech is made up of tones that fall in this range, though

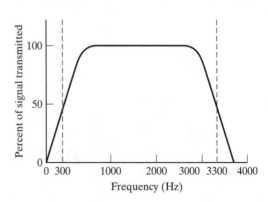

FIGURE 5-5

Telephone channel bandwidth.

a very small percentage of speech falls outside of this range and is not transmitted. This untransmitted portion of speech explains why some people have a "telephone voice," a voice that sounds different on the phone than in person. Another example of the bandwidth limitations of the telephone network can be heard by listening to a radio call-in talk show. The caller always sounds less audible than the host, because only part of the caller's voice reaches the radio station—the portion between 300 Hz and 3300 Hz. The telephone lines could support higher frequencies, but economics dictated that the frequencies between 300 Hz and 3300 Hz were sufficient. Since the highest frequency passed is 3300 Hz and the lowest is 300 Hz, the bandwidth is the difference, or 3000 Hz.

Why all this concern about telephone-line bandwidth when we are studying data communications? In order to transmit ones and zeroes over standard telephone lines, we must first translate the ones and zeroes to audible tones. By understanding the bandwidth limitations of the standard telephone line, we can ensure that the tones used can be transmitted reliably.

TRANSMISSION MEDIA

Many different types of *transmission media* are used in data communications today. Transmission media are the physical paths for carrying information, such as a pair of wires.

A typical local loop between the central office and our home is made up of *twisted pair* wire. Each local loop consists of a pair of wires, continuously twisted throughout its entire length. Typically, the wires are made of copper and are coated with an insulating material, and information is transmitted by sending electrical current through the wires. The twisting of the wires helps minimize the effects of certain types of noise on the voice or data transmission. The effects of twisting wire can be illustrated with most modern clock radios. A clock radio's power cord often acts as the antenna for FM reception; if we straighten the power cord, we get the best radio-signal reception, and twisting it minimizes the signal received from the surroundings. When transmitting voice or data over wire, we want to minimize the interference received. Therefore, we twist the telephone wire to reduce the number of signals received from the surroundings. Not only does this twisting reduce interference from radio stations, but it minimizes other forms of electromagnetic interference as well.

Twisted pair wire is often used at customer facilities, as well as over long distances, to carry voice as well as data communications. Though its bandwidth is limited to 300 Hz to 3300 Hz in the telephone network, this constraint is partly due to the equipment on each end. Higher frequencies can be achieved using special equipment, but twisted pair is generally considered a low-frequency transmission medium. Shielding can be used on twisted pair wire to further reduce the effects of interference and noise, though using it increases the cost. Data rates of several billion bits per second, or *gigabits per second (Gbps)*, are possible for short distances on customer-owned networks, though 56 kbps is the more accepted maximum rate over the standard analog telephone network, which is limited by its bandwidth of 300 Hz to 3300 Hz.

The main advantages of twisted pair wire are that it is relatively inexpensive (it costs only pennies per foot) and easy to install. The wire is flexible enough to be routed through conduit and on cable trays in office buildings, and each pair of wires is usually less than a 16th of an inch in diameter. In many older buildings found in downtown areas of cities, this space requirement is critical, because cables must be run between floors in the narrow space left over in existing elevator shafts. Many pairs of wires are often combined inside a larger cable. In addition, installing twisted pair requires little training, the wire is readily available, and inexpensive (less than $2) modular phone jacks can be used to make connections. Finally, many buildings are already wired with several twisted pairs in each office to allow for phone lines. Separate twisted pairs can be used for voice and data communications, or the two can be combined on a single twisted pair, as found in advanced digital PBXs.

The signal-carrying capacity of twisted pair wire varies, based on the wire itself, the number of twists in a given length of cable, and the type of connectors used. Most often, *unshielded twisted pair*, or *UTP*, wire is used in commercial applications. *Shielded twisted pair*, or *STP*, is available, but it is more expensive, and it is usually reserved only for locations that have an extraordinary amount of electromagnetic interference. These noisy environments may include factories with heavy equipment and hospitals with magnetic imaging devices. While analog voice can be transmitted over almost any twisted-pair cable, data networks have more stringent requirements for the cable and connector specifications.

The most widely used standard for UTP is *ANSI/TIA/EIA-568-B,* which defines several different cable categories that are suitable for data networks. While the cable categories specify frequencies they can carry, users are more interested in the specific data-network applications the cable categories support.

Lower speed data networks (e.g., 10 Mbps) can use *Category 3 cable (Cat3),* which has a specified bandwidth of 16 MHz. *Category 4 cable (Cat4)* was designed with 16-Mbps networks in mind, and it has a specified bandwidth of 20 MHz. *Category 5 cable (Cat5)* was defined specifically for 100 Mbps networks and has a 100-MHz bandwidth. *Category 5e cable (Cat5E)* also has a 100-MHz bandwidth, but it has improved loss and interference characteristics and was intended for 155-Mbps data networks. *Category 6 cable (Cat6)* has a 250-Mbps bandwidth and was designed for Gbps networks, while *Category 7 cable (Cat7)* is expected to have a 600-MHz bandwidth and support even higher speed data networks. All of the standards are *backwards compatible*, meaning that the newer versions can also support the applications of the previous versions. For example, it is possible to run a 10-Mbps data network on a Category 5 cable.

Regardless of the original intentions of the cable-standards bodies, higher speeds than those previously mentioned are often achieved on well-maintained and properly connected cable systems. Advances in network technology have allowed the use of Category 5 for even some Gbps networks, often by using wire pairs in the cable bundle that were unused at 100 Mbps. If the distance is short enough, you can often use a lesser grade of cable at a particular speed and still have good results, though there is no guarantee of signal quality in this case. These data-network speeds are only guidelines, as the cable specifications refer only to the analog bandwidth it supports. Future improvements in network technology might allow more digital bandwidth from these cable types.

The two connectors most commonly used with twisted-pair wire are the *RJ11* and *RJ45* connectors. RJ11 connectors are typically used for analog voice and are available in two-pin, four-pin, and six-pin versions. Eight-pin RJ45 connectors are commonly used in local area networks, as described in Chapter 8. RJ11 and RJ45 connectors are shown in Fig. 5-6.

FIGURE 5-6

RJ11 and RJ45 connectors.

Another type of cabling often used for data communications, video transmission, and some voice communication is *coaxial cable*, or *coax*. Most cable television systems use coax to connect subscribers. A coax cable usually consists of a single wire in the center surrounded by a core of insulating material, with an outer conductive wrapping, usually a copper cylinder, covered by a final insulating sheath. A cross-section of a coax cable is presented in Fig. 5-7, along with a standard coaxial male and female connector. The outer copper cylinder acts as a shield from any external interference, and data can be transmitted electronically on the inner wire. Any noise

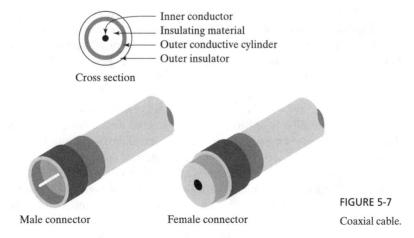

FIGURE 5-7

Coaxial cable.

or interference from the surroundings is absorbed by the copper cylinder and sent to the ground. Coax transmits high frequencies, thus allowing for high data rates, often several hundred Mbps, and it is less susceptible to noise than is twisted pair.

Coax is slightly more expensive than twisted pair wiring, though the connectors are inexpensive and easy to use with little training. The insulating core does add bulk, however, making the coax cables a quarter inch or more in diameter and far less flexible than twisted pair.

Another type of cable, known as *twinaxial cable*, or *twinax*, is almost identical to coax, except that it has two inner conducting wires. Twinax is used in a few special-purpose applications.

Many manufacturers combine different cables to provide an all-purpose wiring scheme for customer premises. The *IBM Cabling System* and the *AT&T Premises Distribution System* are two such schemes; each includes different types of cable with special shielding to meet the needs of particular customer applications.

Fiber optic cable is a popular high-bandwidth transmission medium. Data is transmitted by shining light through a special type of glass fiber. Fiber optic transmission is a modern-day form of the signal lights used to transmit information between ships at sea. The only difference is that in fiber optics, the light travels not through the air, but through glass fiber, and the data rates can exceed a trillion bits per second. One method used to send data through fiber optic cables is simply turning the light on and off. For example, when the light is on, a 1 is transmitted, and when the light is off, a 0 is transmitted. While a single optical channel was traditionally used in fiber optic cable, multiple channels, each on a different color of light, can be used to increase the bandwidth. This technique, known as *wave division multiplexing*, or *WDM*, allows many separate channels of data, each carried by a different color of light in the fiber optic cable. We will discuss multiplexing technologies in more detail later in this chapter.

Fiber optic cable is far more expensive per foot than coax or twisted pair, but the high bandwidth can still make fiber optics economical for high-volume applications. The cost of installing fiber optic cable is also high, with connections costing far more than coax or twisted pair. In addition, special equipment and training are required.

Fiber optic cable is no bulkier than coax, but it is more fragile. It is not affected at all by electrical and radio noise and interference, since the fiber optic transmission uses light, not electricity, to send data. This noise immunity makes fiber optics popular with long-distance carriers seeking to provide high-quality voice and data connections. Some local carriers are already choosing this medium, since the added bandwidth of a fiber optic local loop allows them to provide additional services. On the other hand, existing twisted pair local loops are certainly adequate for most voice and data transmission.

Fiber cable varies in construction, but a typical example is shown in Fig. 5-8. At the center of the cable is a thin glass fiber, known as the *core*. It is surrounded by another glass layer, known as *cladding*, that is specially designed to reflect light back into the core and keep light from escaping. The cladding is surrounded by a *buffer* layer to cushion the fiber. A *strength member* typically surrounds the buffer and provides durability as the fiber is pulled during installation. The last layer is the *jacket*, which is typically made of plastic. Multiple fibers are often grouped together into a larger cable that is then covered with an outer sheath.

Cross section

FIGURE 5-8

Fiber optic cable.

The light source in fiber cables can be either *light-emitting diodes* (*LEDs*) or *lasers*. LEDs cost less and have a longer life, but they are limited in the distance the signal can travel. Lasers are more expensive and have a shorter life, but they allow for longer distances.

There are two major types of transmission in a fiber optic cable. *Single-mode fiber* uses very thin fibers and is useful at longer distances. *Multimode fiber* uses slightly thicker fiber, but is less expensive to produce. Light rays tend to bounce around inside the thicker multimode fiber, shortening the distance a signal can travel. If the maximum transmission distance is reached, repeaters need to be placed in fiber optic lines to regenerate the signal. The tradeoff between single and multimode fiber is made after factoring in the performance (speed and distance) and economic factors (cost of cable and repeaters).

Satellite transmission uses radio waves to transmit data. A *satellite dish*, or antenna, known as the *uplink* station, transmits data to the satellite, which orbits the earth. *Transponders* on the satellite then repeat the signal, which is received by another satellite dish, known as the *downlink* station. Satellite transmission is depicted in Fig. 5-9. Conventional satellites typically orbit approximately 22,230 miles above the earth's surface. Any satellite dish pointed at the satellite can receive the signal, provided that it is tuned to the proper frequency, much in the same way we tune in to a radio station.

To help understand satellites, picture a strange mirror orbiting above the earth. Standing in Florida, we shine a very powerful flashlight pointed right at this mirror, and this special mirror reflects the light over the entire country. Our friend in Oregon can then read outside in the light provided by this mirror. We could not light up the whole country with our powerful flashlight without the help of the mirror to reflect the light everywhere. Similarly, the satellite takes our data and repeats it so that everyone within reach of the satellite can receive the signal. We simply point our dish at the satellite and begin transmitting. Since the satellite is so high, the same satellite can transmit data to almost a third of the world. Transmitting data to the other two-thirds of the world simply requires the signal to be relayed to another satellite. A major advantage of satellites is their ability to communicate from almost anywhere to almost anywhere else.

The bandwidth of satellite transmission depends on the equipment used in the uplink and downlink stations and on the number of satellite channels used. Each satellite is capable of handling many channels at one time, each of different transmission frequencies. Satellite bandwidth can extend from 64 kbps to many Mbps and is almost unlimited if enough channels are used. Satellite transmission is usually cheaper over long distances than fiber optics or twisted pair, because there is no cabling cost

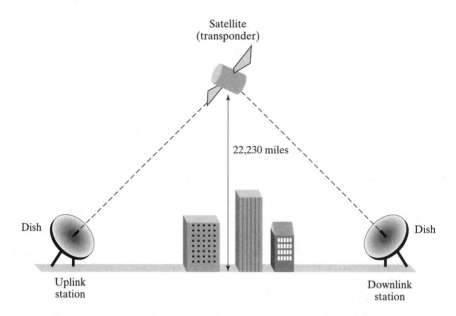

FIGURE 5-9

Satellite transmission.

between the two locations. The satellite dishes are a one-time purchase and do not have to be leased monthly from telephone carriers, though the satellite channels must be leased.

However, satellite transmissions are subject to noise and long delays. Since every transmission must go from the ground to the satellite and back to the ground, each transmission requires approximately a 45,000-mile trip. This transmission occurs at roughly the speed of light, so the trip takes a quarter of a second. Sending a message and receiving a response means at least a half-second delay for the round-trip. A half-second wait may seem trivial to us, but a computer might be able to transmit thousands of bits during that time.

The long delays of satellite transmission can produce the so-called "tunnel effect," where annoying echoes are heard during long-distance calls. Though these echoes can be prevented by using echo cancellers, nothing can be done about the delay between transmission and reception. A transcontinental call over twisted pair wire will probably go no farther than 5000 miles, no matter how convoluted the call routing. The same call using a satellite travels nine times farther and therefore can markedly slow down servers waiting to transmit data.

While these high-altitude satellites have carried voice and data communications for decades, a new breed of satellite, known as a *low-earth orbit* satellite, or *LEO* satellite, has been launched in recent years. These satellites orbit a few hundred miles above the earth. Because they are closer to the earth, more satellites are required to provide global coverage. For example, one such satellite network operates 66 satellites orbiting 485 miles above the earth. Another LEO satellite network operates 48 satellites at an altitude of 736 miles. In between these satellites and conventional satellites is another type, known as a *medium-earth orbit* satellite, or *MEO* satellite. One of these networks operates 12 satellites at an altitude of 6434 miles. In contrast, a conventional satellite system, based on a *geosynchronous-earth orbit* satellite, or *GEO* satellite, requires only three satellites at an altitude of approximately 22,230 miles to cover the globe. This particular altitude is convenient because the satellites orbit at the same speed at which the earth rotates; thus, dish antennas can be aimed once, and the satellite remains in the same relative position. The LEO and MEO satellites are moving with respect to the earth's surface at all times, so these antenna systems are designed to allow for transmission and reception without directly pointing at one particular satellite. The orbiting satellites in these systems hand off calls to one another as they pass near the user. These handoffs are similar in nature to those conducted by a ground-based cellular telephone system, as discussed in Chapter 2.

Satellites are susceptible to noise and interference caused by a variety of sources. Finally, satellite transmission can be heard by anyone with a dish tuned to the right frequency, causing a potential security risk. We discuss methods for minimizing this risk in Chapter 6.

Terrestrial microwave transmission uses radio frequencies similar to those found in satellite transmission. Instead of bouncing radio waves off a satellite, however, the users build tall towers and point the dishes at each other, as illustrated in Fig. 5-10. Alternatively, the dishes can be put on top of buildings, as long as there is a clear *line of sight* between the two dishes. If there is an obstruction (e.g., a mountain or a building) between the receiver and the destination, another tower can be placed on top of the obstruction and used as a repeater. This additional tower simply receives a signal on one side and transmits it to the other side.

The signals used for microwave transmission can be sent only 20 to 30 miles. Longer distances require use of multiple *hops*, with additional towers in between. These intermediary towers act as repeaters, receiving the signal and passing it on. Microwave transmission bandwidth can exceed 250 Mbps.

The key difference between microwave transmission and satellite transmission is that microwave transmission requires a line of sight between the two dish antennas. There can be no obstructions between the two antennas; if we climbed one of the towers on a clear night, we should be able to shine our powerful flashlight at the second tower, and our friend at the top of the second tower should be able to see the light. If the other tower was not the final destination, but instead was only a repeater station, our friend would see our flashlight and then point a flashlight at the next tower.

The cost advantages of microwave transmission lie in relatively short-haul, high-bandwidth applications. The towers and dishes are a one-time purchase cost, there are no satellite channels to lease, and there is currently no shortage of microwave frequencies. Like conventional satellite transmission, there is no cabling cost between the locations, because the signal travels through the air. However, each added hop significantly increases the cost, since every repeater requires a separate tower and two dish antennas, one pointed in each direction. Microwave transmission is subjected to the same noise and interference as satellite transmission, though it is less likely that we will be encountering interference on a 30-mile route than on a 45,000-mile transmission.

Single hop

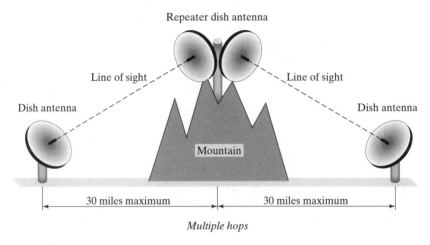

Multiple hops

FIGURE 5-10

Terrestrial microwave transmission.

A chart summarizing the different transmission media, as well as their advantages and disadvantages, is presented in Fig. 5-11.

BASEBAND VS. BROADBAND

There clearly are many different types of transmission media, each suited to certain applications. In addition, there are two methods used to transmit data: baseband and broadband.

In *baseband transmission*, a single data signal is transmitted directly on a wire. The RS-232-C interface, for which a separate wire is used for each signal, is an example of baseband transmission: TD and RD each occupy a separate wire, and the data is transmitted directly on the wires using positive and negative voltages.

Broadband transmission is a technique in which the data to be transmitted are sent using a *carrier signal*, such as a sine wave. Since many different frequency carrier signals can be transmitted simultaneously, more than one signal can be sent on the same wire. This technique is found in cable television, where only a single cable enters our house, but there are many separate signals on that cable; we view the desired station by tuning the particular channel's frequency on our television set or cable box. In

Type	Advantages	Disadvantages
Twisted pair wire	Very inexpensive Easy to install Already installed in many locations	Doesn't pass high frequencies well Relatively low bandwidth
Coaxial cable	Shielded Fairly inexpensive Moderately high bandwidth	Bulky and somewhat inflexible
Fiber optic cable	Transmission unaffected by noise Very high bandwidth	Expensive to install Repeaters often required
Satellite	No line of sight needed No cabling needed between sites High bandwidth	Channels must be leased High initial equipment cost Long delays
Terrestrial microwave	No cabling needed between sites High bandwidth	Line of sight needed Towers and repeaters can be expensive High initial equipment cost

FIGURE 5-11

A comparison of transmission media.

data communications, broadband transmission always uses analog signals to send data. We now explain the most common use of broadband transmission in data communications.

MODULATION

The conversion of digital signals to analog form for transmission is called *modulation*, and converting these analog signals back to digital form is called *demodulation*. A device that performs modulation and demodulation is a modulator/demodulator, or a *modem*.

Why is the conversion of the signals necessary? Typically, modems are used when the server and client are in different locations. Most interface standards, like RS-232-C, transmit data using positive and negative voltages, which form square waves. The square waves used in digital transmission cannot be sent over standard telephone lines without first being converted to analog form, because the public telephone network was designed to carry analog signals, like speech. Typical placement of a modem in a data communications circuit is shown in Fig. 5-12. We depict the communications circuit, using common industry practice, as a lightning bolt. The lightning bolt represents the local loops, the central office(s), and any toll offices present in the connection between the two modems.

In some cases, the telephone line between the two modems is permanent, or *leased*. In other cases, the client is contacting a different server each time or needs to contact the server only occasionally. These situations are suitable for a *dial-up*, or *switched, circuit*, for which a new telephone call is placed for each connection.

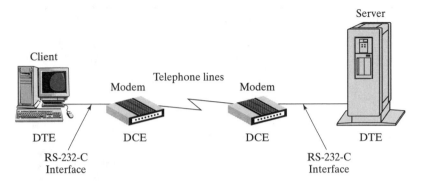

FIGURE 5-12

Using modems in data communications circuits.

In every dial-up connection there are two modems. The modem that places the call is known as the *originate modem*, and the modem that answers the call is known as the *answer modem*. Some early modems were *originate only* (could only place calls) or *answer only* (could only answer calls). Most of today's modems can both place and receive calls and are known as *originate/answer modems*.

Dial-up modem calls can be placed in two ways. Early modems, known as *dumb modems*, performed only modulation and demodulation. In addition to a modem, a telephone instrument had to be attached to the phone line to place calls. The client user picked up the telephone and dialed the number of the answer (remote) modem. After reaching the answer modem, the user could then hang up the phone and hit a "data" button on the originate (local) modem. Doing so put the originate modem in "data mode" and caused it to begin communicating with the answer modem. Some customers used PBXs to automate the dialing process. After dialing the call, instead of hitting a "data" button, a PBX would close a switch connecting a pair of wires coming from the originate modem, known as the *mode indicator leads*, or *MI/MIC leads*. The originate modem would recognize this action as a signal to enter the "data mode" and begin communicating with the answer modem.

A newer generation of modems, known as *smart modems*, can accept dialing instructions directly from the user of the client, dial the call, and perform the necessary modulation and demodulation when the connection is established. Most modems used with personal computers today are smart modems, since the software can instruct the smart modem to dial and disconnect calls. Since the smart modem is able to dial the call itself, using rotary or touch-tone dialing, a separate telephone instrument is not needed for a smart modem.

Typically, modems convert the square waves that represent ones and zeroes to sine waves for analog transmission. There are many different methods for performing this conversion, each with its own advantages and disadvantages. Both the originate and answer modem must use the same modulation methods for successful data communications. We now explain several popular types of modulation.

Today, modems are often used to connect a client to an intermediary data network. In a typical example, a user's modem dials the modem of an *Internet service*

FIGURE 5-13

Using modems to access the Internet.

provider, or *ISP*. The data is then sent over the ISP's network and onto the Internet, which in turn carries the data to the server. A data network like the Internet is often depicted as a cloud, as shown in Fig. 5-13. The modems in this case are just used as a method to access the Internet. ISPs and the Internet are discussed thoroughly in Chapter 8.

Amplitude Modulation

In one modulation technique, known as *amplitude modulation*, or *AM*, the amplitude, or height, of the sine wave varies to transmit the ones and zeroes. Another name for amplitude modulation is *amplitude shift keying*, or *ASK*, since data is transmitted by shifting amplitudes. The bit pattern 00101001 is being transmitted using amplitude modulation in Fig. 5-14. Notice that the sine wave's amplitude is high when transmitting a 1 and low when transmitting a 0. The duration, or width, of each cycle of the sine wave does not change throughout the transmission; in other words, the frequency doesn't vary. In Fig. 5-14, there are two complete cycles of the sine wave (two peaks and two valleys) for each bit transmitted. The number of complete cycles used to send a bit with amplitude modulation is an arbitrary choice and varies depending on the type and speed of the modem.

If we attached a telephone to a modem using amplitude modulation and listened to it transmit the bit pattern 00101001, we would hear a single tone that never varies in pitch (frequency), but that instead gets louder when transmitting a 1 and softer when transmitting a 0. Of course, we would need very sensitive ears, since most modems transmit several thousand bits per second.

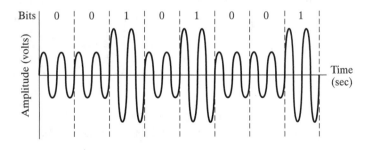

FIGURE 5-14

Amplitude modulation.

One major disadvantage of amplitude modulation is that telephone lines are very susceptible to variations in transmission quality that affect amplitude. Particularly on long-distance calls, we are accustomed to hearing the volume of a person's voice vary during the course of a conversation. If a modem using amplitude modulation is transmitting a 1 when the telephone connection volume fades, the receiving modem will hear a low-amplitude sine wave and may interpret it as a 0.

We have considered only the transmission of data in one direction at a time. In a full duplex communications circuit, a sine wave of another frequency can be used to simultaneously send data in the other direction. The amplitude of this second sine wave also varies to send ones and zeroes in this direction.

Frequency Modulation

Another technique, known as *frequency modulation*, or *FM*, varies the frequency of the sine wave to transmit data while the amplitude remains constant. Another name for frequency modulation is *frequency shift keying*, or *FSK*, since data is transmitted by shifting frequencies. The same bit pattern, 00101001, is being transmitted using frequency modulation in Fig. 5-15. Notice that the amplitude of the sine wave doesn't vary, but the length of each cycle, and hence the frequency, does. A low frequency (1070 Hz) is used to send a 0, and a higher frequency (1270 Hz) is used to send a 1. If we attached a telephone to a modem using frequency modulation and listened to it transmit the bit pattern 00101001, we would hear a low-pitched tone for each 0 and a higher pitched tone for each 1. The volumes, or amplitudes, of both tones would be the same.

Since the receiving modem recognizes only differences in frequency and is not concerned with the amplitude of the signal, small variations in phone-line volume will not cause demodulation errors when frequency modulation is used.

If we need to send data in both directions at once, we need two frequencies (one for a 1 and one for a 0) for each direction, for a total of four frequencies. Frequency modulation is often used for 300-bps transmission according to the *Bell 103/113* specification, also known as *AT&T 103/113*. The originating modem sends a

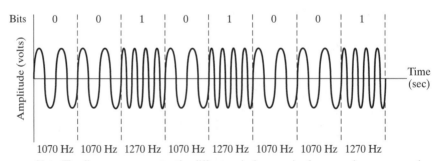

Note: The diagram exaggerates the difference in frequencies for example purposes only.

FIGURE 5-15

Frequency modulation.

one using a 1270 Hz tone or a zero using a 1070 Hz tone. The answering modem sends a one using a 2225 Hz tone or a zero using a 2025 Hz tone. The ITU(CCITT) *V.21* standard describes a 300-bps modem used internationally with a similar modulation scheme.

Phase Modulation

A more sophisticated technique is known as *phase modulation*, or *PM*, because data is transmitted by changing the phase of the sine wave. Another name for phase modulation is *phase shift keying*, or *PSK*, since data is transmitted by shifting phase. A sine wave normally repeats itself indefinitely, with one peak and valley after another. Shifting phase breaks the sine wave abruptly and starts it again a few degrees forward or backward.

We assume 180-degree forward phase shifts for our example, shown in Fig. 5-16. The sine wave continues uninterrupted for two time periods as we transmit zeroes. Then the sine wave stops abruptly at the axis, and we skip forward 180 degrees. In a sine wave, skipping forward 180 degrees moves us halfway across the sine wave, bringing us to the point where the sine wave starts back up to the next peak. In our example, the 180-degree phase shift is used to send ones, and a continuous sine wave is used to send zeroes; however, this is only one possible way to use phase modulation to transmit data. Notice that the amplitude and frequency of the sine waves stay constant throughout transmission. We simply shift phase during a time period to send a 1 or continue the sine wave uninterrupted to send a 0. The receiving modem can monitor the incoming sine wave and determine if the phase shifted during a particular time period.

A forward phase shift is nothing more than skipping ahead in our sine wave. For example, normally a CD player will play an entire album. However, we could decide to skip a song that we don't enjoy. If we wanted to send data using this method, we could arbitrarily say, "If I skip a song, I'm sending a 1. If I play all the songs, I'm sending a 0." The receiver must know what song normally comes next on the album in order to determine if a song was skipped. With phase modulation, the receiver knows exactly what the sine wave should look like. If part of the sine wave is skipped, the receiver can recognize this

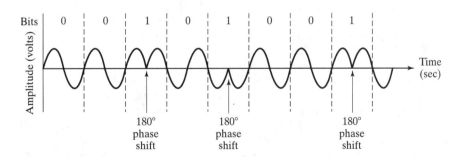

FIGURE 5-16

Phase modulation.

fact, just as we would recognize that a song was skipped. In our CD player example, we skip an entire song; in Fig. 5-16, we skip 180 degrees of the sine wave.

If we need to send data in two directions at once, we use one frequency for each direction. The phases shift on each of these sine waves, as necessary, to send data. Like frequency modulation, phase modulation is not affected by slight variations in amplitude that normally occur on the telephone network. The main advantage of phase modulation is that only a single-frequency sine wave is used to send both ones and zeroes in each direction. In frequency modulation, separate frequencies are required to send a one and send a zero in each direction.

BITS PER SECOND VS. BAUD

So far, we have considered the modulation of only one bit at a time. We have varied amplitude, frequency, or phase to send a one or a zero. In each case, there were two alternatives: a high or low amplitude, a high or low frequency, or a phase shift or no phase shift. We've already discussed the Bell 103/113 standard for 300 bps transmission; for each bit, the transmitting modem needed to decide which frequency to send. The number of decisions, or possible signal changes in a second, is known as the *baud rate* of a modem. The 300-bps modem described by our example is also a 300-baud modem, because the signal could potentially change 300 times in a second, once for each bit.

Some clients communicate at much higher speeds, like 9600 bps. However, a telephone circuit's bandwidth does not transmit frequencies higher than 3300 Hz. If we perform only one amplitude, frequency, or phase change in a given cycle and if a single bit is transmitted with each change, we would be limited to 3300 bps. We could build a more sophisticated modem that would recognize an amplitude, frequency, or phase change after half a cycle, but this modem would still limit us to 6600 bits per second. Clearly, there is a need for faster modulation methods to handle higher speed devices.

What if we could send more than one bit with each shift of amplitude, frequency, or phase? Sending two bits would provide us with four possible combinations: 00, 01, 10, and 11. Therefore, using amplitude modulation, we would need four possible amplitudes; frequency modulation would require four frequencies, and phase modulation would require four phases. Sending two bits in this way is known as *dibit modulation*.

One of the most commonly used forms of modulation today is the dibit phase shift keying described by the *Bell 212A* (AT&T 212A) specification. In this specification, the originate modem transmits data using a 1200-Hz sine wave, and the answer modem transmits data using a 2400-Hz sine wave. Phase shifts of 90, 0, 180, and 270 degrees represent the bits 00, 01, 10, and 11, respectively. The bit pattern 01001110 is being transmitted according to the Bell 212A standard shown in Fig. 5-17. A similar 1200-bps modem standard used internationally is the ITU(CCITT) *V.22*.

With this dibit transmission, the modem could change the signal only every two bits, when it may shift the signal's phase. In this case, Bell 212A described 1200-bps transmission: If 1200 bits are sent in a second, and 2 bits are sent with each possible signal change, the modem is 600 baud. The client and server require a certain bit per second rate and are not affected by the baud rate. A client transmitting 1200 bits per second functions equally well with a 1200-bps/1200-baud modem or a 1200-bps/600-baud modem.

Though we have just described dibit modulation, some modems use tribit (three bits at once) or even quabit (four bits at once) modulation. For example, to use tribit phase shift keying,

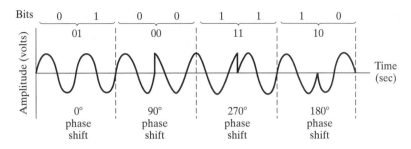

FIGURE 5-17

Dibit phase shift keying using the Bell 212A specification.

we need to use 45-degree phase shifts to give us the eight possible combinations of three bits: 000, 001, 010, 011, 100, 101, 110, and 111. Quabit phase shift keying would require 22.5-degree phase shifts. These smaller phase shifts require more sophisticated modems to detect the subtle changes.

Since most older modems (300 bps and slower) sent only one bit with each signal change, *bps* and *baud* were equivalent terms and were therefore used interchangeably for many years. Even though today most modems use dibit, tribit, or even quabit modulation, the term *baud* is often mistakenly used instead of *bps*, even by modem vendor sales personnel. For example, the Bell 212A modem, though a 1200-bps/600-baud modem, is often mistakenly referred to as a 1200-baud modem. The easiest way to avoid any misunderstanding when purchasing modems is to specify the bps rate of the server or client and request a modem that can handle that transmission speed.

One interesting feature of certain modem specifications is their *multispeed* capability. For example, when a Bell 212A modem begins communications with another modem, it tries to communicate using the 1200-Hz and 2400-Hz tones already mentioned. If the other modem does not provide the appropriate tone, the Bell 212A modem assumes that it has reached a slower modem and tries to communicate using the Bell 103/113 tones we have already presented. In other words, the Bell 212A modem will attempt to communicate at 1200 bps; if unsuccessful, it will fall back to 300 bps. This capability allowed early users of the Bell 212A modem to continue to communicate with older 300 bps modems, while still achieving the increased performance that 1200 bps affords when communicating with other Bell 212A modems. This multispeed capability has become an accepted practice in the industry.

Faster modems often combine different modulation methods to allow for faster transmission rates. The first widely accepted dial-up 2400-bps modem, described by the *ITU(CCITT) V.22 bis* standard, also included a fallback to the older 1200-bps speed of Bell 212A. The V.22 bis standard achieves 2400 bps by combining changes in phase and amplitude at the same time in a technique known as *quadrature amplitude modulation*. Four bits are sent at once, at 600 baud, for a 2400-bps transmission rate. There are four different phases and four amplitudes, for a total of 16 possible combinations, which allows for all the different possibilities of four bits: 0000, 0001, 0010, 0011, 0100, 0101, 0110, 0111, 1000, 1001, 1010, 1011, 1100, 1101, 1110, and 1111.

While it is easy to see the phase shifts in a 1200-bps modem, because phase is the only variable, both phase and amplitude are changing with 2400-bps and later modems. These changes create a sine wave that is difficult for the human eye to decipher, so instead we use a special picture known as a *constellation diagram*, as shown in Fig. 5-18. The degrees of phase shift are laid out around the center point, with 0 degrees at the right position, 90 degrees at the top, 180 degrees at the left, and 270 at the bottom. If an imaginary line were drawn from the center point to each of the dots, the distance would represent the amplitude, and the angle would represent the phase. While Fig. 5-18 shows the 16 points in the V.22 bis constellation, the higher speed modems simply have more possibilities and therefore more dots in their constellation diagrams.

The most widely used modulation standard at 9600 bps is the ITU(CCITT) *V.32* standard. This standard also functions at 4800 bps. It uses quadrature amplitude modulation with *trellis coding*, which can recover from minor transmission problems. Extra information is sent with the data to allow the receiving modem to detect and correct minor errors. At 14.4 kbps, the ITU(CCITT) *V.32 bis* standard is popular; at 28.8 and 33.6 kbps, *V.34* is used. A comparison of the various modem standards and the types of modulation used is shown in Fig. 5-19.

The ITU (CCITT) *V.90* standard can provide transmission speeds of up to 56 kbps from the central office to the analog-line user, while modulating at V.34 speeds in the other direction. Unlike standard analog modems, which operate on any analog line, this modem requires a digital line connected to a digitally equipped central office on the side transmitting at the higher speed. This digital line, like a T-1 or ISDN line, would normally carry digitized voice. In

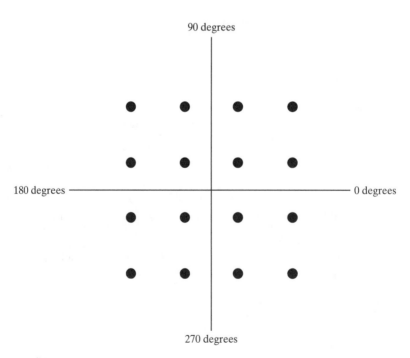

FIGURE 5-18

V.22 bis modem constellation diagram.

Speed	Standard	Modulation method	Maximum baud rate
300 bps	Bell 103/113	Frequency modulation	300 baud
1200 bps	Bell 212A	Phase modulation 600 baud	
2400 bps	V.22bis	Quadrature amplitude modulation	600 baud
4800 bps	V.32	Quadrature amplitude modulation/trellis coding	2400 baud
9600 bps	V.32	Quadrature amplitude modulation/trellis coding	2400 baud
14.4 kbps	V.32bis	Quadrature amplitude modulation/trellis coding	2400 baud
28.8 kbps	V.34	Quadrature amplitude modulation/trellis coding	3429 baud
33.6 kbps	V.34	Quadrature amplitude modulation/trellis coding	3429 baud
56 kbps/ 33.6 kbps	V.90	Digital: G.711 Analog: Quadrature amplitude modulation/trellis coding	Digital: 8000 baud Analog: 3429 baud
56 kbps/ 48 kbps	V.92	Digital: G.711	Digital: 8000 baud

FIGURE 5-19

Common modem standards.

this case, it carries signals that look like voice digitized according to the ITU(CCITT) *G.711* standard, but it actually contains computer data. In the high-speed transmission direction, the V.90 modem sends signals through the digital telephone network until they reach the destination central office. At the central office, these signals are assumed to be digitized voice. Therefore, the central office places the analog equivalent of these digital signals on the user's analog local loop. The receiving modem is expecting analog signal levels that mimic the digital ones typically used in the central office. If the line has little noise, the modem will still be able to detect the original signal levels and determine which ones and zeroes they originally represented. An extremely noise-free analog local loop is required on the receiving end to demodulate data at 56 kbps in this manner. In practice, most users connecting with 56 kbps modems approach this rate only sporadically, when the ideal circumstances occur. In the other direction, standard V.34 modulation is used. The *V.92* standard is similar to V.90, except speeds towards the central office can reach 48 kbps under ideal conditions, when G.711 transmission is used in both directions.

Some modem vendors create their own proprietary modulation schemes and do not follow any established standards. The disadvantage is that these modems communicate only with their counterparts manufactured by the same vendor. However, a standard modem, like a V.90 modem, communicates with any V.90 modem, regardless of the manufacturer.

Error-Correcting Modems

At modem speeds up to 1200 bps, the quality of dial-up phone lines is sufficient to ensure reasonably reliable modem transmission. However, with the advent of 2400-bps modems, the modulation methods became more sophisticated. For example, in the V.22 bis standard, the phase and amplitude both vary, so even slight telephone line noise could cause an error. Most modems operating at speeds of 2400 bps and above have some type of error-correction capability.

Though the higher speed modems use trellis-coded modulation, significant line noise can cause more errors than trellis coding can correct. So even these modems need some additional error checking if we want to ensure reliable transmission.

Two approaches are commonly used today to correct for errors between modems, regardless of the speed or underlying modulation methods. The first, known as *Microcom Network Protocol*, or *MNP*, is a commercially licensed error-checking protocol. The second, ITU(CCITT)'s *V.42*, also known as *Link Access Procedure for Modems*, or *LAPM*, is an international standard for error correction. Most modern modems support one or both of these protocols, and users can configure their modems to use one of them. Both protocols rely on the receiving modem to detect an error and ask the transmitter to send the data again. The user never sees errors, but the user may see delays if the modems must halt transmission to retransmit data. The modems will, if necessary, either lower the CTS signal or send an XOFF character to stop the DTE from transmitting while the modem retransmits the prior block. Errors can also be fixed in DTEs or at other places in the network, as discussed in Chapter 6.

Data Compression in Modems

Many modems today use data compression. The modems don't send bits any faster, but they attempt to send fewer bits by searching for repeated patterns and sending some type of shorthand notation. The receiving modem translates the shorthand back to the original bits, creating the illusion that the two modems are operating at a higher speed.

The fifth version of the previously mentioned MNP standard, known as *MNP 5*, can compress data to half its size under ideal conditions. The ITU(CCITT) *V.42 bis* standard can theoretically compress data to one-fourth its original size under ideal conditions. Since it is hard to predict if the data transmitted will have repeated patterns, compression at these ideal levels should not be expected. In addition, MNP 5 adds some overhead, which actually worsens the transmission of data that is not compressible. V.42 bis, on the other hand, senses if the data is not compressible and suspends operation when it cannot improve the data flow.

Compression features are probably the most oversold feature on modems today. Some vendors claim to have a 134.4-kbps modem, when all they have is a V.34 modem operating at 33.6 kbps with V.42 bis compression, assuming a 4-to-1 compression ratio. This optimistic approach seldom translates to true performance during operation. A newer compression standard, *V.44*, offers theoretical compression ratios approaching 6 to 1. Data compression is discussed in more detail later in this chapter.

Short-Haul Modems

All of the modems presented thus far have been designed for use over the public telephone network. Occasionally, users may have a large building or campus environment where they need to locate devices a few hundred or even a few thousand feet from each other. If these are RS-232-C devices, the user is limited to 50 feet; any greater distance requires the use of modems. If the user can own or lease wires between these devices, *short-haul modems*, also called *limited-distance modems*, can be used.

Short-haul modems transmit data over twisted pair wire, but not through the telephone company's central offices. They modulate data using frequencies greater than the normal telephone channel bandwidth limit of 3300 Hz. By using these high frequencies, higher transmission rates can be achieved using less expensive hardware. However, the resulting sine waves can be passed over twisted pair wire for only a few miles and cannot be passed through the central office switch. The short-haul modem can transmit for a few miles, and the dial-up modem can transmit around the world, with the help of central offices and toll offices in between. Therefore, a user with a client in the basement and a server on the fifth floor could connect the two with a pair of short-haul modems and twisted pair wire. This user would have high data rates and no monthly phone-line costs.

Facsimile and Fax Modems

Facsimile, or *fax*, is the electrical transmission of documents over telephone lines. The standards for fax machines are set by the ITU(CCITT). Different standards offer different transmission quality, or *resolution*, which is measured in lines per inch. ITU(CCITT) *Group 1* and *Group 2* fax machines were purely analog devices, offering only 100 lines per inch of resolution. Transmission of a typical printed page could take 3 to 6 minutes using these techniques.

Modern fax machines employ digital compression technology to shorten the time used for fax transmission. *Group 3* transmission is a common example. Long white spaces or black spaces on a page are described by their dimensions rather than sent one small dot at a time, as with earlier fax machines. This technique, known as *run length encoding*, reduces the time for transmitting a typical page to under a minute. Group 3 fax typically operates at 4800 bps or 9600 bps and offers 200 lines per inch of resolution.

In a modern fax machine, a scanner converts the document into ones and zeroes, which can be sent by the fax modem. A fax machine contains the scanner, modem, and printer in one unit. Separate fax modems are now available that let any computer with the proper software send and receive faxes as well.

Fax modems use special protocols beyond those found in standard data modems. For example, most fax machines produce a header at the top of each page that indicates the transmitting party and the page number. This information is transferred between the two fax machines, or fax modems, at the start of the transmission.

The *Group 4* standard offers increased resolution and speed, operating at up to 64 kbps with resolutions of up to 400 lines per inch. The higher speeds are seldom used because they are not currently economical enough for most office communications.

MULTIPLEXERS

When several connections are needed between two sites, we can use multiple phone lines and pairs of modems. These redundant paths are costly and not very efficient. One of the most widely used devices for improving data communications efficiency in this case is the *multiplexer*, often called a *mux*. A multiplexer allows several devices to share the same communications circuit. This sharing can be accomplished in several ways. For instance, faster modems can be used on the communications circuit, or the communications circuit can be split into several separate channels. Another option is to substitute a single digital phone line with DSU/CSUs for multiple phone lines with slower modems. Throughout the following multiplexer discussion, the analog line and modems are assumed, but a CSU/DSU and digital phone line could be used instead. Typically, bandwidth requirements and the cost of the phone circuits determine whether the shared path is analog or digital.

Multiplexing is useful when there are parallel communications paths between two locations. The main advantage of multiplexing, as shown in Fig. 5-20, is that fewer telephone lines and modems are needed. The one-time purchase cost of multiplexers is usually justified over time by the reduction of monthly costs for telephone lines. The main purpose of multiplexers, therefore, is to minimize communications circuit costs. While we discuss multiplexers now in the context of interconnecting clients and servers, they are also used to minimize voice-communications costs when parallel voice paths exist.

Multiplexers are normally used in pairs, with one multiplexer at each end of the communications circuit. The data from several clients can be sent over a single communications circuit by one multiplexer. At the receiving multiplexer, the data is separated and sent to the appropriate destinations. Multiplexing is a generic technology that is not limited to a particular vendor's servers or clients; it can be applied anywhere parallel paths are present.

We often refer to the low-speed ports of a multiplexer as *branch ports* and to the high-speed port as the *trunk port*. Just like a tree, there are many branches (clients or server ports) and only one trunk (connected to the modems). The branch and trunk ports are labeled in Fig. 5-20.

There are other opportunities to increase efficiency beyond multiplexing when working in an environment with older, legacy communications equipment. Examples of these configurations, using front end processors, port sharing devices, line splitters, remote intelligent controllers, and various multidrop scenarios, are detailed in Appendix B. A new network being installed today would not normally use these configurations, but some existing networks still use these approaches.

Time-Division Multiplexing

Multiplexers that share the time on a fast communications circuit among slower devices use a technique known as *time-division multiplexing*, or *TDM*. In our first example of TDM, shown in Fig. 5-21, the four clients and server ports each operate at 2400 bps. The pair of modems between the multiplexers operates at 9600 bps. The four clients and server ports actually share the modem's 9600-bps bandwidth. For convenience, we discuss the transmission of data from the clients to the server ports, though

FIGURE 5-20

Multiplexing.

the same principles apply in both directions. In addition, the speeds are arbitrarily chosen for our example, and the concepts described will work at any speed; these could easily be four 64-kbps clients communication across a 256-kbps digital phone circuit using CSU/DSUs.

In Fig. 5-21, Each of the clients can transmit and receive at 2400 bps, so if all four are constantly transmitting and receiving data, a total of 9600 bps is transmitted and

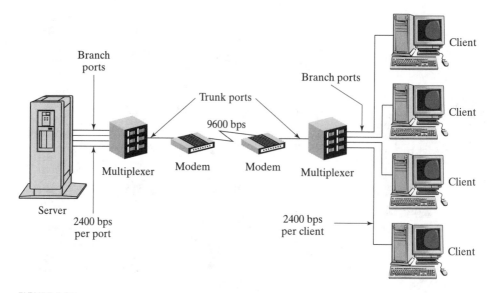

FIGURE 5-21

Time-division multiplexing.

received by the modems. Since all of the clients are probably not transmitting all of the time, there is enough bandwidth between the modems to handle this activity. This technique is known as *pure time-division multiplexing* because there is always enough bandwidth to handle the clients' maximum transmission.

CHARACTER AND BIT INTERLEAVING

How does TDM work? There are two popular methods, known as character interleaving and bit interleaving. The former is the easiest to visualize.

In *character interleaving*, or *byte interleaving*, multiplexing is performed one character at a time. Of course, each character may be made up of eight bits. In Fig. 5-22, each of the clients is sending a message that we have chosen at random. Client 1 sends "Hello," Client 2 sends "Goodness," Client 3 sends "Labor," and Client 4 sends "Nice"; the clients send these words one character at a time. For convenience, we refer to the multiplexer attached to the clients as multiplexer A, and we refer to the multiplexer attached to the server as multiplexer B.

Multiplexer A, using character interleaving, checks each of its branch ports for characters transmitted by clients. These characters can be sent, one at a time, over the high-speed trunk port. For example, multiplexer A scans its ports, discovering the characters *H*, *G*, *L*, and *N*. Multiplexer A sends *HGLN* over its trunk port to multiplexer B. Multiplexer B then sends the characters to each server port at 2400 bps: The *H* to port 1, the *G* to port 2, the *L* to port 3, and the *N* to port 4. Next, multiplexer A sends *eoai* over its trunk port. Multiplexer B sends the *e* to port 1, the *o* to port 2, the *a* to port 3, and the *i* to port 4. This process continues until all of the characters are sent.

FIGURE 5-22

Character interleaving.

We call this process "character interleaving" because every fourth character transmitted over the multiplexer's trunk ports is destined for the same branch port. It is the equivalent of four lanes on a highway alternately merging into one lane, taking one car from lane 1, one from lane 2, one from lane 3, one from lane 4, one from lane 1 again, and so on. At the end of the road, the one lane splits off into four again, and the first car feeds into lane 1 again, the next to lane 2, the next to lane 3, the next to lane 4, the next to lane 1 again, and so on. In character interleaving, characters are merged instead of cars. Remember that each character may be made up of eight bits, but the characters are merged in their entirety.

Each of the clients is allocated one-fourth of the time on the modems in each direction; each time a particular client and server-port pair communicates is called *a time slot*. In our example, Client 1 had the first time slot, Client 2 the second, and so on. At multiplexer B, the character in time slot 1 is sent to Server port 1, the character in time slot 2 is sent to Server port 2, and so on. If we used TDM with 10 devices instead of 4 on each end, there would be 10 time slots instead of 4 in each direction.

Notice in our example that Client 4, with the shortest message ("Nice"), does not use its time slot after it has sent the four characters. We could think of this lack of use as a waste of a time slot, but the vacant time slot does have a purpose. If Client 4 had a longer word to transmit, it would have been guaranteed enough time slots to complete the transmission, because the speed of the trunk port is as large as the sum of the speeds of the branch ports (2400 + 2400 + 2400 + 2400 = 9600). Each client and server pair is guaranteed enough bandwidth to carry on its communications. If some of the pairs don't use all of their bandwidth, some time slots will go unused, even though the full bandwidth capability is there.

Bit interleaving is another way to accomplish TDM. This method takes one bit from each client and sends it on the trunk port. For our example, as shown in Fig. 5-23, we'll assume that there are still four clients and that Client 1 sends the ASCII character *A* (01000001), Client 2 sends a *B* (01000010), Client 3 sends a *C* (01000011), and Client 4 sends a *D* (01000100). We ignore any start and stop bits for the sake of simplicity. Since we first transmit the bit on the right in ASCII code, the first bit received from Client 1 is a 1, from Client 2 is a 0, from Client 3 is a 1, and from Client 4 is a 0. Multiplexer A then sends 1010 on the trunk port. Multiplexer B receives these four bits and sends the 1 to Server port 1, the 0 to Server port 2, the 1 to Server port 3, and the 0 to Server port 4. Rather

FIGURE 5-23

Bit interleaving.

than sending four characters at a time, as in character interleaving, the multiplexer sends four bits at a time. Each time slot is shorter, containing only one bit instead of an entire character, but there are eight times the number of time slots in a second. The speed of the trunk port still needs to be as great as the sum of the speeds of the branch ports ($2400 + 2400 + 2400 + 2400 = 9600$). Once again, the speeds are arbitrarily chosen for our example, and the concepts described will work at any speed. Bit interleaving functions identically to character interleaving, except that there is a bit in each time slot instead of a full character, or byte.

Whether bit interleaving or character interleaving is used, an important feature of pure TDM is that the clients and server ports are unaware that their data is being multiplexed over a single communications line. The 2400 bps of data sent by the client always arrive at the server at the rate of 2400 bps. Neither the client nor the server knows that the data was combined with other clients' data, sped up, and then separated and slowed down. The data is still transmitted to the server at 2400 bps because a full 2400 bps of bandwidth out of the modem's 9600 bps has been reserved for this connection.

Statistical Time-Division Multiplexing

In practice, typical client users do not use all of their clients' bandwidth. Humans take coffee breaks, lunch hours, and long weekends. In addition, client users often type at slower speeds than their clients can transmit, so a few characters may be transmitted, then no characters for a while, then a few more characters, and so on. If we use pure TDM with clients, some of the time slots are left empty when transmission is not occurring from or to one of the clients.

Statistical time-division multiplexing, or *STDM*, takes advantage of the sporadic nature of client users and allocates bandwidth to each client on the basis of demands and needs. For example, a multiplexer using STDM, often called a *stat mux*, shown in Fig. 5-24, can have a transmission speed in the trunk ports that is lower than the sum of the branch-port speeds. In our example, six clients, each at speeds of 2400 bps, are using a trunk port transmitting at 9600 bps. STDM assumes that not all of the devices are transmitting all the time, which is a very reasonable assumption when clients are being used.

With pure TDM, the time slots are allocated on a constant basis: one client always gets time slot 1; the next, time slot 2; and so on. In STDM, clients use time slots only when they are actually transmitting data. How does multiplexer B in Fig. 5-24 know which data goes to which server port? Typically, a statistical multiplexer sends not only the data, but also an *address*, which indicates which of the ports the data is destined for. In our example, a three-bit address is used, which would allow for a maximum of eight ports (000, 001, 010, 011, 100, 101, 110, and 111). In STDM, when a client is not sending data, no time slots are allocated to it, and other clients that are sending data can use these time slots.

The term "statistical" refers to the method by which time slots are allocated. A statistical multiplexer decides how many time slots to allocate in the next second based on the amount of data sent by a given device in the last second. Complicated formulas are calculated constantly, so the time slot use is forever changing based on the user's most recent demands and probable future needs.

What happens when all users try to transmit at the same time? Clearly, the 9600-bps port cannot handle all 14,400 bps (6×2400 bps). Some statistical multiplexers will

FIGURE 5-24

Statistical time-division multiplexing.

buffer, or hold, the data until some of the users stop transmitting and until there are extra time slots on the trunk port. Other statistical multiplexers are able to stop a client from transmitting when there is a shortage of time slots. Once again, the speeds are arbitrarily chosen for our example, and the concepts described will work at any speed.

STDM can be more efficient than pure TDM when there is intermittent transmission from the clients, because it makes better use of the bandwidth on the trunk port. However, if all of the clients are constantly trying to transmit, STDM does not provide acceptable transmission time. Not only are there not enough time slots for the clients' data, but some of the time slots are used up in sending the client addresses.

Pure TDM is often described as being *transparent* to the users, meaning that an immediately available transmission path is guaranteed. STDM is not transparent to users, since their data transmission may be delayed.

Clearly, when a guaranteed transmission path is necessary, pure TDM is the only acceptable form of time-division multiplexing. STDM offers a more economical solution through more efficient use of the trunk ports, though it has the possibility of transmission delays.

Frequency-Division Multiplexing

Another common type of multiplexing is *frequency-division multiplexing*, or *FDM*. Whereas in time-division multiplexing, many clients share time on a high-bandwidth link, in frequency-division multiplexing the clients continually share the bandwidth by dividing the link into many separate frequencies, or channels.

An example of frequency-division multiplexing can be found in cable television, where a single coaxial cable carries all of the television channels simultaneously. Each channel is assigned a separate frequency, which the viewer selects by using the television's tuner. The signals from all of the television stations are multiplexed onto a single link, and each is assigned a different frequency.

In data communications, frequency-division multiplexing transmits the data from each client on a different frequency. As shown in Fig. 5-25, the four clients can communicate with four remote server ports by dividing the telephone circuit into four channels. For our example, Client A communicates with Server port A over multiplexer Channel A, and so on. We choose 1000–1300 Hz for Channel A, 1500–1800 Hz for Channel B, 2000–2300 Hz for Channel C, and 2500–2800 Hz for Channel D. As shown in Fig. 5-25, a 0 transmitted from Client A to Server port A is sent between the multiplexers on Channel A with a 1000-Hz tone; a 1 is sent with an 1100-Hz tone. For data sent in the other direction, from Server port A to Client A using multiplexer Channel A, a 0 is sent with a 1200-Hz tone, and a 1 is sent with a 1300-Hz tone. The other three channels use a similar modulation scheme, as shown in Fig. 5-25. Transmission occurs simultaneously, in full duplex, on all four channels at once, because data is sent using different frequencies for each channel. Although we have chosen four channels for our example, frequency-division multiplexing can be performed with any number of channels. Using too many channels, however, makes the cost of the multiplexer prohibitive.

Notice that the multiplexer using FDM is not only sharing the communications path among many users (multiplexing), but it is also converting the digital data to analog form (modulating). A separate pair of modems is not necessary when FDM is used, because FDM combines multiplexing and modulation. Having modulation and multiplexing built into the same device may be convenient, but it also may be more restrictive in the long run. For example, if advances are made in modem technology, a TDM user could simply purchase a new pair of modems and use the existing TDM multiplexers. An FDM user, however, could only take advantage of new technology by replacing both multiplexers.

Frequency-division multiplexing, like pure TDM, is transparent to the end user. Each user has a full-bandwidth connection at all times. If a particular client does not transmit data, time on its channel is wasted. This scenario is the data-communications equivalent of an off-air television station: when it is off the air, no one else is able to use that open channel.

FIGURE 5-25

Frequency-division multiplexing.

Frequency-division multiplexing can be more expensive to implement than time-division multiplexing because each channel requires separate frequencies. The more channels used over a communications circuit, the closer the frequencies are to each other. If the frequencies are too close together, it becomes extremely expensive to build devices to separate the different frequencies. In our example, each channel used four frequencies. However, if we combined phase shift keying techniques with frequency-division multiplexing, we would need only two frequencies per channel (one frequency in each direction). That said, FDM always requires more frequencies than a standard single-channel modem, thereby increasing the hardware complexity and costs.

Statistical frequency-division multiplexing, or *SFDM*, is sometimes used to make more efficient use of the channels. However, the complexity and cost of sharing channels usually outweigh the benefits. Unlike STDM, which is a practical and economical alternative to TDM, SFDM is rarely used.

DATA COMPRESSION DEVICES

Data compression is another method commonly used to improve data-communications efficiency. The philosophy behind data compression is, "Why send 28.8 kbps when 14.4

kbps will do the job?" The typical arrangement of *data compression devices* is shown in Fig. 5-26. The client, server, and modem are usually unaware that compression is taking place. However, some data patterns occur that cannot be compressed. When such patterns occur, the data compression device must be able to buffer incoming data or to ask the client or server to stop transmitting while it sends data in an uncompressed fashion. Like multiplexers, data compression devices are used to reduce communications circuit costs. Rather than sharing the communications path, a data compression device manages to send the same information using fewer bits. The net result is a higher effective bandwidth for the user.

Data compression devices can be combined with multiplexers for an even greater communications cost savings. For example, three 9600-bps clients connected to a multiplexer using TDM would normally require a pair of 28.8-kbps modems. However, a pair of 2-to-1 data compression devices and 14.4-kbps modems could be used instead. Alternatively, we could increase to as many as six clients with 28.8-kbps modems and 2-to-1 data compression devices. These concepts apply to any other speed of modems or clients as well.

Data compression can be achieved in many different ways. One common method is to use a special shorthand notation for transmitting data. If a certain character is sent frequently, the data compression devices may send an abbreviated form of the character. Just as we use "kbps" instead of "kilobits per second" in this book, a data compression device seeks the same efficiency. Another method used is to send only changes to the data. Many other methods are used to compress data, most of which are proprietary. Therefore, the same vendor's data compression devices are typically used at each end of the circuit. Data compression capability may also be included in a modem, as described earlier in this chapter.

While data can be compressed during transmission, it is even more efficient to store the data in a compressed way before transmitting it. Efficient data storage using optimized file formats significantly reduces the size of the files. *ZIP* files are a general format for storing data of any type. *JPEG* is an example of a compressed format for storing pictures, and *MPEG* is a compressed format for video clips. *MP3* is a commonly used format for storing audio files. We will discuss some of these multimedia formats in more detail in Chapter 10. Data already compressed in one of these formats is unlikely to benefit from any additional compression efforts during transmission.

FIGURE 5-26

Data compression devices.

FIGURE 5-27

Inverse multiplexers.

INVERSE MULTIPLEXERS

Not all data communications applications require minimization of communications circuit costs. In some instances, transmission speed is far more important. For example, as shown in Fig. 5-27, a server is located in a nuclear power plant control room. A client is located 50 miles away, in a remote control center, and is connected to the server through modems and phone lines. It is determined that phone lines in that area can support 14.4-kbps modems, but any higher speed causes low reliability. Safety considerations dictate that the remote user must be able to receive a screenful of information almost instantly, requiring a 28.8-kbps transmission. We can use two telephone lines and an *inverse multiplexer* to combine the bandwidth of the two telephone lines. Rather than sharing one phone line's bandwidth among many clients, as is done with the multiplexers discussed previously, we combine the bandwidth of two phone lines for use by a single client.

Using the arrangement shown in Fig. 5-27, the server could send the word "Warning!" to the inverse multiplexer at 28.8 kbps. The inverse multiplexer would send alternating letters over modems attached to each phone line at 14.4 kbps. At the other end, the receiving inverse multiplexer recombines the letters, resulting in a 28.8-kbps transmission of the word "Warning!" An inverse multiplexer acts just like a regular multiplexer, except that the high-speed trunk port is attached to the clients or servers, and the low-speed branch ports are attached to the modems and phone lines.

In this example, the inverse multiplexer's high-speed transmission requires twice as many modems, twice as many phone lines, and a pair of inverse multiplexers. However, in some cases, as in the example previously cited, high-speed transmission is essential and well worth the extra cost.

SUMMARY

The digital signals from our clients or servers can be sent over special digital circuits provided by the common carriers or through other transmission media. Alternatively, the signals can be modulated and sent in analog form over standard phone lines, using modems. Remote digital transmission over special digital communications circuits requires DSUs and sometimes CSUs at the end of the circuits. The T-1 carrier provides a

1.544-Mbps digital path, which can be broken into 24 separate channels. Integrated Services Digital Network is an evolving standard for digital voice and data communications that provides an all-digital communications network. Packet switching networks, frame relay networks, and the Internet all provide a means for transmitting data to different locations.

A circuit's bandwidth is its carrying capacity. For digital circuits, bandwidth is the number of bits that can be transmitted each second. The bandwidth of an analog circuit is the range of frequencies it can transmit. The bandwidths of different transmission media vary dramatically. Twisted pair, coaxial cable, twinaxial cable, and fiber optic cable are some of the different cabling options. Microwave and satellite transmission media do not require cabling between locations.

In baseband transmission, the data signal is transmitted directly on the wire. Broadband transmission sends data using a carrier signal. Modulation is a common example of broadband transmission, in which digital signals are converted to analog form for transmission over telephone circuits. Modems perform modulation and demodulation and can be used with leased lines or dial-up circuits. Both dumb and smart modems can be used with dial-up lines, and modems can originate calls, answer calls, or both originate and answer calls.

Many different modulation techniques are in use today. In amplitude modulation, a sine wave's amplitude varies to send ones and zeroes. Frequency modulation uses different frequencies to send ones and zeroes. Phase modulation uses shifts in a sine wave's phase to send ones and zeroes. A signal's baud rate is the number of possible changes in a second. If one bit is sent for each signal change, the bit per second rate is the same as the baud rate. Often, the bps rate is faster than the baud rate, because more than one bit is sent with each signal change. Many modems today have built-in error-correction and data-compression features. Short-haul modems are special modems used for short-distance transmission over customer-owned lines, using frequencies outside the bandwidth of the telephone network. Facsimile, or fax, technology electrically transmits documents over phone lines.

Multiplexers improve communications efficiency without any special features or actions on the part of the server or terminal. Multiplexers allow many devices to share one communications circuit, thereby minimizing communications circuit costs. Time-division multiplexing splits the communications circuit by allocating time slots to each device. In pure TDM, each client has an equal share of the communications circuit and is guaranteed an immediately available transmission path. This is possible as long as the speed of the communications circuit is equal to or greater than the sum of the speeds of the attached devices. TDM can be accomplished using character (byte) interleaving or bit interleaving. In character interleaving, a character occupies each time slot, whereas in bit interleaving only a single bit is in each time slot. In statistical time-division multiplexing, devices are allocated time slots based on the amount of data recently transmitted. This process is more efficient than pure TDM when the data transmission is sporadic. However, STDM does not guarantee an immediately available transmission path. In contrast to TDM, frequency-division multiplexing divides the communications circuit into several channels, with data being transmitted on all channels simultaneously, but on different frequencies. FDM combines modulation and multiplexing, so modems are no longer needed; however, the FDM technique can be fairly expensive to implement.

Data compression devices improve communications efficiency by minimizing the number of bits transmitted. Data is often compressed through various abbreviation techniques. Another device, known as an inverse multiplexer, combines the bandwidth of two or more communications circuits to allow for high-speed transmission.

TERMS FOR REVIEW

Address	*Category 7 cable*
AM	*Channel service unit*
Amplitude	*Character interleaving*
Amplitude modulation	*Cladding*
Amplitude shift keying	*Coax*
Analog	*Coaxial cable*
ANSI/TIA/EIA-568-B	*Constellation diagram*
Answer modem	*Core*
Answer-only modem	*CSU*
ASK	*Cycle*
AT&T 103/113	*Cycles per second*
AT&T Premises Distribution System	*Data compression*
Backwards compatible	*Data compression device*
Bandwidth	*Demodulation*
Baseband transmission	*Dial-up circuit*
Baud rate	*Dibit modulation*
Bell 103/113	*Digital circuit*
Bell 212A	*Digital service unit*
Bit interleaving	*Digital subscriber line*
Branch port	*Digital transmission*
Broadband ISDN	*Downlink*
Broadband transmission	*DSL*
Buffer	*DSU*
Byte interleaving	*Dumb modem*
Cable modem	*E-1*
Carrier signal	*Facsimile*
Cat3	*Fax*
Cat4	*FDM*
Cat5	*Fiber-optic cable*
Cat5E	*FM*
Cat6	*Frame relay network*
Cat7	*Frequency*
Category 3 cable	*Frequency-division multiplexing*
Category 4 cable	*Frequency modulation*
Category 5 cable	*Frequency shift keying*
Category 5e cable	*FSK*
Category 6 cable	*G.711*

Gbps
GEO
Geosynchronous-earth orbit
Gigabits per second
Group 1
Group 2
Group 3
Group 4
Hertz
Hz
IBM Cabling System
IEEE
Integrated Services Digital Network
Internet
Internet service provider
Inverse multiplexer
ISDN
ISP
Jacket
JPEG
LAPM
Laser
Leased
LED
LEO
Light-emitting diode
Limited-distance modem
Line of sight
Link Access Procedure for Modems
Low-earth orbit
Mbps
Medium-earth orbit
MEO
MI/MIC lead
Microcom Network Protocol
MNP
MNP5
Mode indicator lead
Modem
Modulation
MP3
MPEG
Multimode fiber
Multiplexer
Multispeed

Mux
Originate modem
Originate/answer modem
Originate-only modem
Packet switching network
Period
Phase modulation
Phase shift keying
PM
PSK
Pure time-division multiplexing
Quadrature amplitude modulation
Repeater
Resolution
RJ11
RJ45
Run length encoding
Satellite
Satellite dish
SFDM
Shielded twisted pair
Short-haul modem
Sine wave
Single mode fiber
Smart modem
Square wave
Stat mux
Statistical frequency-division multiplexing
Statistical time-division multiplexing
STDM
STP
Strength member
Switched circuit
T-1 carrier
TDM
Terrestrial microwave
Time slot
Time-division multiplexing
Transmission medium
Transparent
Transponder
Trellis coding
Trunk port
Twinax
Twinaxial cable

Twisted pair	*V.34*
Unshielded twisted pair	*V.42*
Uplink	*V.42 bis*
UTP	*V.44*
V.21	*V.90*
V.22	*V.92*
V.22 bis	*Wave division multiplexing*
V.32	*WDM*
V.32 bis	*Zip*

EXERCISES

5-1. What is the purpose of the DSU/CSU?

5-2. What is the function of a repeater in a digital circuit?

5-3. What are some common digital-transmission methods?

5-4. What is bandwidth? How is analog bandwidth measured? How is digital bandwidth measured?

5-5. Compare twisted pair wire with coaxial cable. Which is a higher bandwidth medium? Which is already installed in many offices?

5-6. What are the commonly used categories of unshielded twisted pair wire for data networks of 100 Mbps and higher?

5-7. What are the various components inside a typical fiber optic cable?

5-8. Explain the differences between satellite and terrestrial microwave transmission. Which is best?

5-9. What is the difference between baseband and broadband transmission?

5-10. What is modulation?

5-11. What are the different types of dial-up modems? How do they originate calls?

5-12. How does amplitude modulation transmit ones and zeroes? Frequency modulation? Phase modulation?

5-13. What is the purpose of a short-haul modem? How does it compare with dial-up modems, both technically and economically?

5-14. How do modern fax machines reduce the time needed for transmission?

5-15. What is multiplexing? What is its main purpose?

5-16. Explain the difference between TDM and FDM.

5-17. Compare pure TDM with statistical TDM.

5-18. What is the purpose of a data compression device?

5-19. When is an inverse multiplexer used?

C H A P T E R   6

Data Integrity and Security

DATA INTEGRITY

In any data communications network, there is the possibility of errors in data transmission. Preventing or correcting these errors is often referred to as maintaining data integrity.

SOURCES OF ERRORS

Errors in data transmission can occur for many reasons, including electrical interference from thunderstorms or from other transmission lines. In addition, power surges or spikes due to faulty equipment can also cause bits to be lost or changed during transmission.

All of us have placed long-distance phone calls where the connection is crystal clear, as if we are talking to someone across the street. If we used modems over a clear connection like that, we would probably never encounter data errors.

But we have also placed phone calls where the connection is filled with noise, static, echoes, and other sounds. If we used modems over this type of connection, we would likely encounter many errors. Humans can separate static and noise from actual conversation, but modems are easily confused by noise. As we discussed in the section on modulation in Chapter 5, modems may have to detect subtle frequency or phase shifts several thousand times in 1 second. A "little" static that lasts a half-second can easily obliterate 16.8 kilobits if we're transmitting at 33.6 kbps.

ERROR-CONTROL APPROACHES

Regardless of the source and cause of errors, we need some scheme to protect our data. Such methods of maintaining data integrity are often called error-control approaches. Four common approaches are in use today.

One approach is simply *not to check for errors*. This approach may sound frivolous, but it is used by some of the dumb terminals we introduced in Chapter 3. The device assumes that the terminal operator, and not the terminal itself, is able to catch any errors. In this case, a conscious decision has been made that it's more important to build a cheap terminal than an error-free terminal.

For a human example of this approach, picture a court reporter writing down everything said in a courtroom. A witness uses the word "books" during testimony, but the courtroom is fairly noisy, and the reporter thinks she said "bucks." The reporter writes "bucks" into the court record and doesn't even know he's wrong. Hopefully, whoever reads the court record will notice the error and be able to understand the sentence. This scenario provides an example of not checking for errors.

A second approach is *error detection with flagging*. This approach requires that errors be detected, or noticed, when the data is received. This approach requires no correction of these errors; instead, it only indicates that an error exists. Some devices display a question mark or sound a beep when they receive a character that they believe is in error. These devices have no idea how to correct errors, but they are able to alert the user that something has gone wrong.

Using the previous example to illustrate this method, the reporter knows that he did not hear the word properly, but he thinks that he heard "bucks." He therefore writes down "bucks," circles it, and puts a question mark above it to alert whoever reads the record later that this word may not be correct. This scenario provides an example of error detection with flagging.

A third approach is *error detection with a request for retransmission*. After an error is detected by the receiver, some protocols ask the sender to retransmit the message. Protocols are explained further in Chapter 7. A device using one of these protocols would check all incoming messages. If a particular message contains errors, the device asks the sender to transmit another copy of the message. The device does not display the message on the screen until it is received error free.

Using our courtroom example to illustrate this method, the reporter knows that he didn't hear the word correctly, so he raises his hand and says, "Please repeat that sentence. I didn't quite get it the first time." This scenario provides an example of error detection with a request for retransmission.

A fourth approach is *forward error correction*, or *FEC*. In this case, the error is corrected by the receiving device. This method requires the receiving device to have sufficient intelligence to determine not only where the error is, but a' .o how to correct it. In most cases, forward error correction is limited. For example, ˄ scheme can be provided to correct 100% of single bit errors when only one bit in a byte is incorrect, but the same scheme does not correct multiple bit errors in a byte.

Using our courtroom example to illustrate this method, the reporter realizes that he did not hear the word correctly, because "bucks" doesn't make sense in the context of the sentence. The reporter decides that the witness must have said "books" and writes that word down instead. This scenario provides an example of forward error correction.

IMPLEMENTING ERROR CONTROL: THE TECHNICAL DETAILS

There are many ways to detect errors. The most common methods are echo checking, parity checking, checksums, and cyclical redundancy checks.

Echo Checking

In *echo checking*, the receiving device repeats everything it receives to the transmitting device. If the characters "ABC" are transmitted to a device using echo checking, the receiver then transmits "ABC" back to the sending device. The sender can then determine if the data was received correctly and can retransmit it if necessary.

Since echo checking requires every data bit to be repeated back to the originator, it at least doubles the time required for data transmission. Though this method guarantees that data will be received correctly, it is obviously inefficient and is used only in critical applications. For example, if the command "Lower landing gear" is being sent from an airplane's central computer to the landing-gear controller, it is certainly worth repeating the command back and forth a few times to be sure that it has been properly understood.

Parity Checking

Parity checking is one commonly used error-checking method for asynchronous transmission. As we discussed in Chapter 3, in asynchronous transmission a user might send 1 character now, 10 characters 5 minutes from now, no characters for 1 hour, and then 1000 characters 3 minutes later. Any ideal error-detection scheme used with asynchronous transmission should be able to check each character as it arrives, since each character is sent independently.

There are many types of parity checking, including even parity, odd parity, space parity, mark parity, no parity, and ignored parity. Parity checking requires the transmitter to send an extra bit in each character to meet a certain parity requirement. *Even parity* requires an even number of ones in each byte. *Odd parity* requires an odd number of ones in each byte. *Space parity* uses a 0 for every parity bit, and *mark parity* uses a 1 for every parity bit.

Figure 6-1 shows examples of the letters "A", "B", "C", and "D" being transmitted using ASCII code and even, odd, space, and mark parity.

For a parity-checking example, we use a seven-bit ASCII character, as discussed in Chapter 3. The letter "A" is represented by the seven bits 1000001 in ASCII code. Since we are using even parity, an even number of ones must be sent in every byte. There are already two ones in the sequence 1000001, so the parity bit will be 0, and 01000001 is sent. The receiver counts the number of ones in the byte and assumes that

ASCII character	Even parity	Odd parity	Space parity	Mark parity
A	01000001	11000001	01000001	11000001
B	01000010	11000010	01000010	11000010
C	11000011	01000011	01000011	11000011
D	01000100	11000100	01000100	11000100

FIGURE 6-1

ASCII character transmission with different parities.

data was received correctly, since 1 appears twice in the sequence 01000001. Notice that the parity bit is placed in the leftmost position in ASCII code.

If an error occurs during transmission in the previous example (letter "A", ASCII, even parity, 01000001) and the sequence received is 01001001, the receiver counts the number of ones and determines that there are three ones in the sequence. The receiver recognizes that this outcome is an error, since with even parity all characters received should have an even number of ones. In this case, even parity is able to detect that there is an error in the byte.

Odd parity functions in the same way as even parity, except that there is always an odd number of ones. The letter "A" using odd parity and ASCII is transmitted as 11000001.

Even and odd parity have several limitations. First, it is critical that both the sending and receiving devices use the same parity-checking method, be it even or odd. It makes no difference which method is used as long as the same method is used by both sender and receiver.

Second, this type of parity checking detects only an odd number of bit errors in a byte. If an even number of bit errors occurs, parity checking (even or odd) does not detect the error. The only way to be convinced of this point is by repetition. Figure 6-2 shows several examples of errors that occur in transmitting the letter "A" to demonstrate this point. If we expect that errors will occur in a random fashion, we have a 50% chance of detecting errors using either even or odd parity.

Space and mark parity are primitive parity-checking methods. In space parity, the sender always uses a 0 for the parity bit, and the receiver always looks for a 0. If a drastic data error occurs, wiping out enough of the byte to change the parity bit to a 1, space parity will detect the error. Otherwise, as long as the parity bit is 0, the receiving device is oblivious to any error. In fact, if the transmission of a byte only results in one bit error, there is only a one in eight chance that the error occurs in the parity bit, giving us a 12.5% chance of detecting an error. In that case, we have actually detected an error in

Character "A" sent with even parity	Number of ones sent	Received as:	Number of bit errors	Number of ones received	Is error detected by even parity?
01000001	2	01000001	0	2	No
01000001	2	01100001	1	3	Yes
01000001	2	01110001	2	4	No
01000001	2	01110101	3	5	Yes
01000001	2	01110111	4	6	No
01000001	2	01111111	5	7	Yes
01000001	2	11111111	6	8	No
01000001	2	10111111	7	7	Yes
01000001	2	10111110	8	6	No

FIGURE 6-2

Parity checking and bit errors.

our parity bit, while our actual data is fine! Mark parity functions in the same manner as space parity does; however, a 1 is substituted for the 0. Therefore, space and mark parity work only when a lot of bits are wiped out, and they are not really useful for single bit errors.

Ignored parity implies that a 0 is sent as a parity bit and that the receiver does not even check the parity bit. This method allows a receiver that is incapable of parity checking to communicate with another device that is using parity checking. *No parity* implies that no parity bit is sent or checked.

Cyclical Parity

Cyclical parity is a less common variation of parity checking, but it increases the odds of detecting errors. Rather than using only one parity bit to detect errors in a byte, cyclical parity uses at least two parity bits. Each parity bit checks some of the bits in the byte. For example, if we wanted to send the six-bit sequence 101101, we could use cyclical parity checking, as shown in Fig. 6-3. Bits 1, 3, and 5 are checked with the parity bit in position 7, and bits 2, 4, and 6 are checked with the parity bit in position 8. If we use odd cyclical parity checking, there must be an odd number of ones in bits 1, 3, 5, and 7, as well as in bits 2, 4, 6, and 8. In this example, bits 7 and 8 must both be 1 to provide an odd number of ones in both bit groups. The only way for errors to slip by this checking scheme is if errors occur in certain combinations of alternating bits.

Hamming Code

Hamming code, a forward error-correction code devised by Richard Hamming, allows the receiving device not only to detect a single-bit error, but also to correct it with 100% accuracy. However, because this error-correction ability requires several parity bits, it is not as widely used as other parity methods. Hamming code for a 7-bit ASCII character requires 4 parity bits, for a total of 11 bits. The parity bits are placed in bit positions 1, 2, 4, and 8 (all powers of two). The data bits are placed in positions 3, 5, 6, 7, 9, 10, and 11 (none of these are powers of two). Hamming code allows for either even-parity or odd-parity checking. We use even-parity Hamming code for our example.

Figure 6-4 shows the ASCII letter "A", with its seven bits. Notice on the first line of the example that the seven data bits have been placed in the Hamming code data-bit

Type of bit	Bit value	Bit number
Data	1	1
	0	2
	1	3
	1	4
	0	5
	1	6
Parity	1	7
	1	8

FIGURE 6-3

Cyclical parity.

```
ASCII for letter "A" = 1 0 0 0 0 0 0 1

                 1      0   0   0         0   0   1    Before
         —   —   —   —   —   —   —   —   —   —   —    parity
Bit No.  1   2   3   4   5   6   7   8   9   10  11

         0   0   1   0   0   0   0   1   0   0   1    After
         —   —   —   —   —   —   —   —   —   —   —    parity
Bit No.  1   2   3   4   5   6   7   8   9   10  11
```

FIGURE 6-4

Hamming code.

positions. Now we move to line 2 to fill in the parity bits. There must be an even number of ones in the following bit combinations:

Bits 1, 3, 5, 7, 9, 11 (checked with parity bit 1)
Bits 2, 3, 6, 7, 10, 11 (checked with parity bit 2)
Bits 4, 5, 6, 7 (checked with parity bit 4)
Bits 8, 9, 10, 11 (checked with parity bit 8)

There are already 2 ones in bits 3, 5, 7, 9, and 11, so a device using Hamming code places a 0 in bit 1 to maintain an even number of ones in bits 1, 3, 5, 7, 9, and 11. There are already 2 ones in bits 3, 6, 7, 10, and 11, so the device places a 0 in bit 2 to maintain an even number of ones in bits 2, 3, 6, 7, 10, and 11. There are no ones in bits 5, 6, and 7, so the device places a 0 in bit 4 to maintain an even number of ones in bits 4, 5, 6, and 7. There is only a single 1 in bits 9, 10, and 11, so the device places a 1 in bit 8 to give us 2 ones in bits 8, 9, 10, and 11.

The resulting sequence, 00100001001, will be transmitted, and the receiving device can check the four parity bits by the same method we used to create them; there should be an even number of ones in every group. If all of the parity checks are correct at the receiving end, then there have been no errors (or there is more than one error).

If a single bit is in error, one or more of the parity checks will fail. Add up the numbers of the parity bits that failed, and the position of the incorrect bit will be found. For example, if bit 6 was switched during transmission from a 0 to a 1, 00100101001 would be received. Parity check 1 would pass (even number of ones), parity check 2 would fail (odd number of ones), parity check 4 would fail (odd number of ones), and parity check 8 would pass (even number of ones). When we add up the numbers of the parity checks that failed ($2 + 4 = 6$), the result clearly indicates that bit 6 is incorrect. Bit 6 can then be switched from a 1 to a 0, resulting in 00100001001, and the parity bits can be removed, resulting in 1000001, which is the data we sent originally.

Remember, this ingenious method is designed to correct single bit errors. If more than one bit error occurs, the results will not be predictable.

Checksums

A *checksum* is a generic term referring to a type of error detection used when blocks of characters, rather than single characters, are received. Large blocks of data are often sent in synchronous transmission, as we explained in Chapter 3. In a simple example, the transmitting device begins with a checksum equal to zero before transmitting a block of data. As each character in a block is transmitted, the transmitter takes the binary number representing that character (the ones and zeroes) and adds it to the checksum. When the entire block of characters has been sent, the checksum (or a portion of the checksum) is also sent. Meanwhile, the receiver adds up the ones and zeroes that it receives, creating its own checksum. When the checksum arrives, the receiver can then compare it to the checksum it calculated. If these amounts do not match, the receiver knows that an error has occurred. Typically, checksums are used in protocols in which the receiver can ask the sender to retransmit the data if an error has occurred.

Cyclical Redundancy Check

The *cyclical redundancy check*, or *CRC*, is a variation on the concept of the aforementioned simple checksum. Instead of simply adding up the ones and zeroes, the CRC uses a more complicated mathematical formula that combines division and addition. This formula helps exaggerate errors, preventing them from canceling each other out. In simple binary addition, as in the simple checksum discussed previously, a one changing to a zero in one byte can be hidden by a zero changing to a one in a later byte. Although the CRC is more complicated and expensive to implement, it is more reliable and provides a high degree of data integrity. Almost no blocks of characters with an error can slip by a CRC without the error being detected.

SECURITY

Though accurate transmission of data is often essential, in some cases data security can be even more important.

THE IMPORTANCE OF SECURITY

As computers take on a larger and larger share of business transactions, the need for data security becomes evident. Hardly a check or invoice is written today by businesses without the assistance of computers. Even checks written by hand are processed by a computer in a check clearinghouse.

Twenty years ago, it was standard practice for clerks in the accounting department to keep financial records locked away. Similarly, today's computer users are accustomed to using special *passwords* to help "lock up" important information. One common example of a password is the *PIN*, or *personal identification number*, employed in conjunction with our bank card to access an automated teller machine. We tolerate the inconvenience of remembering and using this PIN because we recognize the need to safeguard our bank accounts.

SECURITY CONCERNS

Data communications devices and links are often vulnerable to unauthorized access or intrusion. Many networks, both public and private, include microwave or satellite transmission at one point or another. Anyone with the necessary equipment can eavesdrop on this data, often without the user's knowledge. In addition, phone lines can be tapped, further eroding a data network's security.

There are two common concerns when considering security issues. First, do we expect accidental intrusions, or do we expect intentional intrusions? Precautions taken to prevent someone from stumbling into our network do little to foil a determined intruder.

Second, do we want simply to guard against others eavesdropping on our data, or do we expect someone to attempt to alter the data? Advance knowledge of corporate strategies can be worth millions of dollars to competitors, making eavesdropping a very profitable endeavor for unethical individuals. Similarly, we could all add a few extra zeroes to the end of our bank account balances if we could alter the data on our bank's computer network. There are clearly many motives for breaching a network's security.

SECURITY GOALS

There are several goals to consider when safeguarding data. The *National Institute of Standards and Technology*, or *NIST*, has identified five basic goals for proper data security. A secure data message should be sealed, sequenced, secret, signed, and stamped.

A *sealed message* cannot be modified by an unauthorized party. A sealed message is the data communications equivalent of the tamper-proof packaging that is used on many over-the-counter medications today. The receiver will be able to detect if a message has been tampered with.

A *sequenced message* is protected against undetected loss or repetition. This book is an example of a sequenced message; since the pages are numbered, the reader can determine if any pages are missing.

A *secret message* cannot be understood by an unauthorized party. Secret messages are often sent in coded or scrambled form.

A *signed message* includes proof of the sender's identity. A signature on a check is one example; it is recognizable by all, but it is reproducible only by the sender.

A *stamped message* guarantees receipt by the correct party. Sending a certified letter and requesting a return receipt with the receiver's signature is an example of a stamped message.

SECURITY MEASURES

Most of today's networks do not meet all of these security goals. The level of protection used depends on the value of security in a given application.

Security measures are often distributed throughout data communications networks. These measures can be implemented in clients, servers, modems, special security devices, and even transmission facilities.

Secure Transmission Facilities

One security approach that is often overlooked is the selective use of transmission media. As we discussed in Chapter 5, the characteristics of the various transmission media differ widely. Twisted pair and coax can be tapped easily and cheaply, whereas unnoticed tapping of fiber optic lines requires more training and special equipment. Satellite and microwave transmission are also completely vulnerable to tapping by anyone willing to invest in the appropriate receiving equipment. Sometimes the cost involved in making inexpensive services secure is greater than the economic benefits provided. Careful selection of transmission media is the simplest way to improve security.

Passwords

Passwords are the most common form of security. The biggest drawback of passwords is the carelessness of many users. Some users write down passwords where they can be discovered, and others choose a familiar word, like the name of their dog, which can easily be guessed.

Passwords are usually required by the server, but they can also be required by special security *call-back devices*. These devices help increase the security provided by a password. Remote users attempting to access a server using a modem must first enter their password and name into a call-back device attached between the modems and the server. The device then checks the password for accuracy and, if the password is correct, hangs up and calls the location programmed into the call-back device. In this case, an intruder must not only steal a user's password, but must also break into the user's home or office to be there when the call-back device telephones. Some servers and modems have this call-back feature built in so that a separate call-back device is not necessary. This feature provides increased security, but it unfortunately has an important drawback: The call-back device must know in advance where the user will be calling from. A traveling salesperson would have a hard time accessing the office computer if it is attached to a call-back device.

Another way to make passwords more secure is to incorporate special hardware into the client. For example, an automated teller machine cannot be accessed with a PIN alone; a bank card must be inserted as well.

Historical and Statistical Logging

Another security method is *historical logging*, a complete recording of all data passed through a particular device. All data passing between a client and a server can be captured in the historical log. Historical logging is usually performed by servers, though it can be accomplished at other points in the network as well. The data can be stored on a variety of devices, the most common of which are magnetic tapes or disks.

One example of historical logging is a student taping a professor's lecture. The tape is a complete record of the entire lecture and could be replayed the next week if the student wanted to review a particular topic. Similarly, if a company's personnel computer files have been mysteriously altered, the historical log in the server could be replayed the next day and determine which user changed everyone's salary data, for example. The historical log would contain a complete record of the user's actions. Through review of the log, the user's method of access can be determined, and hopefully the system can be made more secure against future intrusions.

Though this method provides total recall of system events, it also uses a great deal of storage space (disks and tapes). A more efficient but similar method is known as *statistical logging*, whereby statistics are kept on each data port. These statistics might include which users were logged on to which ports, the amount of time users spent logged on, the files accessed, and other information about transactions that occurred. Like historical logging, statistical logging is often performed by servers, though it can be accomplished by other devices as well.

An example of statistical logging is a student trying to determine which topics a professor considers important. The student records in his or her notebook that the professor spent 10 minutes on topic A, 20 minutes on topic B, and then 10 minutes on topic C. The student can later look back at this record to determine what topics the professor emphasized. Similarly, the company with the mysteriously altered personnel files could look back at the statistical log to determine which user accessed the salary files. The statistical log would not indicate exactly what was done to the files. The offending user would be identified, but the exact events that occurred would not be recorded.

When comparing statistical and historical logging, remember that by the time a company consults its logs, the security breach has probably already occurred, and the damage has been done. A statistical accounting that shows which users may have caused the damage is probably just as useful as a play-by-play description of exactly what happened.

Closed User Groups

Many networks restrict user access by establishing *closed user groups*, or *CUGs*. A set of users who need to communicate only with each other and do not want other users to access their computers can form a closed user group. For instance, a company may want to allow its branch offices to connect to the corporate computer to obtain sales price information, while at the same time ensuring that competitors and customers cannot also access this information. The company can establish a closed user group to ensure that only its branch offices have this access. Typically, closed user groups are employed with packet switching networks, which we discuss in detail in Chapter 8.

Firewalls

Another common security measure is the installation of *firewalls* between networks. A firewall examines data and determines whether to pass it through or to discard it based on a set of predefined rules. Firewalls can be used to provide security, as well as to prevent certain error conditions from spreading to neighboring networks.

Firewalls are sometimes separate devices, but firewall functions also can be performed inside existing networking equipment. One example of using a firewall for security purposes would be to place the firewall at the border between a private and public network. The assumption here is that the private network site is trustworthy and secure. However, since there is no way to control a network outside one's premises, a method is needed to screen data that passes between the two networks for security purposes.

A firewall is not typically used to protect against intruders operating on your own network, though it could be used for this purpose. For example, if the executives of a company were concerned about sensitive communications on the company network, they could create an executive network and connect it with a firewall to the network that the rest of the company uses. In this manner, the executives could communicate with others in the company, while also ensuring that their executive network remains secure.

Firewalls are often used inside private networks to prevent the proliferation of errors. For example, if one user on a company-wide network sends a stream of erroneous messages, these messages could fill up the network's capacity. However, if the network is divided into many small department networks, with firewalls in between them, such a problem can be isolated to one department, and the erroneous messages need not be transmitted to the entire company.

Firewalls use several different methods to screen data. One technique is known as *packet filtering*. Packet filtering can be used when messages are already broken into blocks, or packets, as described in Chapter 8. The origin of the data is checked, along with the destination, and sometimes the type of data is also scrutinized. The packet-filtering firewall is programmed by the network manager with a set of rules describing which users on the private network are permitted to exchange packets with which users on the outside network. Any packets that violate the rules are discarded. Some packet-filtering firewalls can check the type of data, in addition to the address, and can make more refined decisions. For example, electronic mail messages could be accepted from everyone, but file transfers could be accepted only from specifically authorized users or other offices of the same company. This system would allow general electronic mail communications with outside organizations, such as vendors or customers, but would prevent program files that contain viruses sent by other organizations from being received. On the other hand, even harmless files from outside organizations would be rejected by this rule, thus posing an inconvenience to users.

This technique of screening the type of data is not possible with all packet-filtering firewalls, because it requires the firewall to recognize all of the possible formats of user data and to maintain different rules for each. On networks that use many different types of applications, it is difficult to program a single firewall with every possible packet format and allowable user address combination.

Another common approach is to use an *application-level firewall* to check messages only for a particular application. For example, an electronic mail firewall could screen only electronic mail messages. Because it is designed to check only this type of data, it can look for malicious behavior, like repeated messages, or even junk mail. Another firewall might check incoming file transfers to ensure that certain types of files are not accepted, thus allowing it to exclude the software viruses discussed later in this chapter. Whereas the packet-filtering firewall screens based on addresses, or perhaps types of data, an application-level firewall can examine the data itself and determine if it is acceptable.

The packet-filtering and application-level examples discussed here are only two of the many possible approaches that can be used to screen data. While no firewall offers an absolute guarantee against network intrusion, a firewall can substantially reduce the risk of such an intrusion occurring. The ultimate security measure is to disconnect the private network from the outside world, but doing so precludes users from enjoying the full benefits of networking.

Client and Server Intrusions

Firewalls often protect users against intrusions on client computers by blocking intrusions at the edge of a network. Numerous possible intrusions can affect a user. Some of the most damaging intrusions plant *malicious software,* or *malware,* inside a user's computers. The most notorious malware is a *virus*, a surreptitiously installed piece of software that attaches itself to legitimate software. While some viruses don't cause much harm, others can destroy data or even send private information to others. Viruses often load with the operating system or with another piece of software on the user's computer, and users may be unaware of their existence until the damage is done. Viruses often replicate themselves by attaching to software that is then spread to other computers over shared networks, disks, or other media. Some viruses aggressively propagate by emailing themselves to everyone in your address book. *Antivirus software* can be installed that detects and eradicates viruses, but it is only useful if it is regularly updated to protect against the latest viruses.

A specific type of virus is a *Trojan horse*, which is a piece of software that hides inside another useful program, but that performs an unexpected function. It might send personal data (e.g., password lists) to the author of the virus, or perform some other malicious task, often without the user's knowledge. Other types of malicious software lie in wait for specific times or events to occur to trigger them into action.

A *virus hoax* can be as dangerous as a virus itself. A user may receive an email warning of a specific virus that is supposedly running rampant. The email gives instructions on how to "clean" the computer of the virus. The "cleaning" might involve the deletion of files that are critical to system operation and that leave the user without a working computer. These hoaxes often forward themselves to everyone in your address book as well, thereby propagating the hoax and the damage.

A *worm* is a type of software that reproduces itself repeatedly without requiring human intervention. It is typically self-contained, meaning that it usually does not attach to other files like a virus does. Worms often flood a network with copies of itself to the point that it cannot carry normal user traffic. The worm continues to replicate, infecting all the vulnerable computers on networks connected to the first network, often in short order. While these worms don't necessarily damage the user's computer (beyond installing themselves), they can render the network it is attached to useless, and they are often the most difficult and expensive viruses for a company to eradicate. If even a single computer remains infected, the propagation can begin again. Antivirus software can also detect and remove worms.

While there are many specific types of malicious software, each with different characteristics, the term "virus" is often incorrectly used by the public and the media to describe them all. This misconception is fostered by the fact that most antivirus software packages routinely detect other types of malicious software as well.

Spyware is another type of software that installs itself on a user's computer, typically without the user's knowledge. The most likely scenario for spyware installation is when the user downloads software for a particular purpose. Spyware is often hidden in a free utility that is hard to resist. During installation, users often accept a lengthy license agreement that indicates that they agree to install the spyware along with the utility, but users seldom read the fine print of the agreement. Once installed, the spyware tracks the users' actions and reports back to a central reporting site, which can then tailor advertisements, promotions, or other commercial material for delivery to the unsuspecting user. While some users don't mind being presented with advertisements that are tailored to their preferences, most resent the intrusion of privacy and the fact that their computer's processing power is wasted. *Spyware detection software* can detect and remove spyware in the same way that antivirus software removes viruses. Spyware detection software must also be updated regularly so that it can detect the latest spyware.

Cookies are a type of tracking mechanism that records specific information about network sites you visit. Cookies can provide useful services, like memorizing your preferences, recent orders, account numbers, etc. They do, however, track your activities, and since they remain on your computer they are subject to detection by a virus or other intruder that could then send your personal information from your computer to another. Most users appreciate the value of cookies, but some opt to alter settings on their computers to disable them. The trade-off between convenience and privacy must be examined in making this decision.

Hackers are sophisticated users who attack the computers of others, often just to prove that they can, but sometimes as a means of making a social or political statement. Hackers can exploit security vulnerabilities in client or server software and operating systems that allow them entry into someone's computer or that simply allow them to crash someone's computer. One such attack, known as a *denial-of-service attack*, involves bombarding a computer with so many messages that it cannot handle the traffic of legitimate users. Regardless whether the computer crashes or simply can't reply effectively to the legitimate traffic, the denial-of-service attack can render the computer useless. These attacks can be launched by malicious software planted on numerous computers, all set to attack a particular network site at a predetermined time or on a signal from the hacker. These attacks are extremely hard to trace because they come from numerous sources, all innocent and unaware of the damage that the malicious software installed on their computer is causing.

Hackers are more likely to attack computers that are always connected to a network than to attack dial-up users, who are only temporarily connected. First, the laws of probability work against continuously connected users, who are more likely to be found if a hacker is searching the network at random. The longer you are connected, the more likely you are to be found. In addition, hackers prefer to plant Trojan horses on computers that are always connected, because hackers can rely on these computers to be connected when they want to start an attack.

It is therefore especially important for users of continually connected computers to use the firewalls previously discussed, either at the edge of their network or as software installed on each client computer. Firewalls, combined with antivirus software, provide a reasonable defense against these intrusions.

Spam is loosely defined as unsolicited commercial email. Some would add "unwelcome" to the definition, because some unsolicited email may be useful to the recipient. While much has been written about the deluge of spam in users' mailboxes, there are few effective means of technically controlling it. Special software, known as *spam-filtering software, spam-blocking software*, or *antispam software*, can be installed in either the email server or client. It typically relies on rules and patterns to identify spam, but some spam always slips through, and some regular mail is misidentified and blocked. There have been various legislative efforts to discourage or prevent it, but none have been effective to date. While increased penalties may help, the worldwide nature of computer networks will make these penalties hard to enforce. It is safe to say that as long as email is practically free to send, some will try to exploit it for commercial purposes.

While spam can interfere with reading email, *pop-up advertisements*, generated by some network sites, can sometimes cover the information that users are trying to read. Pop-up advertisements can be more than annoyances, as they can contain links to download spyware software or even viruses. *Pop-up blocker* software is also available to stop these intrusions.

Encryption and Decryption

One of the most thorough and effective ways to improve data security is to use *encryption*. Encryption is the coding, or scrambling, of data before it is transmitted over the communications link. *Decryption* is the decoding, or descrambling, of the received data.

Encryption and decryption can be performed by clients, servers, or special *encryption devices*. Although these devices actually perform both encryption and decryption, they are commonly referred to as encryption devices.

A client can transmit *clear text*, also known as *plain text*, to an encryption device, as shown in Fig. 6-5. The cloud represents any public data network as an example of an insecure medium. The details of the connection to the public data network (e.g., modems) are not shown because the method is not important for the encryption process. The encryption device takes the clear or plain text and scrambles it, or encrypts it, turning it into *cipher text* before sending it on. At the other end of the communications link, the cipher text is decrypted by the encryption device and sent on to the server as clear or plain text (as originally transmitted).

The advantage of encryption is that those eavesdropping on the data transmission cannot understand the encrypted data. Encryption allows the use of insecure connections without fear of security breaches. Examples of insecure connections include

FIGURE 6-5

Encryption devices.

public data networks, phone lines, and even satellite or microwave links. Of course, almost any code can be broken eventually, given enough time and a powerful-enough computer. The method of encryption chosen determines if it will be practical for an eavesdropper to break a code.

Several terms can be used to describe the process of encryption. An *algorithm* is a set of instructions, in this case for scrambling the data. A *key* is a specific set of codes to be used by the algorithm to perform the encryption.

A child's plastic "code ring" offers a simple example of encryption. Typically, the ring contains the alphabet in proper order on the top row and the alphabet in scrambled order on the bottom. To send a coded message, the user simply finds each letter in the top row and sends the corresponding letter in the bottom row. The receiver must then have an identical ring and decode the message by looking at each letter in the bottom row and finding its counterpart in the top row.

An example of this simple type of encryption is shown in Fig. 6-6. In this example, the encryption algorithm would be "Find the letter in the top row and instead use the corresponding letter in the bottom row." The decryption algorithm is "Find the letter in the bottom row and instead use the corresponding letter in the top row." The key is the two-row alphabet chart. If we changed the order of the letters in the bottom row, we would still use the same algorithm, but we would be using a different key. In this example, the phrase "THIS IS SIMPLE ENCRYPTION" would be encrypted as "JDCU CU UCTNRS SGZYLNJCBG."

Secret keys.   The basis of all encryption systems is that even if the algorithm is known, an eavesdropper cannot interpret an encrypted message without the appropriate key. In the previous example, even with the algorithm, a code ring that is missing the bottom row is useless. We call this type of key a *secret key*; as long as we can keep the key a secret, our data is safe from eavesdroppers. Our example requires that the encryption devices store the entire alphabet and its corresponding code letters. Whereas our example uses only 26 letters, character codes like ASCII and EBCDIC use 128 or 256 characters, respectively. Storing all of these characters and their corresponding coded versions would take a lot of memory space in an encryption device. Therefore, most encryption algorithms and keys are based on mathematical formulas.

One example of an encryption algorithm is "Add the key to the character." The corresponding decryption algorithm is "Subtract the key from the character." For example, as shown in Fig. 6-7, if we choose 0010111 (23 is the decimal equivalent) as our key and if we want to send the letter "A" in ASCII, which is represented by 1000001 (65 is the decimal equivalent), we will send 1011000 (88 is the decimal equivalent). At the receiving end, the key will be subtracted from 1011000, resulting in the original 1000001, or the letter "A." Readers unfamiliar or uncomfortable with binary math can

| Clear text: | A | B | C | D | E | F | G | H | I | J | K | L | M | N | O | P | Q | R | S | T | U | V | W | X | Y | Z |
| Cipher text: | Q | A | Z | X | S | W | E | D | C | V | F | R | T | G | B | N | H | Y | U | J | M | K | I | O | L | P |

FIGURE 6-6

Simple encryption.

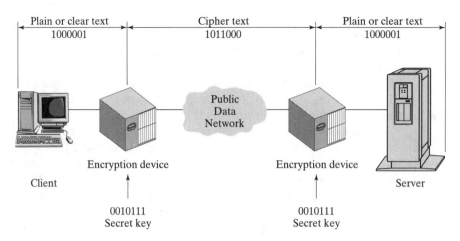

FIGURE 6-7

Secret encryption keys.

use the binary-to-decimal conversion charts in Appendix A, perform the arithmetic in decimal numbers, and then convert the numbers back to binary numbers to determine what pattern of ones and zeroes is sent.

All subsequent examples in this chapter assume that keys used for encryption and decryption are binary numbers, like 10000001. The encryption algorithms are mathematical formulas that in some fashion combine the key with the data to result in cipher text. In some encryption devices, the user can change the key used for encryption or decryption by setting certain switches on the device itself.

The advantage of this type of secret key system is that the key can be changed on a regular basis to ensure that the data is safe. If the transmitter changes the key, the receiver must be notified, or else the received data will not be decrypted correctly. The new key is often sent over a *secure channel*, if one is available. A secure channel is a communications link that is known to be safe from intrusion. More frequently, a new key is sent by courier, or an arbitrary system can be used. For example, we can agree that our key is the number of words in the first paragraph of column 1 of a particular newspaper's front page that day. As long as the sender and receiver are using the same key and as long as no one else knows what the key is or how the key is determined, the data is relatively safe, and the secret key is effective.

The reason that the data is only "relatively" safe is that any code can be broken, given enough time, computing power, and luck. Entire wars have been won or lost by breaking codes. Our example, an addition/subtraction algorithm, would not take long to break. Most algorithms are far more complicated; these algorithms include multiplication, division, and exponents. As long as the keys are changed frequently enough, these complicated algorithms are more difficult to break. Today's computers are much faster than their counterparts of even 5 years ago, and there is reason to believe that their descendants will be even faster and therefore able to break codes more quickly. New algorithms are constantly being developed to outsmart the faster computers, and these algorithms must continue to evolve to ensure data security.

The Data Encryption Standard and Data Encryption Algorithm.   A need for a standard, general-purpose encryption algorithm for use with secret keys was answered in the mid-1970s with the *Data Encryption Standard*, or *DES*. The DES was originally developed by IBM and later adopted by the National Institute of Standards and Technology. The *American National Standards Institute*, or *ANSI*, adopted the same standard under a different name, the *Data Encryption Algorithm*, or *DEA*. The DES has also been endorsed by the *National Security Agency*, or *NSA*, for protecting information that is sensitive but not classified. Classified information is more likely to be encrypted with a secret algorithm, not a standard one like DES, to make unauthorized deciphering more difficult. The DES is relatively inexpensive to implement, and chips that use DES for encryption and decryption are widely available.

The adoption of the DES set a clear direction for the communications industry. Government agencies and many commercial customers began to demand DES encryption of certain data. DES could be incorporated in an encryption device or in servers, clients, modems, or other equipment. The distribution of secret keys would still be up to the individuals transmitting and receiving the data, but at least a standard for encryption devices was established.

A more secure version of DES, known as *Triple DES*, is sometimes used in financial transactions. It executes the DES algorithm three times, thereby increasing the difficulty of breaking the code.

Symmetric and asymmetric keys.   We have already established that secret keys require both users to know which key is being used. The secret keys used in the examples cited so far are based on *symmetric keys*; both the sender and receiver use the same key to encrypt and decrypt the message. In some cases, *asymmetric keys* are used, where the sender and receiver use different keys that are mathematically related in a nonobvious way.

Public keys.   *Public keys* are a common use of asymmetric keys. Though secret keys are easy enough to implement between two users, what if we need to contact many different users and all of the messages need to be encrypted? It is inefficient to call each person and make up a new secret key for each transmission. These calls also jeopardize key security.

The public key encryption method uses asymmetric keys to eliminate this problem. Imagine a company with 100 employees. In the company phone book, in addition to an employee's name and phone number, there is another entry for the employee's unique public key. This public key is used to encrypt messages sent only to that employee. These messages can be decrypted only using that employee's secret key (known only to the employee).

It is assumed that everyone in the company uses encryption devices with the same algorithm. To transmit data to another employee's server, we need to enter that employee's public key into the encryption device, as shown in Fig. 6-8. However, the cipher text that emerges can be decrypted only with the receiver's secret key. Everyone knows the public key, but only the particular receiver knows the secret key.

A public key system requires that the algorithm use asymmetric keys; a different key is used to encrypt and decrypt the data. An eavesdropper who tries to decode cipher text with the receiver's public key does not obtain clear text. The public key system is secure because the public keys used to encrypt the data do not also decrypt the data.

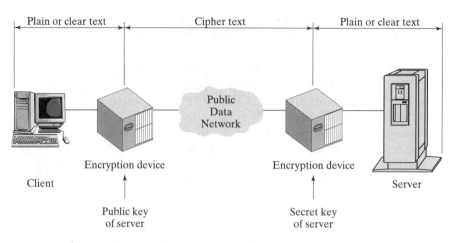

FIGURE 6-8

Data confidentiality using public keys.

DATA CONFIDENTIALITY AND IDENTITY VERIFICATION

All of the encryption methods we have discussed thus far are intended to protect data confidentiality. But what about verifying the identity of the sender? A *digital signature* can be obtained by using the reverse of the system just described. If we encrypt data using our secret key, anyone can decrypt it with our public key, as shown in Fig. 6-9. With this method, we lose all data confidentiality, since the key used for decryption is now public, but we now are assured that no other user can masquerade as us. For example, if someone tries to forge a memo purported to have come from us, he or she would need to know our secret key to encrypt the memo properly so that others decrypting the message with our public key would obtain plain text. Digital signatures can also be used to issue *digital certificates* to authenticate items as genuine. Software, electronic purchase orders, and other items can be validated with these digital certificates. Another application of these signatures is a *digital postmark*, in which a trusted third party receives a message and relays it with an authenticated time and date stamp, which is very useful in legal transactions. These applications of digital signatures help make the exchange of electronic messages as effective as the exchange of signed paper documents.

The two systems just described can be combined to obtain both confidentiality and identity verification. We prepare our memo and then encrypt a certain portion, say the last paragraph, using our secret key. Then we encrypt the entire memo again with the receiver's public key. The receiver then uses his or her secret key to decrypt the message. The resulting message will be in plain text, except for the last paragraph, which we *double encrypted*.

The receiver then decrypts this paragraph using our public key. If the resulting paragraph is then in plain text, then the receiver has proof that the message was sent by us; only someone who knows our secret key could have encrypted that paragraph in such a way that our public key would decrypt it. This double encryption method requires both parties to agree in advance on which part of the message will be double encrypted.

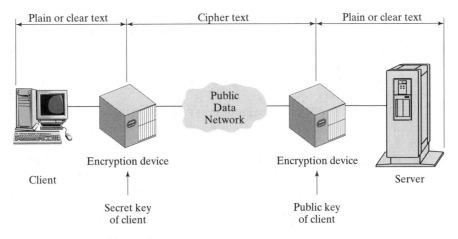

Plain or clear text   Cipher text   Plain or clear text

Public
Data
Network

Encryption device   Encryption device

Client   Server

Secret key   Public key
of client   of client

FIGURE 6-9

Digital signatures using public keys.

Hardware, software, and firmware encryption.   In our examples, we used a method known as *hardware encryption*, where a separate encryption device encrypted and decrypted the data. To change the encryption algorithm, the user usually must purchase a new device. The key can often be changed using special switches on the device itself. This method is fairly secure, because it is hard to determine an algorithm by looking at an encryption device.

Servers and clients can perform encryption and decryption themselves if they are appropriately programmed. This process is known as *software encryption*, and no separate encryption devices are needed. The algorithm can be changed simply by changing the software. The keys are usually also contained in the software. However, this method is vulnerable, because anyone who obtains a copy of the software knows not only the algorithm, but also the key, and can decipher all messages.

A compromise between these two methods is *firmware encryption*. In this case, the software that contains the algorithm or the keys can be stored on preprogrammed chips that can be inserted into an encryption device. If security breaches are suspected, a new set of chips, containing new software, can be installed in the encryption device, thereby changing either the algorithm or the key. This method combines the security of hardware encryption with the flexibility of software encryption.

Common security algorithms and protocols.   Though software encryption is somewhat more vulnerable than the other methods, its ease of use makes it a common choice, particularly in modern electronic mail systems. In most cases, the details of the encryption technology are hidden entirely from the users. The DES and triple DES standards previously described in this chapter are examples of common security algorithms. A widely distributed encryption software product is *Pretty Good Privacy*, or *PGP*. It supports several different encryption algorithms. One of the most widely used public key algorithms is the *RSA* algorithm, named after its three inventors, Rivest,

Shamir, and Adelman. While the selection of a good algorithm is an important step, it is also critical to choose keys of sufficient length to make code breaking difficult. Since these keys are usually generated from user-selected passwords, both the wise choice of these passwords and the maintenance of their security are vital to any network security system. Another common algorithm supported by PGP is *International Data Encryption Algorithm*, or *IDEA*.

In all of the preceding examples, encryption methods are described for the reader. In actual implementations, the key exchange process goes on behind the scenes and is invisible to the user. For example, when accessing a web page over the Internet using *Secure Sockets Layer*, or *SSL*, keys are exchanged between the PC's browser software and the server software of the website. A variety of algorithms can be used with this method. However, all the user does is click on the web page, and the algorithms are selected and the keys are exchanged as part of the Web transaction. This is typically a public key system, where one party must send his or her public key to the other party first, so the return trip (with the data) is encrypted using this public key and can be decrypted using the matching secret key. These public key/secret key pairs are often uniquely generated for a particular transaction and, as such, are hard to break. The next time the user enters into another transaction, a new key set can be created.

Similarly, when sending encrypted email, the user typically clicks on a special security option, and the keys are exchanged automatically. Additional levels of passwords may be required of the user to retrieve the keys from storage on the user's computer to ensure that an intruder could not easily get access to them.

In all of the preceding public key systems, additional secret keys are sometimes used to simplify the computations. Public key systems require very long keys to be secure. Rather than directly encrypting the data with a public key, the public key is sometimes used to send another, system-generated secret key, and the data itself is encrypted with the system-generated secret key. This key is still secure because it is sent in encrypted form. This entire process occurs without the user's knowledge or intervention.

The *IP Security Protocol*, or *IPSec*, allows companies to safely use normally insecure public data networks to interconnect their sites, as we discuss in Chapter 8. The IPSec protocol allows the appropriate encryption techniques to be used to protect this private data as it traverses the public data network. Another use for IPSec is to connect a remote user to a company's network using a public data network like the Internet. Finally, IPSec can be used to interconnect a company with other companies via a public data network.

Point-to-Point Tunneling Protocol, or *PPTP*, is a protocol defined by Microsoft to interconnect remote users through the Internet to their work locations. As it is built into all Windows clients today, it is a popular method for secure remote connections.

The wireless local area networks described in Chapter 8 present another set of security challenges. Wireless networks allow someone sitting in the parking lot of your office building to eavesdrop on all internal corporate network traffic. There have been several attempts to solve this problem.

The first widely distributed security solution for wireless networks was *Wired Equivalent Privacy*, or *WEP*. This mechanism used the *RC4* encryption algorithm, developed by Ronald Rivest. RC4 uses 56-bit secret keys. These keys are configured in the client computers (e.g., laptops) and in the infrastructure devices of the wireless network. Unfortunately, this encryption method is easily broken by the determined intruder and only deters casual intruders. Still, it is better than having no security at all, and it has been widely distributed and deployed. Most wireless network equipment comes with this feature disabled in order to allow users to simply turn on the equipment and begin working. Not having to enter a secret key facilitates installation, but it also leaves the data unencrypted.

To address the weaknesses of WEP, a wireless manufacturers industry group known as the Wi-Fi Alliance created *Wi-Fi Protected Access*, or *WPA*, as an interim step until new standards could be developed and approved. WPA provides a stronger encryption method, the *Temporal Key Interchange Protocol*, or *TKIP*. In addition, it uses *Extensible Authentication Protocol*, or *EAP*, along with a central authentication server to authenticate users, thereby ensuring they belong on the network. A hacker cannot easily spy on your network traffic and will not be able to join your network and send data on it like an authorized member. Many wireless network-infrastructure products can download new software and implement the WPA standard immediately. For this reason, WPA is likely to replace WEP very quickly in existing networks.

A new standard for wireless network security, known as *IEEE 802.11i*, goes beyond WPA in remedying the major deficiencies of WEP. It uses the *Advanced Encryption Standard*, or *AES*, an even stronger encryption technology than WPA. These new advances are significant, and they may make it difficult to upgrade existing WPA devices to 802.11i. Deployment of new technologies in network infrastructures can take years, so even if 802.11i is widely accepted as the better standard, WPA will not disappear overnight.

SUMMARY

Data integrity and security are both important concerns in today's data communications networks. There are many approaches to error control. Errors can simply be detected and flagged. Another approach is to request retransmission when errors are detected. Sophisticated receiving devices can actually correct some errors, a process that is called forward error correction. Methods for implementing error control include echo checking, parity checking, cyclical parity, the Hamming code, and various checksums, including the cyclical redundancy check.

Data security is just as important as error control. Ideally, all messages are sealed, sequenced, secret, signed, and stamped. Security measures include the use of appropriate transmission facilities, passwords, historical and statistical logs, closed user groups, firewalls, and encryption.

Client and server intrusions come in many forms. Hackers often plant malware inside users' computers. Viruses or worms can result in devastating economic and productivity losses, even if data is backed up and recoverable. Hackers can launch denial-of-service attacks, overwhelming a computer's processing capability. Cookies, pop-up ads, and spam, while not always malicious, raise troubling concerns about how companies use others' computers for their own commercial purposes.

Encryption is performed using instructions, known as an algorithm, and with a specific code, known as a key. Secret keys can be used for data confidentiality. The DES, or DEA, is a standard secret-key algorithm. Public keys can be combined with secret keys to provide not only data confidentiality, but also a digital signature. Digital certificates or postmarks can also be issued. The widely used PGP software supports the RSA and IDEA algorithms, among others.

For wireless data security, the WEP standard has been used in recent years. WPA remedies many of the problems with WEP and uses TKIP and EAP. WPA is an interim step on the way to IEEE 802.11i, which uses AES to offer even greater security.

TERMS FOR REVIEW

Advanced Encryption Standard
AES
Algorithm
American National Standards Institute
ANSI
Antispam software
Antivirus software
Application-level firewall
Asymmetric key
Call-back device
Checksum
Cipher text
Clear text
Closed user group
Cookie
CRC
CUG
Cyclical parity
Cyclical redundancy check
Data Encryption Algorithm
Data Encryption Standard
DEA
Decryption
Denial-of-service attack
DES
Digital certificate
Digital postmark
Digital signature
Double encrypted
EAP

Echo checking
Encryption
Encryption device
Error detection with a request for
    retransmission
Error detection with flagging
Even parity
Extensible Authentication Protocol
FEC
Firewall
Firmware encryption
Forward error correction
Hacker
Hamming code
Hardware encryption
Historical logging
IDEA
IEEE 802.11i
Ignored parity
International Data Encryption Algorithm
IP Security Protocol
IPSec
Key
Malicious software
Malware
Mark parity
National Institute of Standards and
    Technology
National Security Agency
NIST

No parity
NSA
Odd parity
Packet-filtering firewall
Parity checking
Password
Personal identification number
PGP
PIN
Plain text
Point-to-Point Tunneling Protocol
Pop-up advertisement
Pop-up blocker
PPTP
Pretty Good Privacy
Public key
RC4
RSA
Sealed message
Secret key
Secret message
Secure channel
Secure Sockets Layer
Sequenced message

Signed message
Software encryption
Space parity
Spam
Spam-filtering software
Spam-blocking software
Spyware
Spyware detection software
SSL
Stamped message
Statistical logging
Symmetric key
Temporal Key Interchange Protocol
TKIP
Triple DES
Trojan horse
Virus
Virus hoax
WEP
Wi-Fi Protected Access
Wired Equivalent Privacy
Worm
WPA

EXERCISES

6-1. Why is data transmission more sensitive to errors than voice transmission?

6-2. How is error detection with flagging different from error detection with a request for retransmission?

6-3. What is the advantage of forward error correction over other error-control approaches?

6-4. What is echo checking?

6-5. How does even-parity checking detect errors? Odd-parity checking? Is one method better than the other?

6-6. If errors occur transmitting bits 3 and 4, will even-parity checking detect the error?

6-7. What type of bit error does the Hamming code correct?

6-8. How is a simple checksum different from the cyclical redundancy check?

6-9. Explain the major goals of proper message security.

6-10. Which transmission media are the most secure? Which are the least secure?

6-11. What is the difference between historical and statistical logging?

6-12. What is a firewall? How does it improve security?

6-13. Explain the difference between clear text and cipher text.

6-14. Compare secret and public keys. How is each used for encryption and decryption?

6-15. What is the difference between symmetric and asymmetric keys?

6-16. What is a digital certificate? A digital postmark?

6-17. What is a virus? A worm?

6-18. What is a denial-of-service attack?

6-19. How are WEP, WPA, and IEEE 802.11i related?

6-20. When is SSL used?

C H A P T E R   7

Architectures and Protocols

We have already discussed clients, servers, terminals, host computers, modems, multiplexers, and many other devices used for data communications. Communications architectures and protocols enable these devices to communicate in an orderly manner, defining precise rules and methods for communications and ensuring harmonious communications among them.

ARCHITECTURES

A *communications architecture* is a manufacturer's strategy for connecting devices. One of the advantages of a well-defined communications architecture is that it cleanly separates the function of communications from the server's other functions. Specifically, a communications architecture can describe special functions that the server's hardware and software must perform to allow applications programs to communicate with the outside world.

For example, there may be many different types of clients attached to a single server. A programmer writing accounting software for the server does not need to know how to communicate with these different clients. The programmer formats the data in a special manner defined by the server's communications architecture. The accounting program then passes the data to the communications software, which, in turn, translates it to a format for each of the different clients. The architecture defines the precise role of each program; the accounting program calculates profits and losses, and the communications program sends data to the clients. Similarly, the author of a word-processing program doesn't need to understand how particular clients function; instead, the programmer simply follows the rules spelled out by the communications architecture and then passes the data onto the communications program for further processing.

An analogy for a communications architecture can be found in a televised football game. The referee calls a penalty and uses hand signals to indicate the infraction and the offending team. The announcer sees these hand signals and translates them into words for the television viewers. In this communications architecture, it is the function of the referee to call the penalty and explain it by using hand signals, and the announcer is responsible for translating the hand signals into words and adding further explanation. Similarly, in communications architectures, each piece of hardware and software has its own task, and they must all function in harmony in order for communications to occur.

Separating the communications functions of a server from its other functions adds flexibility. For example, if we later want to modify our architecture to include other types of clients and devices, we do not need to modify all of the server's software. Since all applications programs communicate through the communications software, only the communications software needs to be modified to accept the new devices. Referring back to our analogy, to televise the same football game in Spain, we would not need to teach the referee to speak Spanish; since only the announcer speaks to the viewers, only the announcer needs to know Spanish.

Thus far in this book, we have considered client-to-server communications. However, users often want to connect servers to other servers, as well as to allow them to share information, transfer files, and so on. A communications architecture describes all types of communications.

THE OPEN SYSTEMS INTERCONNECTION MODEL

The International Standards Organization (ISO) has developed a universal architecture for computer communications. This standard, known as the *Open Systems Interconnection model*, or *OSI model*, breaks down the task of communications into seven independent layers, each with its own tasks. OSI's purpose is to permit communications among devices made by many manufacturers. The exact methods for performing these tasks include some of the protocols we discuss later in this chapter. Almost all of the major players in the industry support the concept of OSI in principle. The *Corporation for Open Systems*, or *COS*, is a nonprofit corporation formed in 1985 that consists of representatives of major host computer manufacturers of that era, including Control Data, DEC, Hewlett-Packard, Honeywell, IBM, NCR, Tandem, Unisys, Wang, Xerox, and others. The corporation's purpose is to facilitate the evolution of intervendor compatibility from a model to a reality. Perhaps the most significant contribution of the OSI model is that it provides all of us with a common language for describing communications tasks and functions.

The seven layers of OSI are shown in Fig. 7-1. Each layer represents a particular function. Sometimes, each function is performed by a separate piece of hardware or software. Other times, a single program may perform the functions of several layers. All of the layers are necessary for communications to occur. The different layer classifications are somewhat arbitrary, and a different standards committee might have chosen to break the communications functions into more or fewer layers. For example, we might describe the process of driving to work as follows: (1) Open the car door, (2) sit down, (3) close the door, (4) insert the key, (5) turn the key, and so on. Another person might describe the same process as follows: (1) Get in the car, (2) start the car, (3) put the car in gear, and so on. We are both describing the same task, and both descriptions are accurate; however, each description chooses to break up the process of driving to

Host computer

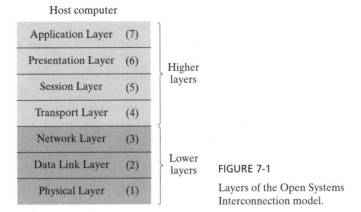

FIGURE 7-1

Layers of the Open Systems Interconnection model.

work into a different set of tasks. Similarly, the ISO–OSI model chooses to divide the function of computer communications into seven layers, though more or fewer layers could easily have been chosen. Rather than examine each layer's functions in detail, we merely highlight each layer's most important functions.

The lowest layer, known as the *Physical Layer*, or *Layer 1*, is responsible for the transmission of bits. The Physical Layer is always implemented using hardware, and it encompasses the mechanical, electrical, and functional interface. This layer is the interface to the outside world, where ones and zeroes leave and enter the device, usually using electronic signals as specified by interface standards. Examples of Physical Layer standards are RS-232-C, RS-449, RS-422-A, and RS-423-A.

The *Data Link Layer*, or *Layer 2*, assembles the data bits into a block, or *frame*, which is then sent to the Physical Layer for transmission. It is often also responsible for ensuring error-free, reliable transmission of data. The Data Link Layer typically scrutinizes the bits received to determine if errors occurred during transmission. This layer is often able to request retransmission or correction of any errors using protocols such as BSC, SDLC, HDLC, and PPP, which are presented later in this chapter.

The *Network Layer*, or *Layer 3*, is responsible for setting up the appropriate routing of messages throughout a network. This layer is the only layer concerned with the types of switching networks used to route the data. The routing of data between networks and through packet switching networks is also handled by the Network Layer. We discuss packet switching networks further in Chapter 8.

The Physical, Data Link, and Network layers of OSI are usually referred to as the *lower layers*. Layers 4 through 7 (Transport, Session, Presentation, and Application) are usually referred to as the *higher layers*, or *upper layers*.

The *Transport Layer*, or *Layer 4*, is responsible for isolating the function of the lower layers from the higher layers. This layer will accept messages from higher layers and break these messages down into messages that can be accepted by the lower layers. For example, a file being transferred may contain thousands of characters. The lower layers may be transmitting data 100 characters at a time, so the Transport Layer breaks the file into many blocks, each 100 characters long. If communications technology changes and longer messages can be accepted in the future, the Transport Layer will need modification; however, the other higher layers will not. The Transport Layer is also responsible for monitoring the quality of the communications channel and for selecting the most cost-efficient communication service based on the reliability required for a particular transmission.

The *Session Layer*, or *Layer 5*, requests that a logical connection be established based on the end user's request. In this case, an end user might be the client operator using the computer. For example, if the user wants to transfer a file, the Session Layer is informed of the location of the file on the user's system and the location of the destination file on the remote server. Any necessary log-on and password procedures are also usually handled by this layer. The Session Layer is also responsible for terminating the connection.

The *Presentation Layer*, or *Layer 6*, provides format and code conversion services. For example, if the server is connected to many different types of printers, each printer may require different character sequences to invoke special features, such as boldface and italics. The Presentation Layer handles all of the necessary formatting. In addition, if files are being transferred from the server of one manufacturer to the server of another, there may be different file formats, or even different character codes. The Presentation Layer would handle any necessary conversion (e.g., ASCII-to-EBCDIC conversion).

The *Application Layer*, or *Layer 7*, provides access to the network for the end user. The user's capabilities on the network are determined by the Application Layer software, which can be tailored to the needs of the user. Some Application Layer software might permit remote clients only to access a server; other Application Layer software might also permit file transfers. Network management statistics, diagnostics, and other online monitoring capabilities can also be implemented in this layer.

We have already mentioned that the Physical Layer must be implemented in hardware. Since this layer is the only part of the model where bits are actually transmitted, it is also the only part of the model that requires hardware implementation. The other layers all manipulate the data in some way, perhaps adding to it or modifying it, but all of these techniques can generally be performed using software. However, since functions can be performed more efficiently and inexpensively by hardware than by software, some functions of the Data Link and Network Layers are sometimes implemented in hardware. The higher layers are almost always implemented in software.

OSI IN ACTION

If two servers use OSI protocols, how would a common transaction, like a file transfer, take place? We trace a file transferred from an imaginary IBM server to an HP server, using the OSI model as a reference.

We begin by examining the path of the data through the layers of the IBM server. As illustrated in Fig. 7-2, a user of a word-processing program on the IBM server issues the file-transfer command to the Application Layer. The Application Layer then passes the file to the Presentation Layer, which may reformat the data. The data is then passed to the Session Layer, which requests that a connection be provided to the destination host and passes the data to the Transport Layer. The Transport Layer breaks the

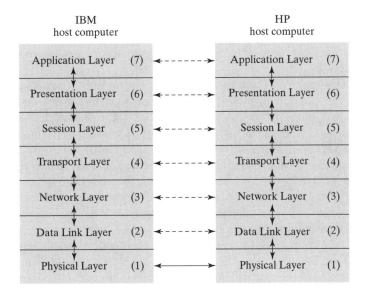

IBM
host computer

HP
host computer

Application Layer (7)	Application Layer (7)
Presentation Layer (6)	Presentation Layer (6)
Session Layer (5)	Session Layer (5)
Transport Layer (4)	Transport Layer (4)
Network Layer (3)	Network Layer (3)
Data Link Layer (2)	Data Link Layer (2)
Physical Layer (1)	Physical Layer (1)

FIGURE 7-2

Transferring a file under the OSI model.

file into manageable chunks of data for transmission and passes them to the Network Layer. The Network Layer selects the data's route and then passes the data to the Data Link Layer. The Data Link Layer adds extra information to the data so that it can be checked for errors at the receiving end and passes the data to the Physical Layer. The Physical Layer takes the resulting data stream and transmits it across the physical link to the other server.

The data transmitted by the Physical Layer includes not only the file from the Application Layer, but also all of the additional information added by each of the other layers. Each layer performs its function by modifying the data. For example, the Network Layer adds extra bits to the data that specify the route that the data is to take. The data finally transmitted by the Physical Layer could be twice as long as the original data, but each of these extra ones and zeroes performs valuable functions. Each of the receiving server's different layers examines the ones and zeroes related to their functions and removes their data before passing the remaining data to the next higher layer. By the time the message reaches the Application Layer on the destination server, it is the same length as the message originally sent by the Application Layer on the originating server.

The HP server's Physical Layer receives the bits and passes them on to its Data Link Layer. The Data Link Layer verifies that no errors occurred and then passes the data on to the Network Layer. The Network Layer ensures that the selected route is proving to be reliable and then passes the data on to the Transport Layer. The Transport Layer reassembles the small chunks of data into the file being transferred and then passes it on to the Session Layer. The Session Layer determines if the transfer is complete, and, if so, it may break down the session, in effect ending communications.

The data is then passed on to the Presentation Layer, which may reformat it, performing any necessary conversion, and then pass it on to the Application Layer. The HP server's users can then access the transferred information through the Application Layer software.

In this example, the transfer of data went smoothly. But what if an error had occurred? For example, if the HP server's Data Link Layer detects any errors, it might request that the data be retransmitted. This retransmission request would be sent back over the HP Physical Layer to the IBM Physical Layer, which would pass it on to the IBM Data Link Layer. The IBM Data Link Layer would respond to the retransmission request, since this layer is responsible for error-free transmission. The IBM Data Link Layer would retransmit the data to the IBM Physical Layer, which then would transmit the data over the physical link. The data would be received by the HP Physical Layer and passed on to the HP Data Link Layer. If there are still errors, the entire retransmission process would be repeated. If the data is now error free, the file transfer would continue as described previously, with the data being passed on to the higher layers.

The OSI model provides for *peer-level communication* between the layers. The Physical Layers of the two servers are the only parts of the two devices that communicate directly. The other layers communicate indirectly, through the lower layers and eventually through the Physical Layer. For example, the Data Link Layer on the IBM server adds bits to the message for error detection that are interpreted by the HP Data Link Layer. Similarly, each layer on the IBM server contributes bits that are interpreted by the corresponding layer on the HP server. Although only the Physical Layers communicate directly, all of the layers communicate indirectly with their peers on the other server by modifying the data and sending messages for interpretation by their counterparts. This peer-level communication is shown with dashed lines in Fig. 7-2.

Our discussion so far has assumed that two servers are directly connected to each other. Sometimes, however, in a network with many servers, there may be intermediary devices between the two servers trying to communicate. Each device on a network can be referred to as a *node*. For example, a message being routed from a server in San Francisco to a server in New York might pass through a switching node in Chicago. Figure 7-3 shows nodes in New York, San Francisco, and Chicago. The nodes at the far ends of the connection—in this case, in San Francisco and New York—are sometimes referred to as the *destination nodes*. The intermediate devices, known as *intermediate nodes*, support only the first three layers of the OSI model. The node in Chicago must receive the message from San Francisco with its Physical Layer, verify with its Data Link Layer that there are no errors, and then determine the appropriate routing to the destination server in New York using its Network Layer. Error-correction information is then added back to the message by the Chicago node's Data Link Layer before it is retransmitted to New York by the node's Physical Layer. Intermediate nodes must support the lower three layers, which are necessary for data transmission and routing. The intermediate node may have higher layers, but since it is not the destination device, the message in this case never reaches those layers in the intermediate node. The Network Layer at the server in New York recognizes that the message has reached its destination and does not send the message to another node; instead, it passes it on to its own higher layers.

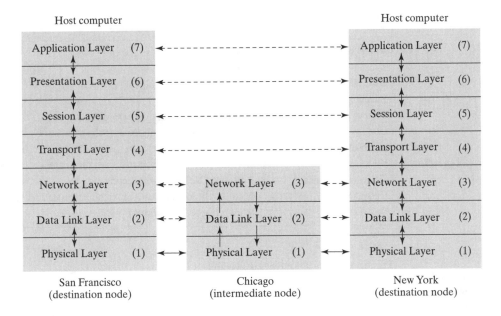

FIGURE 7-3

Multiple node communications under OSI.

PROPRIETARY COMMUNICATIONS ARCHITECTURES

Almost all computer manufacturers or operating system vendors have an architecture for computer communications. It is hard to classify any one architecture as superior to another from a technical point of view. Each is designed to allow particular types of devices to communicate with each other. Some examples of proprietary communications architectures are listed in Fig. 7-4. Almost all systems today are able to communicate with open, standard protocols when connecting with other vendors' equipment.

One architecture that gained significantly more market acceptance than the rest of the proprietary ones is IBM's *Systems Network Architecture*, or *SNA*. While there are few new installations of SNA networks today, there are many existing SNA environments. SNA was revolutionary for its day. Introduced in 1974, it incorporated many of the aspects of today's client/server computing model. Each user attached to the network was able to access a program on any server on the network. This change was significant for that era, for users had previously needed mechanical or electrical switch boxes to connect to two different computers.

SNA's success is usually attributed to its ability to connect a wide variety of devices, each with different capabilities, in a homogeneous network whose workings are hidden from the end user. SNA allows customers to start with a small network and increase its size in a modular fashion. SNA networks can also be connected to other SNA networks. Finally, SNA includes sophisticated network-management functions to simplify fault isolation and problem determination, as well as to provide reports on network usage. A thorough discussion of SNA is provided in Appendix C to aid those who are still working with SNA environments.

Vendor	Architecture
Apple	AppleTalk
Banyan	Vines
DEC (Compaq)	Digital Network Architecture (DNA)
Hewlett-Packard	AdvanceNet
Honeywell	Distributed Systems Architecture (DSA)
IBM	Systems Network Architecture (SNA)
Microsoft	Windows Networking
Novell	Netware
Unisys (Burroughs)	Burroughs Network Architecture (BNA)
Unisys (Sperry)	Distributed Communications Architecture (DCA)
WANG	Wang Systems Networking (WSN)

FIGURE 7-4

Proprietary communications architectures.

PROTOCOLS

While architectures provide a broad framework for communications, describing how different components can be connected, *protocols* precisely define the methods used to communicate. Almost all architectures require the use of certain protocols to ensure reliable data transmission. Protocols are a set of rules for transmitting and receiving data between devices. The OSI model describes different functions required to communicate, with the tasks broken down in a layered fashion. While Layer 1 of OSI is always in hardware, Layer 2 and above may be implemented in software. We will begin our protocol discussion with Layer 2 protocols, or the Data Link Layer.

Data Link Layer Protocols

Sometimes called *line disciplines*, protocols spell out the specific character or bit patterns required for communications between two devices.

An example of a human communications protocol can be found in a classroom. Typically, a professor begins a lecture and controls the communications path. If a student wants to communicate, the student must wait until the professor asks, "Any questions?" Then, the student can raise his or her hand and wait for permission to communicate. The professor can then call on the student, granting control of the communications line to that student. The student then asks the question and grants control of the communications path back to the professor for the response. The protocol in this case is that the student speaks only when called upon; it is customary that the student doesn't interrupt the professor, and vice versa. This type of protocol, commonly used in data communications, is known as a *link-level protocol*, because it precisely defines methods for communicating over a link. In OSI terms, it is known as a Data Link Layer protocol.

Polling and Selecting

Establishing rules for sharing the communications path, known as *communications line control*, is one of the major functions of a Data Link Layer protocol. Often, these rules are established by using polling and selecting methods.

Polling occurs when the server asks the client, "Do you have any data to send?" At this point, a client might send data, or it might simply answer "No." *Selecting* occurs when the server asks the client, "Can you accept data now?" A smart client might then answer, "Go ahead" or "Not now, I'm busy." Not all clients are capable of operating in this way. For example, the dumb terminals described in Chapter 3 cannot respond to these messages. Protocols define the exact characters or bit patterns that must be sent to perform this polling and selecting.

Automatic Repeat Request

Finally, almost all Data Link Layer protocols provide some sort of an *error detection and correction* capability. Most Data Link Layer protocols use an *automatic repeat request* system known as *ARQ*. In this system, when the receiving device recognizes an error, it automatically requests that the data be retransmitted. Both the transmitting and receiving devices usually detect errors by using a checksum or cyclical redundancy check method, as described in Chapter 6.

There are two common types of ARQ in use today. One type, known as *stop-and-wait ARQ*, requires that the receiver respond to each block of data before the next one can be sent. A human example of stop-and-wait ARQ would be an inexperienced secretary taking dictation. After each sentence spoken by the boss, the secretary says, "Okay," indicating that the sentence was received and transcribed properly. The boss does not proceed with the next sentence until hearing the secretary say "Okay." In addition, a secretary who doesn't understand a sentence might ask, "What?" This question is really a request for the boss to repeat the transmission. Similarly, with stop-and-wait ARQ, a device will not transmit the next message until it has received confirmation that the last message was received correctly. It will also repeat messages that were not understood.

In the other method, known as *continuous ARQ*, a device continues sending messages without waiting for confirmation that the last message was received. For example, a boss dictating a letter to a very experienced secretary would probably not pause between sentences to wait for the secretary to say "Okay." We assume that this boss is in the habit of rattling off several sentences at a time, sometimes getting far ahead of the secretary's ability to transcribe. Even though the secretary may continue to say "Okay" after each sentence is transcribed, the boss may already be in the middle of the next sentence. As long as the secretary doesn't say "What?", the boss keeps talking.

If the secretary asks "What?", there are two possible reactions by the boss; therefore, there are two types of continuous ARQ protocols. The first, known as *go-back-N continuous ARQ*, would have the boss return to the last sentence the secretary understood and begin retransmitting the misunderstood sentence, as well as any sentences that followed. The other possible response, *selective repeat continuous ARQ*, would require the boss to repeat only the misunderstood sentence; the subsequent sentences would not have to be retransmitted. In either case, the advantage of continuous ARQ protocols over stop-and-wait ARQ protocols is that the sending device does not have to wait for permission from the receiving device before sending the next block of data. With either type of continuous ARQ, data transmission is never delayed as long as no errors occur. Continuous ARQ, therefore, is more efficient than stop-and-wait ARQ, in which the transmitter must wait for an acknowledgment before proceeding to send the next data block.

COMMON DATA LINK LAYER PROTOCOLS

All common Data Link Layer protocols allow devices to share a communications path and to detect and correct errors. There are two common classes of Data Link Layer protocols, byte-oriented protocols and bit-oriented protocols.

In both types of protocols, the devices must exchange *control information* along with the data transmitted. This control information includes the queries and responses used for polling and selecting, as well as the error-checking information necessary for all types of automatic repeat requests. In *byte-oriented protocols*, also known as *character-oriented protocols*, all control information and data are encoded using entire bytes. *Bit-oriented protocols*, on the other hand, may use single bits to represent both control information and data. Most older protocols were byte oriented, or character oriented, and almost all major character sets, including ASCII and EBCDIC, include control characters.

We choose the first widely used Data Link Layer protocols, BSC and SDLC, as examples. SDLC's close relatives, HDLC and LAP-B, are also included in our discussion. Many other Data Link Layer protocols are in use today, and surely new ones will be proposed in the future. However, these two protocols illustrate classic features. One is byte oriented, and the other is bit oriented; one uses stop-and-wait ARQ, and the other uses continuous ARQ; one allows only half duplex transmission, and the other permits half duplex or full duplex transmission.

Binary Synchronous Communications

The first widely used byte-oriented or character-oriented protocol was IBM's *Binary Synchronous Communications*, or *BSC* (often referred to as *Bisync*). BSC is a half duplex, stop-and-wait ARQ protocol. It permits point-to-point communications, such as a client connected to a server. BSC also permits multipoint communications.

In multipoint use, there is a single *Control station* and many *Tributary stations*. The Control station can communicate with any of the Tributary stations, and any of the Tributary stations can communicate with the Control station; however, the Tributary stations cannot communicate with each other. BSC was originally designed to accommodate three specific character codes: ASCII, EBCDIC, and Transcode. We have already presented ASCII and EBCDIC in Chapter 3; Transcode is a seldom-used six-bit code. The major functions of BSC and other Data Link Layer protocols are to share the communications circuit among two or more devices and to ensure error-free transmission.

Because BSC uses half duplex transmission, along with stop-and-wait ARQ, it is not well suited for use over satellites or for any other transmission media subject to long delays.

For example, if we were to use a stop-and-wait ARQ protocol to communicate over satellites, a block of data, known as a *frame*, would be sent from a server over the satellite to a client. The message might take a quarter of a second to get to the client, at which point the client would determine if the frame contains any errors. Assuming that there are no errors, the client would send an *acknowledgment* that the frame has been properly received, and this acknowledgment message would go back up over the satellite to reach the server, taking another quarter of a second. During this round-trip of a half-second, the server is not permitted to send any more data and must wait for the return acknowledgment. We have not even included any line-turnaround time required due to the half duplex nature of the conversation. These delays make stop-and-wait ARQ unsuitable for satellite transmission.

During our discussion of character codes in Chapter 3, we mentioned that special control codes included in character codes were used by certain protocols. BSC uses many of these control codes to permit devices to exchange *control information*, like an acknowledgment message, and to help divide a BSC frame into several parts. We present here only the basic elements of a BSC frame and only a limited number of BSC features. The purpose of this book is not to make the reader fluent in the BSC protocol, but instead to introduce the types of messages used in a character-oriented protocol.

There are two basic types of BSC frames, one containing user data and the other containing control information. User data frames contain data actually typed by the client user or sent from the server's applications program. Additional information, known as a *header*, may be included in the user data frame by the BSC protocol to allow the message to be addressed to one of several clients. Some error-checking information may also be included in the user data frame.

The other type of frames, known as *control information frames*, are passed between the client and the server to perform polling and selecting, as well as to determine if errors have occurred. A BSC client user does not personally type any control information. The client itself is programmed to respond to BSC control information, but not to pass this information to the user. A BSC client and server actually carry on their own private conversation about the data's accuracy and each other's status, without the knowledge or intervention of the client user.

For example, the client user types data on the keyboard and then hits the ENTER or XMIT (transmit) key. The BSC client sends the data, along with a header, to the server. The server checks the message for errors, and if it is satisfied that none have occurred, it sends back the acknowledgment message. This acknowledgment message is control information, which is received by the client. The client now is certain that its message was received by the server, and the message can be erased from its memory. If the server had found errors, however, the client would at this point retransmit the message. This exchange of control information occurs between the server and client, but the client does not pass the acknowledgment message to the client user. The only way that an end user knows that an error has occurred is if he or she hits the ENTER key again very quickly and doesn't receive a response, which would indicate that the client may be busy retransmitting the last message.

CHARACTERS IN A BSC FRAME

What characters actually make up a BSC frame? We'll begin with a control information frame, which contains the following characters:

```
PAD SYN SYN [control information] PAD
```

The *PAD* character is simply a special pattern of ones and zeroes used at the beginning and end of a frame. The only purpose of the PAD character is to allow time for the transmission line to stabilize. We assume that eight-bit characters are being used for our example, so each PAD character is eight bits in length.

Following the PAD characters are two *SYN* characters, which allow the receiver to "sync up" to the incoming signal and prepare to receive real data. The SYN character can be found in almost all character codes. Since this is a control frame, it contains control information, followed by a PAD character to conclude the frame. Remember that none of these special characters is ever seen by the user, but each is part of the frames sent between the BSC client and server.

What characters make up control information? That depends on whether we are using BSC for point-to-point configurations or for multipoint configurations. Each device is sometimes referred to as a communications *station* in BSC. In point-to-point use, there are only two stations, and the most commonly used control information represents the question "Can I send now?" This question is known as an *enquiry*, and the *ENQ* character is used in the control information portion of the frame. An enquiry frame would be

```
PAD   SYN   SYN   ENQ   PAD
```

The device receiving the enquiry can reply with an *ACK0*, a *NAK*, or a *WACK*. An *ACK0* is a type of acknowledgment indicating that the device is ready to receive; a *NAK* is a negative acknowledgment indicating that the device is not ready to receive; a *WACK* indicates that the device is temporarily busy, but that it will be ready soon. These three possible responses are

```
PAD   SYN   SYN   ACK0 PAD

PAD   SYN   SYN   NAK   PAD

PAD   SYN   SYN   WACK PAD
```

Remember that if we are using an eight-bit character code, the ENQ, ACK0, NAK, and WACK characters may each have an eight-bit representation. If any of these special characters are not available in a character code, a combination of two other characters can be used instead. Assuming that ACK0 was the response, the transmitter can now send data using a data frame, which we will explain in the upcoming discussion. After the data transmission is complete, the transmitter sends an *EOT*, indicating an end of transmission:

```
PAD   SYN   SYN   EOT   PAD
```

At this point, either of the two devices could ask permission to send, using the ENQ character.

Multipoint use complicates the control information exchanged, because there is now a single Control station and several Tributary stations. Typically, a server is the Control station, and the clients are Tributary stations. The Control station performs all of the polling and selecting in multipoint use. The polling and selecting is performed by using the ENQ character plus the address of the Tributary station. Selected stations can respond with acknowledgments, indicating

PAD	SYN	SYN	control information	PAD

PAD	SYN	SYN	SOH	header	STX	data	ETX	BCC	BCC	PAD

FIGURE 7-5

Binary Synchronous Communications frame.

---

their readiness to receive data. Polled stations send data if they have any to send; otherwise, they may indicate that they are done transmitting with a simple EOT message:

```
PAD  SYN  SYN  EOT  PAD
```

So far, we have considered only control information. But how is data transmitted? After a client user hits the ENTER key, the BSC client assembles the data into a data frame. A typical data frame in BSC looks like

```
PAD SYN SYN SOH header STX data ETX BCC BCC PAD
```

The PAD and SYN characters perform the same functions as previously described. The *SOH* character indicates the start of the header, which contains addressing information. The *STX* character indicates the start of the text, or user data, and is followed by the actual user data. The *ETX* character signifies the end of the data and is followed by two *BCC*s, or block check characters, and a final PAD character. The BCC characters vary with each transmission, containing checksums for error correction, like the cyclical redundancy check discussed in Chapter 6. There are other possible data frames that allow control characters to be sent as data in a special *transparent data mode*. This type of transmission is an exception, however. Most data is transmitted as described in the previous frame.

BSC, like any Data Link Layer protocol, is a systematic method for ensuring reliable communications over a shared communications link. There is an appropriate query and response for every possible situation, though we have covered only some basic examples. A comparison of these two most common types of BSC frames is presented in Fig. 7-5.

SDLC, HDLC, LAP-B, and PPP

One of the first widely used bit-oriented protocols is IBM's *Synchronous Data Link Control*, or *SDLC*. SDLC is similar to the ISO *High-level Data Link Control*, or *HDLC*, which contains some additional features. Other similar protocols are ANSI's *Advanced Data Communications Control Procedures*, or *ADCCP*, and ITU(CCITT)'s *Link Access Procedure-Balanced*, or *LAP-B*. The widely used *Point-to-Point Protocol*, or *PPP*, uses virtually the same frame format as SDLC, though it has some differences we will discuss later.

SDLC/HDLC/LAP-B are most often used in full duplex mode, though they can be used in half duplex mode. Since they employ go-back-N continuous ARQ, they are suitable for use over satellite links or other transmission media with long delays. With continuous ARQ, the server does not have to wait for an acknowledgment of the first message before sending more data.

In a full duplex link, the transmitter can send data continuously, while simultaneously receiving acknowledgment messages from the receiver. On a half duplex link, several frames can be sent, at which point the line is turned around and a single acknowledgment message is sent for all of the frames received. This method is more efficient than BSC, in which half duplex mode must always be used, the line must be turned around after each frame, and each frame is acknowledged separately.

In SDLC/HDLC/LAP-B, as in BSC, the control information passed between the server and client never reaches the end user. The user is shielded from all errors by the protocol's ability to correct them, and control information is passed efficiently between stations, using only a few bits. The greatest advantage, however, is that SDLC/HDLC/-LAP-B contain continuous ARQ and a full duplex capability that allows its use with a wide range of transmission media, regardless of delays. The customer can choose the transmission media based on cost, desired reliability, and bandwidth and does not have to be concerned about the effect of delays on the protocol's performance.

The terminology in SDLC/HDLC/LAP-B is slightly different from that used in BSC. Rather than using the terms "Control" and "Tributary Stations," the terms *Primary* and *Secondary stations* are used. All communication is between the single Primary station and the one or many Secondary stations.

SDLC/HDLC/LAP-B, like BSC, also sends data in frames, but data and control information are sent one bit at a time, not one character at time. There are three basic frame formats, known as *Information, Supervisory*, and *Unnumbered*. As in our discussion of BSC, we consider only the most basic elements of SDLC.

Information Format Frames, or *I-Frames*, are used to send and receive data. *Supervisory Format Frames*, or *S-Frames*, are used to transfer control information, including acknowledgment of the accurate receipt of data. *Unnumbered Format Frames*, or *U-Frames*, are used for special functions, including establishing connections, reporting procedural problems, and performing special cases of data transfer. I-Frames and S-Frames are most commonly used together to send data and ensure reliable transmission.

The number of frames that can be sent without receipt of an acknowledgment message, known as the *window*, is either 7 or 127, depending on the number of bits that has been dedicated to count the frames. *Modulo-8* transmission allows 7 frames, while *Modulo-128* transmission allows 127 frames.

BITS IN AN SDLC/HDLC/LAP-B FRAME

All three frame formats follow the same basic pattern shown in Fig. 7-6. Each type of frame begins with a *Flag*, a pattern of eight ones and zeroes (01111110). Then there is the eight-bit *Address Field*, which contains the address of the Secondary station. Since all communication is between a Primary and Secondary station, this address is the destination of a message when the Primary station transmits and the source of the message when the Secondary station transmits. This addressing method allows for proper routing of data to and from Secondary stations in multipoint configurations.

After the address field comes the *Control Field*, which contains either 8 or 16 control bits, depending on the mode of operation. The function of these control bits differs, depending on whether the frame is an I-Frame, an S-Frame, or a U-Frame. After the Control Field is the

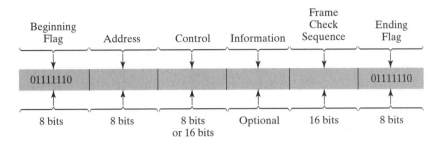

FIGURE 7-6

SDLC/HDLC/LAP-B frame.

Information Field, which occurs only in certain I-Frames and U-Frames. The Information Field is used to transmit data and is variable in length, depending on the amount of data being transmitted. The length of the Information Field is always a multiple of eight bits.

Next in the frame is the *Frame Check Sequence Field*. The Frame Check Sequence, or *FCS*, contains 16 bits for error checking that are calculated using the cyclical redundancy check method presented in Chapter 6. The frame concludes with the ending Flag, also a pattern of eight ones and zeroes (01111110).

Notice that the Flags perform a similar function to the PAD and SYN characters in BSC. The FCS is also very similar to the BCC characters used in BSC. Both BSC and SDLC/HDLC/LAP-B contain addresses. However, the control information is passed in a very different manner than in BSC.

Each bit in the Control Field has a special meaning. For example, Supervisory Format Frames are used to acknowledge receipt of data. The SDLC/HDLC/LAP-B *Receiver Ready*, or *RR*, is similar to the BSC ACK, and it indicates that data has been successfully received. An SDLC/HDLC/LAP-B *Reject*, or *REJ*, is similar to a BSC NAK, and it indicates that a retransmission is necessary. An SDLC/HDLC/LAP-B *Receiver Not Ready*, or *RNR*, is similar to a BSC WACK, and it indicates a temporary busy condition. These different conditions are represented by only a few bits in the SDLC/HDLC/LAP-B Control Field, rather than by entire eight-bit characters, as in BSC.

The remaining bits in the Control Field can be used for other functions. For example, in all types of SDLC/HDLC/LAP-B frames, the Control Field contains a *P/F bit*. The Primary station can require the Secondary station to respond by setting the P/F bit—in this case, the Poll bit. The Secondary station can then transmit data, and, when finished, it can also set this bit. When the Secondary station sets the P/F bit, it is now the *Final* bit, indicating that transmission is complete. This single bit is used for two functions, compared to the BSC use of eight bits for a single function. This high efficiency is another of the advantages of SDLC/HDLC/LAP-B.

The SDLC/HDLC/LAP-B frames are identical. The PPP protocol, which uses a similar frame format, is actually byte oriented in its data field. In other words, it is only possible to send data in eight-bit increments in PPP, so additional bits are added to reach a number divisible by eight. In addition, the first one or two bytes after the Control Field in PPP identifies the layer 3 protocol being carried in the frame, and the rest of the frame (Information field, FCS, Flag) remains unchanged. We include a further discussion of PPP later in the chapter, along with a discussion of the other protocols it is typically used with.

Protocol Converters and Code Converters

If two HDLC devices need to communicate, the HDLC protocol ensures reliable and accurate data transmission. But what if a dumb asynchronous terminal needs to communicate with a server using HDLC? A separate device, known as a *protocol converter*, can act as a translator between the two devices, taking asynchronous data from the client, packaging it into HDLC frames, and transmitting it synchronously to the server. Data from the server is removed from its frame and transmitted asynchronously to the terminal. The same function could be performed for a BSC server, as well as for almost any other protocol.

In some cases, the client may use a different character code from the server. A *code converter* can be used to translate the characters from one character code to another. For example, data sent from an ASCII client can be translated for reception by an EBCDIC server. Sometimes, a *protocol converter* performs both protocol and code conversion.

So far we have focused on Data Link Layer protocols used on serial links. Other protocols will be introduced in Chapter 8 when we discuss local area networks. We now turn to the higher layers, which are dominated by a single suite of protocols.

THE TCP/IP PROTOCOL SUITE AND RELATED PROTOCOLS

The *TCP/IP Protocol Suite* is a collection of protocols originally designed for use on a network connecting U.S. government agencies and universities performing research. The TCP/IP Protocol Suite specifies protocols at various levels of the OSI model and covers a wide variety of tasks likely to be performed on an open network. It is easiest to understand TCP/IP when the two protocols are considered together, even though TCP is not the only protocol that can be used with IP.

The *Transmission Control Protocol*, or *TCP*, and the *Internet Protocol*, or *IP*, are at the heart of this suite of protocols. TCP operates at Layer 4 of the OSI model, the Transport Layer. Since it is concerned with reliable delivery of the user's message, TCP retransmits data lost by the lower layers. It is also responsible for establishing and monitoring the entire connection between the users and is thus called a *connection-oriented protocol*.

IP operates at Layer 3 of the OSI model, the Network Layer. It is concerned with routing and delivering the individual packets, but it does not guarantee delivery. For this reason, IP is called an *unreliable service* that offers *best-effort delivery*. It is possible for the IP packets, known as *datagrams*, to be lost due to errors or failed links in an IP network. When TCP is used in conjunction with IP, TCP takes the necessary actions to ensure proper message delivery to the destination. TCP is also responsible for reassembling and resequencing messages at the destination.

Every packet sent by IP is handled independently, even though it may be part of a larger TCP data *stream*. While TCP monitors the connection, IP handles only individual packets and is therefore called a *connectionless protocol*. An IP network is one type of data transport network discussed in more detail in Chapter 8. All data passed over an IP network is broken into IP datagrams and reassembled into the original user data stream at its destination.

FIGURE 7-7

TCP header.

TCP and IP complement each other very well and are designed to work together. TCP establishes a *connection* between two *endpoints*. An endpoint is defined by both a computer's IP address and a *port number*, which identifies the specific application on the computer. A connection is a data stream between two endpoints. A particular port on a computer can be shared by several connections. For example, if a particular port is reserved for incoming requests to a web server, requests from many users could be destined for the same port on that computer. Unique connections are identified and their data are streams separated, because the streams are identified as coming from, or going to, different endpoints.

The TCP data stream is broken into TCP *segments* to be transmitted. The segments begin with the TCP header, shown in Fig. 7-7, followed by user data. In the case of an IP network, an IP *header* is placed in front of each TCP segment before it is transmitted, resulting in an IP datagram. The TCP header and IP header are shown in Fig. 7-7 and 7-8, respectively. The relationship between the TCP header, TCP segment, IP header, and IP datagram is shown in Fig. 7-9.

FIGURE 7-8

IP header.

FIGURE 7-9

Relationship between TCP header, TCP segment, IP header, and IP datagram.

THE TCP HEADER

The TCP header begins with 16 bits that identify the *source port*, which specifies the applications program and the sending computer that transmitted the data. The following 16 bits identify the *destination port*, thereby specifying the application on the receiving computer that needs to handle the data upon receipt. The next field contains a 32-bit *sequence number*, so the receiver can track the individual TCP segments as they are received, reassemble them later into the original data stream, and acknowledge them to the sender. The 32-bit *acknowledgement number* follows, and it refers to the next group of bytes expected in the opposite direction. The sequence number and acknowledgement number in a given header are not expected to match, as they refer to simultaneous sending and receiving data streams going in opposite directions.

The 4-bit *HLEN,* or *header length* field describes the length of the header in 32-bit increments, with the following 6 bits reserved for future use. The six-bit *code bits* field contains bits used for connection overhead tasks. For example, code bits are used when resetting the connection, synchronizing sequence numbers, indicating the stream is completed, marking data as urgent, indicating an acknowledgement, etc. The 16-bit *Window* field describes the receive buffer size of the sender, so streams in the opposite direction will be limited by this size. The next 16 bits contain the *checksum*, used to verify the data and the header for integrity. The next 16 bits contain the *urgent pointer* field. TCP allows a stream to be interrupted so urgent data can be sent using the existing connection. The urgent pointer field refers to the position in the segment where the urgent data ends and the normal operation begins again. The next 24-bit field contains *options* that allow for any special functions needed for the connection, as well as 8 bits of *padding* to reach the end of the 32 bits required for the header. The user data follows the options and padding, or, if no options and padding exist, the user data follows immediately after the urgent pointer.

IP networks have the advantage of not limiting the destination to a single address, or *station*. A message can be sent from one user to another; this type of transmission is called a *unicast*. Alternatively, a message can be sent to all users in a particular range of IP addresses using a *broadcast*. In a *multicast*, a subset of the network users is configured to be part of a group that recognizes that a message is for them, while those not in the group ignore the message. While a broadcast group is determined in advance by the numerical value of a station's IP address, a multicast can, in effect, be subscribed to. Thus, the user simply chooses to listen to messages with a particular multicast address.

THE IP HEADER

Each IP datagram begins with the *header* shown in Fig. 7-8. The header is at least 20 bytes long and may contain additional optional fields. Following the header is the user data. The entire IP datagram, including the 20-byte header, any optional parts, and any user data, may not exceed 65,535 bytes. Typically, it is limited to far fewer bytes by the underlying transmission-link technology.

The first field in the header is a four-bit *version field*, indicating the version number of IP used in the datagram. It is followed by a four-bit *IHL*, or *Internet Header Length, field*. Since the header may contain optional parts, its length varies; the IHL indicates the length of the header in 32-bit increments. The next eight bits contain the *type of service field* and signal to the network the type of handling this datagram requires. The options include emphasizing priority, low delay, high throughput, or reliability. Many of these measures of network service are discussed further in Chapter 9. There is no guarantee that the network will be able to fulfill these requests. The *total length field* follows in the next 16 bits, indicating the overall length of the datagram, in bytes.

The total length field is followed by a 16-bit *identification field*, which is used by IP to identify datagrams that originally belonged to a single datagram that was *fragmented* at some point in the delivery process. Fragmentation of datagrams, or the breaking of datagrams into smaller datagrams, is a common practice in IP networks, and the identification field allows them to be reassembled at the destination. The next three bits in the header are referred to as the *flags field*. The first of the three bits in the flags field is currently unused. It is followed by a one-bit *DF flag*, or *don't fragment flag*, which is used to instruct the network not to break this datagram into smaller pieces. The next bit is the *MF flag*, or *more fragments flag*, which is used to indicate that this datagram is a fragment of a larger datagram and is not the last fragment. The last fragment— or the only fragment, if the datagram has not been broken down—travels without this MF bit set, and since it contains the same identification field as any prior fragments, the network recognizes it as the last fragment of the original datagram. The next 13 bits contain the *fragment offset field*, which is a special way of numbering fragments so that they can be reassembled in the correct order at some point in the future.

The *time to live field* follows in the next eight bits and indicates the datagram's lifetime. While it is sometimes described in terms of steps, or *hops*, on the network, if a particular device holds on to the datagram for a certain period of time, the time to live field is decreased further. Each time the datagram is passed from one point to another on the network, this *hop counter* is decreased by at least one, and when it reaches zero the datagram is discarded. A warning message may then be sent to the originator. Though discarding an old datagram may sound frivolous, this act is an important feature to prevent datagrams from travelling in circles on the network forever. The next eight bits compose the *protocol field*, which indicates the protocol this datagram encapsulates (e.g., TCP). This information allows the destination host to ensure that the datagram will be handled appropriately (e.g., by the TCP software in the host). A 16-bit *header checksum field* follows, and it allows error detection on the header itself.

The next 32 bits contain the 32-bit *source address* field, which indicates the station that originated the datagram. It is followed by the 32-bit *destination address* field, which describes the station on the network that is to receive the datagram. More details regarding the makeup and use of IP addresses are presented in Chapter 8.

The *options field* was included to allow extensions to IP. If it is used, there are bits to identify the type of user options selected. The IP header must be in 32-bit increments since the IHL counts headers only in 32-bit increments; therefore, the options bits are often followed by *padding bits*. If the options do not use an increment of 32 bits, additional padding bits are added to round up the number of bits to the next increment of 32. If no options are present, the IHL is set to indicate that there are only 20 bytes (5 $\times$ 32 bits) in the header.

When the header is complete, user data follows, up to the length specified in the total length field described previously.

While TCP is typically used in conjunction with IP, it does require the overhead of establishing a virtual connection before transmission begins. The *User Datagram Protocol*, or *UDP*, can be used to send individual messages in IP packets when the connection-oriented features of TCP are not required.

Many other protocols besides TCP and IP were originally included in the TCP/IP Protocol Suite, and dozens have been added in the intervening years. Here, we mention only some of the more commonly used ones. When people discuss TCP/IP, they are often referring to all of the related protocols, rather than just TCP and IP. The enhancement of these protocols is largely supervised by the Internet Engineering Task Force (IETF) previously discussed in Chapter 4. Most of the protocols discussed in the following paragraph operate largely at the Applications Layer of the OSI model, though some that are involved in the operation of the network operate at lower layers. The IETF was concerned, not with following strict OSI model boundaries, but with creating a set of protocols that ran effectively on top of TCP or UDP as the Transport Layer, with IP as the underlying Network Layer.

Several protocols are involved in the transmission and reception of electronic mail. The *Simple Mail Transfer Protocol*, or *SMTP*, provides a universal format and method for exchanging electronic mail. It was originally designed for seven-bit ASCII text messages, and messages were often limited in size. It was later extended to allow for more advanced operations through the use of the *Multipurpose Internet Mail Extensions*, or *MIME*. MIME is not limited to ASCII text. It also allows attachments to text messages, including binary data files, executable programs, audio files, image files, video files, and any other type of data of any size. In addition, MIME standardizes the formatting of the text portion of the electronic mail messages. The uniform treatment of carriage returns, trailing spaces, and other formatting characters in the text portion of the mail is fully defined in MIME to help ensure that mail passing through numerous mail systems will not change during conversions.

Mail formatted with SMTP still needs to be retrieved from the mail server in order to be displayed on the user's client application. One protocol used for this purpose is *Post Office Protocol version 3*, or *POP3*. It provides the mechanisms for a user to log in and authenticate with a mail server, download messages, delete messages, and perform other functions on the mail server. Another similar protocol, *IMAP4*, or *Internet Message Access Protocol version 4*, can also be used for this purpose.

The *Telnet* protocol provides a universal method to access a remote server through a TCP/IP network. Telnet allows remote users to perform many of the same functions on the remote host as can be performed by a client user directly attached to the host. The *Rlogin* protocol is a more advanced remote access procedure than Telnet and is specifically tailored to UNIX-based servers. Both of these protocols are best suited to remotely accessing text-based applications.

The *File Transfer Protocol*, or *FTP*, allows remote viewing of file directories as well as transfer of files in either direction across a TCP/IP network. The user interface provided is not that of the remote machine, but is rather that of the FTP software running on the local machine. For example, a PC user does not need to understand the commands used to operate the file system on a remote UNIX server. FTP hides the UNIX file commands from the user, and the files are transferred, or directories are viewed, with the same FTP software commands that would be used if the files were on another PC.

HyperText Transfer Protocol, or *HTTP*, is probably the best known of the high-level protocols used in conjunction with TCP/IP, because it is the protocol most commonly used when accessing the *World Wide Web*. The World Wide Web is a collection of information accessible on the *Internet*, a global IP network discussed in more detail in Chapter 8. HTTP was designed to allow for efficient transfer of information presented in hypertext format, in which users continually bring up one window after another to get more detailed information or sometimes go back to prior windows when they are satisfied. The information itself does not have to be text, as the name "hypertext" implies. In fact, HTTP often is used to carry information that is a combination of text, image, audio, video, and other information. Often, this information is presented using *HyperText Markup Language*, or *HTML*, a document format popular on IP networks, although HTTP is able to transfer information stored in any format.

With the growth of open networks, security concerns have increased, and numerous protocols have been developed to address these issues. A further enhancement to MIME, known as *Secure/Multipurpose Internet Mail Extensions*, or *S/MIME*, adds the exchange of additional information required for public key encryption features, as described in Chapter 6. These features include the ability to encrypt mail for secrecy and to sign it digitally for authenticity. The Secure Sockets Layer protocol, or SSL, adds security functions to data transferred with HTTP, Telnet, or FTP. The IP Security Protocol, or IPSec, allows companies to safely use normally insecure public data networks to interconnect their sites, as discussed in Chapter 8. Both SSL and IPSec are discussed in more detail in Chapter 6.

The *Simple Network Management Protocol*, or *SNMP*, spells out methods for exchanging network management information and is discussed in more detail in Chapter 9. *ICMP*, or *Internet Control Message Protocol*, is used to send messages about unusual events or error conditions in an IP network. Sample error messages include "destination not reachable" or "time to live expired". ICMP can also be used for troubleshooting purposes in order to check if a given destination is present on the network by requesting a reply to an echo message. These are just some of the possible messages in ICMP. A common use of ICMP for troubleshooting that many users are familiar with is the *ping* function. A ping sends an ICMP *echo request* message to a distant computer, and the distant computer returns an ICMP *echo reply* message. This ping allows the sender to verify the presence of another computer and other characteristics of the connection.

ARP, or *Address Resolution Protocol*, allows a user to find out the physical address of a computer with a given IP address. All users on the network are asked if they answer to a particular IP address, and the one who replies identifies himself with his hardware address so messages can in turn be sent to him. More details on the differences between assigned IP addresses and hardware addresses are discussed in Chapter 8.

DHCP, or *Dynamic Host Configuration Protocol*, allows a computer to ask for an IP address and other configuration information when it is first turned on. A server on the network provides an IP address to be used by this computer for a given length of time, known as a *lease time*. If the computer is still turned on at the end of this time, it typically requests a *lease renewal*. If the computer does not request a renewal, the lease *expires*, and the IP address is released back into a pool for use by other users. This leasing system allows for the conservation of addresses for those who need them, and eliminates the need to configure the IP address in the computer. Fixed resources (like a shared printer) that need to be reached by others on an ongoing basis are not good candidates for *dynamic addresses* and are often assigned *fixed addresses*. In this way, users can easily find these shared resources and, once they are installed, the addresses can be used indefinitely. Care must be taken to ensure that duplicate fixed addresses are not given out and that these fixed addresses are outside the range of the pool of dynamic addresses in order to ensure that a dynamic address is not given out by the DHCP server that matches the fixed address of another user.

A variety of transmission options is available for Layers 1 and 2 in an IP network, and the choice of which to implement is left to the user. IP is often used with local area networks, which will be discussed in Chapter 8. These local area networks have their own Layer 1 and 2 protocols. When connecting to an IP network using a telephone line as a serial link at Layer 1, two possible options at Layer 2 are *Serial Line Internet Protocol*, known as *SLIP*, and *Point-to-Point Protocol*, known as *PPP*. *SLIP* simply sends IP packets one after the other, with an extra byte at the beginning of each packet for framing. There are several different SLIP implementations, and sometimes an extra byte is added after each packet as well. Most SLIP implementations do not offer any error correction or detection, relying instead on higher layers to deal with problems. SLIP's primary drawback is that it can carry only IP datagrams; it is not able to carry other protocols.

Due to the many different SLIP implementations, as well as SLIP's inherent limitations, the IETF devised *PPP*. PPP supports link error detection and multiple protocols. The IETF built on past protocols in designing PPP. In fact, the PPP frame format is virtually identical to the SDLC/HDLC/LAP-B frame format shown in Fig. 7-6, though the lengths of some of the fields are adapted slightly for the particular application. One modification is that two fields in PPP replace the "Information" field in SDLC/HDLC/-LAP-B, which contained only the user data. The first one or two bytes identify the *protocol* (e.g., IP) and the next field contains the *payload*, which would include IP packets (or other packets, depending on the protocol being used). In addition, the address is typically set to eight ones, indicating that the frame should be accepted by all recipients. PPP's simplicity and flexibility have made it the protocol of choice when connecting IP networks over telephone lines. The PPP frame is shown in Fig. 7-10.

Some Application Layer protocols in the TCP/IP suite are shown at the top of the protocol *stack* in Fig. 7-11. The term *stack* refers to the layered nature of the protocols, as one is stacked on top of the other in the diagram. The simplified protocol stack shows the choice of the highest layer protocol first, then TCP or UDP as appropriate,

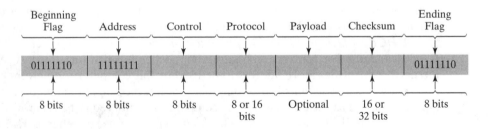

FIGURE 7-10

PPP frame.

Applications Layer	Telnet	SMTP	FTP	DHCP
Transport Layer	TCP			UDP
Network Layer	IP			
Data Link Layer	PPP		Local area network	
Physical Layer	RS-232-C			

FIGURE 7-11

A protocol stack.

followed by IP and the underlying infrastructure. The infrastructure in our example is PPP, assumedly using a modem with an RS-232-C interface. We could also substitute a local area network, which we will discuss further in Chapter 8. The OSI model terminology for the various layers is also included on the side of the figure. The TCP/IP suite was developed independently from the OSI model and is not tied to the OSI definitions, so some protocols in the TCP/IP family do not fit cleanly within the OSI model. We have only chosen a few of the many protocols we have described for this figure just to show an example of a simple protocol stack diagram commonly used in TCP/IP networking discussions. If other protocols had been chosen, there might have been more than one layer needed above the Transport Layer. Creating such a diagram with all of the protocols used today is possible, but it would result in a very large wall chart.

TCP/IP's success can be attributed to several factors. First, the government's communications needs were significant, and the government originally provided funding to develop and refine the technology. The link between government and university research ensured widespread use in the academic community. Since support for TCP/IP was included in most of the popular computer operating systems, it became an easy solution to adopt commercially. In addition, the wide range of protocols, many stretching to the Applications Layer, provides complete solutions for users. From electronic mail to file transfer, the TCP/IP Protocol Suite answered most users' network needs with specific protocols.

This set of specific solutions has helped the TCP/IP Protocol Suite become the most popular standard for universal connection of users in multivendor environments. Is the OSI model still applicable in a TCP/IP-dominated world? The OSI model is still very useful because it provides the common language that allowed networking to evolve to its current state. Clear language alone did not yield full interoperability, however, because at each layer the OSI model allows the user to select among many protocols. The TCP/IP Protocol Suite met users' needs by defining specific protocols for many of these tasks. It took multivendor compatibility out of the model phase and made it a reality.

As with any successful protocol, improvements are always being proposed. Most IP networks today are using IP version 4, also known as *IPv4*. An enhanced version of IP, known as *IPv6*, has been standardized, but its implementation has been slow. It supports longer addresses than IPv4, thereby providing a virtually unlimited supply of addresses. It also provides a shorter header, allowing for faster packet processing. More options are supported, security concerns are better addressed than in the base protocol, and the enhanced service requirements of real-time traffic are handled more effectively. Even with these enhancements, displacing the installed IPv4 equipment would take many years. It is not clear what impact IPv6 will have on the existing IP networks or at what pace it will be deployed.

THE IPv6 HEADER

The *IPv6 header* is simpler than the IPv4 header, because it does not contain all possible information. Other optional extension headers can follow, but the goal would be for the majority of packets to have only the main header shown in Fig. 7-12.

The *Version* field contains four bits identifying this packet as an IPv6 packet. The next eight bits contain the *Traffic class*, which allows different types of traffic (e.g., data, voice, video) to be marked with different classes and therefore handled according to the necessary priority. The next 20 bits contain the *Flow label*, which allows the identification of a particular stream of packets between two computers on the network. If two computers were to exchange voice and data packets simultaneously, this Flow label could be used to distinguish the two separate flows and allow for different bandwidth and delay requirements.

The 16-bit *Payload length* refers to the number of bytes that follow the header in the packet. The header length of 40 bytes is not counted in this Payload length. The *Next header* field contains eight bits and indicates if additional, optional, extension headers follow this header. If this is the last header, this field indicates which layer 4 protocol will need to receive this packet for handling (e.g., UDP or TCP).

The eight-bit *Hop limit* field indicates how many network hops a packet is allowed before being deemed lost and suitable for deletion. This limit prevents lost packets from clogging the network forever. The 128-bit *Source address* indicates the sender of the packet, and the 128-bit *Destination address* refers to the packet's recipient. These long, 128-bit addresses all but ensure enough addresses for the near future.

FIGURE 7-12

IPv6 header.

SUMMARY

A communications architecture is a manufacturer's strategy for connecting its equipment. Most good communications architectures cleanly separate the function of communications from the server's other functions. Originally, each manufacturer had its own proprietary communications architecture, but ISO developed a model for discussing communications between the devices of all manufacturers. The ISO Open Systems Interconnection (OSI) model breaks down the task of communications into seven independent layers, each with its own roles. The Corporation for Open Systems (COS), a group of major computer vendors, was created to facilitate the implementation of intervendor compatibility.

The seven layers of the ISO model, from lowest to highest, are the Physical Layer, the Data Link Layer, the Network Layer, the Transport Layer, the Session Layer, the Presentation Layer, and the Application Layer. The tasks of each layer are clearly defined in the OSI model. Even though the actual transmission of data occurs only at the Physical Layer, all of the other layers communicate with their peers on other devices by modifying or adding to the data being transmitted.

Protocols precisely define the methods used for communications between devices. Most Data Link Layer protocols provide for polling and selecting. Polling is a request for data transmission, and selecting is a request for data acceptance. Most Data Link Layer protocols also use some form of automatic repeat request (ARQ) for error correction. There are different types of ARQ, including stop-and-wait ARQ, in which each frame is acknowledged before the next is sent, and continuous ARQ, in which the next frame can be sent before the previous frame is acknowledged. Continuous ARQ includes go-back-N continuous ARQ, which requires retransmission of all frames sent after an error, and selective repeat continuous ARQ, which requires retransmission only of the frame in error. There are two common classes of protocols, (1) byte-oriented, or character-oriented, and (2) bit-oriented.

IBM's Binary Synchronous Communications, or BSC, is an example of a character-oriented, or byte-oriented, protocol. BSC is a half duplex, stop-and-wait ARQ protocol and is therefore not well suited for satellite transmission. BSC frames can contain user data or control information; control information is sent using entire characters. BSC has a single Control station and one or more Tributary stations.

IBM's Synchronous Data Link Control, or SDLC, is an example of a bit-oriented protocol. SDLC can be used in half duplex or full duplex mode, and it uses go-back-N continuous ARQ; therefore, it can be used for satellite transmission. SDLC is similar to HDLC and LAP-B. SDLC/HDLC/LAP-B frames can be Information Format Frames, Supervisory Format Frames, or Unnumbered Format Frames. In all frames, control information is sent by using individual bits. SDLC/HDLC/LAP-B has one Primary station and one or more Secondary stations.

BSC and SDLC/HDLC/LAP-B are just some examples of common Data Link Layer protocols. Many other protocols are also in use today. Devices that support different protocols can be connected using protocol converters; devices using different character codes can be connected using code converters. The TCP/IP Protocol Suite is a collection of protocols covering a wide variety of tasks likely to be performed on an open network. TCP operates at OSI Layer 4, while IP operates at OSI Layer 3. Some related protocols include SMTP and MIME for electronic mail, Telnet and Rlogin for remote access, FTP for file transfer, HTTP for hypertext, UDP for sending individual packets, and SNMP for network management. S/MIME, SSL, and IPSec are examples of security enhancements that have helped advance the use of the Internet for commercial purposes. At Layer 1 and 2, local area networks are often used as the basis for IP networks. SLIP and PPP are examples of Layer 2 protocols used when IP is sent over serial links like telephone lines. IPv4 is so widely used that the newer IPv6 will have difficulty displacing it.

TERMS FOR REVIEW

ACK0
Acknowledgment
Acknowledgement number
ADCCP
Address Field
Address Resolution Protocol
Advanced Data Communications
  Control Procedures
Application Layer
Architecture
ARP
ARQ
Automatic repeat request
BCC
Best-effort delivery
Binary Synchronous Communications
Bisync
Bit-oriented protocol
Broadcast
BSC
Byte-oriented protocol
Character-oriented protocol
Checksum
Code bits
Code converter
Communications architecture
Communications line control
Connection
Connectionless protocol
Connection-oriented protocol
Continuous ARQ
Control Field
Control information
Control station

Corporation for Open Systems
COS
Data Link Layer
Datagram
Destination address
Destination address field
Destination node
Destination port
DF flag
DHCP
Don't fragment flag
Dynamic address
Dynamic Host Configuration Protocol
Echo reply
Echo request
Endpoint
ENQ
Enquiry
EOT
Error detection and correction
ETX
Expire
FCS
File Transfer Protocol
Final
Fixed address
Flag
Flags field
Flow label
Fragment
Fragment offset field
Frame
Frame Check Sequence Field
FTP

Go-back-N continuous ARQ
HDLC
Header
Header checksum field
Header length field
Higher layer
High-level Data Link Control
HLEN
Hop
Hop counter
Hop limit
HTML
HTTP
HyperText Markup Language
HyperText Transfer Protocol
ICMP
Identification field
I-Frame
IHL
IMAP4
Information Field
Information Format Frame
Intermediate node
Internet
Internet Control Message Protocol
Internet Header Length field
Internet Message Access Protocol version 4
Internet Protocol
IP
IPv4
IPv6
LAP-B
Layer
Lease renewal
Lease time
Line discipline
Link Access Procedure-Balanced
Link-level protocol
Lower layer
MF flag
MIME
Modulo-8
Modulo-128
More fragments flag
Multicast
Multipurpose Internet Mail Extensions

NAK
Network
Network Layer
Next header
Node
Open Systems Interconnection model
Options
Options field
OSI model
P/F bit
PAD
Padding bits
Payload
Payload length
Peer-level communication
Physical Layer
Ping
Point-to-Point Protocol
Polling
POP3
Port number
Post Office Protocol version 3
PPP
Presentation Layer
Primary station
Protocol
Protocol converter
Protocol field
Receiver Not Ready
Receiver Ready
REJ
Reject
Rlogin
RNR
RR
RSVP
S/MIME
SDLC
Secondary station
Secure/Multipurpose Internet Mail
    Extensions
Segment
Selecting
Selective repeat continuous ARQ
Sequence number
Serial Line Internet Protocol

Session Layer
S-Frame
Simple Mail Transfer Protocol
Simple Network Management Protocol
SLIP
SMTP
SNA
SNMP
SOH
Source address
Source address field
Source port
Stack
Station
Stop-and-wait ARQ
Stream
STX
Supervisory Format Frame
SYN
Synchronous Data Link Control
Systems Network Architecture
TCP
TCP/IP

TCP/IP Protocol Suite
Telnet
Time to live field
Total length field
Traffic class
Transmission Control Protocol
Transparent data mode
Transport Layer
Tributary station
Type of service field
UDP
U-Frame
Unicast
Unnumbered Format Frame
Unreliable service
Upper layer
Urgent pointer
User Datagram Protocol
Version field
WACK
Window
World Wide Web

EXERCISES

7-1. What is a communications architecture?

7-2. Name the layers of the ISO–OSI model. Which are the lower layers, and which are the higher layers?

7-3. Explain the functions of each of the layers of the ISO–OSI model.

7-4. What is a protocol?

7-5. Explain the difference between polling and selecting.

7-6. What is ARQ? Compare the different types of ARQ.

7-7. What is the difference between a byte-oriented protocol and a bit-oriented protocol?

7-8. What are main components of an SDLC/HDLC/LAP-B frame?

7-9. What are the main functions of TCP? IP?

7-10. What is the purpose of FTP?

7-11. What was SMTP designed for? What additional capabilities are included in MIME?

7-12. How are HTTP and HTML related?

7-13. How are DHCP and ARP used in IP networks?

7-14. What are the advantages of PPP versus SLIP?

C H A P T E R   8

Data Transport Networks

Data transport networks connect a wide variety of devices located in the same building or across the world. In most cases, data transport networks are not limited by a single vendor's architecture or to a single vendor's equipment, because they provide only the means for transmitting and receiving the data. Data transport networks provide only the OSI model's lower layer functions. As long as the two devices can perform the higher layer functions in a compatible manner, they can use data transport networks to perform the lower layer functions of transmitting and receiving the data.

For example, two French-speaking Americans can send letters written in French to each other through the U.S. Postal Service. The mail carriers do not need to understand French, because they only transport the mail. Packet switching networks, frame relay networks, and local area networks are some examples of data transport networks.

We can classify data transport networks into two types: *wide area networks* and *local area networks*. While wide area networks may span a nation or the globe, local area networks are limited to a single building or campus. Together, they form the basis for most modern networking.

WIDE AREA NETWORKS

Most wide area networks today are based on a technology known as *packet switching*. A *packet switching network*, or *PSN*, provides a *switched service*. For example, a client user can connect to one server now and then connect to a server at a different location later. Data is separated into *packets*, or blocks, and sent through the packet switching network to the destination. At the destination, the packets are combined to form the original stream of data.

Packet switching networks provide a *virtual circuit* between two devices, rather than a continuous connection. In other words, when a packet of data is given to a packet switching network, the network routes the data to its destination. However, if no data is being transmitted, there are no transmission resources being wasted on the connection. Compare this system with the telephone network, through which we can call someone and stay on the line, not saying anything, while still tying up a circuit. In a telephone network, we call this act *circuit switching*. We call a packet switching network's connection a *virtual circuit*, because it appears to the users that they have a virtually continuous connection, and their data always gets to the destination.

Packet switching networks have evolved in recent years. While earlier packet switching networks were based on the *X.25* protocol, the *frame relay* protocol has emerged in recent years as an excellent alternative to X.25. The *Internet* is an even more advanced packet switching network based on the *Internet Protocol (IP)* that has changed the way we communicate electronically. We will discuss all of these protocols and networks later in this chapter. They all share the common principle of breaking data into packets for transmission and reassembling these packets at a later time. We will start our discussion with X.25 packet switching networks and build on these principles with frame relay and IP networks.

Many of today's packet switching networks span great distances. Each location in the network is known as a *switching node*, or simply as a *node*. The switching nodes are connected by *interexchange circuits*, or *IXCs*. A simple packet switching network is presented in Fig. 8-1. These networks can be customer owned, or someone else's packet switching network service can be leased.

Communicating through packet switching networks requires that the devices at each end send data in specially formatted packets. Devices that can communicate by using these packets can be directly attached to a packet switching network. A device known as a *PAD*, or *packet assembler disassembler*, is used to connect devices to an X.25 packet switching network if these devices cannot perform the special packet formatting on their own. A PAD takes data from a client or server, assembles it in a special packet format, and passes it on to the PSN node. Data coming from the packet switching network is disassembled from its packet by the PAD and can then be routed to the server or client.

The PAD might be on the premises of the end user or at the packet switching node itself. A PAD that is part of the packet switching node is often called an *internal PAD*, while a PAD on the premises of the end user is often called an *external PAD* or *terminal handler*. Placement of both types of PADs is also shown in Fig. 8-1.

PSNs combine the advantages of many other transmission methods and add some of their own. Packet switching provides the reliability of a dial-up network, because each packet of data can take a different route. For example, a packet of data could be routed directly from San Francisco to New York, or it might be routed through Chicago. If the transcontinental IXC is not functioning, there are still alternative routes for the packets. Packet switching also has the flexibility of the dial-up network, because users can connect to a different server with each call.

These networks also provide error detection and correction. Packets are checked for errors during transmission and, if necessary, are retransmitted. The packet switching network guarantees that the data received at the destination node is the same as the data transmitted at the source node. The error detection and correction performed by the packet switching network nodes ensure reliable transmission even if the source and destination devices perform no error checking themselves.

Public Packet Switching Networks

Packet switching networks that are owned and operated by service providers for use by their customers are known as *public packet switching networks*. These networks

FIGURE 8-1

Simple packet switching network.

often have entire operations staffs that monitor the network's health. This attention provides a high level of service equivalent to the reliability of the public telephone network. Many of these public packet switching networks have nodes and PADs in numerous cities, affording easy access. For example, a traveling salesperson could access pricing information in a server in the company's home office from anywhere in the country simply by making a local call to the nearest node of the public packet switching network.

One of the first large-scale packet switching networks, known as *ARPANET*, was established to connect U.S. government computing facilities with research universities. Commercial public packet switching networks are operated by various common carriers. For example, SPRINT and MCI now operate the networks originally known as *Telenet* and *Tymnet*, respectively. Each network uses proprietary methods to communicate between packet switching nodes, but they both support similar interface standards.

Packet switching networks are a very cost-effective method of transmitting data. Since no permanent connection is ever established between two devices, users of these networks are typically charged based on the volume of data transmitted. This charge is usually less expensive than comparable dial-up telephone line charges, because the packet switching network effectively shares its bandwidth among many users. For example, the IXCs can be high-bandwidth media, like satellites, microwave, or T-1 circuits. These economies of scale can be passed on to the end users of packet switching networks in the form of lower per-packet costs.

One disadvantage of all packet switching networks, both public and private, is that certain delays may occur, since data may be routed through many nodes before reaching their destination. If an IXC uses satellite transmission, delays are increased even further. A client user in San Francisco, communicating with a server in New York, might notice a 1-second or 2-second delay when using the packet switching network. However, the added benefits of low cost, high reliability, flexibility, easy access, and guaranteed error-free transmission usually outweigh the delay problem in most applications.

The X.25 Standard

The first widely deployed standard for connecting to packet switching networks was the ITU(CCITT) *X.25* standard. Packet switching networks do not have to comply with this standard, but many do. The X.25 standard, which describes all of the functions necessary for communicating with a packet switching network, is divided into three levels. These three levels are similar in function to the lower three layers of the OSI model.

The lowest level, known as the *Physical Level*, describes the actual interface. It conforms to the ITU(CCITT) V.24/V.28 standard, which is similar to the EIA RS-232-C standard, discussed in Chapter 4. The second level, or the *Frame Level*, is the ITU(CCITT) LAP-B bit-oriented data-link protocol that handles error detection and correction, as explained in Chapter 7. The third level, or the *Packet Level*, provides for network-level addressing and call connections.

The X.25 standard defines two types of devices: DTEs, or data terminal equipment, and DCEs, or data circuit-terminating equipment. The packet switching network itself presents an X.25 DCE interface; a server or client that attaches to the packet switching network presents an X.25 DTE interface. For example, a server presenting an X.25 DTE interface would provide a V.24/V.28 type of physical interface, use the LAP-B protocol for transmitting and receiving bits, and then add special packet-level information regarding call setup and addressing.

In addition to the X.25 standard, the ITU(CCITT) developed three standards for describing the operation of an internal PAD. The *X.3* standard defines the PAD's functions and parameters, the *X.28* standard describes the PAD-to-client protocol, and the *X.29* standard describes the PAD-to-server protocol.

The relationship between the X.25, X.3, X.28, and X.29 standards is illustrated in Fig. 8-2. When we discuss the packet-switching network interface standards and protocols, we consider the entire network as a single entity, ignoring the various nodes and IXCs inside.

In Fig. 8-2, client A and server A both communicate to the packet switching network using X.25. Client B, however, is not X.25 compatible and must be attached to the packet switching network through a PAD. Client B communicates with the internal PAD using the X.28 protocol; the PAD's function and parameters are described by X.3. The PAD then communicates with server B using the X.29 protocol. Notice that server B is X.25 compatible and therefore communicates with the network using X.25. Client C is attached to an external PAD on the user's premises. Since the X.25 conversion is done on the user's premises, the packet switching network thinks that client C is X.25 compatible. To the packet switching network, the connection from client C to

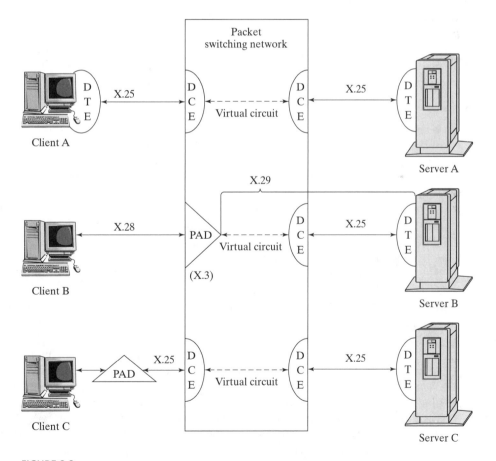

FIGURE 8-2

Interfacing to a packet switching network.

server C is no different than the connection from client A to server A. These examples are just a few combinations, and others certainly are possible.

X.25 packet switching networks can provide many optional services. For instance, a *closed user group* allows users to specify that they want to communicate only with certain users. This service is one security measure used to ensure that only authorized users can access a particular server. For example, a company that links its branch-office computers with headquarters could connect all of its computers through the packet switching network in a closed user group. This configuration permits communication among company computers, but prevents others from accessing these computers. Other possible security services include allowing DTEs to accept *incoming calls only* or to place *outgoing calls only*, depending on the application.

There are two data transmission related services that can be provided by packet switching networks. *Flow control negotiation* allows the DTEs to specify the size of the packet and other parameters. Another service, known as *throughput class negotiation*, allows the DTE to negotiate for a certain bandwidth on a virtual circuit.

Finally, many packet switching networks provide for *reverse charging*, or *collect calls*. This service is the PSN equivalent of a toll-free number, allowing users to contact a particular DTE, with the receiver paying for the service.

While the aforementioned services are referred to by their X.25 names, similar features are available in almost all packet switching networks.

Routing Data in a Packet Switching Network

Perhaps the most interesting facet of packet switching network operation is the routing of data. Earlier, we mentioned that a packet from San Francisco destined for New York might take a direct route or might be routed through a node in Chicago. If we are sending a large block of data through a packet switching network, it will be divided into many packets, or *packetized*. Packets may be of a fixed or variable length, depending on the network. In fact, each packet can take a different route from the source to the destination, though no network tries to vary the routing intentionally.

For example, as shown in Fig. 8-3, packet 1 may leave San Francisco and be routed through Chicago to New York, because the direct transcontinental route to New York may be malfunctioning at that moment. Packet 2, transmitted a tenth of a second later, may take the direct route to New York, because at the moment of transmission, that circuit is available and the other link might be down. Because of the delays involved in routing, it is possible that packet 2 will arrive in New York before packet 1 does.

This method of transmission is analogous to a traveler changing planes in Chicago; not only is the route traveled longer than the direct route, but there also may be some time wasted in Chicago. Traveler 1 may leave San Francisco at 9 AM, change planes in Chicago, and arrive in New York at 7 PM. Traveler 2 may leave San Francisco at 10 AM, take a nonstop flight, and arrive in New York at 6:30 PM. Traveler 2 left later than traveler 1, but arrived in New York earlier. If these travelers were packets, the second 128 bytes of the message would have been received before the first 128 bytes. This sequence of events would be equivalent to reading the second sentence of this chapter before the first. All packets must therefore be *numbered*, and destination packet

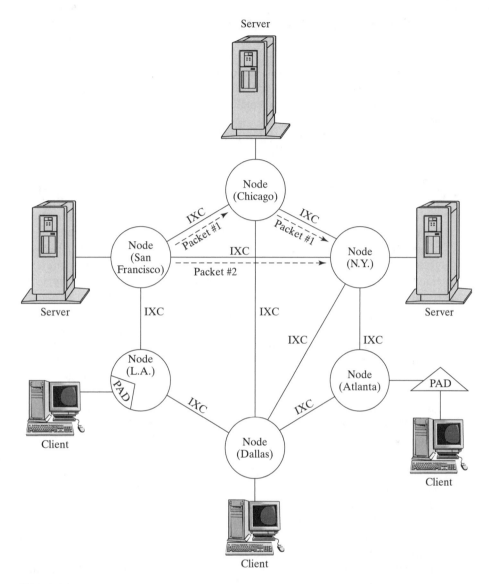

FIGURE 8-3

Routing data in a packet switching network.

switching nodes often provide for the *buffering*, or holding, and *resequencing* of packets Alternatively, the task of buffering and resequencing can be placed in the destination server, depending on the network protocol.

Frame Relay Networks

One of the most important features of the X.25 packet switching networks we have been describing has been error-free delivery of data to its destination. These packet switching networks were developed in an era when unreliable analog modems and analog phone lines were the usual technology on the links between nodes. For this reason, the X.25 protocol included the necessary error-checking and retransmission procedures to ensure that only perfect data were delivered to the destination. Accomplishing this error checking required overhead bits, as well as processing time in each node, even if no error occurred. Any retransmissions that were necessary added even more delay to the data transmission.

With the increased use of digital phone circuits, the chance of errors occurring on the IXCs was dramatically diminished. One type of data transport network that was developed to take advantage of these reliable IXCs is the *frame relay* network. As in X.25 networks, a virtual circuit is provided. The data are broken into pieces—in this case, known as *frames*—and passed through nodes to their destination. However, the nodes do not correct data errors made by the user, and they assume that the users of the network use their own protocol to check for errors and retransmit if necessary. The main advantage of this network is that errors can be resolved once, between the destination and the source, rather than at every node. This feature dramatically reduces the time needed for data to pass through a frame relay network, particularly in comparison to the time needed for data to pass through an X.25 network.

Another difference is that while X.25 operates at Layers 1 through 3 of the OSI model, frame relay operates only at Layers 1 and 2. As long as the protocols used at Layer 3 and above conform to certain frame relay rules, the nodes in the network do not need to open up the frame, look at the entire contents, and generate a new frame. Instead, the frame relay node checks only the frame's header and routes the data accordingly, without creating an entirely new frame. Since the frame is passed on, or relayed, virtually unchanged, the term *frame relay* is used to describe this technique.

This quick relay of frames is possible because the route is calculated initially when the virtual connection is first established. Each frame is marked with a numerical identifier that refers to the next step in the precalculated route. As frames are transmitted through the network, the destination address is not checked; rather, the numerical identifier that refers to the next step in the route is checked and followed. Frame relay switches need to keep a table of active routes, and their numerical identifiers, for quick searching as frames arrive. This table is much smaller than all of the possible routes to all destinations in the network, so frame handling is much faster than a destination-address-based route lookup as is used in X.25 networks. The numerical identifier is broken into two pieces, the *Data Link Path Identifer*, or *DLPI*, and *Data Link Channel Identifier*, or *DLCI*. If multiple connections exist between two locations, they would share the same path identifier, but they would be assigned a unique channel identifier. In this way, connections that follow the same path do not need to generate extra routes and lengthen the lookup table. Simple steps like this one lead to a faster search and provide the speed that makes frame relay popular.

Most of the advantages of packet switching networks are also found in frame relay networks, with the additional benefit of reduced delay and overhead. However, neither packet switching networks nor frame relay networks are ideal for live voice or video transmission, because they lack mechanisms to control delay introduced by the network. While the delay is shorter with frame relay networks, variations in transmission time can pose some problems for voice or video connections if there is excessive traffic. A newer technology, known as *cell relay*, *Asynchronous Transfer Mode*, or simply *ATM*, addresses these timing issues with the help of a supporting transmission infrastructure. Though not as efficient for pure data transmission as frame relay is, ATM is a good technique to use when a mixture of voice, data, and video traffic needs to be carried. ATM is described in detail in Chapter 10.

The Internet

One very widely used data transport network is the Internet. The *Internet*, with a capital "I," uses the TCP/IP protocols. These protocols provide a wide variety of services required in an open network. The Internet began as a network to connect government agencies with universities that were performing research projects, but it has since grown into a large cooperative network, where the users share the operating costs. Many *Internet service providers*, or *ISPs*, interconnect their networks using the protocols of the IETF, as described in Chapter 7. Though the internet now has many commercial users, in addition to governmental and educational users, some of the information accessible from the network has retained the homespun, co-op flavor from its early days.

While the Internet handles the task of delivering data, just as X.25 and frame relay networks do, it has evolved into much more than a data transport network. When people say "the Internet," they are usually referring to the wide range of services and information resources attached to the network, rather than the network itself. Libraries, government agencies, universities, corporations, merchants of all sizes, a variety of information providers, and individuals can be accessed through the Internet. It is also the world's largest public network for transmission of *electronic mail* messages. Another popular application is the use of public bulletin boards, known as *newsgroups*, for exchanging comments, ideas, and information.

The X.25 protocol and frame relay protocol focused solely on delivering data. They were assumed to be a means for large corporations to connect multiple sites, to connect to other corporations, or to simplify remote access to a database. There was no underlying assumption that everyone using an X.25 or frame relay network would use the same Layer 4–7 protocols to provide higher level services. As we described earlier, we can think of these networks as comparable with an overnight letter delivery service, carrying letters in many different languages to people all over the globe. It doesn't matter that the recipient in France can't understand the contents of the letter bound for Italy, because he or she doesn't need to. The letters to France and Italy can travel on the same intercontinental cargo plane, even though their recipients cannot understand each other's languages, because the addressing meets the standards of the cargo company, and the company understands how to deliver these messages.

While IP networks certainly are capable of carrying traffic with different Layer 4–7 protocols, what makes the Internet so useful is that there are worldwide, agreed-upon standards for performing many common Layer 4–7 functions, as described in Chapter 7. The Internet is not necessarily better or worse at transporting data than X.25 or frame relay. However, the Internet is definitely more useful as a global communications infrastructure because it has a better supporting cast of higher layer protocols than either of these other networks, thereby ensuring that the data can be used around the world, not simply transported there.

One example of a product implementing some of these higher layer protocols is a *browser*. A browser is client software that allows a user to view information, typically stored in HTML format, described in Chapter 7. This information stored around the world on computers connected to the Internet is known as the *World Wide Web*. The fact that most browsers support the same higher layer protocols allows users to access any web server attached to the Internet and view the information there. Browsers can be equipped with the public key encryption techniques discussed in Chapter 6 to enhance security, thereby enabling safe online banking, credit-card transactions, and other commercial uses. Another feature common to most browsers is the ability to take on new functions or features by downloading small applications, sometimes called *applets* or *plug-ins*. For example, a plug-in might allow a browser to play a certain type of audio file that the browser was not originally enabled to handle.

Web browsing is enhanced by the capabilities of *search engines*, which index or categorize web data. These search engines have revolutionized research in every field. Most of us are far more likely to enter a phrase in a search engine than to drive to the local library for a quick overview of a topic.

A large website may be represented by a single IP address, but behind the scenes many servers usually handle the traffic. Typically, a large collection of servers, known as a *server farm*, sits behind a *load balancing* device. The load balancing device spreads the traffic evenly among the servers and tracks the connections so the user's session is maintained. Using load balancing, websites can easily be expanded by installing additional servers.

Another popular application is an Internet *chat* session. Supported by the *Internet Relay Chat*, or *IRC* protocol, users can enter into a keyboard chat session with another user, or multiple users. Technology companies, ISPs, and others sometimes offer technical support through chat sessions with a single user. *Chat rooms* refer to publicly established multiuser conversations where people interested in a specific topic can meet electronically. Most chat sessions consist of users typing short messages that others can see, in a keyboarding equivalent of a telephone conference call.

A similar form of conversation in a more private form is the *instant message*, or *IM*. An IM is a short message sent between two users, usually from a separate IM application on their PCs. While a chat session needs to be established with a connection procedure and disconnected when it is finished, an IM can be sent as a stand-alone message, like an email. Unlike an email, instant messages are tied to *presence* information, typically provided by the ISP or corporate presence server. Users create a *buddy list*, or *collaboration group*, of those they like to communicate with. When they log on to the IM or presence server, they and their buddies or colleagues are notified of each other's presence. Users will typically send an instant message only to someone who is logged on, unlike an email, which may be sent without regard to the other user's presence. Instant messaging seems to provide a good compromise between chat and email, because it is sent to someone who is present, but it doesn't need the overhead of an extensive connection setup. Its simplicity has made it a unique electronic conversational medium that has become popular in recent years.

There are several proprietary IM formats today, backed by different service providers. While some efforts are underway to allow conversion between the formats, in most cases you are limited to communicating with customers of the same service you subscribe to. Some IM applications interconnect with cellular phone providers, so IM messages can be translated to text messages on cell phone displays. Unfortunately for users, interoperability between providers remains limited.

Another Internet application is *remote backup*. Even small business or home users can afford offsite data storage using the Internet as their backup medium. Numerous commercial services exist that will store your data and even backup your PC automatically over the Internet. Downloading of audio files, including music, has become another popular application. The *MP3* format for digital audio is a common format used to distribute music electronically. While offering sound quality that is somewhat lower than that of a CD, it provides adequate quality for casual listeners. There are commercial services available that sell music over the Internet legally. There are also numerous *file sharing* networks, where users interconnect their computers and post lists of material they offer to other users. While a convenient way to access free music, the recording artists are not compensated for the copying of files, which has led the recording industry to engage in numerous legal battles. Some users will surely ignore copyright regulations, just as some users copied record albums onto audio cassettes in the analog world.

Rather than using a cumbersome numerical address (e.g., an IP address), we refer to sites with a *Uniform Resource Locator*, or *URL*. An example of a URL is www.prenticehall.com. These URLs are translated into IP addresses by the *Domain Name Service*, or *DNS*. Instead of having to remember 32-bit IP addresses to access web pages, send email, or perform other tasks, we use alphanumeric entries like www.prenticehall.com. DNS servers throughout the Internet help map these easier-to-remember names to their associated numerical IP addresses. There is a hierarchy of servers, beginning with the highest level, known as the *root name servers*. The first request would be to the root name server to find the address of the server containing all of the ".com" domains. This IP address points to the server for the *top-level domain*, in this case ".com". The DNS server at this IP address would, in turn, contain various entries for Prentice Hall's publicly available web resources. In this case, the Prentice Hall DNS server would provide the IP address of its web server. Other entries in the DNS server would include the appropriate destination IP address for Prentice Hall email and any other resources Prentice Hall wanted to make available to Internet users. While Prentice Hall could operate its own DNS server, its ISP could perform the function on its behalf as well.

An analogy to DNS can be found in the public telephone network. Typically the local telephone company offers a directory assistance service where users can dial and request the main phone number for your company. The user dials this number and reaches your company, and then the user can then request your personal phone extension. In a large company, your personal phone number is seldom listed in the phone company's listing, but is instead listed only in this internal directory accessible inside your company. The DNS hierarchy functions in a similar manner. Essentially, you are pointed to one directory after another to narrow in on the information you need, in this case the destination server's IP address.

Retrieving information from the root name server is not usually necessary to process every request. Most DNS servers provide a caching function to remember recent activity and its results. A cache is the computer equivalent of short-term memory, where recent events are stored temporarily until the memory fills, and then new information displaces the oldest information. For example, someone at your company is trying to reach Prentice Hall's website. While no one at your company or ISP may have ever contacted this website before, this is not the first inquiry about a domain name ending in ".com", so the address of the top-level domain's DNS server is already saved, and the request can go directly there without querying the root server. Similarly, if someone else at your company recently contacted www.prenticehall.com, the IP address of Prentice Hall's web server may already be cached at your company's DNS server, and there is no need to ask any other DNS server for it. Your ISP usually has similar caching functions, which explains why some frequently accessed web pages are displayed on your screen almost immediately. The main page for www.verysmallcompany.com may take a lot longer for its first page to display, but subsequent pages tend to display more rapidly.

Access to the Internet from home can be accomplished in many ways. This access is often described as the *last mile* because many people are within a mile of their central office, and it is assumed that a high-speed, digital connection to the Internet is available at the central office. The slowest method is *dial-up access* using an analog phone line and modems to reach up to 56 kbps, as discussed in Chapter 5. A faster approach that uses an existing phone line, but that yields speeds up to several megabits per second by using different modem technology than dial-up modems is known as *digital subscriber line*, or *DSL*, as described in Chapter 10. Cable television lines, described in more detail in Chapter 10, can also be used with special *cable modems* to reach speeds of several megabits per second. Special wireless connections, known as *fixed wireless*, can also reach speeds of several megabits per second for short distances, as described in more detail below. Digital phone lines, known as *ISDN* lines, also described in Chapter 10, are yet another option. In some areas, the local power providers are using technologies to send data over power-lines, though this option is not widely available at this time.

Many people refer to the Internet as the *information superhighway*. Today's Internet, though extremely useful, is certainly not the fastest network imaginable, and it provides only a taste of the advantages of easy access to information. However, it certainly is an excellent model of an open network. Clearly, a much higher speed infrastructure would offer even greater possibilities. Some networking professionals reserve the term "information superhighway" for a future network that will offer a significant increase in capacity over today's Internet and that will seamlessly carry data, as well as high-quality voice and video traffic. Certainly, today's Internet voice and video transmission quality do not satisfy most users. The Internet's capabilities may be expanded and improved to the point where it can offer these services with high quality in the future.

Other packet-based networks offer alternatives for carrying voice and video traffic. One such high-bandwidth network uses ATM protocols for its underlying transmission infrastructure, as described in more detail in Chapter 10. IP and ATM networks will likely coexist for many years to come. More details on the protocols used in routing data in any IP network, not just on the Internet, are provided later in this chapter.

WIDE AREA WIRELESS NETWORKS

There are a variety of wide area wireless network options available. There are numerous broadcast networks, in which short data messages are sent in one direction over specific radio frequencies. Good examples of these types of networks are commercial pager networks, in which beepers are activated and the user even receives information like a phone number to call back. Stock quotes are another example of data broadcast in one direction only—to the users.

For those desiring two-way data communications over wide areas, there are several choices. Considering a portable-computer user as an example, one wireless approach is to use the existing cellular telephone network and a special modem. The special modem is able to interact with the cellular phone network's special dialing commands and signals, but once connected it operates like a normal modem. The transmission and reception capabilities of the user's cellular phone connect this special modem to the cellular network. The cellular network passes the modem signals on to the land-based telephone network, where they will probably reach a standard modem. Unfortunately, signal quality on analog cellular networks is notoriously poor, a problem that could cause frequent retransmissions between error-correcting modems or even cause the connection to be terminated.

This situation improves dramatically on digital cellular systems. Though these systems do not guarantee error-free transmission, they bring cellular systems to a level of quality closer to that of the land-based telephone network. These digital cellular systems, including the 2G, 2.5G, and 3G technologies described in Chapter 2, are excellent options, but not all areas offer consistent coverage and bandwidth.

Many cellular carriers and other wireless data providers offer another service called *Cellular Digital Packet Data*, or *CDPD*. This packet data service can operate over the same channels as the existing analog cellular network, much as X.25 networks can operate over analog phone lines using modems. Instead of using a modem and connecting the computer to a cellular phone, the user connects the computer to a special device that combines the modem, radio transmitter/receiver, and other functions. This device operates independently and does not need to be connected to a cellular phone, although it does communicate with the network operated by a cellular carrier or other provider. This device formats the data according to the CDPD protocol and encrypts it for security. The CDPD network and mobile device can check the data for errors and request retransmission if necessary. If the destination is not a mobile user, most CDPD networks convert the data back to its original format and then transmit it over standard modems on the land-based telephone network. Most CDPD networks take advantage of spare bandwidth on voice channels in the existing cellular networks, minimizing the cost of transmission. CDPD essentially provides the benefits of a packet switching network for the wireless portion of the connection. Another service available in some areas is *General Packet Radio Service*, or *GPRS*. An enhancement to GSM, and it provides data rates up to 170 kbps.

Many other proprietary schemes are used in private networks, and standards continue to evolve in this area. The goal of a universal communications method between wireless devices and land-based networks still seems elusive. There is a broader goal of a *personal communications service*, or *PCS*, in which calls follow a user as the user travels. A single cordless handset that could be used at home, on a mobile basis, and in the office is being widely discussed. At home, the handset would operate as a cordless phone. Outside, or in the car, it would automatically switch to a cellular service, and when you arrive at work it would talk to your company's phone system. Users could also direct their calls to traditional wired phones when they reach their destination. Although most of the technology for providing this type of service exists, choosing which methods to use and making the service commercially viable are still topics of heated debate.

While many products are marketed today under the name "PCS," some are just a combination of existing services that use conventional digital cellular technology, like the TDMA or CDMA systems described in Chapter 2. The GSM standards also discussed in Chapter 2 offer the most promise as a global infrastructure for carrying this PCS service. Wireless data communications schemes will probably be greatly affected by the evolution of PCS standards in the coming years. Though widespread deployment of PCS is envisioned, it is not yet clear if demand will be sufficient to support this deployment in less-developed areas of the world.

Fixed wireless is a technology that can be used to connect residential or business customers to the Internet. An antenna is placed on the customer's premises in order to interconnect with the ISP. Three standards in use today are *WiMax, IEEE 802.16*, and *Local Multipoint Data Services*, or *LMDS*. Typical speeds range from 250 kbps to 1 Mbps, but they vary greatly depending on distance and terrain. Since these technologies are not widely deployed, it is hard to determine which, if any, will prevail in the market over time. As these technologies improve, the advantages of using a wired network may be reduced.

LOCAL AREA NETWORKS

Unlike wide area networks, *local area networks* are limited in their geographic scope. A local area network, or *LAN*, is a privately owned data communications system that provides reliable high-speed, switched connections between devices in a single building, campus, or complex. Networks that extend outside a single building, campus, or complex are not considered local area networks. Like packet switching networks, local area networks provide switched connections, allowing users to connect to different computers at different times. The transmission speed of local area networks is often many millions of bits per second, providing high-bandwidth connections suitable for almost any application, including lengthy file transfers. The limited geographic area of a local area network usually allows the customer to own all of the wiring; therefore, the speed of the LAN is limited largely by the bandwidth of the transmission media chosen.

Most of today's local area networks are highly reliable, with extremely low error rates. Since few local area networks span more than a mile or two, the probability of transmission errors is much smaller than in a wide area network. Local area networks are typically used to connect desktop computers, known as *personal computers*, with each other or with other servers; other clients, workstations, and larger servers can also be connected. A typical application conducted with personal computers over a LAN is the file transfer mentioned previously.

Users of a local area network can exchange files as well as share resources. One example of resource sharing is when several personal computers share a single high-speed laser printer; each user prints infrequently, but each user may need the special features and speed of the laser printer. The printer may be attached to a personal computer, which also must be attached to the network. We say that this personal computer acts as a *print server* for the network because it provides access to the printing services for other users. Sometimes, an entire department accesses a single file-storage device, such as a high-volume disk attached to one personal computer; this personal computer acts as a *file server*. Providing access to remote resources located off the network is the job of a *communications server*. Typically, a communications server is attached to both a modem and the data network, thereby allowing network users to use the modem to access remotely located computers and services. Other specialized server functions can also be provided on a local area network. The servers may be personal computers used for other functions as well as for their role as a server.

A common approach to computing today is the *client/server* architecture. This approach calls for applications to be distributed around an organization's network on servers that users can access as needed. Rather than running all applications on a single mainframe, users can access programs on servers attached to the network when they need a common database or resource.

Information-systems managers have taken advantage of the emerging standards in server platforms to drive down the cost of their computing power. Rather than locking you into a single vendor, as might occur with a mainframe, a client/server architecture allows users to select industry-standard platforms for their applications and provides appropriate computational power for applications and users based on their needs. Client/server architectures typically have some part of the program execute on the user's workstation, executing only the database management system centrally. For example, the graphical user interface may be implemented on the client, and the rest of the operations may be performed on the server.

A client that is very simple, requiring relatively little processing power, is sometimes called a *thin client*. A computer that has very little processing power and little or no local permanent data storage and that is designed to run thin clients is often called a *network computer*. This type of computer puts the burden on the network to exchange the data between the client and server for almost every operation and makes the network computer the modern-day equivalent of a dumb terminal. In this case, the network computer is typically equipped with a graphical user interface, unlike the dumb terminals of the past.

The widespread deployment of the Internet browser has provided a universal client on almost everyone's desktop. Many organizations have chosen to take advantage of this situation, designing their internal corporate applications based on TCP/IP protocols. This system allows the same browser to access both Internet applications and internal applications. The applications or servers accessible only to clients located inside the company, and inaccessible to external users, are sometimes referred to as the *intranet*.

A *demilitarized zone*, or *DMZ*, is an area in between the Internet and an intranet, where some users from the public Internet are provided access to some of a company's servers. For example, servers that allow suppliers to log on and check the status of orders could be placed in the DMZ. The company's proprietary data could remain on servers back in the intranet. Making a portion of your network accessible to outsiders in this limited way creates an *extranet*.

The flow of data between the clients (users) and servers (databases or applications) can generate a tremendous amount of traffic on modern LANs. This traffic level must be carefully considered when installing and managing local area networks.

Local area networks can be implemented using two different types of control. *Centralized control* requires a single device that controls the entire network. Failure of this controller disables the entire network. Changing the number or configuration of devices on the network requires more than simple rewiring. The central controller needs to be notified of any addition, removal, or moving of devices in the network.

Distributed control, used by many of today's local area networks, requires no central device; instead, all of the devices attached to the network actually run the network. The instructions for transmitting and receiving messages must be built into all of the devices attached to the network, usually using a combination of hardware and software. For example, 10 personal computers in a local area network using distributed control all share the responsibility of running the network; each personal computer usually contains a special network interface card and software.

One advantage of distributed control is that adding another user to the network requires only installing the interface card and software in the new user's personal computer and then attaching the personal computer to the network. No central processor or controller needs to be notified of the addition, because each device speaks for itself on the network and shares in the task of operating the network. These networks can therefore be expanded incrementally. Theoretically, the network hardware cost for 101 users is only 1% more than that for a network of 100 users. Companies can start with small networks and enlarge them as their needs increase. There is an upper limit to the number of users on all networks, but this limit varies, depending on the bandwidth of the media, as well as the applications used.

Even with distributed control, if one device attached to the network malfunctions or sends erroneous messages, it can throw the entire network into disarray. Many local area networks make some provision for a centralized monitoring function to shut down network stations that are causing problems.

Local Area Network Topologies

Local area networks can take many different forms or shapes, known as *topologies*. Some of these topologies are illustrated in Fig. 8-4.

In a *mesh network*, each device is connected by a cable to every other device in the network. This configuration may be convenient for small networks, but it becomes awkward and expensive as a network grows to contain more than a few devices.

In a *star network*, all of the devices are connected by cable to a single central point, where some type of controller is located. This centralized control requirement is an often-cited disadvantage of star networks. In a star network, all data is routed through the central point.

A *bus network* has many devices connected to a single cable, known as the *bus*. Typically, there are limitations to the length of the bus in these networks. The point at which a device connects to a bus is known as the *tap*. A *tree network* is similar to a bus network, except that there may be many different branches off the main bus. This configuration allows many closely located devices to attach to the network with only a single tap on the main bus. There is no central control point in a bus or tree network, so new devices can be added simply by tapping onto the network at any point.

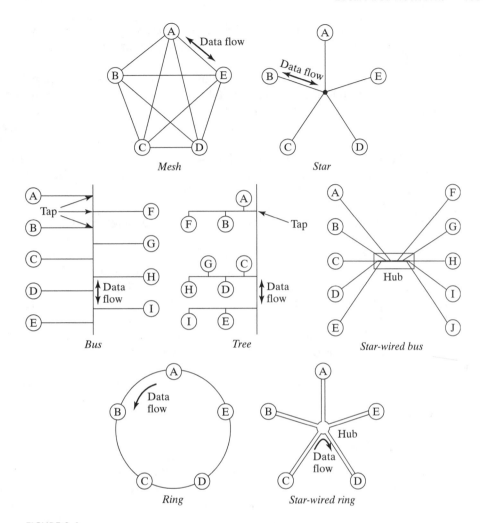

FIGURE 8-4

Local area network topologies.

Disconnecting a tap, in turn, removes a device from the network. Every message placed on a bus travels past all users.

A *ring network* connects all devices in a continuous loop, though it doesn't have to be a perfect circle. Data in a ring network usually flow only in one direction; therefore, data may circle around 90% of the ring to reach a neighboring device. There is no central controller in a ring network either, so devices can be added simply by inserting them anywhere in the ring, or they may be removed from the network by disconnecting them from the ring and closing the ring at that point.

A device known as a *hub* can be used to simplify the wiring of ring or bus networks. In both cases, the hub changes only the physical layout of the network and does not affect the way that the network operates. Messages may go from each user to the hub, but once a message is inside the hub, the original bus or ring topology is simulated.

In a *star-wired bus network*, a miniature bus is created inside the hub. Logically, the network is still a bus, and the hub does not route the messages to any specific destination. Every message is sent to the hub, the hub then retransmits each message to every user, and the user determines whether or not to read and process the message, based on the address in the message header. This type of network physically connects the users to a central hub in a star configuration with twisted pair, coax, or fiber optic cable. In fact, you could think of this network as a three-inch bus with 20-foot taps to the users, rather than as a traditional long bus winding through a building, with short taps to each user. In a *star-wired ring network*, a miniature ring is created inside the hub. Data still flows one way in a continuous loop, but between each user the data return to the hub.

When buildings already have wire running to each office, hubs provide a convenient way to implement bus and ring networks. Users can be removed from or added to the network at the hub, simplifying installation and maintenance. Most hubs can also automatically disconnect a failed device that is generating erroneous data.

In the star-wired bus and star-wired ring topologies, the hub is used to maintain the original network design while also simplifying the wiring. Devices known as *switching hubs*, or simply as *LAN switches*, do not follow this model; instead, they actually repeat the messages only to the correct user. They create true star networks and are used when traffic and performance requirements demand that stations receive only data destined for them. Switching hubs deliver messages based on their address, acting more like a packet switch than like the standard hubs previously described. As the cost of these switches has dropped, they are displacing hubs in most LANs.

Baseband vs. Broadband Transmission

There are two basic types of local area network transmission. *Baseband* local area networks transmit digital signals directly on the cable, while *broadband* local area networks use carrier frequencies to modulate the signal. Whereas baseband LANs allow only a single data conversation or channel at any given time, broadband LANs can be divided into many different channels, allowing for multiple data conversations simultaneously.

Typically, baseband local area networks are less expensive to implement, but they are limited in their capacity and length. Broadband local area networks, though more expensive to purchase and maintain, usually provide higher bandwidth transmission and have less restrictive length limitations. Neither type is clearly superior; thus, the user's applications and cost requirements determine the appropriate choice.

The transmission media chosen depends on whether the LAN is baseband or broadband, as well as on the bandwidth needed. Most local area networks use twisted pair wire or coaxial cable, though some use fiber optic cable for high-speed applications. The relative bandwidths of various transmission media are presented in Chapter 5.

Local Area Network Access Methods

When more than one device needs to share a communications line, *access methods* are required to specify which devices can transmit data at any given moment. We have already discussed one such method, known as *polling and selecting*. This technique is not often used in local area networks, since a central controller is required to poll and select the devices.

Some broadband networks use *frequency division*, separating the communications line into many different frequency channels. Some baseband networks employ *time division* techniques, allocating time slots to each device for transmission. These local area network access methods are similar to their point-to-point multiplexing counterparts, frequency-division multiplexing and time-division multiplexing, explained in Chapter 5.

Contention.   Among the most common types of access methods in use today are the *contention* methods. *Ethernet*, a widely used local area network we will discuss later, uses contention. The various contention methods allow devices to transmit if the line is free; if the line is busy, devices must wait before transmitting. Contention methods are effective because local area networks use high-bandwidth transmission, and a typical message is relatively short. For example, a 40-page file may contain 120 kilobytes, or 960 kilobits, of data, and a 10 Mbps local area network could transmit the entire file in less than a tenth of a second. Since most messages are shorter than a 40-page file and typical devices only use the network occasionally, the network is available most of the time.

Infrequently, two devices transmit at the same time, and a *collision* occurs. Collisions cause data to be lost, and the way the network recovers from a collision depends on the access method. If too many devices are placed on a contention network, many collisions occur and the network's performance deteriorates. A few devices transmitting many large files have the same effect.

One contention method is *random access*, where devices transmit whenever they please. With this method, devices assume that the line is free, because statistically the network is free most of the time. For this method to succeed, there must be some acknowledgment by the receiver that the message arrived; otherwise, the sender cannot be sure that a collision didn't occur.

If we think of a three-way telephone conference call, random access is the equivalent of individuals who speak whatever is on their minds, without regard to whether anyone else is talking or not. If these individuals don't get an answer, they try speaking again.

A more refined contention method is known as *carrier sense multiple access*, or *CSMA*. In CSMA, the device with data to transmit listens to the network to determine if it is being used. If the network is free, the device transmits the data and waits for an acknowledgment from the receiving device. Once the transmitter begins sending data, other devices, also using CSMA, do not transmit, because they are listening and know that the network is busy. Occasionally, if two devices begin transmitting at exactly the same time, collisions may still occur.

When collisions occur, the transmitted data is garbled and the acknowledgment message is not returned by the receiver. Eventually, after a set time limit, the transmitter gives up waiting for the acknowledgment and retransmits the message. CSMA is an improvement over random access, because at least the transmitter makes an attempt to check if someone else is using the network before sending data. However, the transmitter must still wait for a period of time before deciding that the acknowledgment is not forthcoming due to a collision.

Returning to our three-way telephone conference call example, CSMA is the equivalent of a person who checks to see if anyone is talking and, if not, begins speaking and stops listening. After speaking, this person begins listening again.

CSMA is a type of contention method that uses *collision avoidance* techniques. A further improvement on CSMA adds *collision detection*. In this method, known as *carrier sense multiple access/collision detection*, or *CSMA/CD*, the device listens not only before transmitting, but also while transmitting. Ethernet networks, discussed in more detail later, use this CSMA/CD technique. The device first checks to make sure that the network is free and then begins transmitting. If all goes well, the transmitting device hears its own transmission loud and clear. However, if another device begins transmitting at the same instant, both transmitters hear not only their own signals, but also the other signal, or some mixture of the two. Both of the transmitters hear the collision and immediately stop transmitting. After waiting a certain period of time, the transmitters again attempt to send the message. The process of halting transmission, waiting, and then retransmitting is known as *backoff*.

The same method is used for the retransmission after a collision: the transmitter listens both before transmitting, to avoid another collision, and during transmission, to detect if another collision occurs. Remember that collisions are relatively infrequent, since they occur only when two devices begin transmitting at roughly the same time.

In our conference call example, CSMA/CD is the equivalent of a person who first listens to be sure that no one else is talking and then begins speaking. This person keeps listening while talking and realizes when someone else starts speaking at the same time. Both people are using CSMA/CD, and both stop talking, back off, and wait a little while before speaking again. Typically, the more aggressive person jumps in almost immediately and starts talking again, while the other person might wait longer.

An essential aspect of CSMA/CD is the determination of how long a device must wait after detecting a collision before attempting retransmission. Clearly, this waiting time must be different for the two transmitters that collided; otherwise, they would continue to repeat their collision forever. For instance, in our conference call example, if two people's statements collided and each person waited exactly 10 seconds after the collision to speak again, the collision would occur again.

These different contention methods regulate when devices can transmit and how they recover from collisions. How do devices know when to receive data? Whether a network is using random access, CSMA, or CSMA/CD, a device must listen to all data on the network when it is not trying to transmit data. Each message contains a unique address, specifying the intended destination. All devices except the receiver simply ignore the message.

PRIORITY AND RANDOM BACKOFF

It is possible to build devices with different retransmission times, thereby creating a *priority backoff* scheme. After a collision, the device with the shortest retransmission time would always get to retransmit first, and the device with the longest retransmission time would retransmit last.

Priority backoff

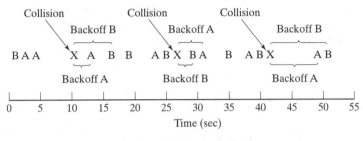

Random backoff

Key: A = transmission successfully completed by device A
        B = transmission successfully completed by device B
        X = collision

FIGURE 8-5

Priority and random backoff.

These devices would be the equivalent of aggressive and shy people in a conversation. More typically, a *random backoff* process is used, in which each device picks a random amount of time to back off for each collision. This system ensures fairness and, as long as the devices are good at picking truly random numbers for each collision, practically eliminates the possibility of repeated collisions.

The difference between priority backoff and random backoff is presented in the two diagrams shown in Fig. 8-5. An "A" represents a transmission completed successfully by device A, a "B" indicates a transmission completed successfully by device B, and an "X" represents a collision between the two devices. As long as each device transmits at a different time, no collisions occur. When a collision does occur, notice that with priority backoff, device A has a higher priority and always gets to retransmit first. In random backoff, sometimes device A gets to retransmit first after a collision, and sometimes device B gets to retransmit first. This random backoff CSMA/CD method is used extensively in Ethernet networks.

Token passing.   Another LAN access method besides contention is known as *token passing*. A *token* is simply a pattern of ones and zeroes with a special meaning, much like the control information used in the link-level protocols presented in Chapter 7. Two common types of tokens are *free tokens* and *busy tokens*; each is a different pattern of bits. All devices in a token-passing network constantly listen to the network. A device can transmit only when it sees a free token.

We assume a ring topology for our example of token passing because this topology is the easiest to visualize. The various steps of transmission using a *token ring network* are shown in Fig. 8-6. Initially, a free token circulates around the ring shown in Fig. 8-6. This token indicates that the network is free and available for use. A device that wants to transmit data must wait for the free token to reach it.

In step 2 of Fig. 8-6, device B sees the free token that is circulating and decides to transmit. Device B then changes the free token to a busy token and adds the data to be transmitted, along with the address of the recipient (device D), its own return address, and some bits for error checking and monitoring. This new package of data now circulates on the ring, and any other devices that want to transmit data have to wait, because there is no free token on the ring. When the data reaches its destination, the receiver (device D) recognizes its address.

As shown in step 3 of Fig. 8-6, device D then copies the data, changing some status bits to indicate that the data was received, and lets the data continue around the ring. When the data reaches the original transmitter, as shown in step 4 of Fig. 8-6, the transmitter removes the data from the ring. The transmitter can then release the network by generating a free token, as shown in step 5. The free token then circulates

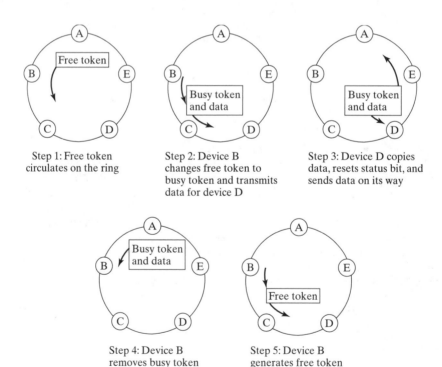

Step 1: Free token
circulates on the ring

Step 2: Device B
changes free token to
busy token and transmits
data for device D

Step 3: Device D copies
data, resets status bit, and
sends data on its way

Step 4: Device B
removes busy token
and data from ring

Step 5: Device B
generates free token

FIGURE 8-6

Operation of a token ring.

around the ring as before, and other devices can transmit their data in the same manner. We are now back to step 1, and the network is free again.

The token-passing networks have several features used to maintain order in the network. Notice that the data makes a complete circle around the ring, giving the transmitter confirmation that the data was not lost. Also, transmitters cannot monopolize the network; instead, they must generate a free token after a certain time period. One of the devices on the network, known as the *active monitor*, in addition to being a user of the network, is responsible for monitoring the network. An active monitor provides the first free token when the network is started. In addition, if a free token is lost due to a transmission error, the active monitor generates a new free token. Other devices on the network act as *standby monitors*, waiting to step in and fill the role of the active monitor if the current active monitor should fail.

Local Area Network Standards

Local area networks provide physical transmission of data, as well as error detection and correction. Therefore, we often think of local area networks as providing the Physical Layer and Data Link Layer functions of the OSI model.

Many of the standards for local area networks were developed by an IEEE committee called *IEEE 802*. This committee divided the Data Link Layer function of local area networks into two main parts. The first, known as *Medium Access Control*, or *MAC*, describes the access methods used in a network, like CSMA/CD or token passing. The second, known as *Logical Link Control*, or *LLC*, describes some other functions that can be used in conjunction with all access methods, like error checking and reliability. Together, the Medium Access Control and Logical Link Control standards describe the way local area networks implement the Physical and Data Link Layers of the OSI model.

Each of the IEEE 802 subcommittees formulates standards on different areas. The *IEEE 802.1* standard provides an overview of local area networks, as well as of methods of connecting networks and systems management. The *IEEE 802.2* standard describes the Logical Link Control methods that can be used in conjunction with all IEEE 802-compatible networks. The *IEEE 802.3* standard describes the CSMA/CD Bus Medium Access Control method already discussed. The *IEEE 802.4* standard describes the *token bus* method for Medium Access Control; the token bus is a variation on the token ring, which is described by the *IEEE 802.5* standard. The *IEEE 802.6* standard describes Medium Access Control methods for a *metropolitan area network*, or *MAN*. A metropolitan area network is larger in geographical scope than a classical local area network and is not considered a local area network at all by many experts.

There are other IEEE advisory groups that make recommendations about specific local area network topics that may affect all of the other subcommittees, though they may not result in standards themselves. These groups include the *IEEE 802.7* committee for broadband transmission, the *IEEE 802.8* committee for fiber optics, and the *IEEE 802.9* committee for integrating voice and data on local area networks. The *IEEE 802.11* standards cover wireless LANs, as discussed later in this chapter.

The *Manufacturing Automation Protocol*, or *MAP*, is a user-defined networking standard originally developed by General Motors. The MAP standard describes a token bus network, like IEEE 802.4. MAP is designed to integrate operations on the factory floor by tying together control computers, robot welders, and other intelligent devices that previously operated independently. Many products are already built by automated equipment, and the MAP network ties all of this equipment together, allowing an engineer who is making a design change to communicate the change automatically to the equipment on the production line in seconds. Some users are demanding MAP compatibility for all future factory equipment.

Another user-defined standard, known as the *Technical and Office Products* specification, or *TOP*, was developed by Boeing Computer Services. TOP is similar to MAP, even though it uses the CSMA/CD bus, much like IEEE 802.3. TOP is designed with the office and computing environment in mind, rather than the factory floor.

Widely Used Local Area Networks

There are many different types of local area networks in use today. Two of these, however, have captured the most attention. Equipment compatible with these networks, *Ethernet* and *token ring*, is available from many different vendors.

Ethernet was originally used by DEC (now Compaq), Intel, and Xerox, among other companies, and it is by far the most widely used LAN today. The original Ethernet is a bus network that uses the CSMA/CD access method found in IEEE 802.3. Ethernet uses baseband transmission, and it initially operated only at 10 Mbps using coaxial cable. The *10BASE-T* standard has become one of the most popular methods of cabling Ethernet networks. It is a 10 Mbps, baseband, IEEE 802.3 standard for transmitting Ethernet over twisted pair wire, hence the name 10BASE-T. It requires the use of hubs in a star-wired bus configuration for half duplex transmission or LAN switches for full duplex transmission. A fiber version, known as *10BASE-F*, is also available, and higher speed versions will be discussed later.

THE ETHERNET FRAME

The latest version of the Ethernet frame, also known as the IEEE 802.3 frame, is shown in Fig. 8-7. It is the most widely used frame in data communications today.

The first eight bytes include the seven-byte *Preamble*, followed by a one-byte *Start-of-Frame Delimiter*, or *SFD*. Together, these eight bytes are composed of an alternating series of 62 ones and zeroes, followed by 2 ones, used to indicate the start of the frame. The receiving device can use these early bits to sync up with the transmission speed. In early versions of Ethernet, the preamble was considered to be eight bytes long, with no Start-of-Frame Delimiter; however, the bit pattern was the same, so the change is in name only.

The next fields contain the six-byte *Destination Address*, or *DA*, and the six-byte *Source Address*, or *SA*. The source address refers to the transmitter's identity, and the destination address refers to the intended recipient. These 48-bit fields uniquely identify every Ethernet device or station on a network. The IEEE assigns blocks of addresses to each device vendor, and the vendor is responsible for uniquely identifying each card inside its address block. When a vendor has produced enough devices to exhaust its block of addresses, the IEEE provides it with a new address

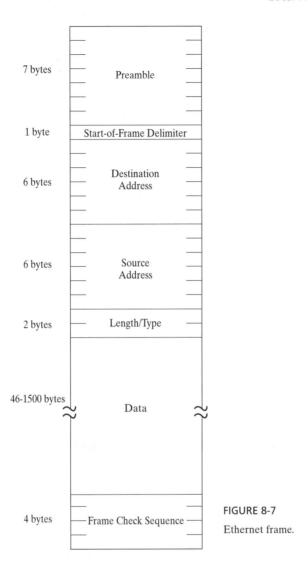

FIGURE 8-7
Ethernet frame.

block. As long as all vendors follow the rules (and they almost always do), every Ethernet device is given a unique address.

Ethernet provides for sending to users singly or in groups. When the first bit of the 48-bit address is a zero, the address is a unicast address, and the message goes to a single station only. When the first bit of the address is a one, it is a multicast address, and multiple stations are able to receive the message. The most widely used multicast address, known as a broadcast address, is made up of all ones. All stations on the network receive a broadcast message.

The next two bytes contain the *length/type field*. Ethernet is often used today without IEEE 802.2 Logical Link Control. In this case, this two-byte field indicates the type of protocol contained in the Ethernet frame (e.g., IP). When Ethernet is used in conjunction with IEEE 802.2, these two bytes indicate the lengths, in bytes, of the *data field* that follows in the Ethernet frame. In that case, the IEEE 802.2 Logical Link Control is responsible for identifying which higher layer protocol in the receiving device must act on this frame.

To accommodate both methods, the types have been assigned numbers greater than the 1500-byte maximum length of an Ethernet data field. The receiving station, upon reviewing the length/type field, can easily determine if it contains the data field length or the protocol type, since numbers 1500 or lower refer to the length and those higher than 1535 refer to the protocol type (1501–1535 were left unused). In most cases, IEEE 802.2 is not used, and the Layer 3 packets (e.g., IP datagrams) are inserted directly into the data field.

The next field contains the *data*, which can be anywhere from 46 to 1500 bytes long. It is followed by a four-byte *Frame Check Sequence*, or *FCS*, which is used for error detection of the destination address, source address, length/type field, and data field. It uses a 32-bit Cyclical Redundancy Check, or CRC, as described in Chapter 6.

Using Ethernet with standards like 10BASE-T allows for half duplex operation. In half duplex operation, as with traditional CSMA/CD, ideally only one user transmits at a time. This configuration is suitable when all users are attached to a single cable, like a coaxial cable in a bus network, or when a simple hub is used, as in a star-wired bus. It is also possible to connect two users with a single 10BASE-T connection using half duplex operation.

When a LAN switch, or switching hub, is used to connect each of the devices in a star configuration, there is no need to restrict how many users talk at one time, as long as the switch has sufficient capacity and buffering. With one LAN user attached to each switch port, full duplex operation becomes possible. There is a dedicated path from the switch to the user and from the user to the switch, and either party can transmit at any time. Similarly, two users can be connected to each other using 10BASE-T in full duplex. The same frame format used in half duplex will work in this configuration, but since no one shares his or her transmission link with anyone else, a user can transmit at any time.

One advantage of full duplex, switched connections is that some traffic problems are reduced. If the problem is caused by traffic evenly distributed among many users, switching can eliminate the collisions that occurred on a shared network. If the traffic is concentrated in one place (e.g., when many users are trying to reach a certain server), then a switched infrastructure will not eliminate the problem. In this case, a higher speed link is required to connect that server to the switch. Otherwise, messages would be queued up in a buffer on the switch at the port to which the busy server is connected, so the users would still notice some performance degradation.

Another popular network used in some special applications is the *token ring network*, which uses a star-wired ring configuration. IBM deployed the first popular commercial version. Token passing is accomplished by conforming to the IEEE 802.5 standard. The *IBM Token Ring Network* used baseband transmission to transmit data first at 4 Mbps and later at 16 Mbps, using unshielded twisted pair cable. Even higher speeds are discussed later. While IBM was the first major vendor to get behind the token ring, many other vendors now offer token ring products.

There were additional local area networks in use during the early years of LANs. The *IBM PC Network* was a 2-Mbps network that used broadband CSMA/CA. AT&T also had two local area networks. AT&T's *Starlan Network* was a star network based on IEEE 802.3, designed mainly for connecting personal computers in the office environment. AT&T's *Information Systems Network*, or *ISN*, provided connections to a wide variety of devices, including servers, clients, terminals, and personal computers, by using a combination of local area network and packet switching network-transmission methods. Most of these networks have now been replaced by Ethernet or token ring networks.

Literally hundreds of vendors produce devices compatible with Ethernet and the token ring. There are also many different special-purpose, proprietary networks that do not meet any particular standard. Most users, however, prefer a standard network.

Higher Speed Local Area Networks

Several IEEE standards have been developed to allow operation at 100 Mbps and above. Fast Ethernet is a version of IEEE 802.3 that operates at 100 Mbps. 100BASE-T operates much like 10BASE-T, using Ethernet protocols, twisted pair wire, baseband transmission, and hubs in a star-wired bus architecture. There are also fiber versions available. Fast Ethernet is now widely deployed, and devices that support both regular 10 Mbps and 100 Mbps are also available. The ability to switch between several speeds based on the highest speed of two connected devices is known as *autonegotiation*.

Gigabit Ethernet operates at a billion bits per second, or 1 gigabit per second (Gbps). While Fast Ethernet simply takes the existing Ethernet protocol and runs it ten times faster, it is not so simple at gigabit speeds. Half duplex CSMA/CD transmission relies on every station detecting a collision every time one occurs. As a result, the maximum distance between stations is limited, because the time it takes for a frame to travel this maximum distance must be less than the time it takes to send the shortest possible frame. If the maximum distance exceeded this limit, it would be possible for a station to finish sending a small frame and sense no collision, when in fact a collision did occur moments later on the far end of the network. At a billion bits per second, the time to send a small frame would be very short, thereby severely limiting this maximum distance between stations. Special techniques are applied to correct this problem, including allowing stations that transmit very short frames to transmit several frames at a time. Since most users of Gigabit Ethernet are interested in high performance, they are likely to be in a switched, full duplex environment. In this environment, where the connection from the switch to the user is dedicated rather than shared, collisions are eliminated and the distance issue is no longer relevant.

The rapidly falling prices of LAN switches are bringing switching technology within the reach of almost all users. Even a home network installed today is likely to use switches rather than hubs. Though switched LANs do not solve all performance problems by any means, they can provide some relief depending on the network configuration. Almost all high-speed LANs deployed today will likely employ a switched architecture.

10-Gigabit Ethernet, or *10G Ethernet*, is also in use, but on a much more limited basis. Most client devices remain at 100 Mbps or 10 Mbps, with gigabit speeds reserved for servers or *backbone networks*. A backbone network is a network that connects other networks, but that has no users attached to it. In wide area or metropolitan area networks, there is some discussion of replacing the SONET and ATM standards, discussed in Chapter 10, with 10-Gigabit Ethernet. While this replacement might serve the needs of data users, the more stringent quality requirements of voice and video users are not specifically guaranteed by the Ethernet protocols. For this reason, it is not likely that even 10-Gigabit Ethernet will displace these other standards in public networks that carry significant quantities of voice or video communications.

There is one ANSI standard for local area networks that has been deployed for many years where continuous operation is essential. ANSI's *Fiber Distributed Data Interface*, or *FDDI*, uses fiber optics to operate at speeds of up to 100 Mbps per channel using a token ring topology similar to IEEE 802.5. FDDI uses two channels, forming an inner and outer ring. One of the rings is used for normal traffic, and the other ring is used for backup purposes when there is a problem with the primary ring. This high-bandwidth network was originally designed for high-speed mainframe computer communications, as well as many other applications. A version of FDDI that operates on copper cable, known as *Copper Distributed Data Interface*, or *CDDI*, is also available. A recently developed IEEE token ring standard, known as the *High-Speed Token Ring*, or *HSTR*, initially was designed to operate at 100 Mbps over copper cable, though higher speeds of up to 1 Gbps and fiber optic versions are planned.

100VG-AnyLAN is an IEEE 802.12 standard, and it uses a *demand priority* scheme that allows certain traffic to be transmitted on a high-priority basis. This approach can improve performance for time-critical traffic on a LAN. This standard also provides mechanisms to facilitate the linking of Ethernet networks with token ring networks. While 100VG-AnyLAN offers excellent solutions for time-critical traffic, Fast Ethernet has been much more popular.

INTERNETWORKING

When LANs reach their distance limitations or become overcrowded with users or traffic, they must be broken into smaller LANs and connected, or *internetworked*. LANs at multiple locations can also be internetworked if users need to communicate. Many different devices are available to internetwork LANs. The most common are *repeaters*, *bridges*, *routers*, and *gateways*.

Repeaters

The simplest internetworking device is a *repeater*. A repeater placed between two LANs, as shown in Fig. 8-8, copies every message it hears on LAN #1 to LAN #2 and vice versa. This device essentially makes the two LANs act like a single LAN. Repeaters operate at Layer 1 of the OSI model, simply receiving and transmitting bits without regard to the content or message address. All traffic is repeated from each LAN onto the other LAN, sometimes unnecessarily. For example, as shown in Fig. 8-8, a message from user A to user C does not need to be sent on LAN #2, but the repeater is unable to recognize this fact and repeats it anyway.

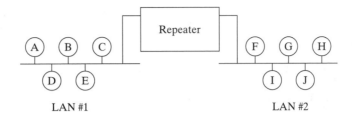

FIGURE 8-8

Internetworking two Ethernet networks with a repeater.

Repeaters are the least expensive internetworking devices and are typically used to extend a LAN beyond its usual distance limitation. If two LANs connected with a repeater do not have a traffic problem, there is no need for a more complex approach. However, most LANs that are long enough to have reached their distance limitation probably have many users, and there could be advantages to using more sophisticated devices than repeaters.

Bridges

A *bridge* can connect two or more networks that use a similar data communications scheme and, specifically, the same addressing method. For example, two Ethernet LANs can be internetworked using a bridge, as shown in Fig. 8-9. The bridge has connections to both networks and listens to all traffic on both networks. Two token rings could also be connected with a bridge, as shown in Fig. 8-10.

In fact, the Ethernet and token ring are both IEEE 802 networks with similar addressing, so they can also be connected to each other with a bridge, with some limitations, as shown in Fig. 8-11. The addressing referred to here is the 48-bit Medium Access Control, or MAC, address, described in the IEEE 802.3 standard for Ethernet or IEEE 802.5 for the token ring. This bridge must switch the data from the Ethernet frame format on one network to the token ring format on the other. If the message is short enough to fit in either format, a bridge theoretically can handle the task. For practical reasons, routers are usually used when connecting Ethernet networks to token ring networks. To simplify our introduction to bridges, we focus on the common case of connecting Ethernet networks. Connecting two token rings with bridges is a similar process with some implementation differences.

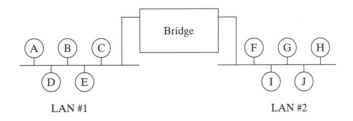

FIGURE 8-9

Internetworking two Ethernet networks with a bridge.

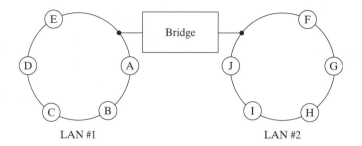

FIGURE 8-10

Internetworking two token ring networks with a bridge.

In theory, a bridge could be installed and manually configured so that it knows which users are on each network. If party A in Fig. 8-9 sends a message to party C, the bridge knows that both users are on the same network, and the message does not need to be retransmitted on the second network. If, however, the message is from party A to party J, the bridge must retransmit the message on the second network. Only traffic that must reach the other network is transferred there. Bridges operate at Layer 2 of the OSI model, known as the Data Link Layer. A bridge simply checks the address at Layer 2 and retransmits the data on the appropriate port. The message is repeated, if necessary, exactly as it was received. This type of bridge is known as a *transparent bridge* and is commonly used to connect Ethernet networks. It is called "transparent" because it makes all of the decisions about routing messages without requiring the participation of the users or their workstations. No higher layer addressing is introduced, and no additional information is added to the message to facilitate its delivery. Directing a message based on its Layer 2 address in this manner is sometimes called *Layer 2 switching*.

Bridges are commonly used when a LAN begins to approach its capacity. In this case, splitting the LAN into two smaller LANs with a bridge between them can alleviate

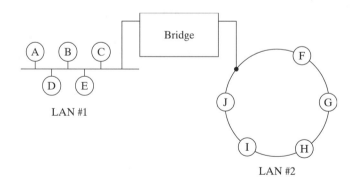

FIGURE 8-11

Internetworking an Ethernet network and a token ring network with a bridge.

the traffic problem, if the users on the two new LANs are carefully distributed. If departments that frequently send messages to each other are grouped on the same LAN, their messages will not need to go through the bridge.

When one Ethernet network is divided into two with a bridge, as in Fig. 8-9, users on opposite sides of the bridge are said to be in separate *collision domains*. Even if user B and user H transmit at the same time, they no longer collide with each other, because they are on two separate LANs. When a particular collision domain becomes overcrowded with traffic, internetworking devices, like bridges, can be used to separate it into many separate collision domains, each with fewer members. This technique is known as *segmenting* the LAN, and the resulting new LANs are often referred to as LAN *segments*.

For example, a 10-Mbps Ethernet with an average traffic load of 50% during the workday probably has certain peak traffic times when response time is unacceptable. This situation is caused by the increased probability that a user will have to wait to transmit, as well as by an increased number of collisions. So if the 5-Mbps average traffic load can be split into two LAN segments, traffic might be reduced to 3 Mbps per LAN. This calculation assumes that of the old 5 Mbps of traffic, 2 Mbps is now between users on the new LAN #1, 2 Mbps is between the users on the new LAN #2, and 1 Mbps needs to be transferred between the LANs. Since the traffic between the LANs must be repeated by the bridge, it will exist on both LANs; therefore, 1 Mbps is added to the 2 Mbps on each LAN for a total average traffic load of 3 Mbps per LAN. An Ethernet network with an average load of 30% of capacity is less likely to have peak traffic problems than one averaging 50% of capacity. Though this example just chooses hypothetical traffic numbers, bridges can be used in most networks to reduce congestion in this way.

Most bridges in use today are able to configure themselves. These bridges, called *adaptive bridges* or *learning bridges*, create a table of user locations by listening to the traffic on all connected networks. When the bridge is first installed, it does not know which users are on which side of the bridge, so it starts by listening to all traffic on connected LANs. When the bridge hears a message, it notices which side it hears it on and checks the return address of the message. This return address is also known as the *source address*. During this learning period, the bridge creates a table showing which users are connected to each LAN based on the source addresses it hears, so it can direct traffic appropriately later on. After a brief learning period, a bridge is ready to operate. However, if some users did not transmit during the initial learning period, the bridge can still learn their location later whenever they first transmit. The bridge always uses the Layer 2, or MAC, address to make its decisions.

For example, in Fig. 8-9, assume that the bridge has completed the learning period and is operating, but that it still does not know where parties A and C are located because they have not yet transmitted messages. If the next message is transmitted by party A and is destined for party C, the bridge must repeat the message on LAN #2, because it does not know where to find party C. But the bridge does now know that party A is located on LAN #1, because it heard the message on that LAN and because party A was listed as the transmitter in the source address field of the message. The fact that the bridge mistakenly repeated the message to LAN #2 is of little consequence. Party C will get the message anyway because it was sent on LAN #1, and no users on

LAN #2 will be interested in the message because it is not addressed to them. In this case, a message is repeated unnecessarily, but the bridge learned in the process and now knows where party A is. In fact, once all users have sent a message, the bridge knows where the parties are and can deliver all future messages to them properly. In order for this simple configuration method to function properly, there can be only one active path between any two users. No active duplicate paths between two users can be allowed using this method.

Other techniques used by bridges to ensure that there is only one active path between two users include the *spanning tree protocol, source routing protocol*, and a combination of the two methods known as *source routing transparent protocol.* All of these methods allow multiple physical paths to exist, but select only a single path to connect each pair of users. Only if a network link fails do the bridges reconfigure themselves to use a different route. The spanning tree protocol is used when transparent bridges are connecting Ethernet networks, while source routing protocols are used when connecting token ring networks. Bridges using the source routing method are not transparent because they require the user or the user's workstation to select the route. The source routing transparent method, designed to connect token rings with Ethernets, is seldom used. As already mentioned, routers are usually used for connecting Ethernet networks to token ring networks.

While all of the figures discussed thus far assume that the LANs being connected are adjacent to each other, it is possible to use bridges between LANs at different locations. These bridges are then connected by some type of phone circuit, which could be a T-1 line, an analog phone line with modems, or some other data networking service. Bridges used in this manner are often called *remote bridges*. The link between the bridges must be of adequate bandwidth to handle the expected traffic between the LANs, or else bottlenecks will develop at the bridges. Bridges are used in this manner in Fig. 8-12.

The simplicity of bridges becomes more evident when there are more than two LANs being connected, as shown in Fig. 8-13. Each bridge operates in the same manner as when there were only two networks. The bridge listens to the traffic and then decides whether or not to repeat it to the other side. In this example, the bridge between LAN #2 and LAN #3 does not need to consider that on one side there is one network and on the other side there are two. It just knows that users A–J are on one side and users K–O are on the other, and it can repeat the messages accordingly.

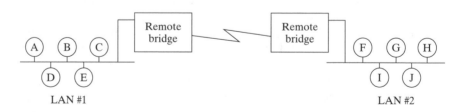

FIGURE 8-12

Internetworking two Ethernet networks with remote bridges.

FIGURE 8-13

Internetworking multiple Ethernet networks with bridges.

Bridges can also have more than two ports, as shown in Fig. 8-14. The bridge still decides where to repeat the messages, based on its knowledge of the users' locations, and the learning techniques and protocols discussed earlier still apply.

There is no difference between a bridge and the LAN switch or switching hub described earlier. The distinction is usually simply made in marketing positioning by the vendor. Both devices switch data based on the Layer 2, or MAC, address. We started our discussion of bridges with the example of dividing a LAN into two segments to reduce traffic issues. A switch with one user on each port creates the smallest possible LAN segments and is known as *microsegmentation*.

In summary, bridges can only connect similar networks using the same addressing method. There must be a unique address for each user on all interconnected networks to enable bridges to use the simple learning methods we have discussed. Bridges are, however, economical internetworking devices and are therefore very popular, in spite of their limitations.

Routers

A *router* can also be used to interconnect LANs. Unlike bridges, routers do not require all users on connected LANs to have unique physical addresses. Routers, like bridges, can direct messages around link failures when duplicate paths are available. For example, in Fig. 8-15, four LANs are connected using routers. To send a message between

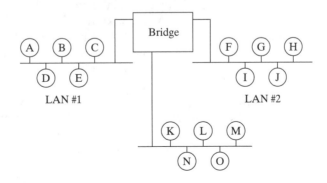

FIGURE 8-14

Internetworking multiple Ethernet networks with a single bridge.

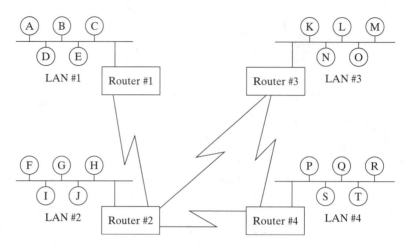

FIGURE 8-15

Internetworking Ethernet networks with routers.

LAN #3 and LAN #4, the routers would most likely send the message over the direct line between the two routers. If this line is not functioning, the message might be routed through the router attached to LAN #2.

Routers operate at OSI Layer 3, the Network Layer, and actually contain a virtual map of the network. Directing a message based on its Layer 3 address in this manner is sometimes called *Layer 3 switching*. One typical network protocol is *Internet Protocol*, or *IP*. Users are identified by a Layer 3 address, in addition to the Layer 2 Ethernet or Layer 2 token ring address already assigned to each LAN user. The Network Layer address is a combination of a *network identifier*, or *netid*, and a *host identifier*, or *hostid*. The netid is used to direct the message to the proper network, and the hostid identifies the particular user on the network.

The use of higher level addresses beyond the individual user's Layer 2 address is a significant difference from the approach used by bridges. Bridges keep a table of Layer 2 addresses of all active users on all interconnected networks. A bridge's ability to find a user depends on its ability to send the message in the right direction based on its table of users on all networks. A router knows about all LANs in the internetwork, but only about the specific users on the LANs directly attached to that router. For example, in Fig. 8-15, the router on LAN #1 knows that users A through E are attached to it and knows that it is part of an internetwork containing four LANs. Each of the routers is assigned its own network address, and we call them Routers #1 through #4 for the purpose of our example. Router #1 must only know how to reach Router #4, and it does not need to learn separate routes for all of the users on LAN #4. Unlike a bridge, which needs to learn how to reach every specific user, once a router learns how to reach another router, it can reach all of the users on the network served by that router.

Most users are unaware of their actual hostid and netid addresses. Instead, protocols are used to associate nicknames with the actual Network Layer address. For example, a user might send a message to "JohnDoe@LAN4", where John Doe is the user's nickname and LAN4 is the name for the particular router of John Doe's LAN. The user's workstation uses special protocols to translate this nickname into the actual hostid and netid before placing it on the network. Specialized address or directory servers can be attached to the network to help users find the addresses of other users. Though these techniques are not directly associated with routing, most router-based internetworks provide these features to increase usability.

Another example of a router function is connecting networks that carry messages of different sizes. Earlier, we discussed internetworking token ring and Ethernet networks with a bridge, but we added the caveat that the messages transmitted must be small enough to fit on either network. The *maximum transmission unit*, or *MTU*, is the longest message allowed on a network. For example, the MTU may be different on token ring and Ethernet networks. Users in these situations must keep their messages smaller than the maximum transmission unit of all networks through which they pass, if they wish to use simple internetworking technology like a bridge. Alternatively, a router that connects the networks could split longer messages into shorter ones, and they could be reassembled at the destination. This fragmenting of messages into smaller ones is a typical function of a router.

Some routers are capable of handling multiple protocols simultaneously, keeping track of which users expect which type of addresses and handling their messages accordingly. Sometimes, routers can act as *firewalls*, screening and filtering incoming traffic, to help maintain security in an open network. This feature is discussed in more detail in Chapter 6.

Some routers actually look into the Layer 3 packets themselves and examine the Layer 4 protocol being used, to optimize their routing choices and packet prioritization. These routers are sometimes said to be performing *Layer 4 switching*. Even though they are still handling individual Layer 3 packets, this term has unfortunately crept into the industry as router vendors try to distinguish their routers as being of higher performance or smarter than their competition. Some router vendors even claim to be doing higher layer switching; however, all packets are still delivered based on their Layer 3 address. Think of these high-performance routers as Layer 3 routers that simply consider the content of the packets when deciding which to handle first or which route to use.

Routing messages in an IP network depends on correlating a user with a particular area in the network. Since mobility is important in today's workplace, the ability to move one's laptop from place to place, maintain the same IP address, and yet still be found easily are in conflict. The *Mobile IP* protocol addresses this problem by adding an extra step in the routing process. A user's location is essentially stored at a single place, regardless of where the user physically moves in the network. If they are not at their regular location, their actual location is available to those trying to reach them so they can be found. It's the IP equivalent of postal mail forwarding when you are on vacation.

As stated earlier, IP version 4 has a small address field, and a shortage of addresses is a problem for corporate enterprises, as well as for the Internet as a whole. While IPV6 solves this problem with a large address space, another approach is *Network Address Translation*, or *NAT*. NAT allows users to utilize an IP address from a special reserved range on their private network, and a device (or software) translates this address when packets are sent outside the private network. Addresses in this reserved range are not allocated to anyone on the Internet itself, so their only use is in private networks using NAT.

A home LAN user, for example, with four computers at home might obtain only one IP address from an ISP. The home router, sitting between the LAN and the Internet, receives all traffic from the Internet and readdresses it with the proper privately assigned address for each PC. To the ISP, it appears that one computer is running four programs concurrently, each accessing the Internet. In reality, four different computers are running one program, and the router uses NAT to help them masquerade as a single user. Outbound traffic is readdressed in a similar manner. Since the NAT device or software can track open sessions with the Internet, it has an added security benefit. Hackers who try to intrude with unsolicited messages will not get these through to any PC on the LAN because they are not part of an established session. The hackers are actually attacking the router, rather than the PCs themselves, and most routers have far simpler and more reliable software than PCs. While this is not a true firewall function as described in Chapter 6, it is enough for most home users.

NAT is almost analogous to the function of your company mailroom. Everyone outside the company uses one postal address to reach everyone in your company. The mailroom sorts and delivers the mail internally. Outgoing mail all uses the same return address. The postal service (analogous to the Internet) is not aware of or involved in the fact that there are multiple individual destinations beyond your mailroom. In a company mailroom, destinations of correspondence are generally not tracked, but otherwise the analogy holds true.

In a large enterprise, traffic is often handled by many routers. Instead of IP addresses being assigned randomly among the users, they can be assigned in a hierarchical fashion. For example, all users on a certain floor of a building can be given IP addresses in a certain range, and one router on that floor supports all of them. In a five-story building, five routers, one for each floor, are connected to a single router that then connects to the Internet. As Internet traffic arrives at this main router destined for a user inside the building, the main router needs to check only five entries in its table and determine within which range the address falls. The traffic is then handed off to the router on the appropriate floor for delivery to the correct user. The router on that floor has its own table that lists only its users, and the list might contain 100 entries. So instead of having one router supporting the whole company, where every packet needs to be checked against 500 entries in a single table, there are two lookups, once in a table of 5, and once in a table of 100. This hierarchical addressing results in much faster sorting. Otherwise, large enterprises generate lengthy tables, and packet forwarding can be slowed down dramatically. This hierarchical assignment of host IP addresses in ranges, known as *subnetting*, is a very common practice. An example of subnettting is shown in Fig. 8-16.

Most IP networks route data using the *Open Shortest Path First*, or *OSPF*, protocol. This protocol does not consider the traffic load on various parts of the network in making its routing decisions. Just as certain main roads can become bottlenecked with traffic in rush hour, while other side streets may remain empty, OSPF may not always find the optimal route at a given moment. Most data traffic, like email, is not time sensitive and can be delayed a few milliseconds without much

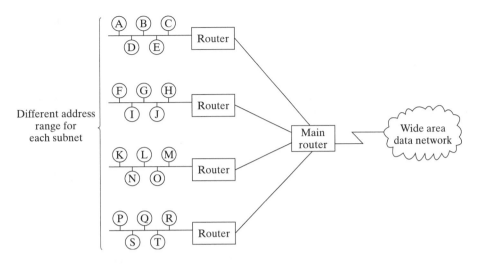

FIGURE 8-16

Using subnets.

impact. Increasing amounts of voice and video traffic, however, are being sent over modern data networks.

Several protocols have been created to improve the performance of these networks when sending this type of time-sensitive information. One such protocol is *Resource Reservation Protocol*, or *RSVP*. RSVP allows paths to be reserved through a network for high-priority data. Though RSVP may ensure enough bandwidth is reserved, it alone cannot prevent the network from introducing significant variable delays; therefore, RSVP is not very widely used.

A typical communications session through an IP network generates many packets between two endpoints. It is wasteful for each router along the way to recalculate the optimal route with the arrival of each subsequent packet. Faster packet handling can be achieved by labeling each IP packet as part of a larger stream of data using a protocol known as *Multiprotocol Label Switching*, or *MPLS*. Some vendors of network equipment have their own proprietary schemes for optimizing the handling of various traffic types.

Another protocol, the IETF *Differentiated Services*, or *Diffserv*, allows packets to be handled differently based on the type of treatment they require. Unlike MPLS or RSVP, packets are not handled as part of a larger flow or stream. Instead, they are each marked for the treatment they need, and each packet is handled individually. Higher priority packets are handled ahead of lower priority packets when congestion occurs.

The IPv6 protocol, discussed in Chapter 7, builds in the necessary features for voice and video that MPLS, RSVP, and Diffserv attempt to add to existing IP networks. Other issues associated with sending real-time traffic over data networks will be discussed further in Chapter 10.

Gateways

Many routers offer more sophisticated services beyond what would be expected of Layer 3 devices. Though sometimes still referred to as routers, these devices probably fall into a more sophisticated class of devices known as gateways. Two separate networks, each using entirely different communications methods, can be connected using a *gateway*. A gateway may be a dedicated device, similar in function to a protocol converter. Many gateways perform functions found as high as Layer 7 in the OSI model, but certainly higher than Layer 3.

One example of a gateway would be a device that connects a packet switching network with a LAN while providing translation between electronic mail formats, as shown in Fig. 8-17. The packet switching network might be carrying electronic mail in one format, while the LAN users might be using another format. The gateway handles the address translations, message translations, and any other conversion necessary to ensure delivery of the mail. A gateway performs any and all functions from Layer 1 through Layer 7 to ensure the compatibility of one or more features on different networks. In this sense, a gateway often acts like a combination of a router and a protocol converter. Unfortunately, the terms "gateway" and "router" are sometimes used interchangeably by vendors.

While Figs. 8-15 and 8-17 show only a single LAN at each site, it is possible, and even likely, that a large organization will use the previously described subnetting technique shown in Fig. 8-16. In this case, the one LAN at each site is replaced in the figure with several LANs, each with their own router, and these routers are in turn connected to a single router or gateway to the Internet or other wide area network.

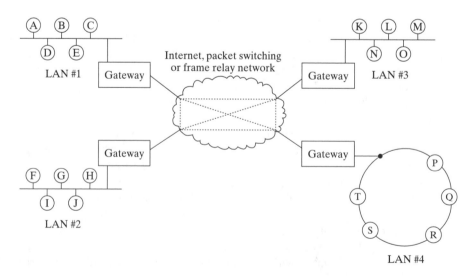

FIGURE 8-17

Internetworking with gateways.

Internetworking Transmission Options

To simplify our introduction to bridges, we assumed that remote bridges are connected by a simple physical pipe, like a leased digital phone line or an analog line with a pair of modems. Routers and gateways can also operate over such a pipe.

However, if there is not sufficient traffic to justify the use of a leased line, it may be appropriate to turn to commercially available networks to connect your LANs. If a public packet switching network is used between the LANs, a *tunnel* is built through the packet switching network by taking the LAN messages and encapsulating them in the packet switching network's protocol, as shown with dotted lines in Fig. 8-17. At the destination side of the data transport network, the X.25, frame relay, or other protocol is removed, leaving the original message.

IP networks, like the Internet, offer another good internetworking choice. Even if the LANs at both sides are using IP as the networking protocol, we may not send the IP packets directly through a vendor's IP network without first protecting them. We may choose to secure the data before sending it across a public IP network like the Internet. In this case, we can build a secure tunnel using a protocol like IPSec. IPSec uses encryption methods described in Chapter 6, like DES and triple DES, to establish a *virtual private network*, or *VPN*, through the public network. The data can take advantage of the economies of scale of the larger public network, while being kept secure inside the IPSec tunnel. A VPN appears to be a private data network to the user, even though the user's packets ride (in secure form) along with other people's data on a public network. VPNs are similar to the closed user groups provided in X.25 networks.

Another transmission option, defined by Bellcore and offered by carriers today, is *Switched Multimegabit Data Service*, or *SMDS*. Designed specifically with internetworking LANs in mind, it is a *connectionless* service that does not attempt to establish a virtual circuit, but that instead simply delivers individual frames. A similar service, *Connectionless Broadband Data Service*, or *CBDS*, is available in Europe. Both of these services are considered by most experts to be intermediate steps on the way to the ATM service mentioned earlier and described in more detail in Chapter 10.

Each of these configurations provides high-bandwidth transmission within each location through local area networks and takes advantage of the economies found in packet switching, frame relay, the Internet, or other wide area networks.

WIRELESS LOCAL AREA NETWORKS

There are many different types of wireless networks available today, and many more are under development. One application of this technology is found in *wireless LANs*, or simply *WLANs*. These LANs allow users in a limited area, typically in the same building, to communicate without cabling. Laptop PCs, PDAs, or other devices equipped with the appropriate interface and antenna can communicate with each other and even with wired networks, depending on the type of wireless LAN being used. In some cases, the antennas are visible and can be aimed in different directions to try to improve the wireless signal. In other cases, the antennas are concealed inside the laptop itself and cannot be aimed in any particular direction.

Most wireless LANs today follow one of the *IEEE 802.11* standards. The original 802.11 standard operates at 2 Mbps. The *802.11a* standard operates at 54 Mbps, *802.11b* at 11 Mbps, and *802.11g* at 54 Mbps. These are all theoretical top speeds, and in various parts of a building, transmission speeds can be significantly lower. For this reason, the original 802.11 was not found to be a viable competitor for wired LANs. The 802.11a standard was expensive in its initial implementation. Therefore, 802.11b made considerable inroads into the market. The 802.11b LANs were the first to be widely deployed, and since they operated on different radio frequencies than 802.11a LANs, it was very costly to build a network infrastructure that was compatible with both standards. For this reason, 802.11b essentially forced 802.11a to the role of a niche player in the market for those who really needed the higher speeds, while 802.11b became the mainstream technology. The 802.11g standard was a later technology adopted to provide the speeds of 802.11a, while using the same radio frequencies of 802.11b. As a result, network-infrastructure vendors were able to build devices that were both 802.11g compliant and backwards compatible with 802.11b. If history is any guide, future improvements in WLAN speeds will also take place on these same frequencies to provide these same advantages. A summary of these speed and radio-frequency assignments is shown in Fig. 8-18. While in this figure 802.11 refers to the original standard, in conversation people refer to "802.11" with the entire family of standards in mind.

In typical wireless LANs, wireless users communicate with an *access point*, which acts as the wireless equivalent of a LAN switch. An access point communicates to the wired LAN using the regular protocols, but it uses a special Medium Access Control on the wireless part of the LAN. Access points can be configured to provide service to any user within wireless reach or only to those who meet certain security requirements. Security considerations in wireless LANs are discussed in Chapter 6.

An access point allows a wireless user to reach all other wireless users and wired users on the network. While this is very convenient and is a logical choice for most businesses that deploy WLANs, what about two colleagues sitting in a train with laptop computers who want to exchange a file? The computers can be configured to operate in an *ad hoc* mode, where no access point acts as an intermediary. Typically, a simple software setting in the computers allows switching between ad hoc and access point modes. The same two wireless users could be sitting in a hotel lobby where an access point is available, but rather than elect to pay the fee charged by the hotel for access

Network	Maximum data rate	Radio Frequency	Distance Limitation
IEEE 802.11 (original)	2 Mbps	2.4 Ghz	50 meters
IEEE 802.11a	54 Mbps	5 Ghz	100 meters
IEEE 802.11b	11 Mbps	2.4 Ghz	100 meters
IEEE 802.11g	54 Mbps	2.4 Ghz	50 meters
Ultrawideband	500 Mbps	3.1-10.6 Ghz	10 meters
Bluetooth	2 Mbps	2.4 Ghz	100 meters
IrDA	4 Mbps	Not applicable	2 meters

FIGURE 8-18

A comparison of some wireless networking standards.

point service, they connect directly instead, eliminating the middleman. Of course, in this ad hoc configuration, they cannot access the Internet or any other services connected to the hotel's access point.

Although wireless LANs reduce the need for building wiring, the radio transmissions cause an added potential for noise and can be thought of as the data communications equivalent of a cordless phone. The workstation must be within a reasonable distance of the access point, or in the case of ad hoc, the other user. The transmission quality will vary dramatically depending on the environment.

In order to speed the deployment and adoption of wireless LANs, a vendor consortium certifies equipment as compliant with *Wi-Fi*, or *Wireless Fidelity*, and users can feel confident knowing that various versions of 802.11 equipment from different vendors will interoperate properly.

While the 802.11 standards were originally envisioned as a corporate LAN solution, they have also been widely accepted by the mobile worker. Many hotels, airports, coffee shops, and even fast food restaurants offer some version of 802.11 service on a fee-for-service or subscription basis, or even for free, to encourage you to patronize their establishments. These publicly available 802.11 access points are often referred to as *hot spots*.

Some have even forecast that these hot spots will become ubiquitous in nature, occupying almost every public place, to the point that any other wide area data network service will be unnecessary. In this scenario, every place you might park your car or every building you might enter would have some hot spot within range. Whether this becomes the case or not, the convenience of the hot spots is already evident, so they are certainly here to stay. In their early deployment, there are many conflicting billing systems, and subscribing to one service does not give you access on the others. Until roaming agreements are worked out among carriers to allow users to move about freely, this technology will provide "spotty" coverage at best.

Wireless LANs have also been widely adopted by home users, who prefer to plug in a wireless access point, rather than crawling in attics and cellars to install LAN cable. Unfortunately, most home users are often unwittingly installing their access points without security features enabled, making their home networks vulnerable, as discussed in Chapter 6.

Wireless technology can also be used to interconnect two wired networks. A *wireless bridge* can be attached to one LAN, and another wireless bridge can be attached to a second LAN. Signals between the two LANs can be relayed using a common standard like 802.11b/g, following the same methods as conventional LAN bridging discussed earlier in this chapter.

Most users of wireless LAN equipment use *omnidirectional* antennas that allow for equally effective communication in all directions. *Directional* antennas, which optimize one direction at the expense of others, may be useful depending on the area being covered. Directional antennas are often used to interconnect a second building or a remote corner of a large building that would be out of reach of an omnidirectional antenna.

It is worth revisiting the Bluetooth interface that was introduced in Chapter 4. While Bluetooth does provide many of the features desirable in a wireless LAN, it is primarily intended for shorter distances than 802.11 LANs, and it is not seen as a competitor for 802.11 for LANs that cover an entire office building.

Wireless LANs that substitute infrared signals for radio waves are also available, using IrDA or similar technology. Though these infrared LANs are not subject to noise caused by electromagnetic interference, they require a clear line of sight between the transmitter and receiver and, as such, are not very widely used.

A new technology known as *Ultrawideband*, or *UWB*, has the potential to revolutionize multimedia connections. Its data rate of up to 500 Mbps is sufficient to transmit audio and video streams, in addition to computer data, reducing the need for interconnecting cables. Televisions, stereo systems, PCs, servers, video recorders, and other devices could all connect with this technology. Its 10-meter distance limitation is, however, a very significant drawback. Consider, however, the tangled web of cabling behind most televisions today, and even a standard that eliminated the need for these interconnections between entertainment devices would be welcome. Technologies like this one take years to succeed in the marketplace, and only time will tell if it will be widely accepted. A comparison of commercially used wireless data networks, including the data rates, distance limitations, and radio-frequency band (if applicable) is shown in Fig. 8-18. The speeds and distance limitations are the maximum typically achievable in normal office environments, though performance can be significantly worse, depending on a building's construction and sources of wireless interference.

In addition to these commercially used wireless transmission options, several residential LAN standards have emerged in an attempt to eliminate the need to install LAN cabling. Each of these standards was initially far less expensive than commercial wireless LANs. Some are true wireless networks designed specifically for the home environment, while others are "wireless" only in the sense that no dedicated LAN wiring must be installed. *HomePNA* 2.0 provides a 10-Mbps LAN using existing phone lines, with version 3 products expected in the range of 128 Mbps to 240 Mbps. *HomePlug* offers a 14-Mbps LAN using the existing power lines, with the next version expected to offer 100-Mbps speeds. *HomeRF 2.0* is a 10-Mbps wireless LAN. As the cost of 802.11b/g wireless LANs has come down dramatically, it is not clear if these residential-specific standards will survive in the marketplace.

SUMMARY

Data transport networks provide the lower layer OSI model functions. Data transport networks are broken into two categories, wide area and local area networks. Packet switching networks, frame relay networks, and the Internet are examples of wide area networks.

Packet switching networks are often used for long-distance data transmission, and they provide a virtual circuit between devices. Packets are routed from one PSN node to another node over interexchange circuits. Devices that are unable to communicate using packets can be attached to an X.25 network with a PAD, which performs the necessary translation. The PAD can be part of the network or completely external and located on the user's premises. PSNs provide the reliability of the dial-up network at a reduced cost, since permanent connections are never established. Packet switching networks can be customer owned or operated by service providers for use by the public.

Most early packet switching networks complied with the X.25 standard. This three-level standard specifies the Physical Level, Frame Level, and Packet Level procedures and protocols for connecting to a packet switching network. There are other related standards that explain the PAD function, known as X.3, X.28, and X.29. PSNs can provide additional services, such as closed user groups, incoming or outgoing calls only, flow control or throughput class negotiation, and reverse charging. The routing of data in a packet switching network may cause delays, and packets can arrive out of sequence.

Frame relay networks are streamlined, more efficient versions of packet switching networks. They take advantage of the reliability of digital links to reduce error checking and to speed the routing of data. The Internet is a data network based on the Internet Protocol. It connects users with numerous services, including the World Wide Web, electronic mail, and news groups. Chat rooms and instant messaging are examples of new collaboration methods the Internet has fostered.

Wide area wireless data networks include pager networks and cellular-based networks. These wireless technologies may all lead to a further deployment of Personal Communications Service, or PCS. Other wireless standards for fixed wireless access include WiMax, IEEE 802.16, and Local Multipoint Data Services, or LMDS.

A local area network is a privately owned data communications system that provides reliable high-speed, switched connections between devices in a single building, campus, or complex. LAN users typically transfer files or share resources known as servers. LANs can be designed using centralized or distributed control. LANs can also be designed using many different topologies, including a mesh, star, bus, tree, ring, star-wired bus, or star-wired ring. Both baseband and broadband transmission can be used in LANs.

The access methods used in LANs also vary widely. LANs can be designed to use polling and selecting, time division, or frequency division, though contention or token-passing methods are more commonly used. Contention methods include random access, CSMA, and CSMA/CD. The most important aspect of these contention methods is the backoff procedure used, which is typically random backoff. Token-passing methods use free and busy tokens to control access to the network; active and standby monitor devices help maintain a reliable token-passing network.

The IEEE 802 committee is responsible for many LAN standards, encompassing both Medium Access Control and Logical Link Control. The Ethernet and token ring networks are two of the most widely used LANs. Fast Ethernet, Gigabit Ethernet, 10 Gigabit Ethernet ANSI's Fiber Distributed Data Interface, Copper Distributed Data Interface, High-Speed Token Ring, and 100VG-AnyLAN are among the higher speed standards available today.

Multiple LANs can be connected by internetworking them with a variety of devices. Repeaters operate at OSI Layer 1, bridges at OSI Layer 2, routers at OSI Layer 3, and gateways at higher layers of the OSI model. Repeaters retransmit all messages from one LAN to another and therefore do not need to know the location of individual users. Bridges usually learn the location of users by listening to traffic, and they choose appropriate paths using a variety of protocols. They are ideal for connecting similar networks using similar addressing methods. Routers use Layer 3 addresses to direct messages and often use network protocols like the Internet Protocol, or IP. Gateways add higher layer functions, similar to protocol converters. Various LAN switching options are available to further segment LANs and improve performance.

Numerous internetworking transmission options are available, including leased phone lines, packet switching networks, frame relay networks, SMDS, and CBDS. The Internet is one popular network used to internetwork LANs today. VPNs are often built by tunneling through the Internet using protocols like IPSec.

Wireless data networks are increasing in use. Wireless LANs can include only wireless users or a mix of wired and wireless users. Wireless LANs typically use an access point, but users can also connect in an ad hoc mode. The IEEE 802.11 standards are predominant, with 802.11b and 802.11g getting the most attention.

TERMS FOR REVIEW

Access method
Access point
Active monitor
Ad hoc
Adaptive bridge
Applet
ARPANET
Asynchronous Transfer Mode
ATM
Autonegotiation
Backbone network
Backoff
Baseband
Bridge
Broadband
Browser
Buddy list
Buffering
Bus
Bus network
Busy token
Cable modem
Carrier sense multiple access
Carrier sense multiple access/collision
  detection
CBDS
CDDI
CDPD
Cell relay
Cellular Digital Packet Data
Centralized control

Chat
Chat room
Circuit switching
Client/server
Closed user group
Collaboration group
Collect call
Collision
Collision avoidance
Collision detection
Collision domain
Communications server
Connectionless
Connectionless Broadband Data Service
Contention
Copper Distributed Data Interface
CSMA
CSMA/CD
DA
Data field
Data Link Channel Identifier
Data Link Path Identifier
Data transport network
Demand priority
Demilitarized zone
Destination Address
Dial-up access
Differentiated Services
Diffserv
Digital subscriber line
Directional

Distributed control
DLCI
DLPI
DMZ
DNS
Domain Name Service
DSL
Electronic mail
Email
Ethernet
External PAD
Extranet
Fast Ethernet
FCS
FDDI
Fiber Distributed Data Interface
File server
File sharing
Firewall
Fixed wireless
Flow control negotiation
Frame
Frame Check Sequence
Frame Level
Frame relay
Free token
Frequency division
Gateway
Gbps
General Packet Radio Service
Gigabit
Gigabit Ethernet
Gigabit per second
GPRS
High-Speed Token Ring
HomePlug
HomePNA
HomeRF 2.0
Host identifier
Hostid
Hot spots
HSTR
Hub
IBM PC Network
IBM Token Ring Network
IEEE 802

IEEE 802.1
IEEE 802.2
IEEE 802.3
IEEE 802.4
IEEE 802.5
IEEE 802.6
IEEE 802.7
IEEE 802.8
IEEE 802.9
IEEE 802.11
IEEE 802.11a
IEEE 802.11b
IEEE 802.11g
IEEE 802.16
IM
Incoming calls only
Information superhighway
Information Systems Network
Instant message
Interexchange circuit
Internal PAD
Internet
Internet Relay Chat
Internet service provider
Internetworked
Intranet
IRC
ISDN
ISN
ISP
IXC
LAN
LAN switch
Last mile
Layer 2 switching
Layer 3 switching
Layer 4 switching
Learning bridge
Length/type field
LLC
LMDS
Load balancing
Local area network
Local Multipoint Data Services
Logical Link Control
MAC

MAN
Manufacturing Automation Protocol
MAP
Maximum transmission unit
Medium Access Control
Mesh network
Metropolitan area network
Microsegmentation
Mobile IP
MP3
MPLS
MTU
Multiprotocol Label Switching
NAT
Netid
Network Address Translation
Network computer
Network identifier
Newsgroup
Node
Numbered
Omnidirectional
100BASE-T
100VG-AnyLAN
Open Shortest Path First
OSPF
Outgoing calls only
Packet
Packet assembler disassembler
Packet Level
Packet switching
Packet switching network
Packetized
PAD
PCS
Personal Communications Service
Personal computer
Physical Level
Plug-in
Polling
Preamble
Presence
Print server
Priority backoff
PSN
Public packet switching network

Random access
Random backoff
Remote backup
Remote bridge
Repeater
Resequencing
Resource Reservation Protocol
Reverse charging
Ring network
Root name server
Router
RSVP
SA
Search engine
Segment
Segmenting
Selecting
Server farm
SFD
SMDS
Source address
Source routing protocol
Source routing transparent protocol
Spanning tree protocol
Standby monitor
Star network
Starlan Network
Start-of-Frame Delimiter
Star-wired bus network
Star-wired ring network
Subnetting
Switch
Switched Multimegabit Data Service
Switched service
Switching hub
Switching node
Tap
Technical and Office Products
Telenet
10BASE-F
10BASE-T
10G Ethernet
10-Gigabit Ethernet
Terminal handler
Thin client
Throughput class negotiation

Time division

Token

Token bus

Token passing

Token ring network

TOP

Top-level domain

Topology

Transparent bridge

Tree network

Tunnel

Tymnet

Ultrawideband

Uniform Resource Locator

URL

UWB

Virtual circuit

Virtual private network

VPN

WAN

Wide area network

Wi-Fi

WiMax

Wireless bridge

Wireless Fidelity

Wireless LAN

WLAN

World Wide Web

X.3

X.25

X.28

X.29

EXERCISES

8-1. What is a virtual circuit in a packet switching network?

8-2. What are the functions of PSN nodes, IXCs, and PADs?

8-3. What are the advantages and disadvantages of a PSN?

8-4. What are the levels of the X.25 standard? What other standards are similar to the lower levels of the X.25 standard?

8-5. How is frame relay different from X.25?

8-6. What is the Internet?

8-7. What is an ISP?

8-8. What is the World Wide Web?

8-9. How is an intranet different from the Internet?

8-10. What is a LAN?

8-11. What is the difference between centralized control and distributed control in LANs? What are the advantages and disadvantages of each method?

8-12. Describe the different LAN topologies. Which topology usually requires centralized control?

8-13. How do baseband LANs differ from broadband LANs?

8-14. What is an access method?

8-15. What is contention? What is a collision?

8-16. Describe random access, CSMA, CSMA/CD, and backoff.

8-17. Describe how token passing can control access to a LAN. What happens if the free token is somehow lost during transmission?

8-18. What transmission speed is used on the original Ethernet? Fast Ethernet? Gigabit Ethernet?

8-19. What is internetworking? Describe the difference between a repeater, a bridge, a router, and a gateway.

8-20. How does CDPD differ from using a modem over an analog cellular phone line?

8-21. What is Layer 2 switching? Layer 3 switching? Layer 4 switching?

8-22. What are the major differences between IEEE 802.11a, 802.11b, and 802.11g?

C H A P T E R   9

Network Management

Any network, whether it is a LAN, the Internet, or a frame relay network, is really a collection of individual components working in harmony. *Network management* helps maintain this harmony, ensuring consistent reliability and availability of the network, as well as timely transmission and routing of data.

NETWORK MANAGEMENT FUNCTIONS

Network management can be accomplished by dedicated devices, by servers on the network, by people, or by some combination of all of these. No matter how network management is performed, it usually includes the following key functions: *network monitoring, network control, network troubleshooting*, and *network statistical reporting*. These functions assume the role of network "watchdog," "boss," "diagnostician," and "statistician," respectively. All of these functions are closely interrelated, and often many or all of them are performed by the same device.

The most important function of network management is *network monitoring*. This function constantly checks on the network and reports on any problems, acting as the network "watchdog." A reported malfunction may be as serious as a completely inoperative communications link to a server and might require immediate action. Another possible report might indicate an unusually high error rate between two modems, indicating either modem problems or a possible degradation in the telephone circuit. Such a report would allow the problem to be corrected before the communications link becomes completely inoperative.

Another function of network management is *network control*. This function, acting as the network "boss," allows for the activation and deactivation of network components and features. Deactivating a faulty modem to prevent network users from accessing it is an example of network control. Network control also allows components to be reconfigured. For example, a client might have its address changed using network control.

There is another network management function, known as *network troubleshooting*, that works closely with the network monitoring and control functions. For example, after network monitoring determines that the link to a server is not operating properly, the network control feature could be used to deactivate that link. The network troubleshooting function, acting as the network "diagnostician," could then be used to isolate the exact cause of the problem. Diagnostic tests could be run on all of the devices in the communications link, perhaps including the cables, modems, and telephone circuits.

Resolving network operations problems almost always requires a combination of the network monitoring, control, and troubleshooting functions. Even if the network is operating flawlessly, there may still be delays, or resources may be inadequate for the users' data traffic. The *network statistical reporting* function can then be one of the most useful in network management.

The network statistical reporting function, acting as the network "statistician," can pinpoint exactly which parts of a network are being used and how often particular components are being used. Overutilization and underutilization problems can be identified and corrected. For example, statistics might reveal that there are not enough communications links between two servers, because the existing links are constantly busy and data is being delayed. Similarly, infrequently used resources can be identified and taken out of service or used elsewhere.

Working in conjunction with the network monitoring function, information about the performance of specific circuits in a network can be collected. Network statistical reporting can then reveal if the network's overall performance requirements are being met.

SERVICE LEVELS

Some criteria for the successful performance of a network are clear-cut. For example, a link that isn't working at all obviously needs to be reported. But in the case of occasional data errors, how many errors are acceptable? What are the criteria for these subjective network management functions?

The performance of a network is typically judged by comparing it with acceptable *service levels* in several key areas. In some areas, there are industry-accepted standards for reasonable service levels; other areas require the user to specify a service level based on the particular application.

Availability

The most important area in which to measure a network's success is its *availability*. We consider the time when it is working properly as its *uptime* and the time when the network is not working properly as its *downtime*. Availability is the ratio of uptime to total uptime and downtime, as shown in Fig. 9-1. A network that works properly for 99 hours and is then down for 1 hour has an availability of 99%.

Since networks are not likely to fail at a set time each day, we usually deal with the average failure rate of a network. The *mean time between failures*, or *MTBF*, is the average time between network failures. Interpreted in a more positive way, MTBF is the uptime, or the average time a network works properly.

In general, the longer the MTBF, the better, though it depends on how crucial the component is. For example, the MTBF of a light bulb may be only 1000 hours; however,

$$\text{Availability } (\%) = \frac{\text{uptime}}{\text{uptime } + \text{ downtime}} \times 100\% = \frac{\text{MTBF}}{\text{MTBF } + \text{ MTTR}} \times 100\%$$

MTBF = Mean time between failures

MTTR = Mean time to repair

FIGURE 9-1

Availability.

this relatively short amount of time is usually acceptable, because light bulbs are easy to replace. However, the MTBF of twisted pair local loops is expected to be many years. This relatively long amount of time is important, because it is not practical to dig up streets to repair telephone wire every few months.

To the network user, the downtime is as important as the uptime. The *mean time to repair*, or *MTTR*, is the average time required to diagnose and correct a problem. The corrective action may be either a repair or a replacement of the defective component. In general, the shorter the MTTR, or downtime, the better. A server with an MTBF of 9 years may seem outstanding, but if its MTTR is 1 year, the availability is only 90%. Some components, like modems, are easily and quickly replaced, provided that spares are kept on hand. Because of this low MTTR, a lower MTBF may be tolerated; thus, it may be acceptable that a modem has an MTBF of only 1 year, since the MTTR may be only 1 day. The availability of this modem could be 364/365, or 99.7%. A summary of the relationship between MTBF, MTTR, and availability is provided in Fig. 9-1.

The MTBF and MTTR of a network are based on the MTBFs and MTTRs of all of the components in the network. A sophisticated server with a long MTBF may sit idle due to a cheap LAN switch with a low MTBF. There is no industry-accepted level of availability for a data communications network; it simply depends on the applications of the end users in a given environment.

The higher a network's availability, the more often the components in the network are functioning properly. However, there are some components that cannot be judged by availability alone. For example, during a thunderstorm, some static may occur on a telephone line. This appearance of static is usually not classified as a failure, since the telephone line is working; however, its performance is momentarily degraded, causing a brief period of errors.

Reliability

The *reliability* of a data communications network is usually measured by its ability to pass data without errors. Acceptable error rates are usually specified for each communications link in the network. Locally, this link might be a LAN; remotely, the link might include telephone circuits and modems.

A special test, known as a *bit error rate test*, or *BERT*, can be performed to determine a communications link's reliability. Typically, a known pattern of ones and zeroes is continually transmitted on the link, and proper reception is verified at the other end.

$$\text{BERT} = \frac{\text{number of bit errors detected}}{\text{total number of bits received}} = \text{bit error rate test}$$

$$\text{BLERT} = \frac{\text{number of block errors detected}}{\text{total number of blocks received}} = \text{block error rate test}$$

FIGURE 9-2

Reliability.

If 1000 bits are transmitted and two bit errors are detected, the bit error rate for that circuit is .002. An acceptable bit error rate for modems using voice-grade circuits might be about one bit in a million, or 0.000001. Most modems perform better than this rate under ideal conditions and worse than this rate under poor conditions.

Another measure of reliability, known as a *block error rate test*, or *BLERT*, measures the ability of a link to pass entire blocks of data, rather than just bits. When link-level protocols are used, the BLERT may be more appropriate than the BERT, since these protocols automatically correct errors anyway, using retransmission. The only issue with link-level protocols is how often the blocks need to be retransmitted.

A BLERT is more indicative of actual link reliability when link-level protocols are used, because even if only a single bit error occurs, the entire block of data will need to be retransmitted by the protocol. In addition, a BLERT distinguishes between bit errors spread randomly during transmission and errors that are clustered together in the same block. When link-level protocols are used, randomly dispersed errors are more troublesome because many blocks may have to be retransmitted. A comparison of BERT and BLERT is presented in Fig. 9-2.

Response Time

In some networks, a consistent *response time* is critical. The definition of response time depends on the devices being used. For example, consider a client connected to a server through a network. The time between the instant when the client user hits the Enter key and when the reply message is received from the server is known as the response time. In this case, response time is really a summation of the time it takes the message to travel from the client to the server, the processing time at the server, and the travel time of the reply. This formula is summarized in Fig. 9-3.

If polling is being used, three response times are usually considered. There is a *minimum response time*, if the client is polled immediately after the user hits the Enter

$$\begin{aligned}\text{Response time} = \ &\text{travel time from client to server}+\\ &\text{processing time at server}+\\ &\text{travel time from server to client}\end{aligned}$$

FIGURE 9-3

Response time.

key. The *maximum response time* assumes that the client was polled just before the Enter key is hit and therefore must wait until all the other clients are polled before it gets another chance to transmit. The *average response time* is halfway between the minimum and the maximum response times, assuming that all clients are using the network equally.

A small local area network might have a response time of only a few hundred milliseconds. On the other hand, a packet switching network with many nodes might have response times of a second or more.

Response time may or may not be important to a user, though for most common applications a 2-second response time is considered adequate. A clerk typing payroll data may not mind waiting an extra few seconds for the next screen of information to be transferred from the server. However, a nuclear power plant operator needs to communicate with the control computer instantly in an emergency, and even a few seconds can be critical.

Throughput

Throughput is perhaps even more important than response time as a measure of network-transmission speed. Throughput is the net bandwidth of a network; it is a measure of the number of information bits per second that can be accepted and transmitted by a network. This rate is typically less than the transmission speed of the individual links. For example, in a network, a particular communications link with 56 kbps modems may have an average throughput of only 40,000 information bits per second, because some of the available bandwidth is used for the extra bits, or *overhead*, associated with protocols. This overhead may include error-checking and addressing information, and it is necessary for data transmission with protocols, although it is not part of the actual user's data.

Throughput is often referred to as *net bandwidth* rather than simply *bandwidth*, because it considers only the number of information bits transmitted per second. Bandwidth considers all of the bits transmitted, including the overhead bits.

One standard measure of throughput is calculated using the ANSI formula for *TRIB*, or *transfer rate of information bits*. This formula, shown in Fig. 9-4, provides a throughput rate in bits per second. It calculates the average rate at which users can expect the network to transport actual information bits to their destination. Throughput is an excellent measure of the efficiency of a particular network or communications link.

$$TRIB = \frac{\text{number of information bits transferred}}{\text{time required for the information bits to be transferred}}$$

$$TRIB = \text{transfer rate of information bits (bits per second)}$$

FIGURE 9-4

Throughput.

NETWORK MANAGEMENT APPROACHES

Setting standards for adequate service levels in the availability, reliability, response time, and throughput areas is an important first step in network management. After these thresholds are in place, the next logical step is to judge the network against these levels.

Although many different methods are used in network management, there are three basic approaches that use varying degrees of automation.

Nonautomated Network Management

The first approach uses minimal automation and requires users to call a network control center to report problems. There is little or no automated network monitoring and control equipment. However, when network problems are reported, specialized test equipment can be used to isolate the problem. This approach relies on users to monitor the network and report problems, and it requires technicians trained in using the test equipment to isolate and diagnose the problems. This specialized network test equipment is usually portable and can be taken to possible trouble spots in the network. We discuss some different types of network test equipment later in this chapter.

Unfortunately, in a large network, it is often difficult to determine where to place test equipment to start isolating the problem. A typical user might report, "I keep getting disconnected from the server." However, there may be 20 links and 10 nodes between the client and the server, so where does the technician start? It's the equivalent of a driver complaining that there was a pothole somewhere on a 50-mile commute and expecting the highway department to find and repair it.

This minimal-automation approach has the advantage of requiring little or no investment in network management tools. However, the ongoing cost in maintaining the network is high, since problems can be difficult to locate and diagnose. Network problem reporting is completely in the hands of the users, and technicians must isolate and diagnose all problems themselves.

Semiautomated Network Management

The second approach uses automatic network monitoring equipment for parts of the network. For example, a server might have network management capabilities that trigger alarms when an unusual number of bit errors occur. In this case, automation is used to report a problem, but a technician still must use specialized test equipment with the server to isolate and diagnose the problem. The problem could be occurring at the server, at the end user's client, or at any of the links or nodes in between.

This compromise approach takes advantage of built-in network management capabilities already in some devices, without the expense of updating the entire network. Some problems will still be difficult to locate, and the burden of fault isolation and troubleshooting still falls largely on the network technician. A network's reliability is improved somewhat with this approach because problems are detected quickly. However, isolating and troubleshooting many problems will still require much expertise on the part of technicians.

Integrated Network Management

The most advanced network management approach ties all equipment in a network together using special network management protocols. Network management functions are integrated into every component of the network, and software used in one server continuously monitors the network; this server acts as a control center. Test messages are sent to each device periodically, and any transmission errors are reported to the control center.

In this integrated approach to network management, a single technician, using the control center server, can perform all of the major network management functions. The technician can monitor the network, is instantly alerted to all network problems, and can usually perform network control functions. Typically, diagnostics can be run directly from the control center, and devices can be deactivated or reconfigured if necessary to work around a simple link problem. Many problems will still require that a technician be dispatched to investigate the problem using specialized test equipment, but in almost all cases the technician at the control center will know about problems before the users do, or at least at the same time.

Many of today's integrated network management tools use graphics extensively to display network status, highlighting problem areas on a map of the network to aid in troubleshooting. Some of these control centers actually use artificial intelligence computer software, known as *expert systems*, to help diagnose and isolate problems. Ideally, a technician's job is simplified by these tools because a defective component is already isolated, or at least the choice is narrowed down to one or two components. The technician can then use the specialized test equipment to determine which of the devices is actually causing the problem.

The integrated network management approach can also provide access at the control center to extensive network statistics on all devices in the network. Such network-wide statistics are almost impossible to compile without an integrated network management approach.

However, it should be noted that with an integrated network management approach, all devices in the network must be compatible with the control center's network management protocols so they can report their problems and statistics. Clearly, a single vendor could establish network management protocols and implement them in all of its devices. However, for integrated network management to be successful, not all of the equipment needs to be from the same vendor; only compatibility is necessary.

Network Management Protocols

Several protocols enable the collection of network management information from devices of different vendors. The most popular network management protocol in use today is the *Simple Network Management Protocol*, or *SNMP*. It is part of the TCP/IP Protocol Suite discussed in Chapter 7. SNMP describes a common set of information needed to manage a network, known as the *Management Information Base*, or *MIB*. SNMP also describes the method by which the network *manager* exchanges information with network management *agents* in the devices being monitored. Although limited in its capabilities, SNMP is relatively easy to implement and has been widely accepted by vendors and users alike. As TCP/IP networks proliferate, so will the SNMP protocol. *SNMPv2*, a later version of SNMP, has been generalized to work on non-TCP/IP networks as well and has added some enhancements, though the principles of operation are the same as those of the original SNMP.

The SNMP agents can report status, or configuration information, about anything contained in the MIB. The MIB also identifies which items the SNMP manager can configure on the remote devices. The simple messages in SNMP can be categorized in three groups: *get*, *set*, and *trap*. The manager can retrieve configuration or status information from the agent by sending a *get* message. The manager can change the configuration or settings of the remote device by sending the agent a *set* message. *Trap* messages are sent by the agent to inform the manager of specific events being monitored at the remote device.

These messages provided by SNMP allow data to be exchanged, but the type of information, and the remote configuration capabilities, may be limited by the MIB. The MIB definition is very flexible, and vendors are free to design their own MIBs. For example, one vendor of networking equipment might choose to offer extensive network management capabilities with a fairly lengthy MIB, while another might offer a small MIB with very little information that can be exchanged. Standards organizations and user groups can also propose standard MIBs for vendors to implement, and one popular MIB is known as the *Remote Network Monitoring* MIB, or *RMON*. RMON was developed by the Internet Engineering Task Force (IETF) to allow for easy monitoring and protocol analysis on Ethernet and token ring LANs.

The first version of RMON, sometimes referred to as *RMON1*, defined some specific traffic statistics and thresholds for reporting certain events. It also provided the ability to capture and filter packets on a remote LAN for viewing at the manager station. Reports about this remote traffic were based on monitoring the MAC address of the LAN stations that were communicating. *RMON2* extended these capabilities by translating the station MAC addresses to higher layer addresses, like IP addresses, as well as monitoring higher level protocols. While RMON1 might report on the overall traffic on a network, RMON2 informed the manager as to which particular types of applications, and which protocols, were making up this traffic. For example, if RMON1 is used to monitor an IP internetwork, a router that carries traffic from other LANs appears to be the source of all traffic from off the local segment, since its MAC address is seen as the origin on the LAN being monitored. RMON2 operates at a higher level, reporting on traffic based on an IP address so that the original source of the traffic coming through the router can be identified. RMON2 is added onto RMON1, and the two MIBs are used together to provide RMON2 functions. RMON1 and RMON2 are just two examples of standardized MIBs; others are sure to be added in the coming years.

ISO has its own protocol for network management, known as the *Common Management Information Protocol*, or *CMIP*. It is far richer and more complex than SNMP, but CMIP is also more costly to implement and operate. For this reason, there is little interest in CMIP, and SNMP is more widely used. While SNMP and CMIP are standard protocols, many vendors also have proprietary protocols for network management.

Most of the network management systems available today support some proprietary protocols, as well as most standard protocols. Many available software packages can act as the network manager and display the management information conveniently for the user. Hewlett-Packard has a popular network management product called *OpenView* that supports a variety of protocols. Another popular product that supports standard protocols is Sun Microsystems' *SolarisNet* (formerly *SunNet) Manager*. Aprisma, formerly Cabletron, offers another network management product known as *Spectrum* that also supports numerous protocols. IBM offers host-computer-based network management software known as *Netview*, which can interface to another IBM software product known as *Netview/PC*. These are two products in IBM's family of *Communications Network Management* (*CNM*) tools. While these products were originally designed to support only Netview protocols, support for other protocols is now included as well. Many other vendors are offering similar products, with a variety of user interfaces and capabilities.

DIAGNOSTIC METHODS

There are several different manual approaches that can be used when diagnosing problems. One of the most common techniques is *loopback testing*, or *echo testing*. Typically, loopback testing is used to test modems or dumb terminals, though other devices can also be tested this way.

For example, a client, like a PC with an RS-232-C-serial port, can be loopback tested with a specially wired connector. This connector, known as a *loopback plug*, has the Transmitted Data and Received Data pins wired together; in addition, several control signals are connected together to simulate normal operation. If a technician suspects that a client is not operating properly, the cable attached to the client can be disconnected and the loopback plug can be attached instead.

The client user types characters, which are translated into bits and then sent over the RS-232-C Transmitted Data pin as positive and negative voltages. Since the Transmitted Data pin is wired to the Received Data pin, the client receives the characters that it just transmitted. If the client is functioning properly, the typed characters are received and then appear on the screen. A typical RS-232-C loopback plug configuration is illustrated in Fig. 9-5; details on the RS-232-C interface itself are provided in Chapter 4.

A loopback test is the equivalent of a person putting one end of a garden hose up to his or her mouth and the other end up to his or her ear; when talking into one end of the hose, the person hears his or her voice at the other end of the hose.

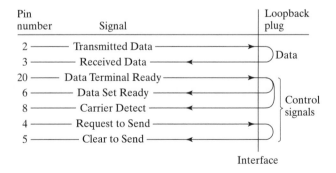

FIGURE 9-5

RS-232-C loopback plug.

ANALOG AND DIGITAL MODEM LOOPBACK TESTING

Many modems are designed with an internal loopback testing capability because users usually are unable to identify where the problem with a data link lies; the problem could be in the local modem, in the remote modem, or in the phone line itself. The loopback testing capability is usually activated by a user or a technician who depresses a switch on the modem or issues a special command.

To help isolate modem problems, there are two types of modem loopback testing, the *local analog loopback test* and the *remote digital loopback test*. Neither test verifies all of a modem's functions, but the two combined reveal almost any modem problem. Modems usually have switches, or commands, to activate each test. To understand these two tests, we take a brief look inside a modem.

As shown in Fig. 9-6, square waves from a DTE in normal operation enter the modem's *decoder* circuitry. At this point, the square waves are translated into an internal representation of ones and zeroes used by the modem. The *modulator* circuitry translates these ones and zeroes into an analog signal, usually a sine wave. This analog signal is then sent out on the telephone line.

At the receiving modem, the sine waves enter the *demodulator* circuitry, where they are translated into ones and zeroes. This digital data then enters the *driver* circuitry, which produces a square wave at the appropriate voltage levels.

If a modem uses an RS-232-C interface, its decoders must be able to receive and interpret RS-232-C square waves, and its drivers must be able to transmit these waves. Similarly, another type of interface could be used simply by changing the decoder and driver circuitry.

In the local analog loopback test, a client is attached to a single modem with a cable, as illustrated in Fig. 9-7. When the local analog loopback switch is depressed, the analog signal is looped back before ever leaving the modem. In a successful test, a user types a key on the client, the client generates a square wave, the data enters the modem and reaches the decoders, and the data is then

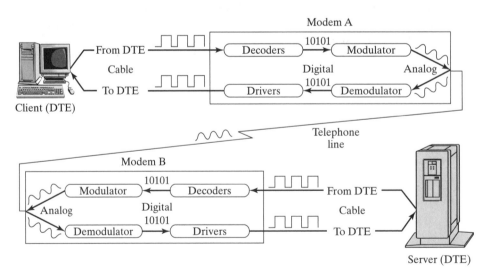

FIGURE 9-6

Normal operation of a modem.

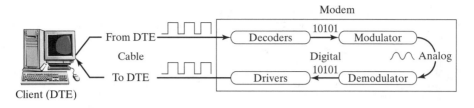

FIGURE 9-7

Local analog loopback test.

converted to digital form and sent to the modulator, where it is converted to analog form. The analog sine wave is then looped back into the demodulator—hence the name *analog loopback.*

In the demodulator, the analog signal is converted back to digital form and passed on to the driver, where it can be translated back to a square wave with the appropriate voltage levels and sent back to the client.

The character then appears on the client screen, and the test is complete. This test verifies the operation of almost all of one modem's components. However, some parts of the modem, including some of the wiring from the modulator/demodulator circuitry to the phone jack are not tested, nor is the phone line itself tested. "Local" refers to the fact that the analog loopback test can be performed locally without another modem and without any phone line. A successful analog loopback test confirms that a modem's decoders, drivers, modulators, and demodulators are probably functioning properly, as well as confirms that the client and cable are working.

A remote digital loopback test can test the phone line itself as well as parts of the modem that are not covered in the local analog loopback method. In this case, two modems, a client, a cable, and a phone line are required, as shown in Fig. 9-8. The remote digital loopback switch is pressed on modem A; modem B is in normal operation mode. The client user strikes a key, and

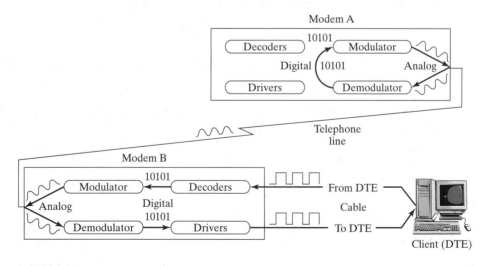

FIGURE 9-8

Remote digital loopback test.

the data is sent by modem B in analog form to modem A, where it enters the demodulator and is translated to digital form. The digital signal is looped back, hence the name *digital loopback*.

The digital signal enters the modulator and is translated back into analog form and sent back over the phone line to modem B and the client. A successful test confirms the operation of the client, the phone line, all of modem B, and the modulator/demodulator circuitry of modem A. The term *remote* in this case simply means that another modem is required at the other end of a telephone line.

By using the local analog loopback and the remote digital loopback testing capabilities of most modems, many obvious problems can be isolated without use of specialized test equipment. Intermittent problems, as well as problems caused by large volumes of data, will not usually be detected by these tests. Also, it is sometimes difficult to determine whether problems lie in the data link or in the attached equipment, such as servers. These cases still require specialized data communications test equipment.

DATA COMMUNICATIONS TEST EQUIPMENT

Regardless of which network management approach is chosen, specialized test equipment is sometimes necessary to isolate and confirm the cause of a problem. Networks using the integrated network management approach seldom need to use specialized test equipment, while networks managed without automation almost always need this equipment to resolve network problems.

The Breakout Box

The simplest form of data communications test equipment is called a *breakout box*. A breakout box typically can be attached at a data communications interface, perhaps between a client and a modem. A breakout box contains light bulbs, called *LEDs*, or *light-emitting diodes*, to monitor interface signals. For example, an RS-232-C breakout box might contain 25 LEDs, one for each signal on the DB-25 connector. A positive voltage might cause the LED for that signal to light; a negative voltage might cause it to turn off. In this way, the status of control signals can be monitored. Data being transmitted by the client causes the Transmitted Data LED to flash on and off, but at a rate much too fast to be read by humans.

The main purpose of the LEDs on a breakout box is to allow monitoring of the control signals, which typically are either on or off and do not change as frequently as the data signals. Breakout boxes can therefore be used to determine if a particular device is presenting a DTE or DCE interface, based on the status of the control signals. This knowledge helps users connect this device to other devices.

Breakout boxes get their name from their switches and jumper wires, which allow technicians to "break out" individual signals. For example, in normal position, all switches are closed and signals are passed straight through the breakout box. However, the switches for the Transmitted Data and Received Data signals can be opened, and wires can be used to cross these signals. In this way, custom cables can be tested to determine the most suitable configuration for connecting two devices. The "breaking out" of signals in this manner is known as *interface modification*.

Some breakout boxes contain a small battery for use in testing cables. A simple continuity test can be performed on each wire in a cable; a lit LED indicates that a wire is conducting electricity, and an LED that doesn't light indicates that a wire is broken.

To summarize, a breakout box is often used for monitoring control signals, DTE/DCE determination, interface modification, and cable testing.

The Datascope or Protocol Analyzer

A more sophisticated device is a *datascope*, or *protocol analyzer*. Like a breakout box, a datascope can be placed in the data communications circuit for monitoring purposes. The datascope generally has all of the features of a breakout box, including switches and jumper wires, and can perform all functions of a breakout box. However, a datascope also has its own display screen to allow technicians to observe the data being transmitted and received.

Datascopes are often called protocol analyzers because they let users see not only the data typed at a client, but also the special control information added by a protocol. Only the actual data typed by the client user or sent by the server appears on the client screen; however, all transmitted data, including the control information, is visible on the datascope's display screen, and this information can aid in troubleshooting network problems.

In addition to monitoring the data transmitted, many datascopes have features that allow data to be trapped in memory when certain conditions or errors occur. When used for troubleshooting intermittent conditions, datascopes can be left in place and configured to sound alarms when protocol errors are detected. Some datascopes, when attached to a phone line, can call a remote office when errors are observed.

Most datascopes can perform the bit and block error rate tests (BERTs or BLERTs) we mentioned earlier. Typically, after a communications problem is isolated and repaired, a datascope is used to run a BERT or BLERT to verify that the problem is corrected.

Some datascopes can even be programmed to simulate or mimic the operation of servers. For example, a datascope can be programmed to poll or ping a server or client to test its operation.

Since datascopes typically contain their own microprocessors, their features are limited only by the software used in them. When a datascope is attached to a LAN, it is sometimes called a *sniffer*. The RMON2 MIB used with SNMP, as described earlier, provides many monitoring features in remote LANs without requiring the user to physically attach test equipment to each LAN. But in some difficult troubleshooting cases, attaching a datascope to the network may be the only way to accurately detect the problem.

Analog Test Equipment

Finally, since many data communications networks include analog telephone circuits at some point, *analog test equipment* is often used. For example, analog test equipment can determine if a particular analog leased line is providing the expected bandwidth. A wide variety of analog test equipment exists today and is capable of measuring distortion, noise, loss, gain, and many other analog circuit characteristics.

SUMMARY

Network management helps maintain network harmony, ensuring consistent availability and reliability, as well as timely transmission and routing of data. Network monitoring, network control, network troubleshooting, and network statistical reporting are the key functions of network management. These functions assume the role of network "watchdog," "boss," "diagnostician," and "statistician," respectively.

Appropriate service levels need to be established for a network in the areas of availability, reliability, response time, and throughput. Availability is the ratio of a network's uptime to its total uptime and downtime. Uptime is also called the mean time between failures, or MTBF; downtime is also called the mean time to repair, or MTTR. Reliability is often measured by using a bit error rate test (BERT) or a block error rate test (BLERT). Response time is the time between the instant when a user strikes the Enter key and when the reply message is received from the server. This time period includes the round-trip travel time, as well as any processing time at the server. If many clients are being polled, there will be a minimum, average, and maximum response time. Throughput is a measure of the net bandwidth of a network. The ANSI standard measure of throughput is known as the transfer rate of information bits, or TRIB. TRIB is the ratio of the number of information bits transferred to the time required for these bits to be transferred.

There are several different approaches to network management, including nonautomated, semiautomated, and integrated network management. Nonautomated network management relies on people to report, isolate, diagnose, and correct problems. Semiautomated network management relies on automation to report many problems, but still requires people to isolate, diagnose, and correct problems. Integrated network management employs automation to report, isolate, diagnose, and assist technicians in correcting network problems. Many vendors use an integrated network management approach, and there are numerous software choices available. Simple Network Management Protocol, or SNMP, is the most widely used network management protocol. Many devices and software products support SNMP. Remote Network Monitoring, or RMON, is a standardized MIB providing network managers with many useful capabilities. The ISO standard Common Management Information Protocol (CMIP) is less popular.

One simple diagnostic method in use today is loopback testing. Some clients can be tested with a simple loopback plug, while modem loopback testing capability is typically built into the modem itself. There are two common types of modem loopback tests, the local analog loopback test and the remote digital loopback test. A combination of these tests can verify the operation of the different parts of a modem, including the decoders, drivers, modulators, and demodulators, as well as the client, cable, and phone line itself.

Sometimes, specialized data communications test equipment is needed to solve problems. The breakout box is used for monitoring control signals, DTE/DCE determination, interface modification, and cable testing. The datascope, also called a protocol analyzer or a LAN sniffer, is a more sophisticated device that can perform all of the functions of a breakout box, as well as monitor data on a display screen. Using a datascope, a technician can view protocol control information, set alarms, trap data, perform tests, and program complex simulations. For telephone line problems, analog test equipment is used to measure distortion, noise, loss, gain, and other analog circuit characteristics.

TERMS FOR REVIEW

Agent
Analog test equipment
Availability
Average response time
Bandwidth
BERT
Bit error rate test
BLERT
Block error rate test
Breakout box
CMIP
CNM
Common Management Information
   Protocol
Communications Network Management
Datascope
Decoder
Demodulator
Digital loopback
Downtime
Driver
Echo testing
Expert system
Get
Interface modification
LED
Light-emitting diode
Local analog loopback test
Loopback plug
Loopback testing
Management Information Base
Manager
Maximum response time
Mean time between failures
Mean time to repair
MIB
Minimum response time

Modulator
MTBF
MTTR
Net bandwidth
Netview
Netview/PC
Network control
Network management
Network monitoring
Network statistical reporting
Network troubleshooting
OpenView
Overhead
Protocol analyzer
Reliability
Remote
Remote digital loopback test
Remote Network Monitoring
Response time
RMON
RMON1
RMON2
Service level
Set
Simple Network Management Protocol
Sniffer
SNMP
SNMPv2
SolarisNet Manager
Spectrum
SunNet Manager
Throughput
Transfer rate of information bits
Trap
TRIB
Uptime

EXERCISES

9-1. Explain each of the key functions of network management.

9-2. What is the difference between availability and reliability?

9-3. What is MTBF? MTTR? When is a short MTBF acceptable?

9-4. What is response time?

9-5. What is throughput? Why is it sometimes referred to as net bandwidth?

9-6. Compare the different network management approaches.

9-7. Which of the network management approaches is the most economical to implement initially? In the long run?

9-8. Does integrated network management require all of the equipment in the network to be supplied by a single vendor? Why or why not?

9-9. Why is SNMP so popular?

9-10. What are the major uses of a breakout box?

9-11. What are the major uses of a datascope? Why is it sometimes called a protocol analyzer?

9-12. What are some differences between RMON1 and RMON2?

C H A P T E R   1 0

The Convergence of Voice and Data Communications

This book began with a discussion of telecommunications and went on to examine various aspects of data communications. Basic data communications concepts, transmission, interfaces, efficiency, security, integrity, architectures, protocols, transport networks, and network management were all considered at length.

A few years into the 21st century, telecommunications and data communications technology continue to come closer together. This process has been occurring gradually over the last 2 decades, though the term *convergence* has only been applied to it recently. In Chapter 2, voice communications technology is presented as a predecessor to data communications. In fact, many of today's voice communications systems depend on digital equipment. Both customer-premises equipment and transmission facilities are increasingly using digital technology.

DIGITAL CUSTOMER-PREMISES EQUIPMENT

The PBX, discussed in Chapter 2, was the first widely used digital customer-premises equipment. Almost all major PBX vendors are currently offering digital PBXs, where voice is *digitized*, or translated, from analog form into ones and zeroes. We present a method for digitizing voice later in this chapter.

Typically, a *digital phone* converts the voice into digital form for transmission to the PBX. A digital phone should not be confused with the DTMF or rotary phones described earlier, which are analog voice communications devices that send dialing signals using tones or pulses. Digital phones use ones and zeroes to transmit voice as well as signaling information. Computer data can also be transmitted through a digital phone as well.

For example, a digital phone equipped for both voice and data communications allows a personal computer user to place a voice call to one person while simultaneously transferring files to the personal computer of another person. This integration of voice and data in a single device, the digital phone, is shown in Fig. 10-1. Another

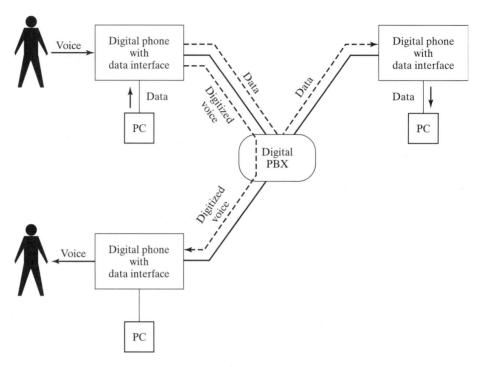

FIGURE 10-1

Integrated voice and data in a digital PBX.

device, known as an *integrated voice/data terminal*, or an *IVDT*, usually combines the capabilities of a digital phone with those of a terminal. Many of today's digital PBXs can be equipped with IVDTs.

While digital PBXs can be used to integrate voice and data, some data communications applications demand extremely high bandwidth. For this reason, the LAN, discussed in Chapter 8, is the more popular data communications solution. LANs can be connected to PBXs, giving LAN users access to servers, terminals, and modems attached to the PBX; PBX users, in turn, can also access devices on the LAN. Both LANs and PBXs can be connected to packet switching or frame relay networks for economical long-distance data communications. These connections are shown in Fig. 10-2.

As discussed in Chapter 2, *facsimile*, or *fax*, was originally an analog communications method for transmitting an image of a printed page. Newer digital facsimile machines convert the image into ones and zeroes, allowing the possibility of high-speed facsimile transmission over digital communications networks, including PBXs, LANs, PSNs, frame relay networks, and other digital transmission facilities.

Transmission of moving images, known as *video transmission*, was originally only an analog technology, like fax. Conventional cable television is an example of analog video transmission. Digital transmission of video is now possible, though it requires a very high digital bandwidth, as we will discuss later in this chapter.

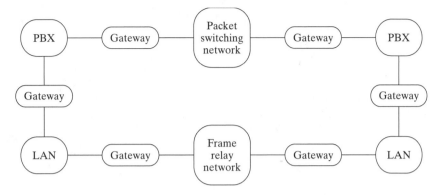

FIGURE 10-2

Interconnecting PBXs and data networks.

Digitizing Voice Using Pulse Code Modulation

In Chapter 5, we explained various modulation methods that allow us to transmit data over analog telephone lines. When digital customer-premises equipment and transmission facilities are used, it becomes necessary to transmit analog signals, like voice, over digital communications facilities. This transmission requires the reverse approach, since the analog signals must now be converted to digital signals for transmission.

Normal telephone conversation can be digitized by using a technique known as *pulse code modulation*, or *PCM*. In PCM, an analog signal is converted to a digital signal for transmission. Typically, the analog signal is sampled 8000 times a second, and an 8-bit representation of the signal is recorded for each *sample*, for a total of 64 kbps. Think of a sample as an audio equivalent of a snapshot of the signal at a given moment; if someone is speaking and we freeze his or her voice at a given instant, we can assign a number that represents the amplitude of the voice signal at that moment. If we repeat this process 8000 times per second, we can then transmit these numbers in binary form. At the other end, we can reconstruct the voice by converting the digital representation back into an analog signal. A simplified, four-bit version of PCM is shown in Fig. 10-3.

The receiver cannot detect any interruptions in the voice because there are so many samples each second. This is the same principle as that on which movies are based. The camera really records many individual snapshots each second on the moving film. When the film is replayed on a projector, it appears that the motion is continuous, because the eye cannot detect the slight jumpiness in the motion between each frame.

High-Bandwidth Digital Transmission Facilities

High-bandwidth digital transmission facilities are playing a major role in communications today. In Chapter 5, we briefly mentioned *T-1 carrier* service. The T-1 standard,

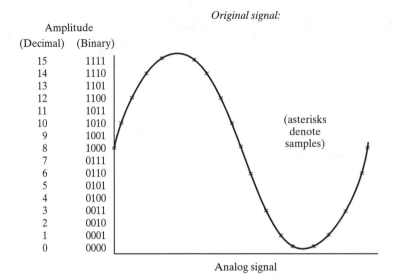

Original signal:

(asterisks denote samples)

Analog signal

Converted to digital form:

1000 1010 1100 1110 1111 1111 1110 1100 1010 1000 0110 0011 0001 0000 0000 0001 0011 0110 1000

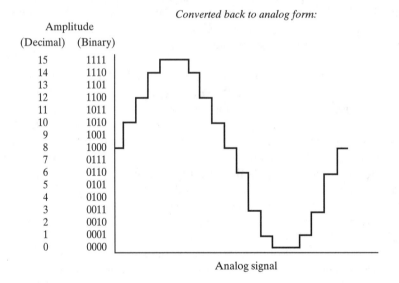

Converted back to analog form:

Analog signal

FIGURE 10-3

Pulse code modulation.

developed by AT&T, provides a 1.544-Mbps digital path now available from all of the common carriers. The electrical characteristics, including the voltage levels for T-1 bit transmission, are specified by the *DS-1* standard. Typically, the 1.544 Mbps is divided into 24 separate channels, using time-division multiplexing.

FIGURE 10-4

T-1 Frame.

T-1 frames. Data is transmitted in *frames*, each 193 bits long; 8000 frames are transmitted each second in a T-1 carrier (1,544,000/193 = 8000). A typical T-1 frame is illustrated in Fig. 10-4. Notice that each of the 24 channels transmits eight bits per frame. In addition, one bit per frame is a *framing bit* used for *synchronization* and sometimes for error checking. The 8000 frames per second include 8 kbps of synchronization and 24 channels each of 64 kbps, adding up to a total of 1.544 Mbps. Each of these 24 channels can be used for either data or digital voice communications.

T-1 SIGNALING

In Chapter 2, we discussed signals passed through the communications network. These analog signals included on-hook and off-hook signals, some dialing signals, and so on. Since T-1 is a digital transmission method, these signals must be passed by using a few bits of the 1.544 Mbps. The 8 kbps of synchronization information is required to separate one frame from the next; however, a bit can occasionally be "stolen" from one of the 24 channels for signaling purposes. One of the most common T-1 signaling methods, known as *robbed-bit signaling*, allows signaling to occur simultaneously with digitized voice or data transmission.

If a particular channel has a bit robbed for signaling, this channel only has seven bits left instead of eight during this frame. With digitized voice, losing an occasional sample does not affect voice quality, since there are 8000 samples per second. This change is equivalent to a speck of dust on one frame of a movie film each second.

However, if a T-1 channel is used to transmit computer data, the bit robbed for signaling purposes will cause data errors. Therefore, when actual data, rather than digitized voice, is transmitted via T-1 carrier, only seven bits per channel should be used for actual data; the eighth bit can be used for signaling, when necessary. With 8000 frames a second and seven actual data bits per channel in each frame, this process results in an effective data rate of 56 kbps per channel. With an analog line and modems, it is very difficult to achieve 56 kbps reliably, and rates closer to 33.6 kbps are more typical. Therefore, the guaranteed 56-kbps capacity of a T-1 data channel still provides a significant advantage to data communications users.

Ironically, with robbed-bit signaling, a digital transmission medium appears to provide 64 kbps per channel for digitized voice, but only 56 kbps per channel for data. In reality, the same bandwidth exists in both cases, but data transmission will fail at 64 kbps with robbed-bit signaling, while voice transmission will not be noticeably impaired. The difference is that a missing bit is always noticed in data transmission.

There have been several generations of T-1, known as *T-1/D1, T-1/D2, T-1/D3, T-1/D4, T-1/D5,* and so on. The "D" part of the T-1 standard specifies exactly how the 1.544 Mbps can be subdivided into separate channels (i.e., the voice digitization and signaling methods used).

T-1 applications.   By combining a T-1 carrier with PCM, 24 voice conversations can be simultaneously transmitted over a single T-1 circuit, which requires only two twisted pairs. With analog voice transmission, 24 pairs would be required. This 12-to-1 advantage does not come without a price, however. In T-1 transmission, repeaters need to be used after a certain distance to prevent the signal from fading, as discussed in Chapter 5. In addition, special digital transmission equipment is required at each end of a T-1 circuit. Analog transmission requires amplifiers and devices known as *loading coils*, instead of digital repeaters.

Even with the added costs of T-1 repeaters and other digital equipment, a T-1 circuit may cost only as much as a dozen analog leased lines, depending on the distance involved. In this case, T-1 offers 24 connections for the price of 12, over only 2 pairs of wires instead of 24 pairs; this results in a 2-to-1 price advantage and a 12-to-1 advantage in terms of wiring requirements. Also, a digital circuit, because of its many repeaters, is less likely to be affected by small amounts of noise. For this reason, a digitized long-distance voice circuit is usually free of any static. In an analog circuit, static and other noise are usually amplified and carried with the signal.

A common application of T-1 is presented in Fig. 10-5, where two PBXs, each at a different site, are connected using a T-1 circuit through a central office. This configuration allows a customer to provide 24 channels between the two PBXs for far less than the cost of 24 analog leased lines. Our figure shows 24 phones at each PBX, implying digitized voice communications on all of the T-1 channels. However, some of these channels could be used to transmit digitized voice, while others are being used simultaneously to transmit data.

T-1 multiplexers and submultiplexing.   Though voice can be neatly digitized into 64 kbps channels, many data communications devices operate at lower speeds, such as 9600-bps clients. Usually, the T-1 transmission rate of 1.544 Mbps is broken into 24 separate channels using a device known as a *T-1 multiplexer*. Any of these channels can be further broken down by *submultiplexing*. Since we have agreed that 56 kbps is the limit of a T-1 channel for data transmission, then five 9600-bps clients could be submultiplexed onto a single channel with bandwidth to spare. Submultiplexed in this manner, the entire T-1 circuit could carry 120 simultaneous 9600-bps client-to-server connections, all on two pairs of wires. Users who need fewer than the T-1 circuit's full 24 channels can often subscribe to *fractional T-1* from a carrier at a reduced rate.

Voice and data compression.   Even greater economies can be achieved by using a more efficient method than standard PCM to digitize voice. There are methods that can digitize voice using only 32 kbps, 16 kbps, or 4 kbps. As technology improves, these numbers will be driven even lower. However, there is already a great deal of 64-kbps PCM equipment installed, and compatibility is often more important than efficiency in telecommunications.

Data compression, explained in Chapter 5, can also be used in conjunction with T-1 circuits. This combination can greatly increase the effective bandwidth for certain applications.

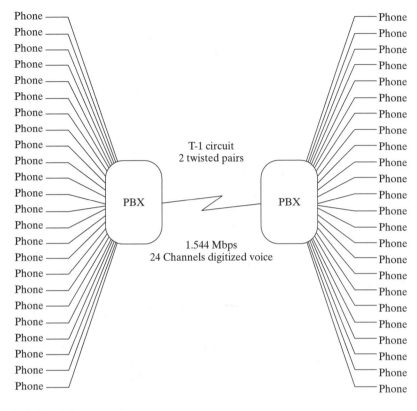

FIGURE 10-5

Connecting PBXs with a T-1 circuit.

Beyond T-1 speeds.   While T-1 offers a 1.544-Mbps digital path, there are other, less widely used, higher bandwidth standards. *T-1C* has a bandwidth of 3.152 Mbps and offers 48 channels. *T-3* offers 672 channels and a 44.736 Mbps bandwidth. However, few companies need 672 channels between two locations; clearly, one or more T-1 lines provides ample bandwidth for all but the largest organizations. The bandwidths of the T-1C and T-3 standards are not exact multiples of the T-1 bandwidth, because they require extra bits for framing and synchronization. Examples of some North American transmission standards are shown in Fig. 10-6.

Digital Networks

Today, digital customer-premises equipment is often combined with digital transmission facilities to form a completely digital private telecommunications network. For example, a company with digital phones attached to digital PBXs at two locations can connect the two PBXs by using a T-1 circuit.

Many companies still use analog equipment in at least part of their network. For example, most digital PBXs today still use some analog lines for central office

Digital signal type	Carrier type	Data rate	Number of channels
DS-1	T-1	1.544 Mbps	24
DS-I C	T-IC	3.152 Mbps	48
DS-2	T-2	6.312 Mbps	96
DS-3	T-3	44.736 Mbps	672
DS-4	T-4	274.176 Mbps	4032

FIGURE 10-6

Some North American digital transmission standards.

trunks. In addition, almost all residential customers still use analog telephone service. The technology is available, however, to create an entirely digital public telecommunications network that serves businesses of all sizes, as well as residential customers.

INTEGRATED SERVICES DIGITAL NETWORK

The *Integrated Services Digital Network*, or *ISDN*, is a set of standards for a digital network that carries both voice and data communications. Today, most residential and some small business communications are carried over analog local loops. Only mid-size and larger businesses with high volumes of telecommunications traffic currently use T-1 carrier. ISDN extends the advantages of digital transmission to all users, large and small, by including many different sizes of digital transmission paths.

The ITU(CCITT) took the lead in defining international ISDN standards. The ISDN standards are really a collection of many standards that specify interfaces for connecting to the public network, as well as a set of services that the network will provide to users. By standardizing interfaces through ISDN, the ITU(CCITT) hopes to make end-to-end digital connections between all devices a reality. Communications networks operated in different countries can all be connected under ISDN standards, allowing for a worldwide integrated digital network. In addition, ISDN provides special services to the users, such as call forwarding, voice mail, and calling-party identification.

We discuss only the more common ISDN standards here. Variations are occurring in different countries; in fact, services differ regionally even in the United States. However, the fundamental interfaces should be the same, allowing device portability and universal attachment within large regions. This fundamental similarity is equivalent to today's modular jack, which is accepted as the universal method for attaching a telephone to the public network. Ideally, ISDN allows computers and telephones to attach to the network with similar ease.

ISDN Channels

To accommodate large and small users, ISDN provides different sizes of transmission paths, known as *channels*. These channels can be combined in different ways to satisfy user requirements.

The *B-channel*, also called the *bearer channel*, is a 64-kbps digital channel. The B-channel can carry user data or digitized voice.

The *D-channel* is a digital channel used to carry signaling information. The capacity of the D-channel can be 16 kbps or 64 kbps, depending on the type of circuit used. These bits are reserved for signaling information, such as on-hook and off-hook status, dialing information, busy signals, and so on, and they are also used in T-1 signaling. However, most T-1 transmission uses *in-band signaling*, where the signaling bits are interspersed in the same channels as the data bits. ISDN uses *out-of-band signaling*, or *common-channel signaling*, meaning that a separate channel (the D-channel) is used for the signaling bits.

Since most signaling typically occurs at the beginning and end of a connection, the D-channel may be idle most of the time. Therefore, certain low-priority user data can also be passed on the D-channel when it is free. A typical example of low-priority data for the D-channel might be electronic mail sent in a packet format. There is usually no urgent need for rush delivery, so these messages can be sent when the D-channel is available, rather than using the high-speed B-channel.

The B-channel and D-channel are the basic building blocks of ISDN transmission, although several other channels are already defined. The *A-channel* is similar to today's analog telephone circuit and provides a means for analog signals to be carried in an ISDN. Since not everyone discards his or her analog customer-premises equipment overnight, some method of carrying analog signals will still be necessary, hence the need for the A-channel. Another channel, known as the *C-channel*, provides a low-speed (up to 16 kbps) data channel for older, pre-ISDN data devices, such as many dumb terminals. A summary of these ISDN channel types is provided in Fig. 10-7.

The Basic-Rate Interface

ISDN provides service to residential and business users with the *basic-rate interface*, or *BRI*. This interface consists of two B-channels and a single D-channel. Usually, one B-channel is used for digitized voice, the other B-channel is used for high-speed data, and the D-channel is used for signaling and low-speed data packets. The basic-rate interface is commonly referred to as $2B + D$.

In the basic-rate interface, the D-channel can carry 16 kbps of signaling information, and each B-channel can carry 64 kbps of data or digitized voice, for a total of 144 kbps. However, an additional 48 kbps is used for overhead, which includes

Channel	Type	Bandwidth	Typical use
A	Analog	Voice grade	Voice
B	Digital	64 kbps	Digitized voice or high-speed data
C	Digital	Up to 16 kbps	Low-speed data
D	Digital	16 or 64 kbps (depending on circuit type)	Signaling or data packets

FIGURE 10-7

ISDN channel types.

synchronization and framing bits. Therefore, the basic-rate interface requires 192 kbps of digital transmission capacity, even though the effective bandwidth is actually 144 kbps.

The basic-rate interface is intended to provide voice and data transmission to the office desktop or the home for the typical individual user. A 64-kbps data transfer rate is adequate for basic client and PC applications, although a higher bandwidth may be desirable as processor speeds increase. The basic-rate interface provides the user with a simultaneous voice and data-communications capability, along with an advanced signaling capability. The 64-kbps data rate is far superior to traditional data transmission, which uses modems and analog lines. Much of the signaling information in the basic-rate interface is not available to the user in today's public network. Certainly, the basic-rate interface is a marked technological improvement over today's analog local loops.

The Primary-Rate Interface

ISDN also provides a higher bandwidth service for business users, known as the *primary-rate interface*, or *PRI*. This interface normally is used to connect PBXs to central offices, PBXs to PBXs, PBXs to LANs, and LANs to LANs. It is also used in other high-bandwidth applications. The primary-rate interface consists of either 23 or 30 B-channels for user data and a single 64-kbps D-channel for signaling.

In North America and Japan, where T-1 transmission is already popular, the *23 B + D* method is used. Since the capacity of each of the 23 B-channels is 64 kbps and since the D-channel capacity is also 64 kbps, existing T-1 transmission equipment that transmits 24 channels of 64 kbps each can also accommodate this primary-rate interface. Since a separate D-channel is used for signaling, no bits are taken from the B-channel for this purpose, and each B-channel has a full 64-kbps capacity, unlike the channels in T-1. A framing arrangement similar to that found in T-1 transmission is used in this version of the primary-rate interface. Therefore, there are 24 channels each of 64 kbps and an additional 8 kbps used for framing, for a total of 1.544 Mbps.

In Europe, where high-speed digital transmission is done today using 2.048 Mbps, the *30 B + D* arrangement is used. Though at first this arrangement may seem to cause a fundamental incompatibility between North American and European networks, this is not the case. Each country, or continent, can use its own methods for digital transmission as long as gateways exist to connect the different networks. It certainly makes sense to maximize the use of existing digital transmission equipment between central offices and toll offices in each country, which is permitted by the two different primary-rate interfaces.

Other Channel Arrangements

The A-channel and C-Channel can be combined in a *hybrid interface* to allow users without ISDN phones and terminals to receive at least some of the ISDN features. These users will have voice and data communication, but they will not have access to some of the ISDN services.

Individual channels may be offered separately in some instances in order to comply with regulatory requirements in the United States and other countries. For example, a customer might be able to lease 35 B-channels and 6 D-channels. However, it is expected that most customer-premises equipment will be designed to take advantage of either the basic-rate or primary-rate interfaces. A comparison of typical ISDN interfaces is shown in Fig. 10-8.

ISDN Equipment Functions and Reference Points

The equipment in an ISDN network and attached to an ISDN network is classified by the functions that it performs. We consider here only the customer-premises equipment, not the details of the central office in the ISDN environment. On the customer's premises, there is both ISDN *Terminal Equipment*, or *TE*, and *Network Termination equipment*, or *NT*.

There are different types of ISDN Terminal Equipment. In this case, the word *terminal* does not refer only to the dumb, smart, or intelligent terminals discussed so far in this book. Instead, terminal equipment in the ISDN nomenclature refers to any device attached to the end of an ISDN circuit. This device could be a dumb terminal, but it could also be a telephone, a personal computer, or any device attached to the ISDN network that transmits or receives voice, data, or other information.

Terminal equipment that is compatible with the ISDN network is known as *Terminal Equipment Type 1*, or *TE1*. An ISDN-compatible digital telephone, an ISDN-compatible personal computer port, and an ISDN-compatible workstation are all examples of TE1. A device that is not compatible with ISDN, such as an RS-232-C or Ethernet device, is known as *Terminal Equipment Type 2*, or *TE2*. This equipment can be attached to an ISDN network only by using a special *Terminal Adapter*, or *TA*, which acts as a converter between the TE2 and the ISDN network.

The TE1, or TE2/TA combination, is attached to the Network Termination equipment, as illustrated in Fig. 10-9. The point between the Network Termination equipment and the TE1 or TA is known as the *S reference point*. The point between the TE2 and the TA is known as the *R reference point*.

There are also several different types of Network Termination equipment. They provide functions similar to those found in the lower layers of the ISO-OSI model, and some users need only certain functions. *Network Termination 1* equipment, or *NT1*, provides only OSI Layer 1 (Physical Layer) functions, including the electrical and physical termination of the network on the customer's premises. The NT1 function allows the

Name	Channel composition	Bandwidth needed	Typical use
Basic-rate interface	2 B + D	192 kbps	Desktop or residence use: one digitized voice and one data channel
Primary-rate interface	23 B + D or 30 B + D	1.544 Mbps or 2.048 Mbps	PBX to PBX, PBX to CO, PBX to LAN, LAN or to LAN
Hybrid interface	A + C	Analog voice and up to 16-kbps data	Used during the transition to ISDN

FIGURE 10-8

Typical ISDN interfaces.

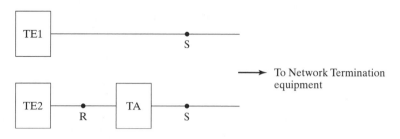

FIGURE 10-9

ISDN Terminal Equipment.

rest of the customer-premises equipment to be isolated from the technology used in the local loop. For example, if the local exchange carrier currently uses twisted pair wire for local loops, an NT1 compatible with this transmission medium can be used. If fiber optic local loops later become available, only the NT1 needs to be changed, since it is the only equipment that attaches directly to the circuit.

There is no exact equivalent of the NT1 in the analog telephone network in our homes today; however, consider the box in our house where the phone company's local loop is connected to our house's telephone wiring. This box, terminating the public network circuit, is the rough equivalent of the NT1, though it performs fewer functions. The NT1 is similar in function to the CSU discussed in Chapter 5.

Network Termination 2 equipment, or *NT2*, can provide OSI Layers 2 and 3 (Data Link and Network Layer) functions, including concentration and switching, if needed. Routers, PBXs, and other controllers are examples of NT2 equipment. While residential users would not always need their own NT2 equipment, business users would for the economical and practical reasons previously explained.

Finally, *Combined Network Termination 1 and 2*, or *NT12*, contains both NT1 and NT2 functions in a single device. Some economies can be gained by purchasing a single device that performs both functions, but if the local loop transmission technology changes, the entire NT12 may need to be replaced. Though the NT12 is less flexible than separate NT1 and NT2 devices, some users may choose NT12 for economical reasons.

The relationship between the Network Termination equipment is shown in Fig. 10-10. The point between the NT1 and the rest of the ISDN network is known as the

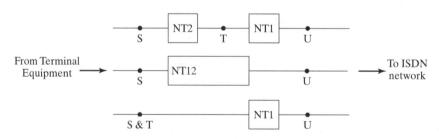

FIGURE 10-10

ISDN Network Termination equipment.

U reference point. The point between the NT1 and the NT2 (if an NT2 is used) is known as the *T reference point.* If an NT1 is used without an NT2, the S and T reference points coincide where the NT1 is connected directly to the terminal equipment.

In the United States, both TE and NT are usually considered customer-premises equipment. Outside the United States, however, the local exchange carrier almost always provides the NT1 function. Even in the United States, the customer usually has the option of leasing some of the NT functions from the local exchange carrier.

The current ISDN standards specify that the S and T reference points require two twisted pairs for transmission, while the U reference point requires one pair for the BRI and two pairs for the PRI. The exact nature of transmission at the S, T, and U reference points is clearly defined in the ISDN standards. The standard at the R reference point depends on the interface standard of the TE2.

Understanding the details of the ITU(CCITT) S, T, and U reference point standards is not as important as understanding the functions performed by the TE1, TE2, TA, NT1, NT2, and NT12. In an ISDN environment, customer-premises equipment is classified according to this terminology. Examples of interconnection of various combinations of equipment are shown in Fig. 10-11.

Circuit and Packet Switching in ISDN

The B-channels in an ISDN network are circuit switched, but D-channel messages are packet switched. D-channel signaling messages that pass between central offices and users in the network are placed in packets according to certain protocols.

All of the switches in an ISDN network are interconnected by a packet switched network to exchange signaling information. If a user wants to place a call from San Francisco to New York, the appropriate call-request packet is sent from the user through the

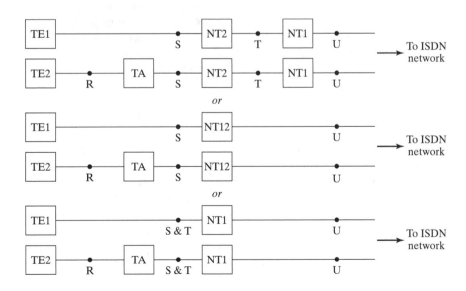

FIGURE 10-11

Interconnecting ISDN Terminal Equipment and Network Termination equipment.

D-channel to the packet-switched signaling network. If the user in New York answers the phone, a call-connect packet returns on the signaling network, and a B-channel is enabled by the network to support this call. This B-channel is circuit switched and remains active for the duration of the call, while the signaling occurred in the separate packet switched signaling network.

It is also technically possible for users to send data messages on the D-channel if spare bandwidth is available, but not all carriers offer this service. The predominant use today of the D-channel is to carry the network's signaling messages.

ISDN Services

While an integrated digital network is a sound technical concept, there is little reason for users to discard existing analog equipment in the interests of technical purity alone. To motivate users to support a new type of network, special user services are included in addition to digital transmission.

ISDN's signaling capabilities are significantly superior to those of today's public network. The D-channel can carry information about the call's destination, the calling party, billing instructions, and other information. This signaling is passed throughout the ISDN network, so the central office at the destination knows not only who is being called, but also where the call came from. The central office can relay this information on the D-channel to the customer with an ISDN digital phone.

In an ISDN world, when the telephone rings, it displays information about the caller, like "(516)-555-1234 John Smith." The user can then choose to answer or ignore the call. In addition, the user could send instructions to the central office to block all calls from John Smith or to forward them to an answering service.

Another example of an often-cited ISDN feature is similar to the PBX camp-on feature. When calling a friend across the country, if we hear a busy signal, we can touch a button on our digital phone that instructs our central office that we really want to reach our friend. Our central office then sends special signaling information to our friend's central office, asking it to inform our central office when our friend is off the phone so that our call can be placed again automatically.

ISDN signaling is carried between switches in the network according to the standard known as *Signaling System 7*, or *SS7*. This standard for network signaling, developed in 1984, is already in widespread use throughout the United States. SS7 information includes the call's origin and destination phone number, as well as instructions for the network handling the call. In most cases today, SS7 is used only between switches in the network. If a call is being placed to an ISDN subscriber, the SS7 signaling information is translated to the appropriate D-channel format before transmission to the end user.

This signaling technology is often used to assist in call routing. For example, a chain of retail outlets advertises a central, toll-free phone number. A potential customer calls this number and is automatically routed to the nearest store. The network signaling messages identify the caller and, based on the caller's phone number, either public or private switching equipment can route the call to the proper store.

Most end users today still use analog phones. While almost all central and toll offices have the capability to pass on signaling information, not all subscribers today are able to take advantage of it. Some analog customers today subscribe to a *Caller ID* service, enabling them to use their existing analog phones with a special display to indicate the number—or sometimes the name and number—of the party calling them. These devices are not ISDN phones, and they provide only a single feature similar to one of the many found in ISDN. The ISDN network carried the signaling message to the central office, making it possible for the information to be delivered to the user using Caller ID.

The availability of these services has sparked many interesting discussions in the United States about the use of telecommunications technology. Many customers have raised questions about their privacy rights and would prefer not to be identified as the calling party. Numerous approaches have been proposed in an attempt to solve these issues. This debate is one example of the type of social issues that ISDN will continue to confront during its deployment.

Using ISDN for residential Internet access is another popular application. In some regions, ISDN pricing is very reasonable, and it has caught on for Internet access, as well as for remote access to the corporate LAN. In other areas, however, the cost of ISDN is still prohibitive. One recent ISDN service for accessing the Internet or the corporate LAN is particularly interesting. Known as *Always On/Dynamic ISDN*, or *AODI*, it uses the ISDN D-channel to send up to 9600 bps of data packets to the Internet or corporate LAN. When user demand exceeds 9600 bps, B-channels are then connected to provide higher bandwidth, and the data flow switches to the B-channels. When the traffic drops below 9600 bps, it is switched back to the D-channel again. This creative use of the available ISDN bandwidth allows a continual connection to the data network over the available D-channel, without tying up the network's B-channels when they are not needed. This system results in lower connection charges from the carrier and increased network efficiency. It is one example of how ISDN is being used to meet the needs of applications that were not even considered during its original development.

An endless number of features can be provided to the customer with ISDN. The extensive signaling capabilities provided in ISDN allow new features to be added later simply by modifying the software in the existing central-office switches.

National ISDN

ISDN implementation in the United States has been facilitated by the introduction of the *National ISDN* standards. These are Telcordia (formerly Bellcore) standards designed to ensure the consistent deployment of ISDN in a user's entire private network, regardless of carrier or equipment manufacturer. National ISDN-N, where N is the number of the standard, can be thought of as a snapshot of ISDN's technology as it evolved and was implemented. It captures an agreed-upon set of ISDN features, provides necessary implementation details, and freezes these features and details long enough for vendors, providers, and users to deploy networks. A few months or years later, the next set of features are agreed upon, and improvements are deployed. For example, the first version, National ISDN-1, has already been deployed, as has National ISDN-2. Plans for deploying future National ISDN versions are already under discussion. In Europe, a similar standard, known as *EuroISDN*, defines a set of features implemented there.

Video and ISDN

There are many different standards committees working on developing ideal methods for transmitting moving images as well as still images. One committee working on moving pictures, or video, is ISO's *Moving Pictures Expert Group*, or *MPEG*. The group provides a variety of standards with different quality levels. One example is the *MPEG II* standard, which offers varying degrees of quality based on the bit rate used. While uncompressed broadcast-quality video might require 21 Mbps bandwidth, on average the MPEG II compression technique reduces this requirement to only 7 Mbps. Neither the basic-rate nor the primary-rate interface of ISDN can provide the bandwidth required for true broadcast-quality video.

Broadcast quality, however, is not required for successful videoconferencing. Many users have found existing ISDN interfaces suitable for videoconferencing applications, and equipment is available using ISDN's basic-rate interface. Typically, the equipment uses both B-channels in a basic-rate interface to carry the video and audio signals. Primary-rate videoconferencing, using 23 B-channels, is also available.

In a typical videoconference, most of the picture is composed of stationary items, like the table and the wall. Typically, the only moving items are people's mouths, arms, and heads. Most videoconferencing equipment takes advantage of this lack of great movement and transmits only the changing parts of the picture, allowing reasonable transmission on a basic-rate interface. If participants start moving around the room, there is usually a perceptible degradation of quality.

Use of a primary-rate instead of a basic-rate interface improves the situation but still falls far short of the 7 Mbps needed for broadcast-quality video. Many users do not require broadcast quality and are satisfied with a speed somewhere between the basic-rate and primary-rate interfaces. The term $N \times 64$, or *multirate ISDN*, has evolved to describe the usage of multiple B-channels for a single connection. While theoretically any number of B-channels can be associated in multirate ISDN, some channel combinations are more commonly used than others. For example, six B-channels, for a total of 384 kbps, is very popular. Some examples of common channel combinations, and the names used to refer to them, are shown in Fig. 10-12. Multirate ISDN can also be used to carry any type of data, including the video example discussed here.

Clearly, ISDN is useful for videoconferencing applications, but it is not considered suitable for broadcast video. As compression technology improves, so will the quality of video transmission, but most experts believe that a higher bandwidth than that associated with ISDN will be necessary to fully develop video applications.

FIGURE 10-12

Some common channel combinations in multirate ISDN.

Service name	Number of B-channels	Data rate
H0	6	384 kbps
H11	24	1.536 Mbps
H12	30	1.920 Mbps

The Realities of ISDN

ISDN is based on proven technologies. For example, the basic-rate interface is similar to that used by many PBX manufacturers in their digital phones today. The 23 B + D version of the primary-rate interface is similar to the T-1 carrier scheme used in the United States. Almost all of the ISDN features are already being used in digital PBXs, so their operation is well understood.

Will ISDN evolve from a set of international standards into a worldwide telecommunications network? Or, will ISDN be the next RS-449, a standard that provides for everything, but that fails to gain widespread acceptance? For ISDN to be fully implemented, new customer-premises equipment and transmission equipment will need to be purchased or existing equipment will need to be modified. Existing digital central offices and toll offices can certainly be modified to accommodate ISDN. But who will pay for ISDN?

In some countries, the government strictly regulates the telecommunications industry and sometimes also runs the public network. In these cases, the government could simply insist that all communications equipment in that country conform to ISDN, and the standard could be implemented quickly. The government, and ultimately the citizens, would bear the expense of the conversion.

In the United States, however, it is likely that the FCC and PUCs will require common carriers to continue to offer basic telephone service at reasonable prices. While ISDN technology is being used extensively by the carriers in their internal networks, ISDN is still just one of the many options customers have for accessing the public network.

Simple economics will dictate how fast ISDN is implemented in customer-premises equipment in the United States. For example, the primary-rate interface is almost identical to T-1 carrier; the main difference is that one of the 24 channels is used for signaling instead of data transmission. Assuming that it continues to be priced reasonably close to the price of the T-1 transmission offerings, the ISDN primary-rate interface will continue to be a very attractive alternative to T-1. By giving up one of the 24 data channels, the customer gains incredible signaling power for the other 23 channels. A customer with PBXs at two locations can tie them together with an ISDN primary-rate circuit; the signaling passed between the two PBXs over the ISDN signaling channel makes it appear to users that they are on a single PBX.

The basic-rate interface may be only of limited appeal to business users. In Centrex-type installations, in which the central office provides the switching function for a customer, the basic-rate interface is a reasonable method of providing digital voice and data service to the desktop.

PBX customers, however, may have already invested in their PBX vendor's own proprietary desktop data interfaces that perform functions similar to those provided by the basic-rate interface. These PBXs will likely be compatible with ISDN interfaces to the central office, but may still use proprietary digital interface standards internally. Some PBX vendors, however, will also choose the ISDN basic-rate service for transmission between the PBX and the desktop.

Finally, residential telephone users make up the biggest unknown for ISDN. Will we welcome basic-rate service in our homes? Is there a need for a second channel for data in most residences? Clearly, many professionals would benefit from remote access to their corporate LAN. Home-based businesses could also benefit from high-speed access. Only a minority of today's telephone customers takes advantage of custom calling services, such as call waiting and call forwarding. Will ISDN's services be any more attractive to residential users? Until the growth of the Internet, ISDN was largely a failure in the residential market. It definitely offers a higher speed connection to the Internet than do dial-up phone lines, but other options for digital connection to the Internet, discussed later, surpass ISDN in speed. For now, ISDN does not appear to be a significant force in the residential market.

DIGITAL SUBSCRIBER LINE SERVICES

The need to connect residences and businesses to the Internet, or to attach them remotely to the company LAN, increased the demand for digital connections. While ISDN is one alternative, another technology is *Digital Subscriber Line*, or *DSL*. Originally developed by Bellcore (now Telcordia), DSL was intended to deliver high-speed digital connections over copper cable from the central office to the residential or business user without the expensive repeaters found in T-1 lines. DSL was offered in many variations, hence the term *xDSL*, where the *x* defines the type of service being offered. All variations operate over twisted pair wire, but not all variations and speeds are offered in all areas.

Asymmetric Digital Subscriber Line, or *ADSL*, offers a transmission path that is of a higher speed in one direction than in the other. The central office sends data to the user of the ADSL line with a higher speed than the speed at which the user sends data to the network. Applications like residential Internet access can certainly benefit from this arrangement, since in most cases the majority of data flows from the Internet to the user. ADSL is available over a single twisted pair at speeds ranging from 1.5 to 9 Mbps in the high-speed direction and 16 to 640 kbps in the low-speed direction. One popular combination is 6.1 Mbps/640 kbps for specific distances and over certain-quality wire. *Rate-Adaptive Digital Subscriber Line*, or *RADSL*, simply scales back the speed of ADSL based on the quality of the wire and the distance between the user and the central office. A newer version of ADSL, known as *Universal Asymmetric Digital Subscriber Line*, or *UADSL*, and also as *ADSL Lite*, *DSL Lite*, and *G.Lite*, is an attempt to standardize ADSL deployment across all carriers, since early implementations had so many speed and transmission differences. It operates using a 1.544 Mbps/384 kbps combination. *ADSL2+*, a new extension of the ADSL standard, can reach speeds of up to 25 Mbps under ideal conditions.

High-bit-rate Digital Subscriber Line, or *HDSL*, offers 1.544 Mbps or 2.048 Mbps transmission in both directions, but requires two twisted pairs. *HDSL2* is a recent version of HDSL that operates at the same speeds and distances as HDSL does, but over a single twisted pair. *Single-line Digital Subscriber Line*, or *SDSL*, offers speeds ranging from 384 kbps all the way to HDSL speeds, but over shorter distances, using only a single twisted pair. One application of HDSL, HDSL2, and SDSL is to connect businesses to the Internet.

Very-high-bit-rate Digital Subscriber Line, or *VDSL*, offers even higher speeds, but it is asymmetric, with the high speeds ranging from 12.96 to 51.84 Mbps and the low speeds ranging from 1.6 to 2.3 Mbps. Its distance is very limited, and one popular application is as a local connection to a higher speed fiber optic network.

There are numerous other xDSL versions, all with their own speeds and distance limitations, and the technology is continually improving. No single DSL choice is clearly superior to the others. Rather, it is a question of matching the transmission speed with the user's application.

In the case of residential DSL and the lower end business DSL services, voice and data coexist on the same twisted-pair wire. Typically, the data signals are modulated at frequencies higher than the normal 3300-Hz limit of the analog voice channel, so as not to interfere with the voice signals. In order to prevent these higher frequency data signals from creating an audible buzz or static on the phone line, two techniques are employed. In the first technique, shown in Fig. 10-13, a *splitter* is installed where the phone line enters the residence. The various frequencies (voice and data) are separated at the splitter; the lower frequency (voice) signals are sent to all of the existing house wiring, and the higher frequency (data signals) are sent to a DSL modem on a dedicated twisted pair. In another technique, shown in Fig. 10-14, the existing house wiring is maintained as is, but a separate *filter* is placed in front of every telephone to prevent the DSL signals from reaching the phone. Only the DSL modem itself is plugged directly into a phone jack without a filter.

FIGURE 10-13

Residential DSL using a splitter.

FIGURE 10-14

Residential DSL using filters.

Early DSL installations almost always used a splitter, which required a service technician to install the splitter and also required new, dedicated wiring for the DSL modem. The filter approach allows for a self-install kit to be sent to the customer; the kit contains the DSL modem and several filters to plug in between the phone jacks and the phones. Carriers prefer filters to be used because they reduce the installation cost dramatically.

Regardless of the method used at the residence, at the central office a splitter separates the voice and data signals, as shown in Fig. 10-15. The voice signals are passed to the central office switch, while the data signals flow into a *Digital Subscriber Line Access Multiplexer*, or *DSLAM*. The DSLAM contains a carrier DSL modem, as well as a multiplexer. Signals from many subscribers' DSL lines are combined in the DSLAM, with a single, high-speed digital connection to the Internet on the other side. This high-speed connection to the Internet is typically made over a T-1, ISDN, or other digital phone circuit, as described elsewhere in this chapter. There is almost never sufficient bandwidth in the DSLAM connection to the Internet to accommodate everyone using their DSL modem at top speed at the same time. Carriers play the law of averages, and it is not uncommon for the bandwidth on the connection from the DSLAM to the Internet to be one tenth, or even less, than the bandwidth of the sum of the attached DSL lines. By sharing the bandwidth among many users, DSL offers a

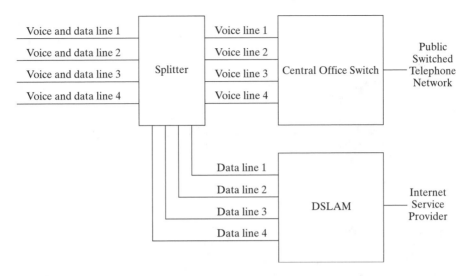

FIGURE 10-15

DSL at the central office.

high bandwidth at an affordable price, though not everyone can use the connection at its top speed at the same time.

CABLE MODEMS

Another possibility for local access to data networks like the Internet is provided by *cable modems*. Most cable modems operate by taking some of the bandwidth available on a cable television system away from television signals and instead dedicating that bandwidth to data traffic. On most cable television networks, data signals are modulated onto sine waves in unused analog channels. The transmission speed of these modems is much higher than conventional modems, because they are not limited by the 3000-Hz bandwidth of the telephone line. Each allocated television channel provides a bandwidth of 6 Mhz for the cable modem.

Most cable television systems deploying data services have converted at least part of their networks to use fiber optic cables. A typical network topology is shown in Fig. 10-16. The *head end* is the cable television equivalent of the phone company's central office. All of the programming, Internet access, etc., is routed through this head end before going to the customers. Originally, coaxial cabling was used from the head end all the way to customer's homes or businesses. To allow for greater bandwidth and provision of additional services like Internet access, fiber optic cable is typically installed between the head end and the neighborhood. A *cable modem termination system*, or *CMTS*, sits either at the head end or somewhere between the head end and the neighborhoods in order to interconnect cable modem customers to the Internet. The boxes in the neighborhood, known as *fiber nodes*, convert the optical signals to electronic ones (and vice versa). A typical node might serve 1000 households, though half or twice as many are also possible. Data intended for a user served

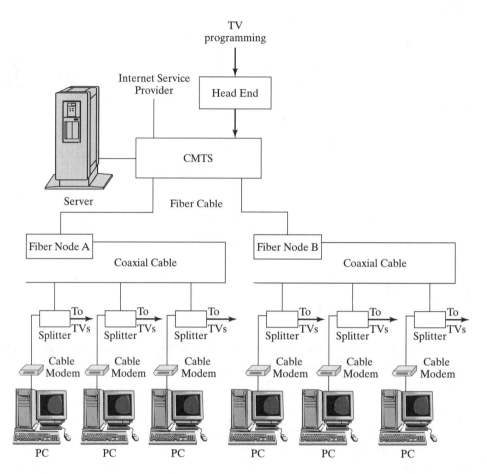

FIGURE 10-16

A cable modem system.

by fiber node A in Fig. 10-16 will be received by fiber node A, and placed on the coaxial cable attached to fiber node A. All of the households attached to that coaxial cable in neighborhood A receive that signal, but only the appropriate user's cable modem delivers it to that user's PC. Therefore, a data signal from the head end destined for a user in neighborhood A would not be delivered to users served by fiber node B. If there is too much data traffic in a particular neighborhood, the cable operator can add an additional node in the area and split one of the existing areas in half, or the operator can allocate additional channels on the cable system to serve data users. Once the cable enters the household, a *splitter* is often used to separate the cable modem signals from the television signals. The cable modem is attached to the appropriate side of the splitter.

Using these various techniques, competing technologies offer many different speeds. In most cases, the transmission speed to the subscriber is much higher than the transmission speed to the network. In many cases, the bandwidth in a neighborhood is shared, just like an office LAN, so the user never has access to all the bandwidth. There is always the risk that a neighbor may be downloading huge amounts of data, slowing down the entire neighborhood, but cable-system providers can monitor this usage and place reasonable restrictions on customers to prevent abuse. As with a LAN, anyone electronically monitoring the cable with test equipment can see the data sent by anyone else on this particular network. To maintain privacy, conventional encryption technology is often built into the cable modems to protect any sensitive data.

While early cable modems were proprietary in nature, most in North America today meet one of the *Data Over Cable Service Interface Specifications*, or *DOCSIS*, standards. The *DOCSIS 1.0* modems were the first standards-based cable modems deployed. *DOCSIS 1.1* has some security enhancements, and it allows the user to request additional bandwidth when needed, presumably at a higher cost from the cable provider. While speeds of up to 30 Mbps are commonly available on most cable systems, most cable providers do not allow any one user to have access to all of this bandwidth. Speeds to the home in the range of 1-4 Mbps and from the home in the range of 256 kbps-784 kbps are attractively priced. Higher speeds are sometimes available at rates more suitable for business users. Another version of DOCSIS, known as *EuroDOCSIS*, is compatible with the cable television systems in Europe.

Cable modems typically connect to the user's computer via an Ethernet or USB interface connection. It is not uncommon for users with a home LAN to connect a router between their PC and the Internet, thereby connecting all PCs in their house through a single cable modem. Cable providers prefer the standards-based modems, because they can send customers to retail outlets to purchase their own modems and self-install kits. The self-install process eliminates a costly technician visit and makes cable modem installation and operation a more profitable venture for the providers.

Cable networks can also dedicate channels for voice transmission, offering an alternative to the local telephone company for telephone service. Cable television networks offer one possibility for combining voice, broadcast video, and data on a single connection to the residence. However, the ability to send high quality video in both directions, as in video conferencing, requires more bandwidth than today's cable television systems provide to individual cable modems. Another network, known as *Broadband ISDN*, offers more promise in this area.

BROADBAND ISDN

The basic-rate and primary-rate ISDN interfaces were once considered extremely high-bandwidth interfaces. However, with improvements in transmission technology and the advent of fiber optic cables, much faster transmission rates are now possible. An even faster class of ISDN interface standards, referred to as *Broadband ISDN*, or *BISDN*, is currently being developed by the ITU(CCITT) to handle much higher transmission speeds. When compared to this new BISDN, the basic-rate and primary-rate ISDN interfaces are sometimes called *Narrowband ISDN*. However, Narrowband ISDN still provides a higher effective bandwidth than that of today's existing analog telephone facilities.

BISDN is already widely available to business users. The extremely high band-width of BISDN permits digitized video signals to be transmitted, as well as digitized voice and data. BISDN could eventually integrate our telephone and cable television networks into a single network that delivers information to businesses and residences.

The business applications of BISDN would include inexpensive high-quality videoconferencing. Digital video telephones would cost no more than a small television set does today. Residential applications could revolutionize entertainment. Rather than going to the video store to rent a movie, a BISDN user would call the video store's computer, scan a catalog of available movies on the television screen, and make a selection. The rental fee would be automatically deducted from the user's bank account, and the movie would be transmitted to the home from the video store.

With BISDN, many office workers could effectively work at home and could even attend meetings through high-quality videoconferencing. Other work could be performed on their home computer and transferred to their boss, who might also be at home. The telephone would still exist for everyday voice conversations.

Compared with today's analog service, Narrowband ISDN simply adds a data channel and signaling, uses digital voice transmission, and provides additional services. BISDN, on the other hand, could actually revolutionize the way in which we communicate. For this reason, some people believe that BISDN will eventually achieve greater residential penetration than Narrowband ISDN will. Many feel that Narrowband ISDN will be used mainly by businesses and that most residential users will not be interested in it. BISDN, however, may provide such clear advantages to residential users that it will be hard to resist. On the other hand, many see BISDN as a technology primarily for use by carriers that are building their wide area networks. A further discussion of BISDN technology will clarify its usefulness.

Broadband ISDN Transmission Media

As discussed in Chapter 2, the trend towards deregulation in the telecommunications and cable television industries should speed up the deployment of combined voice and video networks. The timetable for widespread implementation of BISDN will be accelerated by deregulation. The infrastructure necessary to be successful in this market is significant, so the more companies—and, hence, the more capital committed to its deployment—the sooner BISDN will be widely deployed.

Fiber optic cable has been replacing copper cable in many of these companies' long-distance lines for years because it is an affordable method of transmitting a very high bandwidth. Recognizing that a high-bandwidth infrastructure is the key to success in the BISDN market, some local phone companies and cable companies are already extending their fiber optic networks to locations that are very near to the customers. When the fiber optic cable reaches the customer premises, it is often called *fiber to the premises*, or *fiber to the home* in residential applications.

Most networks use fiber optic cable for much of the distribution, but return to copper cable of some form before reaching the customer premises. Copper cable can support high bandwidths, but for much shorter distances than fiber optic cable can. Most of the distribution schemes take advantage of this fact and do not demand the use of fiber optic cable to every phone jack and cable box. While rewiring the network is difficult enough, rewiring customer premises makes it even more difficult to sell new services. Therefore, both phone and cable companies will probably use the existing copper wiring inside residences and businesses and switch to fiber only after leaving the building.

Fiber to the curb is the term used to describe one approach taken by phone companies, where fiber optic cable is used to connect the central office to a section of a particular street. A special device then converts the optical signals to electrical signals for transmission to the customer on ordinary twisted pair wire. *Fiber to the neighborhood* describes a similar approach taken by cable television companies. This method is sometimes called *fiber to the feeder* or *fiber to the vault*. In this scheme, the fiber optic cable reaches only as far as the neighborhood and does not reach each customer's street. In this case, the device converting the optical signals to electrical ones serves the entire neighborhood, typically transmitting this electrical signal to the customers over coaxial cables. There are other hybrid distribution schemes being used, and all seek to balance the benefits of fiber optics with the economic reality of already installed copper cable in customer premises.

ASYNCHRONOUS TRANSFER MODE

The transmission technology used to implement BISDN is *Asynchronous Transfer Mode*, or *ATM*. Although this is not the only technology suitable for BISDN, it is the one that was chosen by all major standards committees. ATM technology can also be used as a transmission technology for purposes other than BISDN. ATM does not require any fixed channel rate, or speed. Instead, it describes how to fragment data into fixed-size chunks, or *cells*, so that voice, video, data, or any other information can be sent over the same network.

For example, a user might subscribe to ATM at 45 Mbps, similar to the T-3 rate, or might instead choose a speed of several hundred Mbps or even many gigabits per second, or Gbps. The higher the bandwidth of the link, the greater the number of cells that can be transmitted. Though fiber optic cable is not required, the higher bandwidth that it affords is clearly an advantage for any network trying to carry video transmission or other demanding applications. There are many standards using twisted pair wire for a limited distance at speeds up to 100 Mbps and beyond, which suggests that twisted pair wire will play a significant role in future networks. However, some *multimedia* applications may outstrip twisted pair's capability. For example, would the users be satisfied with broadcast-quality video, or would they prefer something closer to *High-Definition Television*, or *HDTV*? Regardless of the underlying physical transmission media used, ATM can be the format, or protocol, used to transmit the cells.

Why was ATM selected for BISDN by all major standards bodies? Much of this acceptance can be credited to the work of the *ATM Forum*, a group of member companies, organizations, and users whose sole purpose is to promote the rapid development and deployment of the ATM specification. Founded in October 1991, this group grew quickly, and it works with national and international standards bodies to encourage ATM activities. Some ATM specifications have been agreed upon in months, whereas prior networking committees have often taken years to settle detailed implementation issues.

Major standards bodies, such as ISO, ITU(CCITT), and ANSI, have recognized ATM as the standard of choice for BISDN. Inevitably, there will be another standard as yet unknown that will offer additional promise and performance. But for now, it appears that ATM will be the standard that ushers us into the BISDN era.

ATM Cells

The fundamental building block of an ATM link is a 53-byte cell. In ATM, and in telecommunications in general, bytes are often referred to as *octets*. The word *cell* is just a different name for a group of data bits, just as the words *packet* and *frame* are used in other standards. The word *cell* is generally used only with respect to the 53 bytes found in ATM.

The 53-byte cell is made up of two parts, the *header* and the *payload*, as shown in Fig. 10-17. The header consists of 5 octets, and the payload consists of the remaining 48 octets. Depending on the type of data being sent, the 48 octets may contain additional overhead to help partition and reassemble longer messages so that the user may be able to use as few as 44 octets of each cell.

There are different types of headers, depending on the endpoints on each link. For example, one type of header is used at the *User–Network Interface*, or *UNI*, where customer-premises equipment connects to a provider network. Another type of header is used at the *Network–Network Interface*, or *NNI*, where two provider networks are connected together. While the detailed formats of the headers are not important for our discussion, it is important to know that there are different formats, depending on the type of interface.

Physical Transmission in ATM

The asynchronous part of ATM does not refer to the physical transmission of the bits. In fact, the bits are transmitted synchronously. Rather, it refers to the fact that the arrival of the next cell does not occur at a predictable, fixed rate, much as characters arrive at any time in asynchronous data transmission.

How is it possible to send a synchronous bit stream composed of asynchronously arriving cells? Consider the bit stream to be continuous, but the data sporadic. Two methods are used to maintain the continuous bit stream. If no user data needs to be transmitted, then either a special pattern of bits representing an idle line can be sent, or idle cells can be transmitted. The receiver gets a continuous stream of bits, some of it cells containing user payloads and others representing idle time, either in the form of idle bits or idle cells. The physical transmission medium can impose other overhead bits to separate timing from data and to help position cells within the continuous bit stream.

Header	Payload
5 octets	48 octets

FIGURE 10-17

An ATM cell.

Many different telecommunications network standards for transmitting data at high speeds would be suitable for carrying ATM cells. The T-3 rate of 45 Mbps was already mentioned. The *Synchronous Optical Network* standard, or *SONET*, is an ANSI standard commonly discussed as a transmission method for ATM. Line speeds in SONET are usually designated by the term *Optical Carrier-N*, or *OC-N*, where $N \times 51.84$ Mbps is the speed of the line. For example, *OC-1* refers to a 51.84 Mbps speed, *OC-3* refers to 155.52 Mbps, and *OC-12* refers to 622.08 Mbps. OC-3 is literally the combination of three OC-1 signals, and OC-12 is made up of twelve OC-1s. The electrical equivalent of the OC-N signals is referred to as *Synchronous Transport Signal-N*, or *STS-N*. The data carried is the same in both cases, but we use the OC-N label when it is in optical form, and we reserve STS-N for the electrical transmission. When a circuit is being used as a single channel, we add a "c," for *concatenated*, to the end of the label. For example, OC-3c means that we use the entire bandwidth of 155.52 Mbps as a single channel, rather than as three separate 51.84-Mbps channels.

These OC-N/STS-N signals are similar to the ITU(CCITT) standard known as *Synchronous Digital Hierarchy*, or *SDH*. The lowest multiple available in SDH is 155.52 Mbps. These signals are labeled as *Synchronous Transport Module-N*, or *STM-N*, where N is the number of multiples used. For example, the OC-3 speed of 155.52 Mbps would be the equivalent of an *STM-1*. The relationships between some common speeds and the standards that apply are shown in Fig. 10-18.

SONET and SDH provide physical transmission paths on which ATM cells can be transmitted, but they can also be used to transfer information in other formats, including traditional circuit-switched digital voice. SONET and SDH, however, provide conveniently available high-speed paths that offer the bandwidth needed for advanced applications. Numerous other standards, including T-1, T-3, 25 Mbps, and 100 Mbps standards, could also serve as the physical pipe that carries ATM cells. Undoubtedly, many other standards will evolve, especially at the UNI, to meet the widely varying bandwidth demands of users. ATM can operate at any speed, making it a very flexible technology that can fit any application, and it can take advantage of future improvements in transmission methods.

Routing Cells in an ATM Network

In Chapter 8, we discussed packet switching networks in detail. Some of the characteristics of traditional packet switching networks that made voice transmission impractical were the long delays and the uncertainty of route. Since packet #3 might arrive before packet #2, an additional delay might occur at the destination while the packets are resequenced.

Rate	OC	STS	SDH
51.84 Mbps	OC-1	STS-1	n/a
155.52 Mbps	OC-3	STS-3	STM-1
622.08 Mbps	OC-12	STS-12	STM-4
1.24416 Gbps	OC-24	STS-24	STM-8
2.48832 Gbps	OC-48	STS-48	STM-16
9.95328 Gbps	OC-192	STS-192	STM-64

FIGURE 10-18

Some synchronous transmission standards.

ATM does not have this resequencing problem, since all cells follow the same route. Also, several assumptions in ATM help reduce the delay to a bare minimum. First, it is assumed that the underlying transmission media is digital in nature and is relatively error free. Therefore, ATM does not require the link-error recovery found in protocols like X.25. The lowest layer of the network assumes that the data arrives without errors and relies on higher layers at the source and destination to rectify any problems with data integrity, if necessary. Some basic error checks are performed on the header to ensure that the cell is not misrouted, but the user data is not checked inside the ATM switches.

With the assumption of no payload errors and the guarantee that all cells follow the same route, the major remaining causes for delay are travel distance and the time spent in each node of the network. The travel distance cannot be avoided and would be present in a traditional circuit-switched network as well. So the key is to minimize the routing time at each node. ATM switches accomplish this task by establishing the route for cells at the beginning of each conversation. Once the routing decision is made for a call, the individual switches can be preprogrammed with instructions for handling cells for the duration of the conversation. When cells do arrive at an ATM switch, the switching can be performed mostly by hardware, because the routing decision has been made in advance and stored in a table in each switch. The ATM switch checks the header of the incoming cell and, based on this header, looks up the correct port on which to transmit the cell on the next leg of its journey. As the cell is transmitted, the header can be modified at each step to point to the correct entry in the table in the following switch.

The header consists of *Virtual Channel Identifiers*, or *VCIs*, and *Virtual Path Identifiers*, or *VPIs*, which are modified as necessary by each node in the network to ensure proper transmission of the cell to its destination. Rather than each node making an independent routing decision, as in traditional packet switching, the nodes simply follow their preprogrammed instructions and modify the VPIs and VCIs accordingly as they transmit the message.

In some ways, ATM is similar to the frame relay method discussed in Chapter 8. They both assume inherently reliable physical networks and therefore have minimal error recovery in the network. However, ATM relies on fixed cell sizes, while frame relay allows for various frame lengths. ATM also has different data formats to accommodate a wide variety of message types, including voice, video, and data, while frame relay is largely a data-transport mechanism. One significant difference between an ATM network and a frame relay network is that ATM is very well suited to carry *isochronous* traffic. In the case of voice traffic, this means that the approximate timing between cells, as well as the order of the cells, is maintained as the cells flow through the network. If 53-byte cells were placed into the network at a certain rate, they would come out at roughly the same rate and in exactly the same order. If the cells had a 3-msec gap between them when they entered an ATM network, they would have approximately a 3-msec gap when they leave the network. While a frame relay network with little or no traffic might perform this way by chance, an ATM network has special timing mechanisms to increase the likelihood that this performance happens. This factor makes ATM networks ideally suited to voice and video communications.

Video Transmission and ATM

While ATM might provide an infrastructure for transmitting video, it says little about how to turn video images into ones and zeroes. The MPEG standard discussed earlier in this chapter is an excellent example of a digitization technique for video that will be carried on ATM networks. Since ATM is scalable in terms of speed, it certainly could accommodate video signals of varying quality, depending on the bandwidth the user is willing to pay for. While compression techniques and algorithms may improve, this improvement does not affect ATM itself, because the digitized video is merely the payload carried on the ATM network.

ATM and the OSI Model

One can think of ATM as providing service at least at Layers 1 and 2 of the OSI model. However, some higher layer activities, like routing, do occur on an ATM network as well. Most users treat ATM as a physical link, ignoring the internals of the network, and add higher layer protocols to ensure the integrity of the network. If the user is comfortable with the reliability of the digital links, then OSI Layers 1 and 2 can be considered to be satisfied by ATM and the underlying links, and only OSI Layers 3 and 4 need to be considered to complete the transport picture. One good example of ATM use is to interconnect LANs with routers using an ATM network between them. TCP/IP can then be used as the OSI Layers 4 and 3 protocols, with ATM as the underlying service for OSI Layers 2 and 1.

ATM Layers

The ATM standard itself describes its functions in three layers, as shown in Fig. 10-19. These layers are not identical to the first three layers of the OSI model. The lowest layer is the *Physical Layer*, where the cells are actually transmitted. This layer is similar to OSI Layer 1, although it transmits cells rather than individual bits. The cells transmitted over a standard such as SONET make up this Physical Layer. The next layer is the *ATM Layer*, which is responsible for handling the mechanics of cell transport. This job includes separating cells from different connections, reading and interpreting the headers, and routing information. The ATM Layer is responsible for manipulating the VPI and VCIs as the cells travel through the network to direct them to their destination. The highest layer is the *ATM Adaptation Layer*, or *AAL*, which breaks down user data into 48-octet payloads so that it can be packaged into cells and then reassembles the cells into the original data stream at the destination. The AAL may also perform other functions, depending on the service required of the ATM network.

ATM Adaption Layer
ATM Layer
Physical layer

FIGURE 10-19

Layers in ATM.

ATM Capacity Issues

Theoretically, an ATM network could accommodate any mix of voice, video, and data traffic, as long as the user does not exceed the bandwidth of the physical link to the network. It can even handle a source of data that varies in speed, often referred to as *variable bit rate* data.

ATM is particularly useful when data is combined from many sources. For example, a user with a 64-kbps voice connection, a 10-Mbps Ethernet data stream, and a 7-Mbps compressed video transmission would have no problem breaking these messages into ATM cells and transmitting them on the same 45-Mbps ATM link. A large pipe, through which users can transmit data at varying rates, provides *bandwidth on demand*. ATM exhibits this characteristic in theory, but in practice there are limitations.

The network may have the bandwidth to receive all of these messages over the initial pipe, but the capability to transmit them across the entire network can be limited by other factors. For example, a highway on-ramp might support 60 cars per minute entering an empty highway. But at rush hour, there might already be so many cars on the highway that only 10 per minute can enter and find a place on the highway. So, network capacity may not always be available, even though your link to the network may have the available bandwidth.

To understand ATM capacity issues, it is useful to contrast ATM with traditional voice networking, like T-1 or even Narrowband ISDN's B-channel service, both of which require fixed channels to be established. These 64-kbps channels are reserved for an entire call, whether or not anyone is talking or anything is being transmitted. Similarly, several of these 64-kbps channels are sometimes grouped together to provide medium-quality videoconferencing. In both cases, these are circuit-switched connections. Once a call is established, the channel is allocated and the bandwidth is reserved.

Rather than establishing fixed B-channels for the duration of the voice or video call, ATM simply accepts cells on one side of the network and delivers them to the other side. A video call would naturally generate many more cells than a voice call would. The variable bandwidth demand of ATM is harder to predict than the simple 64 kbps required for a voice connection in traditional networks, so the carriers running the network are faced with an interesting dilemma. Should the network be sized to accommodate low-bandwidth voice calls, high-bandwidth video calls, or both at the same time? In between are data calls, which require a wide range of bandwidth, from a simple electronic mail message to a database file that contains many megabytes. This classic statistical multiplexing problem is caused, not by ATM, but by the variability of the traffic requirements. The network used must be prepared for any combination of traffic from 64 kbps up to the speed of the physical link, perhaps as high as many gigabits per second.

ATM Tariff Issues

Pricing ATM appropriately is a problem that plagues many carriers who hope to deliver commercially viable service. While traditional networks price voice calls based on distance, connection time, and time of day, ATM must also consider the type of service provided. For example, a video call will clearly cost more than a voice call, but the price will not be directly proportional to the number of bits transmitted.

A 2-hour movie, transmitted using MPEG II video and requiring 7 Mbps, is approximately 50.4 gigabits. Assuming $3 is charged to view this movie, the cost translates to roughly 6 cents per gigabit. With voice at 64 kbps, you could speak for 4 hours and 20 minutes before reaching 1 gigabit. Six cents for a 4-hour phone call sounds low by traditional measures, but with many carriers now offering flat-rate long-distance plans, it is not hard to imagine this scenario: unlimited voice calls for a flat rate, with a reasonable charge (e.g., $3.00) for downloading a movie.

Carriers will need to strike a balance between call setup, quality of service or bandwidth, call duration, and time-of-day usage charges. One possibility is the notion of the bandwidth contract, where users pay a certain rate to guarantee availability of a given bandwidth, but can burst to higher speeds when there is additional demand and the network has space available. Premium rates could be charged for bursting above your guaranteed rate at high traffic times.

Issues such as traffic, congestion control, and tariffs will probably be refined during deployment of these networks. Clearly, today's approaches to traffic, congestion control, and tariffs as used in circuit-switched networks are not appropriate to handle the wide range of bandwidth possible in the ATM networks of the future.

VOICE OVER IP

In the 1990s, IP became the most widely used protocol for local area networks. As bandwidth on these networks increased, many users became interested in combining voice and data on these networks. *Voice Over IP*, or *VOIP*, is a general term that refers to any transmission of voice on a network that uses the IP protocol. VOIP has several interesting commercial uses. The first, in the business environment, is as an alternative to a traditional PBX. The second is as a means of transmitting voice over an IP network instead of through the PSTN to save long-distance costs, especially for users who already own or lease an IP network for data transmission. These two cases both have their own implementation issues and challenges. With appropriate network planning and design, these issues and challenges are easily overcome, allowing the user to reap the benefits of the convergence of voice and data on a single network.

Quality of Service

Businesses, especially ones that are extremely conscious of maintenance costs, liked the idea of a single network in the workplace. It eliminated the need to maintain and administer separate voice and data wiring infrastructures and switching platforms. In theory, the same data network could provide for all of a company's voice and data needs. In practice, voice has more stringent requirements than data, with the three most important requirements being *delay, jitter*, and *packet loss*. The *Quality of Service*, or *QoS*, requirements for a particular type of traffic impose limits on the acceptable delay, jitter, packet loss, and other performance characteristics.

A half-second *delay* in transmission would cause no issues for email traffic, but it could present significant problems for a voice conversation. The delay might be introduced by congestion in an IP network at a particular router or on a particular link, causing IP packets to be held in a buffer for some time before being transmitted. In addition, a large number of hops across the network through various routers and links can introduce substantial delay. Voice connections with long delays can result in echoes and difficulty conversing. Long delays often cause one user to inadvertently interrupt the other, because the first user thinks the other has finished talking. In fact, the other user may have just paused for a moment and may already have resumed talking. Due to the delay, however, the first user begins talking, thereby interrupting the other user. While the impact of delay on a conversation is subjective, somewhere between 100 msec and 200 msec, almost all users cite it as a frustration and a concern.

A second characteristic that is important for voice calls on an IP network is *jitter*. Jitter refers to the variability of delay through a network. For example, when an IP packet passes through a network in 200 msec one time and then later passes through in 300 msec, the variance in this delay pattern is known as jitter. A voice conversation could be interrupted by this jitter, because as the delay increases in the middle of the conversation, there would be a time when the next expected voice packet doesn't arrive. This variable delay could cause a gap or a brief moment of silence in the conversation. While buffers can be used to mask this problem, their use introduces additional delay, thus fixing one problem by introducing another.

In addition, network congestion can result in *packet loss*, typically when buffers in network-switching equipment are exhausted. An occasional lost packet will not degrade voice quality significantly, as it results in only a brief silence or even a barely audible click on the line. Multiple lost packets, however, will pose a problem, and steps must be taken to reduce congestion in the network if this problem becomes serious. It is necessary to balance the delay, jitter, and packet loss characteristics for successful transmission of VOIP traffic. These factors are not as important when sending email or browsing the Internet. For this reason, networks that are suitable for data use may not be suitable for voice use without some redesign.

Problems with jitter and delay can be solved in several ways. In some cases, either additional bandwidth or a different routing topology can be used to reduce congestion which in turn helps reduce delay, jitter, and packet loss. Another helpful approach is to use switches and routers that are designed to recognize the various traffic types and to always put voice ahead of data traffic in their buffers when congestion occurs. Sometimes this feature can be turned on in already existing equipment, while in other cases, new equipment may need to be purchased that supports this traffic sorting. It is much simpler to provide for this feature inside a single building or campus environment than across a wide area network. Over the WAN, where you have no control over the carrier's equipment, you can rely on one of several protocols that are available for requesting and achieving the necessary QoS. If IPv6 is available in the WAN, QoS concerns are easily addressed. Even with IPv4, protocols like RSVP and Diffserv, previously discussed in Chapter 8, can be helpful. Carriers typically offer a variety of service contracts to address the different traffic requirements.

Implementation Considerations

The first generation of VOIP solutions concentrated largely on reducing operating costs by having a single, converged voice and data network. The second generation of VOIP solutions uses applications that combine voice, data sharing, video, instant messaging, and email in order to provide the user with an enhanced communications experience. For example, telecommuters can work from home with a single data connection. By using a virtual private network (VPN) and appropriate software, they can conduct all of their business over this one connection. The combination of all of these media does put additional demands on the network, and care must be taken to ensure QoS is appropriate for voice traffic.

VOIP presents additional security concerns. The various security threats discussed in Chapter 6, including viruses and worms, can generate so much network traffic that they could interrupt VOIP service. In case of an attack by an email virus or worm, the automatic traffic prioritization in the switching equipment might succeed in protecting the voice traffic. Appropriate security devices can protect a network in most cases, but there is always the chance these devices may themselves be overwhelmed by a malicious attack.

Even if a VOIP system is implemented at your business or by your ISP, it is safe to assume that not everyone you communicate with will have a VOIP device. A *gateway* is used to interconnect VOIP users with non-VOIP users, such as PSTN users. A business with a VOIP system might use IP to carry all voice internally and attach a gateway to the IP network to interconnect to the central office of the PSTN using a standard trunk, such as the analog or T-1 lines described in Chapter 2. Gateways can be divided into two pieces, with the call signaling handled in one component, and the media (e.g., analog to digital conversion) handled in another. Protocols like *Media Gateway Control Protocol*, or *MGCP*, and *MEGACO*, are used to *decompose* gateways into these two pieces. Another device, known as a *Multipoint Control Unit*, or *MCU*, is used to mix voice streams from several users to allow for conference calls, as well as to handle other media-processing tasks. MCUs can also be decomposed into separate signaling and media-handling units.

Voice quality on VOIP systems can vary dramatically. While the PSTN traditionally uses 64 kbps to digitize voice, VOIP systems offer a wide range of *codecs*, or *coder/decoders*. Industry standards are available with various compression techniques ranging from as low as 4 kbps to 64-kbps PSTN quality voice and beyond. One modern codec, *G.722*, can provide near-CD quality audio with only 16 kbps, resulting in a superior experience to the PSTN quality, 64-kbps *G.711* codec. When connecting to a network from home with a dial-up modem, users are often willing to give up voice quality to reduce the bandwidth requirements.

In addition, implementing VOIP in a building or campus environment requires high availability. For example, while the user's PC might shut down during a power failure, the user expects the VOIP phone to continue working. So the office LAN, which was originally designed to interconnect PCs, now has the added burden of operating during a power failure. If backup power is provided for this LAN, it can also be used to power LAN-attached phones. Therefore, any data network can be designed to support voice, even under extreme conditions, though some thought, planning, and additional expense may be involved.

SIP and H.323

While the PSTN had numerous protocols (e.g., SS7) for placing voice calls, similar mechanisms had to be established to allow call signaling over an IP network. Two protocols for VOIP signaling are the IETF's *SIP* and the ITU's *H.323*. Some vendors opt for proprietary call-signaling methods other than SIP or H.323, though these methods lock users into a single vendor's equipment. While H.323 was the earlier standard, SIP is more widely used today. *SIP*, or *Session Initiation Protocol*, provides great flexibility in addressing schemes, as phone numbers, email addresses, or IP addresses can be used to identify the called or calling party. The type of connection (e.g., voice, video, or both) is identified at call setup time, and the recipient can accept or reject any part of the connection. Some of the basic components in a typical SIP system are shown in Fig. 10-20. A *registrar* function, usually required in each SIP network, is where users sign in and are authenticated. A *location server* tracks the IP address from which the user signed in, allowing a user to receive their SIP calls wherever they are. *Proxy servers* and *redirect servers* are also used to assist in forwarding call requests to the appropriate location. A single computer may perform all of these functions, though they are described separately in the SIP standard to allow them to be implemented separately. Other information, including *presence*, which indicates you are online and available, can be kept on a *presence server* and can be exchanged with

FIGURE 10-20

A typical SIP-based VOIP system.

SIP messages. While presence is not part of basic VOIP service, many SIP environments contain it today. Essentially, all of the functions found in a traditional office PBX can be reconstructed in the SIP world, though they are typically based on industry standards and contain the enhanced mobility that SIP affords. Any Internet connection can be used to link back to your home SIP system, allowing great flexibility for the user.

The first widely used VOIP protocol, predating SIP, was the ITU's *H.323*. This standard uses similar call signaling to ISDN networks. The signaling packets, however, are passed through the IP networks in this case. While users can contact each other directly to place calls, it is impractical to assume you will always know everyone's IP address. Therefore, a *gatekeeper* often is used to provide authentication and to track a user's location in an H.323 network, similar to the registrar and location server in SIP. While SIP is a protocol designed by the IETF specifically with IP networks in mind, H.323 is an adaptation of a circuit-switched signaling protocol superimposed on IP networks. Some of the basic components in a typical H.323 system are shown in Fig. 10-21.

Both SIP and H.323 take advantage of *Real-time Transport Protocol*, or *RTP*, which is designed to transfer time-sensitive information, like voice or video, over a data network. RTP provides functions needed for real-time transport, like time-stamping of packets. SIP and H.323 both support video conferencing, as well as basic voice calls.

IP phones can look like ordinary PSTN telephones, though they typically use an RJ45 connector to interconnect with a LAN. Some users opt instead for *soft clients*, where a PC application provides a dial pad and other calling capabilities, and where a headset/microphone or handset is attached to the PC's sound card or USB port. Soft clients can easily include phone book and contact list lookups and other convenient functions, including integration with other office applications. Soft clients are especially useful when you are travelling, because they allow you to make a phone call from your laptop computer or even your PDA. In spite of these conveniences, some users still prefer the user interface of a stand-alone IP telephone.

While the required functions of SIP and H.323 are often found on servers on a customer's premises, ISPs or carriers can offer these services on a centralized basis as well. *Hosted communications* solutions, sometimes called *IP Centrex*, centralize the network intelligence in the carrier's or ISP's site, using their equipment. These subscription-based services free the customer from buying and maintaining equipment in exchange for monthly service fees.

THE FUTURE OF CONVERGENCE

When home computers were originally introduced in the 1970s, manufacturers touted the computer as an information organizer that would be widely used to store recipes and help manage the household. Over time, however, many people decided that it was easier to keep recipes in a book or card file. Similarly, ISDN advocates originally believed that we would use the data channel to send instructions from our office computer to our home, to turn on the air conditioner, to ask our VCR to record a television show we forgot to program, and to transfer computer files so that we would not have to carry a briefcase. None of these predictions have come true.

FIGURE 10-21

A typical H.323-based VOIP system.

How will the *information superhighway*, so often discussed in the media at the beginning of this century, evolve in the future? Will the Internet, with its wide array of databases attached to a relatively low-speed network, increase in bandwidth and carry even more voice and video traffic? Will the full promise of Broadband ISDN ever be realized, with its possibility for efficient sharing of bandwidth to allow for cost-effective transmission of voice, video, and data? Will ATM networks extend to residences, or will cable modems, DSL services, and Narrowband ISDN continue to provide local access to the Internet? The answers to these questions depend largely on the speeds and services the users demand and the prices charged by the competing telephone and cable companies.

In our first decade of the 21st century, there is no need to choose between IP and ATM networks. In fact, it is clear that the two will coexist for some time. Most voice carriers have chosen ATM as the transmission technology behind their voice networks, and IP has been chosen by local area and wide area networks as the standard for data communications networks. IP network standards continue to evolve, and they eventually will offer many of the features for guaranteeing bandwidth that isochronous ATM networks do. Conceivably, we could continue forever with separate networks for voice, video, and data communications, but most people expect the technologies to continue to converge.

There are definitely two strong points of view in the industry on the direction that this convergence will take, though probably neither technology will conquer the other. If no networks were already installed, ATM would clearly win, since it carries all types of traffic with ease. Since IP data networks are widely deployed today, however, the problem is not so easy to solve. If data traffic were to continue to grow to the point that it was far greater than voice or video traffic, it might be practical to base the world's communications networks solely on IP. A small portion of the IP networks, then, could be set aside to carry voice and video traffic. Since IP doesn't provide the features required to reliably carry isochronous traffic in its current IPv4 implementations, however, IPv6 would need to be deployed and equipment would need to be changed or reprogrammed. Alternatively, IP could be used as the local access technology for data users, with the IP datagrams stuffed into ATM cells over the wide area networks that carried voice, video, and data traffic. Voice technology could use ISDN as the local access technology, while carriers could convert the B-channels to ATM cells for the wide area. Real networks that use all of these techniques are being deployed today.

Wireless networks have also blurred our picture of the future. While digital cellular capabilities have expanded slowly, wireless data hot spots have exploded onto the scene in densely populated areas. Today, this access offers great convenience to people in the work environment, as well as to business travellers and remote workers, but it has yet to transform our everyday life. The mere existence of high-speed wireless data connections can create new applications, some not even thought of yet today. Any of these new applications could be the so-called "killer app" that makes wireless connections a must for everyone. For example, today we seldom shop for a major appliance without checking advertisements or reviews in the weekend newspaper, on the Internet, or in consumer magazines. With universal wireless data access, you could bring up price and review information on your wireless PDA in the store as you shop.

The main question for the future will be the direction the Internet takes. Interestingly enough, most people discuss what is attached to the network, rather than discussing the network itself. The exciting new multimedia databases that can be accessed from the Internet are typical examples, and they garner much more public attention than IP protocols or any ATM congestion-control scheme ever will. This new marvel of technology, a high-bandwidth network, is not as impressive to the general public as what gets attached to it.

In a sense, we have returned to the origin of telecommunications. Surely, neither Samuel Morse nor Alexander Graham Bell was able to interest the general public in the voltages on their transmission lines. Rather, the potential uses of the information that could now be transmitted acted as the motivating force to lay the infrastructure for the new technologies. Just as users of early telephones could not even begin to imagine the pervasive role of telecommunications in today's world, we cannot predict all of the applications of a Broadband ISDN network or a global IPv6 Internet.

So, as standards committees continue to ponder the future of data communications, new technologies are sure to emerge. The driving force behind the implementation of these networks of the future will be the potential applications rather than the technology itself.

SUMMARY

In our first decade of the 21st century, telecommunications and data communications are converging. Both customer-premises equipment and transmission facilities increasingly use digital technology. Digital PBXs are being used to integrate voice and data with digital phones. LANs and PBXs can be connected to packet switching networks, frame relay networks, and IP networks, allowing communications among devices attached to any of them. In addition, transmission of still images, using fax, or of moving images, using video, once performed only by analog transmission methods, can now be done digitally. Digital transmission of voice is possible by using a digitizing method known as pulse code modulation, or PCM. In PCM, an analog signal is typically converted to a 64-kbps digital signal, using 8000 samples per second and eight bits per sample.

High-bandwidth digital transmission facilities are playing a major role in communications today. The T-1 standard, developed by AT&T, provides a 1.544-Mbps digital path now available from almost all of the common carriers. A T-1 carrier can provide 24 channels, each able to carry 64 kbps of digitized voice or 56 kbps of data over two twisted pairs; analog transmission of 24 voice channels would require 24 pairs of wires.

Even with the added expense of repeaters and digital transmission equipment, T-1 is an economical alternative for users with high-volume communications traffic. There are several different methods for carrying signaling information using a T-1 carrier. The T-1 channels can also be broken down into several lower speed channels by submultiplexing. In addition, voice and data compression can further increase the effective bandwidth of T-1 circuits. Finally, there are higher speed digital transmission facilities than T-1, such as T-1C and T-3, which provide 48 and 672 channels, respectively.

The Integrated Services Digital Network, or ISDN, is a set of standards for a digital network that carries both voice and data communications. The ITU(CCITT) led the international standards development effort, specifying both interface standards for connecting to the public network and network services. ISDN provides different types of transmission paths, known as channels. The B-channel, or bearer channel, is a 64-kbps digital channel for digitized voice or data. The D-channel is a 16-kbps or 64-kbps digital channel used for signaling information and sometimes for low-priority data packets. The A-channel is similar to today's analog voice circuits, and the C-channel provides a low-speed 16-kbps data channel for use with low-speed devices.

The basic-rate interface includes two B-channels and one D-channel, and it is intended for residential or individual business users. This interface provides voice and data communications, as well as an extensive signaling capability, for an individual user. The primary-rate interface contains 23 or 30 B-channels and 1 D-channel, and it is aimed primarily at larger business users. The 23 B + D version is intended for use in North America and Japan, where the 1.544-Mbps T-1 carrier is already prevalent, and the 30 B + D version is intended for use in Europe, where 2.048-Mbps transmission equipment currently exists. The hybrid interface contains both an A-channel and a C-channel and provides analog phone users with some of the benefits of ISDN.

Equipment attached to an ISDN network is classified into two basic categories: Terminal Equipment (TE) and Network Termination equipment (NT). In addition, several reference points are defined where various NT and TE devices are interconnected. Terminal equipment that is compatible with ISDN is known as TE1; terminal equipment that is not compatible with ISDN is known as TE2, and it can be attached to an ISDN network using a Terminal Adapter, or TA. The R reference point is between the TE2 and TA, and the S reference point is between the TE1, or TA, and NT equipment. The NT equipment that provides OSI Layer 1 services and terminates the network circuit on the customer's premises is known as NT1; OSI Layer 2 and 3 services, providing concentration and switching if needed, can be provided by NT2. Both the NT1 and NT2 functions can be combined in a single device, known as NT12. The point between the NT1 and NT2 (if an NT2 is used) is known as the T reference point; if no NT2 is used, then the S and T reference points coincide where the NT1 is directly connected to the Terminal Equipment. The U reference point occurs where the NT1 connects to the rest of the ISDN network.

PBXs and LANs can take advantage of an ISDN network's digital transmission facilities. However, to further motivate users to support ISDN, special services are provided. Many of these services are based on the extra signaling information available in the D-channel. The Signaling System 7, or SS7, is used to pass this information through the ISDN network. ISDN services can include call waiting, call forwarding, calling-party identification, camp-on, and message notification.

It is clear that ISDN can provide functional advantages to certain business users at a reasonable cost within existing technology. ISDN is already being implemented in the United States through National ISDN and in Europe through EuroISDN, though it is intended mainly for business users. Always On/Dynamic ISDN, or AO/DI, is particularly useful for remote access to corporate LANs or the Internet. The real potential of the residential market is not yet understood, and a completely digital telephone network may never be realized.

Digital Subscriber Line, or DSL, provides numerous ways to connect the user to the central office by digitally using twisted pair wire. Speeds vary from hundreds of kbps all the way to many Mbps, depending on the transmission option chosen. Many DSL implementations are asymmetric, offering higher transmission speeds from the central office to the user than in the other direction. DSL can be installed in residences using a splitter or with filters at each phone. At the central office, a splitter separates the voice and data, with the data going to a DSLAM and the voice going to the CO.

Most cable modems also provide an asymmetric, high-speed data connection, typically offering speeds as high as 30 Mbps in the high-speed direction and a few Mbps in the low-speed direction. The DOCSIS standard is the most widely accepted cable modem standard. Both DSL and cable-modem services are ideal for connecting residential users to the Internet or to the corporate LAN.

Broadband ISDN, or BISDN, is an even faster class of interface standards. BISDN, which can handle higher transmission speeds, can easily carry digitized video transmission, along with digitized voice and data. A mixture of fiber optic and copper cable is being used for BISDN. The transmission technology that is used to implement BISDN is Asynchronous Transfer Mode, or ATM. ATM fragments data into fixed-size chunks, or cells, so that voice, video, data, or any other information can be sent over the same network. The ATM Forum is promoting the rapid development and deployment of the ATM specification. ISO, ITU(CCITT), and ANSI have all recognized ATM as the standard of choice for BISDN.

The 53-octet ATM cell is made up of a 5-octet header and a 48-octet payload. One type of header is used at the User–Network Interface, or UNI, where customer-premises equipment connects to a provider network. Another type of header is used at the Network–Network Interface, or NNI, where two provider networks are connected.

In ATM, the bits are transmitted synchronously, although the cells may not always arrive at a fixed rate. Synchronous Optical Network, or SONET, is an ANSI standard commonly discussed as a transmission method for ATM. Line speeds in SONET are usually designated by the term Optical Carrier-N, or OC-N, with electrical equivalents referred to as Synchronous Transport Signal-N, or STS-N. These OC-N and STS-N signals are similar to the ITU(CCITT) standard known as Synchronous Digital Hierarchy, or SDH. Other transmission methods are also possible.

ATM establishes the route for cells at the beginning of each conversation. When cells arrive at an ATM switch, the switching can be performed mostly by hardware, since the routing decision has been made in advance and stored in a table that resides in each switch. Based on the header of the incoming cell, the ATM switch looks up the correct port on which to transmit the cell on the next leg of its journey. The header consists of Virtual Channel Identifiers, or VCIs, and Virtual Path Identifiers, or VPIs, which are modified as required by each node in the network to ensure proper transmission of the cell to its destination. ATM networks have special timing mechanisms that make them ideal for isochronous traffic.

ATM provides service at least at Layers 1 and 2 of the OSI model, though some higher layer activities, such as routing, are included. The ATM standard itself describes its functions in three layers: the Physical Layer, the ATM Layer, and the ATM Adaptation Layer, or AAL. A cell-relay network such as ATM presents a variety of capacity, traffic, and tariff issues far different from those encountered with a circuit-switched network. ATM and IP networks will continue to coexist for years to come.

Voice Over IP, or VOIP, is making significant inroads into business networks. If the data networks are properly designed to provide adequate Quality of Service, or QoS, voice quality can be superior to that offered by traditional phone networks. To achieve the required QoS, delay, jitter, and packet-loss characteristics must all be carefully controlled. Typical VOIP systems have an MCU for conferencing features, and a gateway to connect to non-VOIP systems like the PSTN. SIP and H.323 are two protocols found in VOIP systems. SIP systems may contain a registrar, location server, proxy server, and a redirect server, and they usually contain a presence server. H.323 systems often contain a gatekeeper. Users of SIP or H.323 systems can choose between IP phones or soft clients.

TERMS FOR REVIEW

AAL	*Asynchronous Transfer Mode*
A-channel	*ATM*
ADSL	*ATM Adaptation Layer*
ADSL Lite	*ATM Forum*
ADSL2+	*ATM Layer*
Always On/Dynamic ISDN	*Bandwidth on demand*
AO/DI	*Basic-rate interface*
Asymmetric Digital Subscriber Line	*B-channel*

Bearer channel
BISDN
BRI
Broadband ISDN
Cable modem
Cable modem termination system
Caller ID
C-channel
Cell
Channel
CMTS
Codec
Coder/decoder
Combined Network Termination 1 and 2
Common-channel signaling
Concatenated
Convergence
Data Over Cable Service Interface
    Specifications
D-channel
Decompose
Delay
Digital phone
Digital Subscriber Line
Digital Subscriber Line Access Multiplexer
Digitized
DOCSIS
DOCSIS 1.0
DOCSIS 1.1
DS-1
DSL
DSL Lite
DSLAM
EuroDOCSIS
EuroISDN
Facsimile
Fax
Fiber node
Fiber to the curb
Fiber to the feeder
Fiber to the home
Fiber to the neighborhood
Fiber to the premises
Fiber to the vault
Filter
Fractional T-1

Frame
Framing bit
G.711
G.722
G.Lite
Gatekeeper
Gateway
H.323
HDSL
HDSL2
HDTV
Head end
Header
High-bit-rate Digital Subscriber Line
High-Definition Television
Hosted communications
Hybrid interface
In-band signaling
Information superhighway
Integrated Services Digital Network
Integrated voice/data terminal
IP Centrex
IP phone
ISDN
Isochronous
IVDT
Jitter
Loading coil
Location server
MCU
Media Gateway Control Protocol
MEGACO
MGCP
Moving Pictures Expert Group
MPEG
MPEG II
Multimedia
Multipoint Control Unit
Multirate ISDN
N × 64
Narrowband ISDN
National ISDN
Network Termination 1
Network Termination 2
Network Termination equipment
Network–Network Interface

NNI
NT
NT1
NT2
NT12
OC-1
OC-3
OC-12
OC-N
Octet
Optical Carrier-N
Out-of-band signaling
Packet loss
Payload
PCM
Physical layer
Presence
Presence server
PRI
Primary-rate interface
Proxy server
Pulse code modulation
QoS
Quality of Service
R reference point
RADSL
Rate-Adaptive Digital Subscriber Line
Real-time Transport Protocol
Redirect server
Registrar
Robbed-bit signaling
RTP
S reference point
Sample
SDH
SDSL
Session Initiation Protocol
Signaling System 7
Single-line Digital Subscriber Line
SIP
Soft client
SONET
Splitter
SS7
STM-1
STM-N

STS-N
Submultiplexing
Synchronization
Synchronous Digital Hierarchy
Synchronous Optical Network
Synchronous Transport Module-N
Synchronous Transport Signal-N
T reference point
T-1 carrier
T-1 multiplexer
T-1C
T-1/D1
T-1/D2
T-1/D3
T-1/D4
T-1/D5
T-3
TA
TE
TE1
TE2
Terminal Adapter
Terminal Equipment
Terminal Equipment Type 1
Terminal Equipment Type 2
30 B + D
23 B + D
2 B + D
U reference point
UADSL
UNI
Universal Asymmetric Digital Subscriber
    Line
User–Network Interface
Variable bit rate
VCI
VDSL
Very-high-bit-rate Digital Subscriber Line
Video transmission
Virtual Channel Identifier
Virtual Path Identifier
Voice Over IP
VOIP
VPI
xDSL

EXERCISES

10-1. What are some examples of digital customer-premises equipment?

10-2. Explain how pulse code modulation can be used to digitize voice.

10-3. What is the total bandwidth of a T-1 circuit? What portion of this bandwidth is dedicated to framing and synchronization?

10-4. What are the advantages of using a T-1 circuit instead of 24 analog leased lines for PBX-to-PBX communications?

10-5. Why is submultiplexing sometimes used with T-1?

10-6. What are the names, functions, and bandwidths of the major ISDN channels?

10-7. What are the two major digital interfaces specified in the ISDN standards? What combination of channels are used in each? What are their intended functions?

10-8. Compare the different types of ISDN Terminal Equipment and their functions.

10-9. How do the functions of the various types of ISDN Network Termination equipment correspond to the lower layers of the OSI model?

10-10. What is the major difference between Narrowband and Broadband ISDN?

10-11. What is DSL? What makes ADSL different from a traditional digital phone line?

10-12. What is a cable modem?

10-13. What is ATM? What are the layers of ATM?

10-14. What is VOIP? What are some of its commercial uses?

10-15. What are some factors that influence QoS in VOIP?

10-16. What are two standards used for signaling in VOIP?

10-17. Which components are found in a typical SIP system?

The Binary Number System

In the binary number system, all numbers are represented using only zeroes and ones. Computers typically use the binary number system to represent information because it is easy for computer hardware to represent an off/on, or 0/1 condition.

The binary number system is based on powers of 2, while the more familiar decimal number system is based on powers of 10. There are many charts available for converting decimal numbers to binary numbers, and vice versa. However, most people can do without these charts. Like multiplication tables, they are a useful learning tool, but no one wants to have to consult a multiplication table every time one wants to multiply.

Fortunately, converting numbers between the binary number system and the decimal number system is an easy task. We first examine the decimal number system, and then the binary number system.

In the decimal number system, the digits 0, 1, 2, 3, 4, 5, 6, 7, 8, and 9 are used to represent all numbers. Each place or position in a number has a value that is a power of 10. The value of the first place is 1 or 10^0, the value of the second is 10 or 10^1, the value of the third is 100 or 10^2, the value of the fourth is 1000 or 10^3, and so on. For example, in the decimal number system, the number 5048 is really 5 times 1000, plus 0 times 100, plus 4 times 10, plus 8 times 1.

In the binary number system, numbers are represented in the same way, but powers of two are used for the places, and only a 0 or a 1 is used for each digit. Each place or position in a number has a value that is a power of two. The value of the first place is 1 or 2^0, the value of the second is 2 or 2^1, the value of the third is 4 or 2^2, the value of the fourth is 8 or 2^3, and so on. For example, in the binary number system, the number 1011 is 1 times 8, plus 0 times 4, plus 1 times 2, plus 1 times 1.

We consider only binary numbers up to eight bits long to simplify our discussion, although the same principles are applicable for a number of any size. In an eight-bit binary number, the place values are as follows:

Digits								
Values	*128*	*64*	*32*	*16*	*8*	*4*	*2*	*1*
Powers	2^7	2^6	2^5	2^4	2^3	2^2	2^1	2^0

The eight-bit number 10010110 could be placed in these positions this way:

Digits	1	0	0	1	0	1	1	0
Values	*128*	*64*	*32*	*16*	*8*	*4*	*2*	*1*
Powers	2^7	2^6	2^5	2^4	2^3	2^2	2^1	2^0

This number could be converted to decimal simply by multiplying the digits by the values and adding the results:

$$(1 \times 128) + (0 \times 64) + (0 \times 32) + (1 \times 16) + (0 \times 8) + (1 \times 4) + (1 \times 2) + (0 \times 1) = 150$$

$$128 \; + \; 0 \; + \; 0 \; + \; 16 \; + \; 0 \; + \; 4 \; + \; 2 \; + \; 0 \; = 150$$

For another example, consider the binary number 11101101:

Digits	1	1	1	0	1	1	0	1
Values	*128*	*64*	*32*	*16*	*8*	*4*	*2*	*1*
Powers	2^7	2^6	2^5	2^4	2^3	2^2	2^1	2^0

This number could be converted to decimal simply by multiplying the digits by the values and adding the results:

$$(1 \times 128) + (1 \times 64) + (1 \times 32) + (0 \times 16) + (1 \times 8) + (1 \times 4) + (0 \times 2) + (1 \times 1) = 237$$

$$128 \; + \; 64 \; + \; 32 \; + \; 0 \; + \; 8 \; + \; 4 \; + \; 0 \; + \; 1 \; = 237$$

Using eight bits, the binary number system can represent decimal numbers from 0 to 255. In other words, 0 in decimal converts to eight zeroes in binary, and 255 converts to eight ones in binary. Anything larger requires more bits. Any binary number can be converted to a decimal number using the preceding addition and multiplication technique.

Converting decimal numbers to binary numbers requires only subtraction and a simple decision: Is one number greater than or equal to another? For example, to convert the decimal number 185 to binary form, we must start at the left of our binary number form, which is shown as follows:

Digits								
Values	*128*	*64*	*32*	*16*	*8*	*4*	*2*	*1*
Powers	2^7	2^6	2^5	2^4	2^3	2^2	2^1	2^0

We then ask ourselves if 185 is greater than or equal to 128, the value of the digit on the left of our form. The answer is yes, so we need 128 in the number 185, and we use a 1 for that digit, which is shown as follows:

Digits	1							
Values	*128*	*64*	*32*	*16*	*8*	*4*	*2*	*1*
Powers	2^7	2^6	2^5	2^4	2^3	2^2	2^1	2^0

We then subtract 128 from 185, leaving us with 57. We now ask ourselves if 57 is greater than or equal to 64, the value of the next digit. The answer is no, so we don't need 64 in the number 185, and we use a 0 for this digit, which is shown as follows:

Digits	1	0						
Values	*128*	*64*	*32*	*16*	*8*	*4*	*2*	*1*
Powers	2^7	2^6	2^5	2^4	2^3	2^2	2^1	2^0

Since we didn't use 64, there is no subtraction necessary. We then ask ourselves if 57 is greater than or equal to 32, the value of the next digit. The answer is yes, so we need 32 in the number 185, and we use a 1 for that digit, which is shown as follows:

Digits	1	0	1					
Values	*128*	*64*	*32*	*16*	*8*	*4*	*2*	*1*
Powers	2^7	2^6	2^5	2^4	2^3	2^2	2^1	2^0

We then subtract 32 from 57, leaving us with 25. We now ask ourselves if 25 is greater than or equal to 16, the value of the next digit. The answer is yes, so we need 16 in the number 185, and we use a 1 for this digit, which is shown as follows:

Digits	1	0	1	1				
Values	*128*	*64*	*32*	*16*	*8*	*4*	*2*	*1*
Powers	2^7	2^6	2^5	2^4	2^3	2^2	2^1	2^0

We then subtract 16 from 25, leaving us with 9. We now ask ourselves if 9 is greater than or equal to 8, the value of the next digit. The answer is yes, so we need 8 in the number 185, and we use a 1 for this digit, which is shown as follows:

Digits	1	0	1	1	1			
Values	*128*	*64*	*32*	*16*	*8*	*4*	*2*	*1*
Powers	2^7	2^6	2^5	2^4	2^3	2^2	2^1	2^0

We then subtract 8 from 9, leaving us with 1. We now ask ourselves if 1 is greater than or equal to 4, the value of the next digit. The answer is no, so we don't need 4 in the number 185, and we use a 0 for this digit, which is shown as follows:

Digits	1	0	1	1	1	0		
Values	*128*	*64*	*32*	*16*	*8*	*4*	*2*	*1*
Powers	2^7	2^6	2^5	2^4	2^3	2^2	2^1	2^0

Since we didn't use 4, no subtraction is necessary. We now ask ourselves if 1 is greater than or equal to 2, the value of the next digit. The answer is no, so we don't need 2 in the number 185, and we use a 0 for this digit, which is shown as follows:

Digits	1	0	1	1	1	0	0	
Values	*128*	*64*	*32*	*16*	*8*	*4*	*2*	*1*
Powers	2^7	2^6	2^5	2^4	2^3	2^2	2^1	2^0

Since we didn't use 2, no subtraction is necessary. We now ask ourselves if 1 is greater than or equal to 1, the value of the next digit. The answer is yes, so we need 1 in the number 185, and we use a 1 for this digit, which is shown as follows:

Digits	1	0	1	1	1	0	0	1
Values	*128*	*64*	*32*	*16*	*8*	*4*	*2*	*1*
Powers	2^7	2^6	2^5	2^4	2^3	2^2	2^1	2^0

We then subtract 1 from 1, leaving us with 0, so we know we have accounted for all of the values in the number 185. If our result is not zero at this point, we know that we made an error in our calculation or that the number we chose is too large to be represented in eight bits (greater than the decimal number 255).

Based on our calculations, the binary number 10111001 is the equivalent of the decimal number 185. To double-check our efforts, let's convert it back to decimal:

$$(1 \times 128) + (0 \times 64) + (1 \times 32) + (1 \times 16) + (1 \times 8) + (0 \times 4) + (0 \times 2) + (1 \times 1) = 185$$

$$128 + 0 + 32 + 16 + 8 + 0 + 0 + 1 = 185$$

Converting between the binary and decimal number systems is a matter of following a simple set of rules. It allows us to easily convert between the decimal world we are familiar with and the binary world of computers.

For those who prefer to use a chart rather than performing the simple calculations, a conversion chart is provided in Fig. A-1 for the decimal numbers from 0 to 255.

Binary	Decimal	Binary	Decimal	Binary	Decimal	Binary	Decimal
00000000	0	00010001	17	00100010	34	00110011	51
00000001	1	00010010	18	00100011	35	00110100	52
00000010	2	00010011	19	00100100	36	00110101	53
00000011	3	00010100	20	00100101	37	00110110	54
00000100	4	00010101	21	00100110	38	00110111	55
00000101	5	00010110	22	00100111	39	00111000	56
00000110	6	00010111	23	00101000	40	00111001	57
00000111	7	00011000	24	00101001	41	00111010	58
00001000	8	00011001	25	00101010	42	00111011	59
00001001	9	00011010	26	00101011	43	00111100	60
00001010	10	00011011	27	00101100	44	00111101	61
00001011	11	00011100	28	00101101	45	00111110	62
00001100	12	00011101	29	00101110	46	00111111	63
00001101	13	00011110	30	00101111	47	01000000	64
00001110	14	00011111	31	00110000	48	01000001	65
00001111	15	00100000	32	00110001	49	01000010	66
00010000	16	00100001	33	00110010	50	01000011	67

FIGURE A-1

Binary	Decimal	Binary	Decimal	Binary	Decimal	Binary	Decimal
01000100	68	01110011	115	10100010	162	11010001	209
01000101	69	01110100	116	10100011	163	11010010	210
01000110	70	01110101	117	10100100	164	11010011	211
01000111	71	01110110	118	10100101	165	11010100	212
01001000	72	01110111	119	10100110	166	11010101	213
01001001	73	01111000	120	10100111	167	11010110	214
01001010	74	01111001	121	10101000	168	11010111	215
01001011	75	01111010	122	10101001	169	11011000	216
01001100	76	01111011	123	10101010	170	11011001	217
01001101	77	01111100	124	10101011	171	11011010	218
01001110	78	01111101	125	10101100	172	11011011	219
01001111	79	01111110	126	10101101	173	11011100	220
01010000	80	01111111	127	10101110	174	11011101	221
01010001	81	10000000	128	10101111	175	11011110	222
01010010	82	10000001	129	10110000	176	11011111	223
01010011	83	10000010	130	10110001	177	11100000	224
01010100	84	10000011	131	10110010	178	11100001	225
01010101	85	10000100	132	10110011	179	11100010	226
01010110	86	10000101	133	10110100	180	11100011	227
01010111	87	10000110	134	10110101	181	11100100	228
01011000	88	10000111	135	10110110	182	11100101	229
01011001	89	10001000	136	10110111	183	11100110	230
01011010	90	10001001	137	10111000	184	11100111	231
01011010	90	10001010	138	10111001	185	11101000	232
01011100	92	10001011	139	10111010	186	11101001	233
01011101	93	10001100	140	10111011	187	11101010	234
01011110	94	10001101	141	10111100	188	11101011	235
01011111	95	10001110	142	10111101	189	11101100	236
01100000	96	10001111	143	10111110	190	11101101	237
01100001	97	10010000	144	10111111	191	11101110	238
01100010	98	10010001	145	11000000	192	11101111	239
01100011	99	10010010	146	11000001	193	11110000	240
01100100	100	10010011	147	11000010	194	11110001	241
01100101	101	10010100	148	11000011	195	11110010	242
01100110	102	10010101	149	11000100	196	11110011	243
01100111	103	10010110	150	11000101	197	11110100	244
01101000	104	10010111	151	11000110	198	11110101	245
01101001	105	10011000	152	11000111	199	11110110	246
01101010	106	10011001	153	11001000	200	11110111	247
01101011	107	10011010	154	11001001	201	11111000	248
01101100	108	10011011	155	11001010	202	11111001	249
01101101	109	10011100	156	11001011	203	11111010	250
01101110	110	10011101	157	11001100	204	11111011	251
01101111	111	10011110	158	11001101	205	11111100	252
01110000	112	10011111	159	11001110	206	11111101	253
01110001	113	10100000	160	11001111	207	11111110	254
01110010	114	10100001	161	11010000	208	11111111	255

FIGURE A-1
(Continued)

Legacy Communications Equipment

We have already described the basic hardware components required for data communications. These include clients or terminals, host computers or servers, and sometimes modems and telephone circuits. We now turn to other components that improve the efficiency of data communications, thereby reducing costs and increasing performance. This equipment is typically found in configurations where mainframe computers, or minicomputers, are the host computers and where terminals are used as the client devices.

FRONT-END PROCESSORS

Host computers are well suited to performing numerical calculations, storing and retrieving documents, and accomplishing other tasks in a few millionths of a second. Human terminal operators, however, may type only a few characters in a second. It would be a waste of valuable computer time if the host computer had to spend all of its time monitoring the attached terminals. One of the terminal operators might go on a coffee break, and the host computer would then be tied up with unnecessary monitoring.

A *front-end processor*, or *FEP*, is a communications assistant for the host computer. The front-end processor handles all of the host computer's communications with the outside world, while the host computer concentrates on other things, like calculating this week's payroll deductions. The front-end processor is actually a small, special-purpose computer that is dedicated to a single mission. It communicates with the host computer at a very high speed (often several Mbps), while the terminals usually operate at a much lower speed (several kbps). Front-end processors are often referred to as *front ends*.

As an example, consider a brilliant, aloof professor whose mind works so quickly that she considers speaking with students to be a waste of time. Rather than asking the class if they have any questions and then waiting to see if students raise their hands, she hires a teaching assistant to deal with the students. Anyone with questions must write them down and hand them to the teaching assistant as he walks around the room. The assistant writes all of the questions on one sheet of paper, and the professor then grabs the sheet, quickly reads it, writes down all the answers on another sheet of paper, and hands the sheet back to the assistant. It's up to the assistant to walk around the room again, separating out each of the answers and handing them to the correct students. The professor is pleased because she didn't have to deal with the students, and she can continue to think great thoughts while they digest her answers. The teaching assistant has acted as a front-end processor for the professor; like the host computer, this brilliant professor has better things to do with her time.

In this example, the communication between the students and the teaching assistant occurred at a slow speed, while the communication between the professor and the assistant occurred at a much faster speed. This situation is analogous to the process by which front-end processors communicate. The front-end processor is made up of different logical components, as shown in Fig. B-1. The *channel interface* connects the front-end processor to the high-speed *input/output (I/O) channel* of the host computer. The *processing unit* contains the front-end processor's intelligence; it is a special-purpose computer programmed to perform communications functions. Often, the network control programs are loaded into the processing unit on disk or tape, allowing for future modifications to the software and, hence, the front-end processor's features. Finally, the *line interfaces*, or *front-end ports*, are the relatively low-speed interfaces that usually connect to terminals. If a terminal is located remotely, a pair of modems and a communications circuit can be inserted between the line interface and the terminal.

Since the number of computer ports is often limited by the host computer's architecture, front-end processors can greatly increase the number of terminals that can be attached to a host computer. A front-end processor allows many low-speed devices to share a single high-speed host computer port or channel. Since the channel interface operates at a relatively high speed compared to the line interfaces, the front-end processor may need to hold data destined for the terminals until it can transmit it to the terminals at a slower speed. Holding data in this manner is known as *buffering*.

Some front-end processors schedule terminal communications using special rules, known as *protocols*, which we discuss in detail in Chapter 7. The process by which the flow of communications between a host computer and smart or intelligent terminals is controlled by a front-end processor is known as *polling and selecting*. *Polling* occurs when the front-end processor asks a terminal, "Do you have any data to send to the host computer?" At this point, a smart terminal might send data or instead might simply answer "No." *Selecting* occurs when the front-end processor asks the terminal, "Can you accept data now?" A smart terminal might then answer "Go ahead" or "Not now, I'm busy." Only smart or intelligent terminals can respond to these messages; dumb terminals cannot be controlled using polling and selecting. The host computer could do the polling and selecting, but it is not necessary to waste a host computer's time on such a tedious, repetitive task when a front-end processor can accomplish it easily and cost effectively.

Returning to the previous analogy, polling is performed by the teaching assistant when he walks around the classroom, collecting papers from students who have questions. Selecting would be the approximate equivalent of the teaching assistant distributing the

FIGURE B-1

Using a front-end processor.

answers to those questions. Technically speaking, selecting would require the teaching assistant to ask each student, "Are you ready to receive your answer now?" The assistant would then hand the student the answer when the response is positive.

Many front-end processors can perform special functions that vary with each manufacturer and model. One popular function is error detection and correction. Front-end processors with this feature can detect, and sometimes correct, any bit transmission errors that occur. This function is explained in detail in Chapter 6.

Another function that some front-end processors can perform is *data conversion*. This type of conversion can include *code conversion*, in which the host computer and the terminal device each use a different character code. For example, an ASCII terminal could connect to an EBCDIC host computer using a front-end processor with a code conversion feature. Sometimes, *protocol conversion* is also needed; connecting a dumb asynchronous terminal, which doesn't understand protocols, to a host computer that uses synchronous protocols requires protocol conversion. Finally, *parallel/serial conversion* can be performed by some front-end processors. All of these conversion functions can be performed by separate devices, such as *protocol converters* or *parallel/serial converters*, but it is often less expensive to build these functions directly into the front-end processor. Front-end processors can be configured differently for each port, allowing different types of terminals to communicate with the same host computer.

Front-end processors can often perform *historical logging* or *statistical logging*. Logging provides a record of the users of the front-end processor, including various kinds of information about the users' actions. These two functions are explained in detail in Chapter 6.

Front-end processors are available with many different combinations of the aforementioned features. The number of line interfaces that a front-end processor can support varies by manufacturer and host computer model.

PORT-SHARING DEVICES

Though front-end processors allow terminals to share a high-speed host computer channel, sometimes the front-end ports can operate at faster speeds than the attached terminals. Other times, there may be more terminals than front-end ports. A *port-sharing device*, often called a *concentrator*, allows many terminals to share one front-end port, as shown in Fig. B-2. For example, the front-end port might be operating at 9600 bps, while the four terminals attached to the port-sharing device might each be operating at 2400 bps. In other configurations, all of the terminals might be operating at 9600 bps, but only one can transmit at any one time. A user with an eight-port front end and 10 terminals might opt to purchase a front end and a port-sharing device, rather than purchasing a second front end. The speeds are chosen for our example arbitrarily, and the concepts described will work at any speed.

Port-sharing devices are located near the front-end processor, and they usually require special intelligence in the front end that allows many terminals to communicate through a single front-end port. For example, if polling and selecting were being used, the front-end processor would need to know that several terminals are attached through a port-sharing device on a particular port. This information allows the front-end processor to send the polling and selecting messages for all of these terminals over a single front-end processor port. This polling and selecting intelligence is usually found in the front-end processor's software. If a terminal is located remotely, then the required pair of modems and a communications circuit are inserted between the port-sharing device and the terminal.

LINE SPLITTERS AND REMOTE INTELLIGENT CONTROLLERS

A *line splitter* performs the same function as a port-sharing device, though line splitters are located remotely from the front-end processor and host computer. The major advantage offered by line splitters is that only one pair of modems and one communications circuit are needed for many remote terminals in the same location. Typically,

FIGURE B-2

Using a port-sharing device.

terminal users in a given area of a building might all be attached to a line splitter, which is then connected to a remote front-end processor using a telephone circuit and modems, as shown in Fig. B-3.

A line splitter's cost can be justified because it reduces the number of modems and telephone circuits needed. Line splitters also require a front-end port that can accept more than one terminal. As with port-sharing devices, the front-end processor needs to know that several terminals are accessing the host through that single front-end port so that the proper polling and selecting messages can be transmitted to that port.

A *remote intelligent controller* is just like a line splitter, except that it can also perform some functions of front-end processors. For example, part of the front-end processor's task when communicating to smart or intelligent terminals through a line splitter is to poll the terminals constantly. Since humans type slowly compared to the speed at which a front-end processor can poll, most of the time the poll receives the following response: "No, I have nothing to send now." Normally, a front-end processor sends these polling questions and receives the answers over the single pair of modems to the line splitter, which routes the messages to each of the terminals. If one of the terminals has data to transmit, it still must share time on the modems with all of the other terminals that are simply sending back negative answers to the polling. Remote intelligent controllers, however, can usually perform the terminal polling themselves so that only real data is passed over the modems to the front-end processor. As a result, the

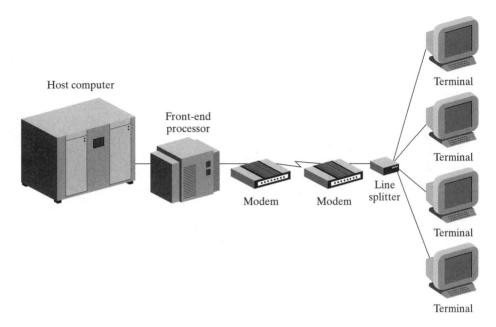

FIGURE B-3

Using a line splitter.

modems are free to perform real data transmission and the front-end processor has more time to concentrate on some of its other ports. The appropriate placement of a remote intelligent controller is shown in Fig. B-4.

Some manufacturers use names other than "port-sharing device," "line splitter," and "remote intelligent controller" for equipment that performs the functions just described. These generic terms, however, serve to describe functions that are common and universal throughout the industry.

All of these methods for improving data communications efficiency, whether with front-end processors, port-sharing devices, line splitters, or remote intelligent controllers, require a special compatibility with the attached host computer or terminals. For example, a front-end processor can be attached only to a host computer that is designed with special high-speed data channels for that purpose. Port-sharing devices, line splitters, and remote intelligent controllers usually require smart or intelligent terminals that can be controlled using polling and selecting. We now turn to other means of improving data communications efficiency that do not require any special features or action on the part of the host computer, front-end processor (if present), or terminal.

MULTIDROP CONFIGURATIONS

One type of configuration, known as *multidrop*, is unlike any we have discussed thus far. We have considered only a host computer or server port, attached to a single

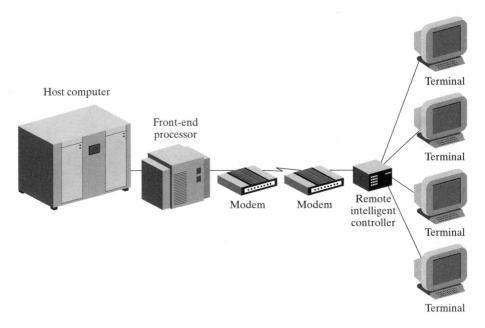

FIGURE B-4

Using a remote intelligent controller.

terminal or to a single device, such as a line splitter that could accommodate several terminals. Some host computer architectures, however, can directly accommodate several terminals on the same line. When used locally, these multidrop configurations typically have a single computer or server port with a cable running into the first terminal. The cable then runs from the first terminal to the second, and so on, as shown in Fig. B-5. Local multidrop configurations are most advantageous when terminals are located near each other and when the front-end processor is located in another room. Rather than running long cables from each terminal to the front-end processor, only one long cable and several short ones are needed.

The key to multidrop operation is that the host computer must "address" each message to a particular terminal, and each terminal must be able to determine which messages are destined for it. Similarly, terminals must mark their messages with their "return address" so that the host computer can determine the sender. Polling and selecting are necessary to prevent two terminals from trying to use the line at once. In addition, a host computer can send a *broadcast message* to all terminals on the line by using a special address recognized by all of the terminals.

Remote multidrop configurations can also be cost effective. As shown in Fig. B-6, a company with locations in San Francisco, New York, and Connecticut needs a communications circuit between the West Coast location and each of the East Coast locations. If we used two phone lines and two pairs of modems, the company would pay for two long-distance telephone lines, each about 2500 miles long. However, if we used a multidrop configuration, one 2500-mile line would be needed, and the second line would be only 40 miles long.

FIGURE B-5

Local multidrop configuration.

A message from San Francisco bound for Connecticut is routed through New York. The message is not displayed on the terminal in New York because the message is addressed to Connecticut; we could say that the terminal in New York simply ignored the message. There is a potential security risk with multidrop configurations, however, since a determined New Yorker could use special monitoring devices to eavesdrop on all of the communications sent to and from Connecticut.

Clearly, the long-distance communications costs are reduced; however, the multidrop capability must be present in the host computer or front-end processor and in the terminals used. The economic benefits of this configuration vary for each user, depending on the geographic layout of the user's network. Because there are so many other options for wide area networking, as described in Chapter 8, multidrop configurations are no longer as popular as they once were.

FIGURE B-6

Remote multidrop configuration.

APPENDIX C

Systems Network Architecture

IBM's *Systems Network Architecture*, or *SNA*, introduced in 1974, is one of the most widely used communications architectures in the world. SNA's success is usually attributed to its ability to connect a wide variety of devices, each with different capabilities, in a homogeneous network whose workings are hidden from the end user. SNA allows customers to start with a small network and increase its size in a modular fashion. SNA networks can also be connected to other SNA networks. Finally, SNA includes sophisticated network management functions to simplify fault isolation and problem determination, as well as to provide reports on network usage. We explain these functions in Chapter 9.

Like OSI, SNA functions can be divided into different layers. These layers roughly parallel the OSI model, but some SNA layers perform more or fewer functions than the corresponding OSI layers. The SNA layers are shown in Fig. C-1, along with a rough approximation of their OSI equivalents.

Because of SNA's flexibility and complexity, a thorough discussion of SNA requires several volumes. We therefore concentrate on some of the basic terminology and language of SNA, as well as describe its major functions. Since SNA is the architecture of a particular manufacturer (IBM), some of its terminology is slightly different from the terminology used previously in this book. For example, what we have often called "host computers" are known in SNA as *Host Processors*. Similarly, SNA *Workstations* are equivalent to the devices that we have called "terminals."

THE STRUCTURE OF SNA

The components or devices interconnected by an SNA network are known as *Nodes*. The Nodes are connected by data communications *Links*. For instance, a Host Processor and Workstation could be considered Nodes in SNA, and the two Nodes are connected by a communications Link. The *network* includes the components and the communications Links.

SNA layers

| Transaction Services |
| Presentation Layer |
| Data Flow Control |
| Transmission Control |
| Path Control |
| Data Link Control |
| Physical Control |

OSI layers

| Application Layer |
| Presentation layer |
| Session Layer |
| Transport Layer |
| Network Layer |
| Data Link Layer |
| Physical Layer |

FIGURE C-1

SNA layers vs. OSI.

SNA clearly separates the network from the users. In other words, the users do not have to understand how the network functions to use the network. For example, assume that an accountant is using a Workstation in an SNA network to access an accounting program on a Host Processor in the same network. There are two *End Users* in this communications path, the accountant and the accounting program. The accountant sends data to the SNA network and receives data from the SNA network. Similarly, the accounting program, which is a specific *Application Program* on the Host Processor, also sends data to the SNA network and receives data from the SNA network. The two End Users, the Application Program and the accountant, are isolated from the routing and transmission of data, which is handled entirely by the SNA network. Neither the accountant nor the accounting program need to understand how the data is routed or transmitted.

Often, there is a *Communications Controller* between the Host Processor and the Workstation, as illustrated in Fig. C-2. The Communications Controller's responsibilities include routing data through a network and controlling the communications Links. For example, the Communications Controller could be linked to several other Host Processors, allowing the same Workstation user to access several different computers.

Cluster Controllers are often added to allow several Workstations to share a single point of access to the network, as shown in Fig. C-3. A Cluster Controller is similar in function to the generic remote intelligent controller we presented in Appendix B. The Cluster Controller is often located many miles from the Communications Controller; however, the length of the communications Link is not important, and Links can even include telephone circuits and modems.

There are different types of Nodes in SNA, depending on their function. For example, as illustrated in Fig. C-4, the Host Processor is often referred to as the *Host Node*. A Communications Controller is referred to as the *Communications Controller Node*. A Workstation, or a Cluster Controller with several Workstations, is referred to as a *Peripheral Node*. A Peripheral Node is always the source and destination of data. Another type of Peripheral Node is a *Distributed Processor*, which is similar to a Host Processor, though more limited in function.

FIGURE C-2

Using a Communications Controller in an SNA network.

Host Processor

Communications Controller

Workstation   Workstation

NETWORK ADDRESSABLE UNITS

The SNA network components we have already discussed can be further broken down into the various functions that they perform. Each Node may contain several *Network Addressable Units*, or *NAUs*. Network Addressable Units have unique addresses so

Host Processor

Communications Controller

Cluster Controller

FIGURE C-3

Using a Cluster Controller in an SNA network. Workstation Workstation Workstation Workstation

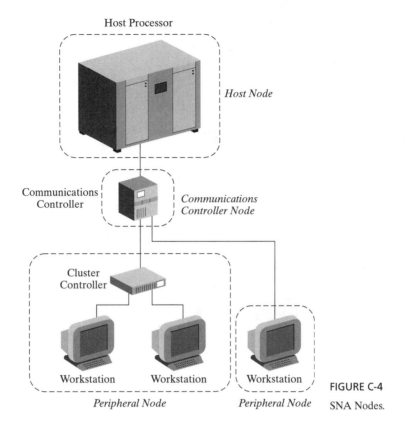

FIGURE C-4

SNA Nodes.

that data can be routed to a particular NAU. Network Addressable Units are a combination of hardware and/or software in a Node that manages a particular function. There are three types of Network Addressable Units: a *Logical Unit*, a *Physical Unit*, and a *System Services Control Point*.

A *Logical Unit*, or *LU*, is the End User's access point to an SNA network. For example, the End User of a Workstation in a Peripheral Node types data on the keyboard, which is then passed to the Logical Unit for routing to its destination, which is a Host Node in the SNA Network. When the data reaches the Host Node, it is passed to the Logical Unit in that Host Node. At the Host Processor, the End User is an Application Program, so the Application Program receives the data from a Logical Unit on the Host Node. Data enters and leaves the SNA network at the Logical Unit.

End Users are not part of the SNA network; instead, they each communicate with the SNA network through the network's Logical Units. When two End Users communicate in SNA through their respective Logical Units, it is known as an LU–LU *Session*, as shown in Fig. C-5. An SNA session is a communications path through an SNA network.

Workstations that are capable of communicating directly with an SNA network contain a Logical Unit. Some Workstations do not possess sufficient intelligence to communicate directly with the SNA network and are instead attached to a Cluster

Host Processor

Application Program
(End User)

Host Node

LU

Communications
Controller

Communications
Controller Node

End User

LU

Peripheral
Node

Workstation

FIGURE C-5

SNA LU–LU Session between
Logical Units in the
Workstation and Host.

Controller; in this case, the Cluster Controller contains the Logical Unit, as illustrated in Fig. C-6. Notice that the Communications Controller does not contain a Logical Unit, because there are no End Users at the Communications Controller Node, and data is only routed through the Communications Controller.

Every Node contains a *Physical Unit*, or *PU*, which manages and monitors that Node's resources. For example, the telephone lines and modems connecting two Nodes are not part of the SNA network. The Physical Unit represents these devices to the network, in much the same way that the Logical Unit represents the End User to the network. A simple SNA network with its Physical Units and Logical Units is shown in Fig. C-7. Notice that the Workstations connected to the Cluster Controller do not contain a Physical Unit, because the Cluster Controller is managing that Peripheral Node's physical resources.

Finally, the *System Services Control Point*, or *SSCP*, is a part of the Host Node that acts as a central control point for monitoring and controlling a network's resources. The System Services Control Point communicates with all of the Physical Units in the Network using SSCP–PU Sessions and all of the Logical Units in the Network using SSCP–LU Sessions. The SSCP can communicate with the PUs and LUs to ensure that they are operating properly; any malfunctions can be logged by the SSCP. Finally, the SSCP can help establish sessions between two LUs, thereby allowing End Users to communicate.

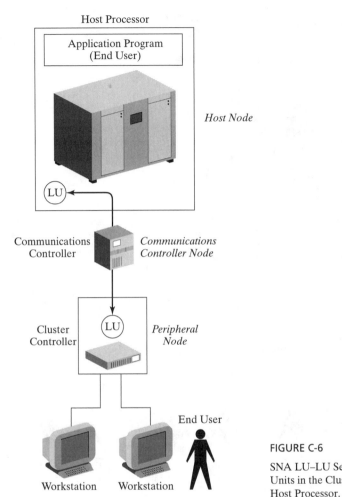

Host Processor

Application Program
(End User)

Host Node

LU

Communications
Controller

*Communications
Controller Node*

Cluster
Controller

LU

*Peripheral
Node*

End User

Workstation   Workstation

FIGURE C-6

SNA LU–LU Session between Logical
Units in the Cluster Controller and
Host Processor.

DOMAINS AND SUBAREAS

The SSCP can be thought of as the ruler of the SNA network, commanding all of the
PUs and LUs in its *Domain*. Each domain has only one SSCP. To establish an LU–LU
Session in which each LU is in a different Domain, the SSCPs of each Domain must
first communicate through an SSCP–SSCP Session. Two SSCPs and their respective
Domains are illustrated in Fig. C-8.

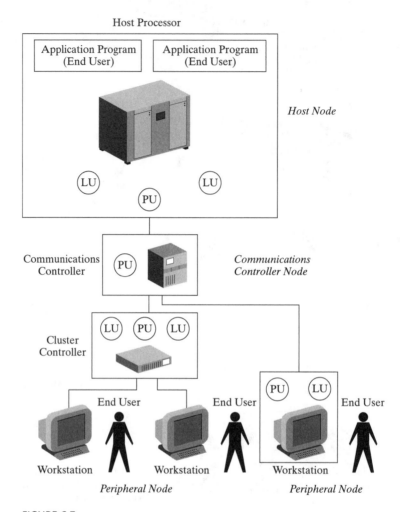

FIGURE C-7

SNA network with its Physical Units and Logical Units.

Domains can be subdivided into *Subareas*, each containing a *Subarea Node* and the resources that the Node controls. Host Nodes and Communications Controllers are both classified as Subarea Nodes. Therefore, as shown in Fig. C-9, each Host

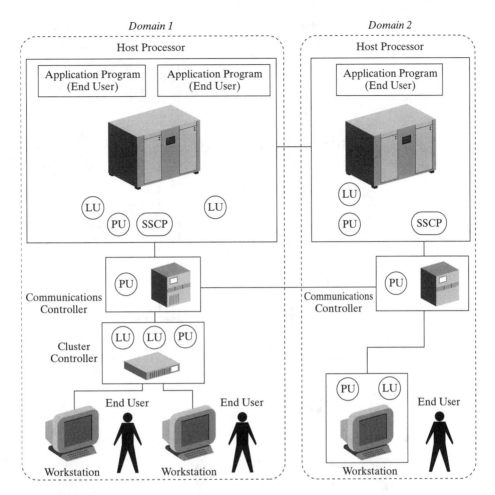

FIGURE C-8

Two-Domain SNA network.

Processor is a Subarea, and each Communications Controller, with its attached Workstations and Cluster Controllers, is also considered to be a Subarea. Also shown in Fig. C-9 are the Links between Subarea Nodes. These Links are known as *Transmission Groups*. If there are several Links in a Transmission Group and one should fail, communications are automatically routed over one of the other Links in the Transmission Group.

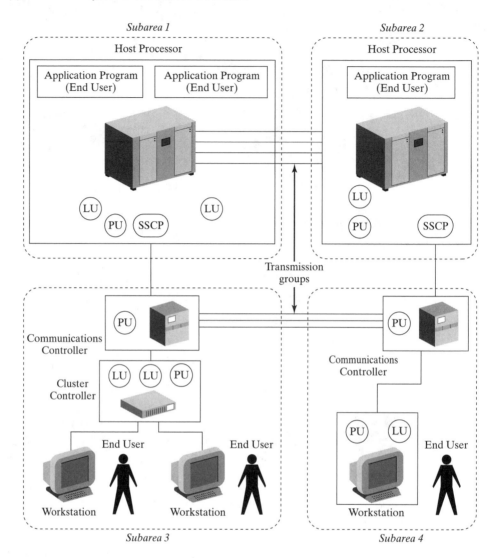

FIGURE C-9

Subareas and Transmission Groups.

Bibliography

A general listing of data communications books is provided first, followed by a suggested reading list of books and articles for each chapter in this text.

GENERAL DATA COMMUNICATIONS BOOKS

Black, Uyless D., *Computer Networks: Protocols, Standards, and Interfaces* (2d ed.). Englewood Cliffs, NJ: Prentice Hall, Inc., 1993.

Black, Uyless D., *Data Communications and Distributed Networks* (3d ed.). Englewood Cliffs, NJ: Prentice Hall, Inc., 1993.

Glover, I. A., and P. M. Grant, *Digital Communications*. Upper Saddle River, NJ: Prentice Hall, Inc., 1998.

Martin, James, *Telecommunications and the Computer* (3d ed.). Englewood Cliffs, NJ: Prentice Hall, Inc., 1990.

Panko, Raymond R., *Business Data Networks and Telecommunications* (4th ed.). Upper Saddle River, NJ: Prentice Hall, Inc., 2003.

Roden, Martin S., *Analog and Digital Communications* (4th ed.). Upper Saddle River, NJ: Prentice Hall, Inc., 1996.

Stallings, William, *Business Data Communications* (4th ed.). New York, NY: Macmillan Publishing Company, 2001.

Stallings, William, *Data and Computer Communications* (6th ed.). Upper Saddle River, NJ: Prentice Hall, Inc., 2000.

Tanenbaum, Andrew S., *Computer Networks* (4th ed.). Upper Saddle River, NJ: Prentice Hall, Inc., 2003.

CHAPTER 2: UNDERSTANDING TELECOMMUNICATIONS

Garber, Lee, "Will 3G Really Be the Next Big Wireless Technology?" *Computer*, January 2002.

Garg, Vijay, K. Smolik, and Joe Wilkes, *Applications of CDMA in Wireless Personal Communication*. Upper Saddle River, NJ: Prentice Hall, Inc., 1997.

Matthews, Blesson, "Generation Wireless," *Network Computing*, June 11, 2001.

Messmer, Ellen, "FCC Divides U.S. for New Wireless Providers," *Network World*, September 27, 1993.

Oliphant, Malcolm W., "Radio Interfaces Make the Difference in 3G Cellular Systems," *IEEE Spectrum*, October 2000.

Rappaport, Theodore S., *Wireless Communications: Principles & Practice*. Upper Saddle River, NJ: Prentice Hall, Inc., 1996.

Ricci, Fred J., *Personal Communications Systems Applications*. Upper Saddle River, NJ: Prentice Hall, Inc., 1997.

Samjani, Azim, "General Packet Radio Service (GPRS)," *IEEE Potentials*, April/May 2002.

Stallings, William, *Wireless Communications and Networks*. Upper Saddle River, NJ: Prentice Hall, Inc., 2002.

Weisman, Carl J., *The Essential Guide to RF and Wireless* (2d ed). Upper Saddle River, NJ: Prentice Hall, Inc., 2002.

Zeng, M., A. Annamalai, and Vijay K. Bhargava, "Harmonization of Global Third-Generation Mobile Systems," *IEEE Communications Magazine,* December 2000.

CHAPTER 3: BASIC DATA COMMUNICATIONS CONCEPTS

Data Communications Concepts (2d ed.). White Plains, NY: International Business Machines Corporation, 1987.

Touring Datacomm, A Data Communications Primer. Cupertino, CA: Hewlett-Packard Company, 1983.

CHAPTER 4: DATA INTERFACES

Bisdikian, Chatschik, "An Overview of the Bluetooth Wireless Technology," *IEEE Communications Magazine,* December 2001.

Black, Uyless D., *Physical Level Interfaces and Protocols*. Washington, DC: IEEE Computer Society Press, 1988.

Bray, Jennifer, and Charles F. Sturman, *Bluetooth 1.1* (2d ed.). Upper Saddle River, NJ: Prentice Hall, Inc., 2002.

Liu, Peiya, "IEEE 1394: Changing the Way We Do Multimedia Communications," *IEEE Multimedia*, April–June 2000.

Putman, Byron W., *RS-232 Simplified*. Englewood Cliffs, NJ: Prentice-Hall, Inc., 1987.

Sairam, K.V.S.S.S.S., N. Gunasekaran, and S. Rama Reddy, "Bluetooth in Wireless Communication," *IEEE Communications Magazine*, June 2002.

Severance, Charles, "FireWire Finally Comes Home," *Computer*, November 1998.

CHAPTER 5: DATA TRANSMISSION

Boyd, Robert S., "Commercial Satellites Launch 'Unwired Planet,'" *The San Jose Mercury News*, May 18, 1997.

Cochrane, P., R. Heckingbottom, and David Heatley, "The Hidden Benefits of Optical Transparency," *IEEE Communications Magazine*, September 1994.

Forney, G. David, Jr., Les Brown, M. Vedat Eyuboglu, and John L. Moran III, "The V.34 High-Speed Modem Standard," *IEEE Communications Magazine*, December 1996.

Greene, Tim, "Wave Division Multiplexing (WDM): Follow the Light," *Network World*, September 7, 1998.

Harbaugh, Logan, "Gigabit Ethernet: Gigabit Ethernet Over Copper Nears Reality," *Information Week*, May 8, 2000.

Johnson, Johna Till, and James K. Hurd, "High Speed Modems: A Price Worth Paying?" *Data Communications*, July 1993.

Kiniry, Joseph R., "Wave Division Multiplexing: Ultra High Speed Fiber Optics," *IEEE Internet Computing*, March–April 1998.

Kuciel, Jim, "Cat 5 Cable Can Handle Gigabit Ethernet," *Network World*, October 16, 2000.

Palais, Joseph C., *Fiber Optic Communications* (4th ed.). Upper Saddle River, NJ: Prentice Hall, Inc., 1998.

Pelton, Joseph N., *Wireless and Satellite Telecommunications: The Technology, the Market and the Regulations*. Englewood Cliffs, NJ: Prentice Hall, Inc., 1994.

Politi, C., and John A. Stein, "VSATS Give Corporate Networks a Lift," *Data Communications*, February 1991.

Senior, John M., *Optical Fiber Communications: Principles and Practice* (2d ed.). Englewood Cliffs, NJ: Prentice Hall, Inc., 1992.

Sweeney, Terry, "Time to Test That Cat-5 Cabling," *Internet Week*, May 8, 2000.

CHAPTER 6: DATA INTEGRITY AND SECURITY

Arar, Yardena, "Better 802.11 Security," *PC World*, August 2003.

Bellovin, S. M., and William R. Cheswick, "Network Firewalls," *IEEE Communications Magazine*, September 1994.

Chokhani, Santosh, "Toward a National Public Key Infrastructure," *IEEE Communications Magazine*, September 1994.

Denning, D. E., and Miles Smid, "Key Escrowing Today," *IEEE Communications Magazine*, September 1994.

Erlanger, Leon, "Real Security for Wireless LANs," *PC Magazine*, August 5, 2003.

Ford, Warwick, *Computer Communications Security*. Englewood Cliffs, NJ: Prentice Hall, Inc., 1994.

Geier, Jim, "WPA Plugs Holes in WEP," *Network World*, March 31, 2003.

Gupta, Vipul, and Sumit Gupta, "Securing the Wireless Internet," *IEEE Communications Magazine*, December 2001.

Hellman, Martin E., "Commercial Encryption," *IEEE Network*, April 1987.

Janowski, Davis D., and Matthew D. Sarrel, "Simpler, Safe Remote Access," *PC Magazine*, August 19, 2003.

Kara, Atsushi, "Secure Remote Access From Office to Home," *IEEE Communications Magazine*, October 2001.

Kluepfel, Henry M., "Securing a Global Village and Its Resources," *IEEE Communications Magazine*, September 1994.

Miller, Sandra Kay, "Facing the Challenge of Wireless Security," *Computer*, July 2001.

Newman, D. B. Jr., J. K., Omura, and Raymond L. Pickholtz, "Public Key Management for Network Security," *IEEE Network*, April 1987.

Park, Joon S., and Derrick Dicoi, "WLAN Security: Current and Future," *IEEE Internet Computing*, September–October 2003.

Paulson, Linda Dailey, "Group Considers Drastic Measures to Stop Spam," *Computer*, July 2003.

Paulson, Linda Dailey, "Vendors Push Wireless LAN Security," *Computer*, January 2003.

Salamone, Salvatore, "Internetwork Security: Unsafe at Any Node?" *Data Communications*, September 1993.

Sherman, Erik, "Walk-By Hacking," *The New York Times*, July 13, 2003.

Stallings, William, *Network Security Essentials* (2d ed.). Upper Saddle River, NJ: Prentice Hall, Inc., 2003.

CHAPTER 7: ARCHITECTURES AND PROTOCOLS

Black, Uyless D., *Data Link Protocols*. Englewood Cliffs, NJ: Prentice Hall, Inc., 1993.

Bonnet, Luther, *SNA Fundamentals*. Chicago, IL: Science Research Associates, An IBM Company, 1987.

Martin, J., with Kathleen Kavanagh Chapman, *SNA: IBM's Networking Solution*. Englewood Cliffs, NJ: Prentice Hall, Inc., 1987.

Systems Network Architecture, Concepts and Products (4th ed.). White Plains, NY: International Business Machines Corporation, 1986.

Waddington, Daniel G., and Fangzhe Chang, "Realizing the Transition to IPv6," *IEEE Communications Magazine*, June 2002.

CHAPTER 8: DATA TRANSPORT NETWORKS

Arar, Yardena, "DSL Speeds, Cellular Coverage," *PC World*, October 2003.

Armitage, Grenville, "MPLS: The Magic Behind the Myths," *IEEE Communications Magazine*, January 2000.

Bertsekas, D., and Robert Gallager, *Data Networks* (2d ed.). Englewood Cliffs, NJ: Prentice Hall, Inc., 1991.

Bhushan, Brij, "A User's Guide to Frame Relay," *Telecommunications Magazine*, July 1990.

Black, Uyless D., *Internet Architecture*. Upper Saddle River, NJ: Prentice Hall, Inc., 2000.

Black, Uyless D., *Networking 101*. Upper Saddle River, NJ: Prentice Hall, Inc., 2002.

Blau, John, "Wi-Fi Hotspot Networks Sprout Like Mushrooms," *IEEE Spectrum,* September 2002.

Chao, H. J., D. Ghosal, D. Saha, and Satish K. Tripathi, "IP on ATM Local Area Networks," *IEEE Communications Magazine*, August 1994.

Cherry, Steven M., "Pesky Home Networks Trouble Cable Behemoths," *IEEE Spectrum*, April 2002.

Cherry, Steven M., "The Wireless Last Mile," *IEEE Spectrum*, September 2003.

Comer, Douglas E., *Computer Networks and Internets* (3d ed.). Upper Saddle River, NJ: Prentice Hall, Inc., 2001.

Comer, Douglas E., *Hands on Networking with Internet Technologies*. Upper Saddle River, NJ: Prentice Hall, Inc., 2002.

Comer, Douglas E., *The Internet Book* (3d ed.). Upper Saddle River, NJ: Prentice Hall, Inc., 2000.

Comer, Douglas E., *Internetworking with TCP/IP (Volume 1): Principles, Protocols, and Architecture* (4th ed.). Upper Saddle River, NJ: Prentice Hall, Inc., 2000.

Cooper, Edward, *Broadband Network Technology: An Overview for the Data and Telecommunications Industries* (2d ed.). Englewood Cliffs, NJ: Prentice Hall, Inc., 1991.

Costa, Janis Furtek, *Planning and Designing High Speed Networks*. Englewood Cliffs, NJ: Prentice Hall, Inc., 1994.

Cox, T., and Frances Dix, "SMDS: The Beginning of WAN Superhighways," *Data Communications*, April 1991.

Crow, Brian P., Indra Widaja, Jeong Geun Kim, and Prescott T. Sakai, "IEEE 802.11 Wireless Local Area Networks," *IEEE Communications Magazine*, September 1997.

Csenger, Michael, "Two Vendors Plan Products Based on 100Base-VG Technology," *Communications Week*, September 20, 1993.

Frank, Edward H., and Jack Holloway, "Connecting the Home with a Phone Line Network Chip Set," *IEEE Micro*, March/April 2000.

Frazer, Howard, "The 802.3z Gigabit Ethernet Standard," *IEEE Network*, May/June 1998.

Gerla, Mario, "High-Speed Local Area Networks," *IEEE Spectrum*, August 1991.

Henry, Paul S., and Hui Luo, "WiFi: What's Next?" *IEEE Communications Magazine*, December 2002.

Janowski, Davis D., and Stephanie Chang, "The Wireless LANscape," *PC Magazine*, June 30, 2003.

Johnson, Howard W., *Fast Ethernet: Dawn of a New Network*. Upper Saddle River, NJ: Prentice Hall, Inc., 1996.

Johnson, Johna Till, "Wireless Data: Welcome to the Enterprise," *Data Communications*, March 21, 1994.

Kapp, Steve, "802.11 Leaving the Wire Behind," *IEEE Internet Computing*, January/February 2002.

Kehoe, Brendan P., *Zen and the Art of the Internet*. Englewood Cliffs, NJ: Prentice Hall, Inc., 1993.

Lin, Yu-Ju, Haniph A. Latcham, and Minkyu Lee, "A Power Line Communication Network Infrastructure for the Smart Home," *IEEE Wireless Communications*, December 2002.

Lindstrom, Annie, "Birmingham Users Turn to SMDS," *Communications Week*, May 17, 1993.

Malamud, Carl, *Exploring the Internet*. Englewood Cliffs, NJ: Prentice Hall, Inc., 1993.

Miller, Arthur, "From Here to ATM," *IEEE Spectrum*, June 1994.

Perkins, Charles, "Mobile IP," *IEEE Communications Magazine*, May 1997.

Seifert, Rich, *Gigabit Ethernet: Technology and Applications for High-Speed LANs*. Reading, MA: Addison Wesley Longman, Inc., 1998.

Seifert, William, "Bridges and Routers," *IEEE Network*, January 1988.

Shah, A., and G. Ramakrishnan, *FDDI: A High Speed Network*. Englewood Cliffs, NJ: Prentice Hall, Inc., 1994.

Sharma, Roshan L., "Interconnecting LANs," *IEEE Spectrum*, August 1991.

Shimada, Karl, "Fast Talk About Fast Ethernet," *Data Communication*, March 21, 1994.

Stamper, David A., *Local Area Networks* (3d ed.). Upper Saddle River, NJ: Prentice Hall, Inc., 2001.

Steenstrup, Martha, *Routing in Communications Networks*. Englewood Cliffs, NJ: Prentice Hall, Inc., 1995.

Varshney, Upkar, "The Status and Future of 802.11-Based WLANs," *Computer*, June 2003.

Vaughan-Nichols, Steven J., "Will 20-Gigabit Ethernet Have a Bright Future?" *Computer*, June 2002.

Venkateswaran, R., "Virtual Private Networks," *IEEE Potentials*, February/March 2001.

CHAPTER 9: NETWORK MANAGEMENT

Chiu, D. M., and Ram Sudama, *Network Monitoring Explained: Design and Application*. Chichester, UK: Ellis Horwood, 1992.

Fisher, Lawrence M., "Having a Network Nightmare? Let the Software Take Over," *The New York Times*, September 18, 1994.

Rose, Marshall T., *The Simple Book: An Introduction to Management of TCP/IP-based Internets* (2d ed.). Englewood Cliffs, NJ: Prentice Hall, Inc., 1993.

Terplan, Kornel, *Communications Network Management* (2d ed.). Englewood Cliffs, NJ: Prentice Hall, Inc., 1992.

Voruganti, Ram Rao, "A Global Network Management Framework for the '90s," *IEEE Communications Magazine*, August 1994.

CHAPTER 10: THE CONVERGENCE OF VOICE AND DATA COMMUNICATIONS

Black, Uyless D., *Emerging Communications Technologies*. Englewood Cliffs, NJ: Prentice Hall, Inc., 1994.

Black, Uyless D., *Internet Telephony*. Upper Saddle River, NJ: Prentice Hall, Inc., 2001.

Black, Uyless D., *Voice Over IP*. Upper Saddle River, NJ: Prentice Hall, Inc., 2000.

Brunet, Craig J., "Hybridizing the Local Loop," *IEEE Spectrum*, June 1994.

Cheung, Nim K., "The Infrastructure for Gigabit Computer Networks," *IEEE Communications Magazine*, April 1992.

Day, Andrew, "International Standardization of BISDN," *IEEE LTS—The Magazine of Lightwave Telecommunications Systems*, August 1991.

Delisle, D., and Lionel Pelamourgues, "B-ISDN and How It Works," *IEEE Spectrum*, August 1991.

DePrycker, Martin, *Asynchronous Transfer Mode* (2d ed.). Chichester, UK: Ellis Horwood, 1993.

DSL Source Book (2d ed.). Paradyne Corporation, 1999.

Dutta-Roy, Amitava, "An Overview of Cable Modem Technology and Market Perspectives," *IEEE Communications*, June 2001.

Fellows, David, and Doug Jones, "DOCSIS Cable Modem Technology," *IEEE Communications Magazine*, March 2001.

Fischer, W., E. Wallmeier, T. Worster, S. P. Davis, and Andrew Hayter, "Data Communications Using ATM: Architectures, Protocols, Resource Management," *IEEE Communications Magazine*, August 1994.

Goode, Bur, "Voice Over Internet Protocol (VoIP)," *Proceedings of the IEEE, Vol. 90, No. 9*, September 2002.

Kovarik, K., and Payam Maveddat, "Multi-Rate ISDN," *IEEE Communications Magazine*, April 1994.

Lane, James, "ATM Knits Voice, Data on Any Net," *IEEE Spectrum*, February 1994.

Li, Bo, Mounir Hamdi, Dongyi Jiang, and Zi-Ren Cao, "QoS-Enabled Voice Support in the Next-Generation Internet: Issues, Existing Approaches and Challenges," *IEEE Communications Magazine*, April 2000.

Liu, Hong, and Petros Mouchtaris, "Voice Over IP Signaling: H.323 and Beyond," *IEEE Communications Magazine,* October 2000.

Mehta, Princy, and Sanjay Udani, "Voice over IP," *IEEE Potentials*, October/November 2001.

Pancha, P., and Magda El Zarki, "MPEG Coding for Variable Bit Rate Video Transmission," *IEEE Communications Magazine*, May 1994.

Partridge, Craig, *Gigabit Networking*. Reading, MA: Addison-Wesley, 1994.

Perry, Tekla S., "Telephone Challenges: A Plethora of Services," *IEEE Spectrum*, July 1990.

Powers, J. T., Jr., and Henry H. Stair II, *Megabit Data Communications: A Guide for Professionals*. Englewood Cliffs, NJ: Prentice Hall, Inc., 1990.

Riezenman, Michael J., "Extending Broadband's Reach," *IEEE Spectrum,* March 2003.

Ruiu, Dragos, "Testing ATM Systems," *IEEE Spectrum*, June 1994.

Schulzrinne, Henning, and Jonathan Rosenberg, "The Session Initiation Protocol: Internet-Centric Signaling," *IEEE Communications Magazine,* October 2000.

Stallings, William, ed., *Advances in ISDN and Broadband ISDN*. Los Alamitos, CA: IEEE Computer Society Press, 1992.

Stallings, William, ed., *Broadband Switching: Architecture, Protocols, Design, and Analysis*. Los Alamitos, CA: IEEE Computer Society Press, 1991.

Stallings, William, *ISDN and Broadband ISDN with Frame Relay and ATM* (3d ed.). Englewood Cliffs, NJ: Prentice Hall, Inc., 1995.

Tanzillo, Kevin, "ATM Users Don't Need to Worry about Data Eavesdroppers," *Communications News*, July 1994.

Verma, Pramode K., ed., *ISDN Systems: Architecture, Technology, and Applications*. Englewood Cliffs, NJ: Prentice Hall, Inc., 1990.

Vickers, B. J., and Tatsuya Suda, "Connectionless Service for Public ATM Networks," *IEEE Communications Magazine*, August 1994.

Walters, Stephen M., *The New Telephony*. Upper Saddle River, NJ: Prentice Hall, Inc., 2002.

Glossary

AAL *See* ATM Adaptation Layer.

Access method A means used to allow LAN users to transmit data.

Access Point A type of wireless LAN attached to a wired LAN that uses regular protocols. It uses a special MAC on the wireless part of the LAN.

A-channel The analog voice channel in ISDN.

ACK0 In BSC, the control character indicating an acknowledgment.

Acknowledgment Typically used in protocols, it is sent by the receiving device to the transmitter to confirm successful receipt of data.

Acknowledgment number In TCP, the number used to confirm receipt of individual segments.

Active monitor The station on a token ring network responsible for watching for the token and for generating a new token if the token is lost.

Ad hoc A type of wireless LAN containing only wireless users with no underlying wired LAN technology.

Adaptive bridge A type of bridge that can learn the locations of users and deliver messages accordingly based on their Layer 2 address. Also known as a learning bridge.

ADCCP *See* Advanced Data Communications Control Procedures.

Address Typically used to identify different devices, either in a polling and selecting environment or in a local area network.

Address Field The part of an SDLC frame that contains the eight bits that represent the identity of the Secondary station.

Address Resolution Protocol (ARP) A protocol used to find out the physical address of a computer with a particular IP address.

ADSL *See* Asymmetric Digital Subscriber Line.

ADSL Lite *See* Universal Asymmetric Digital Subscriber Line.

ADSL2+ An enhanced version of the ADSL standard, it can reach speeds up to 25 Mbps.

Advanced Data Communications Control Procedures (ADCCP) A bit-oriented ANSI protocol.

Advanced Encryption Standard (AES) The strong encryption algorithm used in IEEE 802.11i to offer better security than TKIP used in WPA.

Advanced Mobile Phone Service (AMPS) A popular analog cellular system used in the United States, South America, Australia, China, and other countries.

AES *See* Advanced Encryption Standard.

Agent The remote partner to a central station, or manager, in a network management protocol.

Algorithm A set of instructions for performing a task.

Always On/Dynamic ISDN (AO/DI) An Integrated Services Digital Network option that allows a continual D-channel connection, with the option to substitute higher bandwidth B-channels as traffic increases.

AM *See* Amplitude modulation.

American National Standard Code for Information Interchange (ASCII) The ANSI seven-bit character code, with an eighth bit for parity checking.

American National Standards Institute (ANSI) An umbrella organization for all standards organizations in the United States. These organizations can submit standards to ANSI for acceptance as a national standard.

American Telephone & Telegraph (AT&T) Now a long-distance company; formerly, the parent company of the Bell System, which also included many local phone companies.

Amplitude The strength of an electronic signal (in volts), or the volume of a tone (in decibels).

Amplitude modulation (AM) Transmission of information by varying the volume of a tone (the amplitude of a sine wave).

Amplitude shift keying (ASK) Another name for amplitude modulation.

AMPS *See* Advanced Mobile Phone Service.

Analog A signal that can vary infinitely over a given range, like voice.

Analog cellular A traditional cell-based wireless telephone service, in which the signals are transmitted to users in analog form.

Analog test equipment Devices used to diagnose voice-grade telephone circuits.

ANSI *See* American National Standards Institute.

ANSI/TIA/EIA-568-B The most widely used standard for unshielded twisted pair wire.

Answer-only modem A type of modem that can only receive calls.

Antispam software Software that prevents spam from reaching the user.

Antivirus software Software that eradicates and detects viruses.

AO/DI *See* Always On/Dynamic ISDN.

Applet Applications software that downloads when needed; typically used with a browser.

Application Layer Layer 7, the highest layer of the OSI model. It provides access to the network to the end user.

Application Program In SNA, a software program running on a Host Processor that communicates through an SNA network.

Application-level firewall A firewall that screens messages only for a particular application, like electronic mail.

Applications software User programs running on a host computer, such as word-processing programs, spreadsheets, and accounting programs.

Area code A three-digit code used in the public network to route calls to a particular geographical area.

ARP *See* Address Resolution Protocol.

ARPANET The packet switching network used to connect U.S. government computing facilities.

ARQ *See* Automatic Repeat Request.

ASCII *See* American National Standard Code for Information Interchange.

ASK Amplitude shift keying. *See* Amplitude modulation.

Asserted state The state of an RS-232-C control signal when it is ON, raised, or true.

Asymmetric Digital Subscriber Line (ADSL) A digital access technology that provides a link from the user to the central office over twisted pair wire that has a higher speed in one direction than in the other.

Asymmetric keys An encryption technique that uses a different key to encrypt a message than is used to decrypt the message.

Asynchronous Transfer Mode (ATM) A technology used to fragment data into cells so that voice, video, data, or any other information can be sent over the same network. ATM is used to implement BISDN.

Asynchronous transmission A method of data transmission requiring start and stop bits.

AT&T *See* American Telephone & Telegraph.

AT&T Premises Distribution System AT&T's method for wiring office buildings with standard cable.

ATM *See* Asynchronous Transfer Mode.

ATM Adaptation Layer (AAL) The third layer in ATM, it breaks down user data into 48-octet payloads so that it can be packaged into cells and reassembles them at the destination. It can also perform other functions, depending on the service required.

ATM Forum A group of member companies, organizations, and users whose sole purpose is to promote the rapid development and deployment of the ATM specification.

ATM Layer The second layer in ATM, it is responsible for handling the mechanics of cell transport.

Attendant The operator of a PBX console.

Automatic repeat request (ARQ) An error-control method in which the receiving device detects an error in data transmission and asks for a retransmission of the block of data.

Autonegotiation The ability to automatically switch to the correct speed between two devices.

Availability The ratio of uptime to the total uptime and downtime.

Backbone networks A network that connects other networks and that no end users directly attach to.

Backoff The length of time a device waits after a collision occurs before attempting retransmission.

Balanced transmission A method of sending data requiring two wires, as in RS-422-A.

Bandwidth The carrying capacity of a circuit, usually measured in bits per second for digital circuits or Hertz for analog circuits.

Bandwidth on demand A term describing a large pipe through which users can transmit data at varying rates.

Baseband transmission The transmission of a data signal directly on a wire.

Basic service element (BSE) A feature or service provided by the local exchange carrier to the public, as part of Open Network Architecture.

Basic-rate interface (BRI) The preferred method for attachment to ISDN by individual users, it includes two B-channels, one for digitized voice and one for data, and one D-channel for signaling.

Baud rate The number of possible signal changes in a second. It is sometimes equivalent to the bps rate, but not always.

Baudot code One of the first character codes, it uses five bits to represent characters.

BCC In BSC, a block check character used for error detection.

BCD *See* Binary Coded Decimal.

B-channel The bearer channel in ISDN, it carries 64 kbps of digitized voice or data.

Bearer channel *See* B-channel.

Bell 103/113 AT&T's 300-bps frequency modulation method, now widely accepted as an industry standard.

Bell 212A AT&T's 1200-bps dibit phase shift keying method, now widely accepted as an industry standard. It falls back to the Bell 103/113 300-bps frequency modulation method when communicating with Bell 103/113 modems.

Bell Communications Research The research arm of the RBOCs formed after divestiture, also known as Bellcore.

Bell Labs The research arm of AT&T.

Bell Operating Company (BOC) An individual local exchange carrier, previously owned by AT&T before divestiture.

Bell System The name used to designate the combination of the Bell Operating Companies and AT&T's long-distance business before it was broken up by divestiture.

Bellcore *See* Bell Communications Research.

BERT *See* Bit error rate test.

Best-effort delivery As found in IP, the network attempts to deliver the packet, but does not guarantee that the packet will not be lost.

Binary Coded Decimal (BCD) An early character code used internally by computers to represent information.

Binary number system A numeric system based on powers of two. All numbers are represented using only the digits 0 and 1.

Binary Synchronous Communications (BSC) IBM's character-oriented (or byte-oriented) half duplex, stop-and-wait ARQ protocol.

BISDN *See* Broadband ISDN.

Bisync *See* Binary Synchronous Communications.

Bit A binary digit, either a 1 or a 0.

Bit error A transmission error in which a 1 is received as a 0, or vice versa.

Bit error rate test (BERT) An industry-standard measure of reliability, it is the ratio of the number of bit errors detected to the total number of bits received.

Bit interleaving A time-division multiplexing method in which each time slot contains a bit from each channel.

Bit-oriented protocol A protocol that uses single bits to communicate control information.

Bits per second (bps) A typical measurement of data speed, it is the number of bits transmitted (or received) in a second.

BLERT *See* Block error rate test.

Block A group of characters, or bytes.

Block error rate test (BLERT) An industry-standard measure of reliability, it is the ratio of the number of block errors detected to the total number of blocks received.

Bluetooth A wireless data standard operating up to 1 Mbps for 30 feet.

BOC *See* Bell Operating Company.

Bps *See* Bits per second.

Branch port The low-speed port of a multiplexer, usually attached to the terminal or front-end processor.

Breakout box The test equipment used to monitor the interface status, determine if a device is a DTE or DCE, modify interfaces, and test cables.

Break-up The divestiture of the Bell Operating Companies from AT&T.

BRI *See* Basic-rate interface.

Bridge A device that connects two or more networks and that operates at Layer 2 of the OSI model.

Broadband ISDN (BISDN) A set of interface standards being developed by the ITU(CCITT) for high-speed transmission.

Broadband transmission A transmission method in which data is modulated on a carrier signal, such as a sine wave.

Broadcast A message sent to all users on a network.

Broadcast message Data intended for multiple users, as on a multidrop circuit.

Browser Software that allows a user to view information that is typically stored in HTML format.

BSC *See* Binary Synchronous Communications.

BSE *See* Basic service element.

Buddy list Also known as a collaboration group, it is a list of users whose presence we want to track. We inform these users of our presence when we log on.

Buffer The area surrounding the cladding in a fiber optic cable.

Buffering Holding data temporarily, usually until it is properly sequenced, as in packet switching networks, or until another device is ready to receive it, as in front-end processors.

Bus network A network topology in which all devices are connected to a single cable.

Busy signal A signal provided by the central office to the user, indicating that the called party is already using the phone.

Busy token A pattern of bits used to indicate that another station is already using the token passing network.

Byte A group of bits, usually eight.

Byte interleaving A time-division multiplexing method in which each time slot contains a byte from each channel.

Byte-oriented protocol A protocol that uses entire bytes to communicate control information.

Cable modem An access technology that dedicates channels on a cable television system to data transmission. It is usually used to provide Internet access.

Cable modem termination system (CMTS) A device for interconnecting the cable modems with the Internet, it can be located at the head end or in the neighborhoods.

Cache Memory containing recently accessed information.

Call-back device Data security equipment used with dial-up modems that calls users to verify their location.

Caller ID A service available with analog telephone lines that allows users to see the phone number of the incoming caller on a special display.

Carriage return A special character used to send a terminal's cursor or printer's head to the left margin.

Carrier Detect (CD) *See* Data Carrier Detect.

Carrier sense multiple access (CSMA) A collision-avoidance contention method often used with local area networks, it requires the transmitting device to check if the network is free before transmitting.

Carrier sense multiple access/collision detection (CSMA/CD) A contention method often used with local area networks, it requires the transmitter to check if the network is free before transmitting and to continue monitoring to determine if there is a collision during transmission.

Carrier signal An electronic signal used to modulate data in broadband transmission, usually a sine wave.

Cat3 *See* Category 3 cable.

Cat4 *See* Category 4 cable.

Cat5 *See* Category 5 cable.

Cat5E *See* Category 5E cable.

Cat6 *See* Category 6 cable.

Cat7 *See* Category 7 cable.

Category 3 cable (Cat3) An unshielded twisted pair wire with 16 MHz bandwidth.

Category 4 cable (Cat4) An unshielded twisted pair wire with 20 MHz bandwidth.

Category 5 cable (Cat5) An unshielded twisted pair wire with 100 MHz bandwidth.

Category 5E cable (Cat5E) An unshielded twisted pair wire with 100 MHz bandwidth, but with improved loss and interference characteristics compared with those of Category 5.

Category 6 cable (Cat6) An unshielded twisted pair wire with 250 MHz bandwidth.

Category 7 cable (Cat7) An unshielded twisted pair wire expected to have 600 MHz bandwidth.

Category I The RS-449 signals that require two wires, allowing for RS-422-A transmission.

Category II The RS-449 signals that require only a single wire and a common return and that use RS-423-A transmission.

Cathode ray tube (CRT) Another name for a terminal.

CBDS *See* Connectionless Broadband Data Service.

CC *See* Control codes.

C-channel The low-speed data channel in ISDN, carrying up to 16 kbps.

CCITT *See* Consultative Committee on International Telephone and Telegraph.

CD Carrier Detect. *See* Data Carrier Detect.

CDDI *See* Copper Distributed Data Interface.

CDMA *See* Code Division Multiple Access.

CDMA 2000 *See* Code Division Multiple Access 2000.

CDMA 2000.X *See* Code Division Multiple Access 2000.X.

CDPD *See* Cellular Digital Packet Data.

Cell When used in wireless communications, a cell is a zone served by a particular transmitter. When used in ATM, it is a data packet containing 53 bytes, including a 5-byte header and a 48-byte payload.

Cell relay Another name for the technique used in ATM.

Cellular A wireless communications technique that divides an area into cells, each served by a transmitter. Calls are handed from one cell to the next as users move.

Cellular Digital Packet Data (CDPD) A wireless data service that sends packet data over the existing analog cellular network while providing added functions, like error detection and correction.

Central office The local exchange carrier's office where the central-office switch is located. It provides power, routing, and signaling functions for the user.

Central processing unit (CPU) Often used as another name for a host computer, it actually refers only to the heart of the host computer.

Centralized control A control method in which a single device runs a network.

Central-office switch The device in the central office that provides the power, routing, and signaling functions for the user.

Central-office trunk A local loop between the central office and a PBX.

Centrex A service with which the local exchange carrier handles both external and internal calls for a customer.

Channel interface The high-speed port of a front-end processor that connects directly to the host computer's high-speed input/output channel.

Channel service unit (CSU) The device terminating the common carrier's digital circuit on the customer's premises.

Channel A transmission path used in ISDN; available in various sizes.

Character A letter of the alphabet, number, punctuation mark, or special key used by different terminals. It also includes special codes used by devices to communicate.

Character code Methods of representing characters, typically with ones and zeroes.

Character interleaving Another name for byte interleaving.

Character-oriented protocol Another name for byte-oriented protocol.

Chassis ground The RS-232-C pin used to connect cable shields to the electrical ground.

Chat An Internet application for conversational, text-based communications.

Chat rooms A known address for Internet-based conversations, often topically oriented.

Checksum An error-checking method in which bits are added before and after transmission and then compared.

Cipher text Data that has been encrypted for transmission.

Circuit switching Establishing a path and reserving resources for the duration of a connection regardless of whether or not any transmission actually takes place (e.g., in the telephone network, in which a call is connected and channels are set aside in both directions even if no one is talking).

Cladding The glass layer in a fiber optic cable surrounding the core, it is designed to reflect light back into the core.

Clear text Data that is not encrypted.

Clear to Send (CTS) The RS-232-C control signal generated by the DCE, it indicates that the DTE can transmit data.

Client/server An architecture in which portions of a program operate on a local workstation, with centralized databases operating on a shared server.

Closed user group (CUG) A security measure often used in packet switching networks, it restricts access to a certain set of users.

Cluster Controller A device used in SNA to allow several Workstations to have a single point of access to the network.

CMIP *See* Common Management Information Protocol.

CMTS *See* Cable modem termination system.

CNM *See* Communications Network Management.

Coax *See* Coaxial cable.

Coaxial cable A transmission medium consisting of a single wire in the center, which is surrounded by a core of insulating material with an outer conductive wrapping, and in turn is covered by an insulating sheath.

Code bits In TCP, bits reserved for overhead tasks like resetting the connection.

Code conversion To translate from one character code to another, thereby allowing certain incompatible devices to communicate.

Code Division Multiple Access (CDMA) A digital cellular standard used in the United States, it shares channels with the analog AMPS system.

Code Division Multiple Access 2000 (CDMA2000) An enhancement to CDMA, it provides data rates up to 2.4 Mbps.

Code Division Multiple Access 2000.X (CDMA 2000.X) An enhancement to CDMA that provides data rates up to 144 kbps.

Codecs *See* coder/decoders.

Coder/decoders Software or hardware devices that convert signals (e.g., voice or video) between analog and digital formats.

Collaboration group Also known as a buddy list, it is a list of users whose presence we want to track. We inform these users of our presence when we log on.

Collect calls A packet switching and public network service that bills call costs to the called party.

Collision The result of two devices transmitting at the same time, usually causing data to be lost.

Collision avoidance A contention technique in which devices check if the network is free before transmitting.

Collision detection A contention technique in which devices check whether collisions occur during transmission.

Collision domain A part of a network where users share a transmission media and could accidentally talk simultaneously.

Combined Network Termination 1 and 2 (NT12) ISDN equipment that combines the Network Termination 1 and Network Termination 2 functions.

Common carrier A company that provides voice and/or data communications transmission services to the general public.

Common Management Information Protocol (CMIP) An ISO protocol for network management that is far richer than SNMP, but less widely used.

Common return A single wire serving as a shared path for returning electrical signals, as in RS-423-A transmission.

Common-channel signaling A method in which a separate channel is used for signaling bits.

Communications architecture A manufacturer's strategy for connecting its host computers, terminals, and communications equipment, it defines the elements necessary for data communications between devices.

Communications Controller In SNA, a device responsible for routing data through a network and controlling the communications links.

Communications Controller Node An SNA node containing a Communications Controller.

Communications line control Rules for sharing a communications path.

Communications Network Management (CNM) A series of IBM tools for managing networks.

Communications server A device that provides local area network users with access to resources located off the network and vice versa, through modems or other communications circuits.

Concatenated The combination of several channels into a single channel, as in a SONET OC-Nc circuit.

Concentrator Another name for a port-sharing device.

Conditioned line A type of leased line suitable for high-speed data transmission, requiring extra hardware and available at an added cost.

Connection In TCP, a negotiated set of parameters that describes the way in which packets are exchanged between two endpoints.

Connectionless A term used to describe the process of delivering each piece of data independently, without establishing a connection.

Connectionless Broadband Data Service (CBDS) A European service similar to Switched Multimegabit Data Service.

Connection oriented A term used to describe the process of establishing a physical or virtual connection, rather than just delivering individual pieces of data independently.

Constellation diagram A visual representation of modem phase shifts and amplitudes.

Consultative Committee on International Telephone and Telegraph (CCITT) An international telecommunications standards organization, whose members include regulating bodies from member countries, representatives from leading companies, and representatives from other organizations. *See* International Telecommunications Union.

Contention A method used to share a communications path.

Continuous ARQ An automatic repeat request method in which the transmitter continues sending data blocks without waiting for acknowledgment messages, until a set number of unacknowledged blocks has been sent or a negative acknowledgment is received.

Control character A character used in character codes to perform special functions.

Control codes (CC) ASCII characters used to convey control information in protocols.

Control Field The part of an SDLC frame that contains control information.

Control information In a protocol, the data sent to perform polling, selecting, ARQ, and error checking, as well as to convey status information to devices.

Control key A specific key on a terminal that will cause a special character to be generated when that key is struck in conjunction with another key on the terminal.

Control signal In RS-232-C and RS-449, the pins indicating the status of a given connection.

Control station In BSC, the single station that can communicate with all of the other (Tributary) stations.

Convergence The combination of voice and data technologies on today's networks.

Cookies A type of tracking mechanism that records specific information about network sites you visited and stores it on your computer. It is accessible to websites you visit later.

Copper Distributed Data Interface (CDDI) A copper version of Fiber Distributed Data Interface.

Cordless The simplest type of wireless communications, it typically consists of a handset and base station that use radio waves between them instead of cable.

Core The innermost section, it is a glass strand inside a fiber optic cable.

Corporation for Open Systems (COS) A nonprofit corporation consisting of major host computer manufacturers whose purpose is to facilitate the implementation of OSI.

COS *See* Corporation for Open Systems.

CPE *See* Customer-premises equipment.

CPU *See* Central processing unit.

CRC *See* Cyclical redundancy check.

Crossover A function performed by DCEs in a communications circuit, it takes the transmitted data from one DTE and delivers it to the other DTE for reception.

CRT *See* Cathode ray tube.

CSMA *See* Carrier sense multiple access.

CSMA/CD *See* Carrier sense multiple access/collision detection.

CSU *See* Channel service unit.

CTS *See* Clear to Send.

CUG *See* Closed user group.

Customer-premises equipment (CPE) Devices either leased or owned, that are used at the customer site.

CX *See* Data Carrier Detect.

Cycle A full repetition of a sine wave, including one peak and one valley.

Cycles per second A measure of frequency, the number of cycles of a sine wave in a second.

Cyclical parity A parity checking method designed to detect two sequential bit errors in a byte.

Cyclical redundancy check (CRC) A sophisticated version of a checksum, it uses a complex mathematical formula that combines division and addition to detect errors.

DA *See* Destination Address.

Dash In Morse code, a long beep used to send characters.

Data Carrier Detect (DCD) The RS-232-C control signal generated by the DCE that indicates that the DTE should expect to receive data at any time.

Data circuit-terminating equipment (DCE) The type of interface typically found on modems and some multiplexers.

Data communications The exchange of digital information between two devices using an electronic transmission system.

Data compression devices Equipment that allows more data to be transmitted per second than the speed of the link would normally allow.

Data conversion Protocol and/or code conversion.

Data Encryption Algorithm (DEA) The name used by ANSI for the Data Encryption Standard.

Data Encryption Standard (DES) A standard, general-purpose encryption algorithm that uses secret keys developed by IBM and later adopted by the National Institute of Standards and Technology.

Data Field The user data in an Ethernet frame.

Data Link Layer Layer 2 of the OSI model, it is responsible for ensuring error-free, reliable transmission of data.

Data Over Cable Service Interface Specifications (DOCSIS) The widely used North American cable modem standards.

Data rate The speed at which bits are transmitted and received, usually measured in bits per second, or bps.

Data Rate Select (DRS) The RS-232-C control signal used by devices to change each other's speed.

Data Set Ready (DSR) The RS-232-C control signal generated by the DCE to indicate that it is powered on and ready to begin communications.

Data terminal equipment (DTE) The type of interface usually found on terminals, host computers, and printers.

Data Terminal Ready (DTR) The RS-232-C control signal generated by the DTE to indicate that it is powered on, online, and ready to begin communications.

Data transport network A general term describing a system that carries data communications, like local area networks and packet switching networks.

Datagram An individual data packet, as in IP.

Datascope A type of data communications test equipment that provides all of the functions of a breakout box and also provides a display screen for monitoring data and analyzing protocols. It can also trap events and sound alarms, and it can be programmed for complex simulations.

DB9 A 9-pin connector, available in male and female versions, defined in the ISO standard 4902 and in the RS-449 standard, and used with the secondary channel of the RS-449 interface.

DB25 A 25-pin connector, available in male and female versions, defined in ISO standard 2110, and often used with the RS-232-C interface.

DB37 A 37-pin connector, available in male and female versions, defined in ISO standard 4902 and in the RS-449 standard, and used with the primary channel of the RS-449 interface.

DCD *See* Data Carrier Detect.

DCE *See* Data circuit-terminating equipment.

D-channel In ISDN, the signaling channel, carrying 16 kbps or 64 kbps, depending on the circuit type.

DDD network *See* Direct distance dial network.

DEA *See* Data Encryption Algorithm.

Decoder circuit The part of a modem's circuitry that translates incoming square waves to an internal representation of ones and zeroes.

Decompose To break down into smaller pieces.

Decryption The decoding, or descrambling, of received data.

Default A term often used to describe a customer's standard long-distance carrier.

Delay The elapsed time between transmission and reception of data.

Demand Priority A transmission scheme that allows certain traffic to be transmitted on a high-priority basis.

Demilitarized zone (DMZ) The area between a company's intranet and the Internet where some of the company's servers are located in order to allow limited access.

Demodulation Converting analog signals back to digital form.

Demodulator circuit The part of a modem's circuitry that converts analog signals back to digital form.

Denial of service attack Bombarding a computer with so many erroneous messages that it is overwhelmed and cannot process legitimate traffic.

DES *See* Data Encryption Standard.

Destination Address (DA) In IP, a field indicating the location to which the datagram is to be delivered. In Ethernet, the 48-bit field indicating the location to which the frame is to be delivered.

Destination node In the OSI model, it is the host computer at each end of a connection, and it is often used to describe the transmitting and receiving computers that implement the higher layers; in a packet switching network, it is the node attached to the DTE that is receiving the data.

Destination port In TCP, the port number of the receiving endpoint.

DF *See* Don't fragment flag.

DHCP *See* Dynamic Host Configuration Protocol.

Dial tone A signal provided by the central office to the user indicating that it is ready to accept digits.

Dial-up A telephone circuit connection that requires the user to place a new call each time, allowing destination flexibility.

Dial-up access Using modems and conventional telephone lines to access the Internet.

Dibit modulation A technique for modulating two bits for every baud or signal change.

DID trunk *See* Direct inward dial trunk.

Differentiated Services (Diffserv) An IETF protocol that allows packets to be handled differently based on the treatment they require.

Diffserv *See* Differentiated Services.

Digital A way of representing information using ones and zeroes.

Digital cellular A new type of wireless telephone service, in which the signals are transmitted to users in digital form.

Digital certificate A type of digital signature used to verify the authenticity of a file, often for downloaded software.

Digital circuit Special lines provided by the common carriers, they are suitable for transmitting data directly in square-wave form without modulation.

Digital PBX A computer that treats telephones and trunks as specialized input and output devices. Voice is either digitized in the phone or at the PBX, and voice as well as data communications can be switched.

Digital phone A device that digitizes voice and is attached to either a digital PBX or an ISDN-type public network.

Digital postmark A method of verifying the time and date a message was sent, based on a digital signature and with the help of a trusted third party.

Digital service unit (DSU) A device connected between the user's DTE and the common carrier's digital circuits, which are typically terminated by a channel service unit.

Digital signature A method of verifying message authenticity or sender identification by encrypting with a secret key and decrypting with a public key.

Digital Subscriber Line (DSL) A broad title covering an array of digital access technologies that connect the central office to the user with twisted pair wire.

Digital Subscriber Line Access Multiplexer (DSLAM) A combination DSL modem and multiplexer, it connects DSL users with the Internet.

Digital transmission Sending data in square wave form rather than by using modulation over analog circuits.

Digitize To convert voice to ones and zeroes, or digital form.

Direct distance dial (DDD) network Another name for the public network.

Direct inward dial (DID) trunk A local loop between the central office and a PBX that allows for automatic call routing, in which the central office signals the PBX to indicate the called party's extension.

Directional An antenna that is optimized to transmit or receive in a particular direction at the expense of other directions.

Display station Another name for a terminal.

Distributed control A design for spreading the responsibility of running a network throughout the attached devices, as in some local area networks.

Distributed Processor In SNA, a device similar to a Host Processor, though more limited in function.

Divestiture The breakup of the Bell System, whereby AT&T lost its local phone companies, but kept its long-distance business, Bell Labs, and Western Electric.

DMZ *See* Demilitarized zone.

DNS *See* Domain Name Service.

DOCSIS *See* Data Over Cable Service Interface Specifications.

DOCSIS 1.0 The first standard for cable modems.

DOCSIS 1.1 An enhancement to DOCSIS 1.0, it has additional security features and allows users to request more bandwidth if needed.

Domain In SNA, a System Services Control Point and all of the devices it controls.

Domain Name Service (DNS) A directory that associates Internet domain names with IP addresses for various services.

Don't fragment (DF) flag In IP, a one-bit flag in the flags field indicating that the datagram should not be fragmented further.

Dot In Morse code, a short beep used to send characters.

Double encrypted When a message is encrypted with the sender's secret key and the receiver's public key and is decrypted with the sender's public key and the receiver's secret key, to provide both data confidentiality and authenticity.

Downlink The satellite dish receiving information from the satellite.

Downtime The time when a system or network is unavailable.

Driver circuit The part of a modem's circuitry that translates the modem's internal representation of ones and zeroes to square waves at the appropriate voltage levels.

DRS *See* Data Rate Select.

DS-1 The standard specifying the electrical characteristics for 1.544 Mbps transmission over four wires, as in T-1 transmission.

DSL *See* Digital Subscriber Line.

DSL Lite *See* Universal Asymmetric Digital Subscriber Line.

DSLAM *See* Digital Subscriber Line Access Multiplexer.

DSR *See* Data Set Ready.

DSU *See* Digital service unit.

DTE *See* Data terminal equipment.

DTMF *See* Dual-tone multifrequency dialing.

DTMF register Equipment that can recognize DTMF digits.

DTR *See* Data Terminal Ready.

Dual-mode phone A cellular phone that can operate according to two different standards.

Dual-tone multifrequency (DTMF) dialing Also known as touch-tone, a dialing method using two simultaneous tones of different pitches to represent digits.

Dumb modem A modem that performs only modulation and demodulation, but that is not able to dial calls. The user needs a separate phone to dial the calls, or a PBX can automate the process.

Dumb terminal A terminal that receives data from a host computer and displays it on its screen, but that is unable to change or modify the data. Similarly, any data typed using the keyboard is sent directly to the host computer without major modifications.

Dynamic addresses Assigning a new IP address, typically using DHCP, each time a device is turned on.

Dynamic Host Configuration Protocol (DHCP) A protocol used to assign an IP address to a computer when it is first turned on.

E-1 carrier A standard for 2.048 Mbps digital transmission often used in Europe, it is similar to the T-1 standard more commonly used in North America.

EAP *See* Extensible Authentication Protocol.

EBCD *See* Extended Binary Coded Decimal.

EBCDIC *See* Extended Binary Coded Decimal Interchange Code.

Echo canceller A device used to remove echoes from conversations on voice-grade lines by actually subtracting the echo before it reaches the user.

Echo checking An error-detection method in which the receiver repeats everything received to the transmitting device.

Echo reply A common ICMP message, it is the response to an echo request or ping.

Echo request A common ICMP message, it requests a reply from another IP device. It is also known as a ping.

Echo suppressor A device used on voice-grade lines to prevent echoes by allowing transmission in only one direction at a time, in a half duplex fashion.

Echo testing Another name for loopback testing.

ECSA *See* Exchange Carriers Standards Association.

EDGE *See* Enhanced Data rates for Global Evolution.

EIA *See* Electronic Industries Association.

EIA-232-D A revision to RS-232-C, its new features are seldom implemented.

EIA-232-E A revision of EIA-232-D, its new features are seldom implemented.

800 number Another name for a toll-free number.

Electronic Industries Association (EIA) A standards organization representing many manufacturers in the U.S. electronics industry.

Electronic mail A messaging method in which text, files, images, and any data storable on a computer can be transmitted to another user.

Email *See* Electronic mail.

Encryption Scrambling or coding data for transmission.

Encryption device Equipment that scrambles or codes data for transmission.

End office Another name for a central office.

End User In SNA, the parties on the end of each LU–LU session, including Application Programs and people at Workstations.

Endpoints In TCP, a connection is made between two of these; each endpoint is defined by an IP address and a port number.

Enhanced Data rates for Global Evolution (EDGE) A system providing data rates up to 384 kbps on GSM or TDMA networks.

Enhanced service provider (ESP) In Open Network Architecture, a company that delivers a special function or service to the customer through the public network.

ENQ In BSC, the control character used as an enquiry.

Enquiry In a protocol, when a device asks permission to send data.

EOT In BSC, the control character signifying the End of Transmission.

Equal access The ability to choose a default long-distance carrier and still access all other long-distance carriers by using a simple dialing method.

Error detection Determining that one or more bits changed from a 1 to a 0, or vice versa, during transmission.

Error detection and correction Determining which bits changed from a 1 to a 0, or vice versa, during transmission and changing the bits back to their original form.

Error detection with a request for retransmission Determining that one or more bits changed from a 1 to a 0, or vice versa, during transmission and asking that the block of data be repeated.

Error detection with flagging Determining that one or more bits changed from a 1 to a 0, or vice versa, during transmission and notifying the user of the error.

ESP *See* Enhanced service provider.

ETACS *See* European Total Access Communications System.

Ethernet The CSMA/CD bus local area network originally used by Xerox, DEC, and Intel and now used by many other vendors as well.

ETX In BSC, the control character signifying the end of actual user data.

EuroDOCSIS A version of DOCSIS used in Europe.

EuroISDN The regional implementation of ISDN used in Europe.

European Total Access Communications System (ETACS) A popular analog cellular standard used primarily in Europe.

Even parity An error-detection method requiring an even number of ones in each byte.

Exchange Carriers Standards Association (ECSA) A standards organization consisting of telephone equipment manufacturing companies formed after the AT&T divestiture, it continues to work on standards previously developed by the Bell System.

Expert system A type of artificial intelligence computer software tool often used in network management to help isolate and diagnose problems.

Expires The term used to describe that the time for an IP address lease from a DHCP server elapses.

Extended ASCII A version of the ASCII character code that provides eight data bits, allowing for graphics or foreign language characters, but at the expense of the parity bit.

Extended Binary Coded Decimal (EBCD) The predecessor of the Extended Binary Coded Decimal Interchange Code.

Extended Binary Coded Decimal Interchange Code (EBCDIC) An eight-bit character code developed by IBM.

Extensible Authentication Protocol (EAP) A centralized authentication method used in WPA to ensure that only authorized users are able to access a wireless LAN.

External PAD A PAD located on the user's premises, outside a packet switching network.

External Transmit Clock (XTC) The RS-232-C Timing Signal generated by a DTE that times its own data transmission.

Extranet A network accessible to a limited set of external users.

Facsimile (Fax) A method of sending still images, like printed pages, over telephone lines.

False state The state of an RS-232-C control signal when it is OFF or lowered.

Fast Ethernet The version of the IEEE 802.3 network that operates at 100 Mbps, it is simply the original version operating 10 times faster.

Fax *See* Facsimile.

FCC *See* Federal Communications Commission.

FCS *See* Frame Check Sequence field.

FDDI *See* Fiber Distributed Data Interface.

FDM *See* Frequency-division multiplexing.

FE *See* Format effectors.

FEC *See* Forward error correction.

Federal Communications Commission (FCC) The body regulating all interstate communications in the United States.

Federal Information Processing Standards (FIPS) A set of specifications that must be met to supply the U.S. government with computing and data communications equipment.

FEP *See* Front-end processor.

Fiber Distributed Data Interface (FDDI) A high-speed local area network using fiber optic cable to form an inner and outer token ring suitable for mainframe computer communications and other applications.

Fiber nodes The boxes in the neighborhood in a cable modem system.

Fiber optic cable A high-bandwidth transmission medium that allows data to be transmitted by shining a light through a special glass fiber.

Fiber to the curb One of many cabling approaches used to combine fiber optic cable for long distances with copper cable for short distances, it uses fiber to the customer's street and copper to the customer's premises.

Fiber to the feeder One of many cabling approaches used to combine fiber optic cable for long distances with copper cable for short distances, it uses fiber to reach somewhere in the neighborhood of the customer and copper to the customer's premises. It is also known as fiber to the vault or fiber to the neighborhood.

Fiber to the home A cabling approach in which fiber optic cable connects a central office or cable television company directly with the customer's home. It is also known as fiber to the premises.

Fiber to the neighborhood One of many cabling approaches used to combine fiber optic cable for long distances with copper cable for short distances, it uses fiber to reach somewhere in the neighborhood of the customer and copper to the customer's premises. It is also known as fiber to the vault or fiber to the feeder.

Fiber to the premises A cabling approach in which fiber optic cable connects a central office or cable television company directly with the customer's premises. It is also known as fiber to the home.

Fiber to the vault One of many cabling approaches used to combine fiber optic cable for long distances with copper cable for short distances, it uses fiber to reach somewhere in the neighborhood of the customer and copper to the customer's premises. It is also known as fiber to the feeder or fiber to the neighborhood.

Figures A special character in the Baudot character code indicating that future transmission will be from the Upper Case set of characters.

File server A shared storage device for local area network users, typically in the form of a personal computer with a high-volume disk attached to the network.

File sharing A technique for exchanging data where users offer a list of available files to an indexing service, which then makes them available to other users who are logged on to that service.

File Transfer Protocol (FTP) A part of the TCP/IP Protocol Suite, it allows remote viewing of file directories as well as transfer of files in either direction across a TCP/IP network.

Filter In a DSL system, a device that prevents data signals from reaching conventional phones, fax machines, and answering machines.

FIPS *See* Federal Information Processing Standards.

Firewall A technique used to screen messages passing between two networks to protect against security breaches or the spreading of certain error conditions.

Firewire *See* IEEE 1394.

Firmware encryption An encryption method in which software containing the algorithm, or the keys, can be stored on preprogrammed chips in an encryption device.

First generation (1G) The classification for traditional analog cellular phones.

Fixed addresses Using the same IP address every time a device is turned on.

Fixed wireless Using radio signals and stationary antennas instead of cabling to interconnect to locations, it can be used for Internet access.

Flag In SDLC, the pattern of eight bits beginning each frame.

Flags field In IP, a three-bit field containing one unused bit, the don't fragment flag, and the more fragments flag.

Flow label In IPv6, the field identifying a stream of packets between two computers on a network.

Flow-control negotiation A packet switching service allowing DTEs to specify the size of the packet and other parameters.

FM *See* Frequency modulation.

Foreign exchange A voice communications service offered by common carriers for business users who want phone numbers in areas other than their actual location.

Format effectors (FE) The ASCII control characters that perform special functions on printers and terminals.

Forward error correction (FEC) Another name for error detection and correction.

Four-wire communications Communicating over two pairs of wires. This term is often incorrectly used as a synonym for full duplex, as full duplex communications no longer requires four wires.

Fractional T-1 A carrier service offered for customers who do not need all 24 channels available in T-1.

Fragment In IP, a new datagram that is actually a piece of a larger datagram.

Fragment offset field In IP, a 13-bit field used to number a datagram fragment for later reassembly.

Frame A block of data sent using a protocol, like BSC or SDLC, or a group of bits representing data from many channels, as in T-1 transmission.

Frame Check Sequence (FCS) field In many protocols, the part of the frame containing the CRC error-checking bits.

Frame ground Another name for chassis ground.

Frame Level The second level of the ITU(CCITT) X.25 standard, it conforms to the ITU(CCITT) LAP-B Protocol.

Frame relay A technique used in data transport networks in which error checking is performed end-to-end instead of on each individual link.

Framing bit In T-1 transmission, a bit used for synchronization and sometimes for error checking.

Free token A pattern of bits on a token passing network, indicating that the network is available for use.

Frequency The pitch of a tone, or the number of cycles per second of a sine wave.

Frequency division A local area network contention method based on the frequency-division multiplexing technique.

Frequency modulation (FM) The transmission of information by varying the pitch of a tone (the frequency of a sine wave).

Frequency shift keying (FSK) Another name for frequency modulation.

Frequency-division multiplexing (FDM) A multiplexing method in which devices continually share the bandwidth of the link by dividing the communications circuit into many separate frequencies, or channels.

Front end Another name for a front-end processor.

Front-end port Another name for the line interfaces of a front-end processor.

Front-end processor (FEP) A device that acts as a communications assistant for the host computer, handling all communications with terminals and other devices and allowing the host computer to concentrate on calculations.

FSK Frequency shift keying. *See* Frequency modulation.

FTP *See* File Transfer Protocol.

Full duplex communications A simultaneous, two-way communications path.

Full-Speed USB *See* USB 1.1.

G.711 The ITU(CCITT) standard codec for digitized voice signals used in T-1 and ISDN and upon which V.90 and V.92 modems are based.

G.722 An example of a codec that provides near-CD quality audio with only 16 kbps.

G.Lite *See* Universal Asymmetric Digital Subscriber Line.

Gatekeeper A common component in an H.323 VOIP system, it is used to authenticate a user and track the user's location.

Gateway A device used to connect two separate networks that use different communications methods (e.g., a VOIP gateway that interconnects VOIP and non-VOIP users).

Gbps *See* Gigabits per second.

General Packet Radio Service (GPRS) An enhancement to GSM that provides data rates up to 170 kbps.

GEO *See* Geosynchronous-earth orbit.

Geosynchronous-earth orbit (GEO) A satellite that orbits at approximately 22,230 miles above the earth.

Get A type of SNMP message sent from the manager to the agent to request configuration or status information.

Gigabit Ethernet The version of the IEEE 802.3 network that operates at 1 Gbps, it includes some additional changes to allow transmission to be 100 times faster than the original Ethernet.

Gigabits per second (Gbps) A billion bits per second.

Global System for Mobile (GSM) A digital cellular standard first deployed in Europe, it is now in use throughout the world.

GND Ground. *See* Chassis ground.

Go-back-N continuous ARQ A type of automatic repeat request in which transmission continues until too many frames are unacknowledged or until a negative acknowledgment is received. The frame in error, and all succeeding frames, must be retransmitted.

GPRS *See* General Packet Radio Service.

Group 1 An early ITU(CCITT) fax standard, it was purely analog, it offered 100 lines per inch of resolution and took approximately 6 minutes to transmit a typical page.

Group 2 An early ITU(CCITT) fax standard, it was purely analog, it offered 100 lines per inch of resolution and took approximately 3 minutes to transmit a typical page.

Group 3 A commonly used ITU(CCITT) fax standard, it converts the image to digital form and compresses it before transmission. It typically operates at 4800 or 9600 bps, offers 200 lines per inch of resolution, and takes under a minute to transmit a typical page.

Group 4 An advanced ITU(CCITT) fax standard, it converts the image to digital form, operates at speeds up to 64 kbps, and offers 400 lines per inch of resolution.

GSM *See* Global System for Mobile.

H.323 The first standard VOIP signaling protocol.

Hackers Sophisticated users who attack the computers of others.

Half duplex communications An alternating transmission path that goes two ways, but only one direction at a time.

Hamming code A method devised by Richard Hamming for detecting a single bit error in a byte and correcting it with 100% accuracy.

Handshaking The interaction of control signals between devices.

Hardware encryption The encryption and decryption of data using a separate device; the algorithm is changed by purchasing a new device.

HDLC *See* High-level Data Link Control.

HDSL *See* High-bit-rate Digital Subscriber Line.

HDSL2 A version of HDSL that operates at the same speeds and distances, but over a single twisted pair.

HDTV *See* High-Definition Television.

Head end In a cable television system, the equivalent of a telephone company central office.

Header In most protocols, it is the beginning of a package of data used for routing. For example, in ATM, the first five octets of a cell are known as the header. In IP, the first 20 bytes (plus any options bytes) make up the header.

Header checksum field In IP, the 16-bit field used to verify if the header contains any errors.

Header length In TCP, the length of the header in 32-bit increments.

Hertz Another name for cycles per second.

High Performance Serial Bus *See* IEEE 1394.

High-bit-rate Digital Subscriber Line (HDSL) A digital access technology that provides a link from the user to the central office over two twisted pairs. The link runs the same speed in both directions, typically 1.544 Mbps or 2.048 Mbps.

High-Definition Television (HDTV) A standard for very high-quality television transmission, far superior to traditional broadcast quality.

Higher layers Layers 4 though 7 of the OSI model (the Transport, Session, Presentation, and Application Layers).

High-level Data Link Control (HDLC) The ISO bit-oriented protocol, similar to SDLC, but with some additional features.

High-Performance Serial Bus *See* IEEE 1394.

High-Speed Token Ring The new version of the IEEE 802.5 network that operates at speeds above 16 Mbps, including 100 Mbps and above.

High-usage intertoll trunk A trunk connecting toll offices that can carry many conversations simultaneously.

Hi-Speed USB *See* USB 2.0.

Historical logging A security method that provides a complete recording of all data passed through a particular device.

HLEN *See* Header length.

HomePlug A residential LAN that operates over power lines.

HomePNA A residential LAN that operates over existing telephone wiring.

HomeRF 2.0 A residential wireless LAN that operates at 10 Mbps.

Hop A step in delivering messages in a network. In packet networks, like IP networks, each handoff to the next router is a hop; in terrestrial microwave transmission, a repeater station is used for each hop.

Hop counter Typically, a field in a protocol that is incremented or decremented with each step in routing to track the number of routing steps.

Hop limit In IPv6, the number of routing steps a packet is allowed to have on a given network before it is discarded.

Host computer The heart of a data communications network, it can perform numerical calculations, store and retrieve data, and perform a variety of tasks known as applications.

Host identifier (Hostid) A part of the Network Layer address in IP, it uniquely describes a particular host on a network. The network itself is identified by the netid.

Host Node In SNA, a node containing a Host Processor.

Host Processor The SNA term for a host computer.

Hosted communications A VOIP system where servers are operated and maintained by a service provider, it is sometimes called IP Centrex.

Hostid *See* Host identifier.

Hot spots A publicly available wireless LAN access point.

Howler signal The signal sent by the central office to the user to indicate that the phone has been left off the hook.

HSTR *See* High-Speed Token Ring.

HTML *See* HyperText Markup Language.

HTTP *See* HyperText Transfer Protocol.

Hub A device used to simplify the wiring of bus or ring networks by using a physical star topology while maintaining the original logical bus or ring.

Hybrid interface An ISDN interface that combines the A-channel and C-channel, providing a user with analog voice and low-speed data, along with access to some of the ISDN services.

HyperText Markup Language (HTML) A document format that links items in a hierarchical fashion, it can link text, audio, video, image, or any collection of items to allow for easy browsing.

HyperText Transfer Protocol (HTTP) A protocol used with TCP/IP to transfer information, typically data prepared in the HTML format.

Hz Hertz. *See* Cycles per second.

IBM International Business Machines Corporation.

IBM Cabling System IBM's method for wiring office buildings with standard cable.

IBM PC Network An IBM local area network available in baseband and broadband CSMA/CD versions.

IBM Token Ring Network An IBM local area network that uses token passing on a baseband, star-wired ring, similar to the IEEE 802.5 standard.

ICMP *See* Internet Control Message Protocol.

IDEA *See* International Data Encryption Algorithm.

Identification field In IP, the 16-bit field used to identify the original datagram so that the fragments can later be reassembled.

IEC *See* Interexchange carrier.

IEEE *See* Institute of Electrical and Electronics Engineers.

IEEE 802 An IEEE local area network standards committee made up of several subcommittees.

IEEE 802.1 A standard providing an overview of local area networks, methods for connecting networks, and systems management.

IEEE 802.2 A Logical Link Control standard for local area networks.

IEEE 802.3 A CSMA/CD bus Medium Access Control standard for local area networks.

IEEE 802.4 A token bus Medium Access Control standard for local area networks.

IEEE 802.5 A token ring Medium Access Control standard for local area networks.

IEEE 802.6 A metropolitan area network Medium Access Control standard for local area networks.

IEEE 802.7 An advisory subcommittee on using broadband transmission in local area networks.

IEEE 802.8 An advisory subcommittee on using fiber optics in local area networks.

IEEE 802.9 An advisory subcommittee on integrating voice and data in local area networks.

IEEE 802.11 An example of a special protocol used in wireless LANs.

IEEE 802.11a A wireless LAN standard operating at 54 Mbps and 5.0 GHz.

IEEE 802.11b A wireless LAN standard operating at 11 Mbps and 2.4 GHz.

IEEE 802.11g A wireless LAN standard operating at 54 Mbps and 2.4 GHz.

IEEE 802.11i An enhanced security method for wireless LANs, it uses AES to provide stronger security than WPA.

IEEE 802.16 One of the available fixed wireless standards, it can operate at speeds of several hundred kbps, depending on distance and terrain.

IEEE 1394 A data communications interface designed to connect peripherals to desktop computers, it operates at speeds up to 400 Mbps in its first version and is also known as High Performance Serial Bus, or Firewire.

IEEE 1394A A data communications interface designed to connect peripherals to desktop computers, it operates at speeds up to 400 Mbps and is also known as High Performance Serial Bus, or Firewire.

IEEE 1394B The next version of IEEE 1394, it operates at speeds up to 3200 Mbps.

IETF *See* Internet Engineering Task Force.

I-Frame *See* Information Format Frame.

IHL *See* Internet Header Length field.

IM *See* Instant message.

IMAP4 *See* Internet Message Access Protocol version 4.

In-band signaling Interspersing signaling bits with user data instead of transmitting signaling on a separate channel.

Incoming calls only A packet switching network service allowing DTEs to accept calls, but not to place them.

Independent Telephone Company (ITC) A local exchange carrier not formerly controlled by AT&T before divestiture.

Information Field In SDLC, the part of the Information Frame containing user data.

Information Format Frame (I-Frame) In SDLC, the type of frame used to send and receive user data.

Information separators (IS) In ASCII, the control characters used by host computers in storing and retrieving data.

Information superhighway A high-bandwidth network providing cost-effective transmission of voice, video, and data, it will probably be based on BISDN.

Information Systems Network (ISN) AT&T's combination of local area network and packet switching network transmission methods to provide connections to a wide variety of devices.

Infrared Data Association (IrDA) A widely available wireless data standard based on infrared light waves.

Input/output channel The high-speed port of a host computer, usually connected to a front-end processor.

Instant message (IM) A message sent between two users who are logged on to an IM service.

Institute of Electrical and Electronics Engineers (IEEE) A professional organization of engineers, consisting of specialized societies whose committees prepare standards in their areas of specialty.

Integrated Services Digital Network (ISDN) An evolving set of standards for a digital network that carries both voice and data communications.

Integrated voice/data terminal (IVDT) A device, usually attached to a PBX, combining the capabilities of a digital phone with those of a terminal.

Intelligent terminal A programmable smart terminal.

Interexchange carrier (IEC) Another name for a long-distance company.

Interexchange circuit (IXC) Another name for an intertoll trunk, as well as the link-connecting nodes in a packet switching network.

Interface The point at which one device connects to another.

Inter-LATA call A call between two local access transport areas, also known as a long-distance call.

Intermediate node The device between two communicating host computers that implements the lower layers of the OSI model.

Internal PAD A PAD located inside a packet switching node.

International Baudot A version of the Baudot code with a sixth bit added for parity checking.

International Data Encryption Algorithm (IDEA) A common encryption algorithm support by PGP.

International Standards Organization (ISO) A standards organization in which each member country is represented by its own national standards organization.

International Telecommunications Union (ITU) The parent organization of the ITU-T (formerly CCITT). An international telecommunications standards organization, whose members include regulating bodies from member countries, representatives from leading companies, and representatives from other organizations.

International Telecommunications Union–Telecommunications Standardization Sector (ITU–T) The official name that the CCITT now uses to describe its activities and new standards. Usually referred to simply as "ITU."

Internet When the "I" is capitalized, it is a popular wide area network using TCP/IP protocols. When the "i" is in lowercase, it can be any collection of connected networks.

Internet Control Message Protocol (ICMP) A protocol used to send messages about unusual events or error conditions in an IP network.

Internet Engineering Task Force (IETF) An international organization dedicated to the evolution and smooth operation of the Internet.

Internet Header Length field (IHL) In IP, the 4-bit field used to indicate the length of the header, in 32-bit increments.

Internet Message Access Protocol version 4 (IMAP4) A protocol for retrieving and sending mail from a mail server.

Internet Protocol (IP) A part of the TCP/IP Protocol Suite, it operates at Layer 3 of the OSI model, the Network Layer, routing individual packets, known as datagrams.

Internet Relay Chat (IRC) The protocol used for chatting on the Internet.

Internet service provider (ISP) A company operating a packet switching network based on IP protocols, attached to other IP networks, as part of the global Internet.

Internetworking Connecting two or more separate networks.

Interoffice trunk (IOT) A communications circuit connecting two central offices in a local area.

Intertoll trunk A communications circuit connecting two toll offices.

Intranet The servers and applications attached to a company's TCP/IP-based network that are accessible only to internal users.

Inverse multiplexer A device used to combine the bandwidth of two or more communications circuits to meet high-bandwidth requirements.

Inward WATS trunk Another name for a toll-free number.

IOT *See* Interoffice trunk.

IP *See* Internet Protocol.

IP Centrex A VOIP system where servers are operated and maintained by a service provider, it is sometimes called hosted communications.

IP phones A telephone that operates on VOIP systems.

IP Security protocol (IPSec) A protocol used to allow secure private networking across insecure public data networks.

IPSec *See* IP Security protocol.

IPv4 The current version of the Internet Protocol that is most widely deployed.

IPv6 A new version of the Internet Protocol that offers many enhancements; however, it may be years before it changes the networking landscape.

IRC *See* Internet Relay Chat.

IrDA *See* Infrared Data Association.

IS *See* Information separators.

ISDN *See* Integrated Services Digital Network.

ISN *See* Information Systems Network.

ISO *See* International Standards Organization.

ISO Standard 2110 A standard describing the DB25 connectors.

ISO Standard 4902 A standard describing the DB37 and DB9 connectors.

Isochronous A type of data traffic in which data order and timing is critical, as in real-time communications like voice and video.

ISP *See* Internet service provider.

ITC *See* Independent Telephone Company.

ITU *See* International Telecommunications Union.

ITU-T *See* International Telecommunications Union–Telecommunications Standardization Sector.

IVDT *See* Integrated voice/data terminal.

IXC *See* Interexchange circuit.

Jacket The protective coating surrounding the buffer in a fiber optic cable.

Jitter The variability of delay through a network.

JPEG A popular image compression format.

Key A specific set of codes used by an encryption algorithm to encode data and by a decryption algorithm to decode data.

Key system A customer-premises equipment solution to small-business telecommunications needs, it eliminates the inefficiencies of Centrex, but is smaller and less sophisticated than a PBX.

Keyboard The part of a terminal where data is entered by the user.

LAN *See* Local area network.

LAN Switch A device that creates a true star network and in which data is delivered to the appropriate user only based on the destination address. It is also known as a switching hub.

Landline A telephone line that uses wires, as opposed to a wireless or cellular connection.

LAP-B *See* Link Access Procedure-Balanced.

LAPM *See* Link Access Procedure for Modems.

Lasers A light source ideal for fiber optic transmission.

Last mile The interconnection from the Internet or central office to our home or business.

LATA *See* Local access and transport area.

Layer Division according to function as found in the OSI model. *See* also Application Layer, Presentation Layer, Session Layer, Transport Layer, Network Layer, Data Link Layer, and Physical Layer.

Layer 2 switching A device that delivers messages based on their Layer 2 address (e.g., Ethernet MAC address).

Layer 3 switching A device that delivers messages based on their Layer 3 address (e.g., IP address).

Layer 4 switching A device that delivers messages based on their Layer 3 address (e.g., IP address). It is aware of the Layer 4 protocol being used (e.g., TCP), and it handles, routes, and prioritizes the Layer 3 packet accordingly.

Learning bridge A type of bridge that can learn the locations of users and deliver messages accordingly based on their Layer 2 address. Also known as an adaptive bridge.

Lease renewal The process by which a device requests a DHCP server to extend the lease time for an IP address.

Lease time The time for which a DHCP-supplied IP address is valid.

Leased line A circuit rented from the common carriers for a flat monthly fee, with no usage charge per call.

Least cost routing A PBX system feature that chooses the least expensive trunk for a given call at a particular time of day.

LEC *See* Local exchange carrier.

LED *See* Light-emitting diode.

Length/type field The field in an Ethernet frame that refers to the data field length or protocol type.

LEO *See* Low-earth orbit.

Letters A special character in the Baudot character code indicating that future transmission will be from the Lower Case set of characters.

Light-emitting diode (LED) A small light bulb, about an eighth of an inch in diameter, typically found on a breakout box.

Limited-distance modem Another name for a short-haul modem.

Line discipline Another name for a protocol.

Line feed A special character used to send a terminal's cursor or printer's head to the next line.

Line interface The low-speed port on a front-end processor that is typically attached to terminals.

Line of sight The requirement that there be no obstructions between two dish antennas in terrestrial microwave transmission.

Line splitter A device that allows many terminals to share one front-end port and that is located remotely from the front-end processor.

Link Access Procedure for Modems (LAPM) The ITU(CCITT) standard for modem error correction, also known as V.42.

Link Access Procedure-Balanced (LAP-B) The ITU(CCITT) bit-oriented protocol similar to SDLC.

Link level protocol A set of rules precisely defining methods for communicating over a communications circuit, or link.

Link A communications circuit.

LLC *See* Logical Link Control.

LMDS *See* Local Multipoint Data Services.

Load balancing A device that shares load among multiple servers, as in a server farm.

Loading coil A device used in some analog telephone circuits to improve voice quality at longer distances.

Local access and transport area (LATA) A geographical region where the local phone company provides the user with entry, or access, to the public network and carries or transports calls.

Local analog loopback test A modem diagnostic technique that can be performed with a modem, a cable, and a terminal.

Local area network (LAN) A privately owned data communications system that provides reliable high-speed, switched connections between devices in a single building, campus, or complex.

Local exchange Another name for the central office.

Local exchange carrier (LEC) Another name for the local phone company that provides service inside the LATA.

Local loop The pair of wires that runs from the central office into our home or business.

Local Multipoint Data Services (LMDS) One of the available fixed wireless standards, speeds of several hundred kbps can be achieved depending on distance and terrain.

Location server A common component in a SIP VOIP system, it tracks the IP address from which the user signs in.

Logical Link Control (LLC) The IEEE 802.2 subcommittee standard relating to local area network functions like error checking and reliability.

Logical Unit (LU) In SNA, the Network Addressable Unit that is the End User's access point to the network.

Long-distance call Another name for an inter-LATA call.

Loopback plug A special connector used to perform echo testing with an asynchronous dumb terminal.

Loopback testing A diagnostic technique in which transmitted data is returned to the sender for comparison with the original message.

Low The state of an RS-232-C control signal when it is off or false.

Low-earth orbit (LEO) A satellite that orbits at approximately a few hundred miles above the earth.

Lower Case The portion of the Baudot character code used for the letters of the alphabet.

Lower layers Layers 1 through 3 of the OSI model (Physical, Data Link, and Network Layers).

Low-Speed USB *See* USB 1.0.

LU *See* Logical Unit.

MAC *See* Medium Access Control.

Mainframe A host computer usually serving a large organization.

Malicious software Software designed to harm a user's computer or network, like a virus or a worm.

Malware *See* Malicious software.

MAN *See* Metropolitan area network.

Management Information Base (MIB) The common set of information needed to manage a network, as described in SNMP.

Manager The central station partner of the remote agent in a network management protocol.

Manufacturing Automation Protocol (MAP) A user-defined networking standard originally developed by General Motors.

MAP *See* Manufacturing Automation Protocol.

Mark In RS-232-C, transmission of a 1, using an electrical signal between −3 and −15 volts.

Mark parity An error-detection method in which the parity bit is always a 1.

Maximum transmission unit (MTU) The longest message allowed on a particular network.

Mbps Millions of bits per second.

MCI One of many common carriers offering a variety of services.

MCU *See* Multipoint Control Unit.

Mean time between failures (MTBF) The average time between network failures, or uptime.

Mean time to repair (MTTR) The average time required to diagnose and correct a problem, or downtime.

Media Gateway Control Protocol (MGCP) A VOIP protocol used to decompose gateways into call signaling and media components.

Medium Access Control (MAC) A group of IEEE standards that relate to local area network access methods and that describe how devices share time on a network.

Medium-earth orbit (MEO) A satellite that orbits a few thousand miles above the earth.

MEGACO A VOIP protocol used to decompose gateways into call signaling and media components.

MEO *See* Medium-earth orbit.

Mesh network A network topology in which each device is connected by a cable to every other device in the network.

Metropolitan area network (MAN) The IEEE 802.6 standard describing Medium Access Control for networks that span a city.

MF *See* More fragments flag.

MFJ *See* Modified Final Judgment.

MGCP *See* Media Gateway Control Protocol.

MI/MIC lead *See* Mode indicator lead.

MIB *See* Management Information Base.

Microcellular A type of cellular system using small zones, such as areas of a building.

Microcom Network Protocol (MNP) A commercial modem protocol licensed by Microcom to many vendors to perform error correction and sometimes compression, depending on the version of the protocol.

Microcomputer A host computer usually serving only a single user.

Microsegmentation Using a LAN switch with only one station connected to each port.

MIME *See* Multipurpose Internet Mail Extensions.

Minicomputer A host computer usually serving a group of users, such as a department or a division.

MNP *See* Microcom Network Protocol.

MNP 5 The first version of MNP to provide the data compression feature.

Mobile IP A protocol that allows IP users to be reached at various locations.

Mode indicator (MI/MIC) lead A pair of wires connected to a dumb modem. When closed by a PBX, they cause the modem to begin communicating with a remote modem.

Modem A device that performs modulation and demodulation, allowing data communications to occur in analog form over telephone circuits.

Modified Final Judgment (MFJ) The edict requiring AT&T to divest itself of the Bell Operating Companies.

Modulation Converting digital signals to analog form for transmission.

Modulator circuit The part of a modem's circuitry that performs modulation.

Modulo-8 As used in protocols like SDLC, the ability to transmit up to seven frames without waiting for an acknowledgment message.

Modulo-128 As used in protocols like SDLC, the ability to transmit up to 127 frames without waiting for an acknowledgment message.

More fragments (MF) flag In IP, a single bit in the flags field used to indicate that this is not the last of the fragments of a particular datagram.

Morse code A character code used in telegraph transmission, in which long and short tones are used to represent characters.

Moving Pictures Expert Group (MPEG) An ISO committee providing a variety of standards for video transmission.

MP3 A popular compressed audio format often used for music files.

MPEG *See* Moving Pictures Expert Group.

MPEG II One of the standards of the Moving Pictures Expert Group that provides varying degrees of quality based on the bit rate used.

MPLS *See* Multiprotocol Label Switching.

MTBF *See* Mean time between failures.

MTTR *See* Mean time to repair.

MTU *See* Maximum transmission unit.

Multicast A message sent to a group of users on a network; sometimes it is sent to everyone, but is ignored by those not in the group.

Multidrop A configuration in which several terminals are directly attached to, and share, a single communications line leading to a single front-end or host computer port.

Multimedia A term commonly used to describe applications or transmissions containing some combination of voice, video, image, and data.

Multimode fiber A type of fiber optic cable using thicker cable, which is ideal for shorter distances.

Multiplexer (Mux) A device used to allow a single communications circuit to take the place of several parallel ones. It is often used to allow several remotely located terminals to communicate with several front-end processor ports over a single circuit.

Multipoint Control Unit (MCU) In VOIP, a device that can mix voice streams from several users to allow for conference calls, as well as handle other media processing.

Multiprotocol Label Switching (MPLS) A protocol that labels each packet as part of a larger data stream to enable faster handling.

Multipurpose Internet Mail Extensions (MIME) A set of enhancements beyond SMTP that allow for a variety of items, including text, executable files, audio, video, and binary files, to be exchanged in electronic mail messages.

Multirate ISDN The usage of multiple B-channels for a single connection, also known as N × 64.

Multispeed A capability found in many modems that allows them to communicate at different speeds.

Mux *See* Multiplexer.

N × 64 The usage of multiple B-channels for a single connection, also known as Multirate ISDN.

NAK In BSC, the control character signifying a negative acknowledgment.

Narrowband ISDN The ISDN standard currently being implemented, including the basic-rate, primary-rate, and hybrid interfaces. *See* Integrated Services Digital Network.

NAT *See* Network Address Translation.

National Bureau of Standards (NBS) *See* National Institute of Standards and Technology.

National Electrical Code A widely used standard for electrical wiring and safety practices.

National Institute of Standards and Technology (NIST) The federal standards organization in the United States, it produces the Federal Information Processing Standards. It was formerly known as the National Bureau of Standards (NBS).

National ISDN A series of Bellcore standards that ensure consistent deployment of ISDN regardless of carrier or equipment manufacturer.

National Security Agency (NSA) A federal agency that has adopted the Data Encryption Standard for protecting sensitive, but not classified, information.

NAU *See* Network Addressable Unit.

NBS *See* National Bureau of Standards.

Netid *See* Network identifier.

Netview IBM's host-computer-based network management software.

Netview/PC IBM's personal computer-based network management software that allows any device conforming to IBM's standard set of protocols to transmit network management information to Netview.

Network A group of interconnected, communicating devices.

Network Address Translation (NAT) A technique where a private address range is used on a LAN either to conserve address space or to provide additional security.

Network Addressable Unit (NAU) In SNA, a device with a unique address to which data is routed.

Network computer A host with very little processing power and designed to run thin clients, it is the modern-day equivalent of a dumb terminal.

Network control The network management function that acts as the network "boss," allowing for the activation and deactivation of network components and features.

Network identifier (Netid) A part of the Network Layer address in IP, it uniquely describes a particular network. The specific host on the network is described by the hostid.

Network Layer Layer 3 of the OSI model, it is responsible for setting up the appropriate routing of messages throughout a network.

Network management Ensuring consistent reliability and availability of a network, as well as timely transmission and routing of data, it can be performed by dedicated devices, by host computers, by people, or by some combination of all of these.

Network monitoring The network management function acting as the network "watchdog" that constantly checks on the network and reports on any problems.

Network statistical reporting The network management function acting as the network "statistician" that pinpoints which parts of a network are being used and how often.

Network Termination 1 (NT1) In ISDN, the equipment providing only OSI Layer 1 (Physical Layer) functions, including the electrical and physical termination of the network on the customer's premises.

Network Termination 2 (NT2) In ISDN, the equipment providing OSI Layers 2 and 3 (Data Link and Network Layer) functions, including concentration and switching, if needed.

Network Termination (NT) equipment In ISDN, equipment providing functions similar to those found in the lower layers of the OSI model.

Network troubleshooting The network management function acting as the network "diagnostician" that assists in isolating and diagnosing problems.

Network–Network Interface (NNI) The ATM interface specification describing how to connect two provider networks.

Newsgroup A popular Internet application in which users post, review, and subscribe to information on an electronic bulletin-board system.

Next header In IPv6, it indicates if additional, optional headers follow the current header.

NIST *See* National Institute of Standards and Technology.

NNI *See* Network–Network Interface.

Node In SNA, the component or device interconnected by the SNA network; in a packet switching network, the device that switches and routes calls at each location.

NSA *See* National Security Agency.

NT *See* Network Termination equipment.

NT1 *See* Network Termination 1.

NT2 *See* Network Termination 2.

NT12 *See* Combined Network Termination 1 and 2.

Null modem cable A special cable used to connect two DTEs together in RS-232-C, it simulates the operation of two DCEs and the network between them.

Numbering In a packet switching network, the method of tracking the proper sequence of packets.

OC-1 An OC-N signal operating at 51.84 Mbps.

OC-3 An OC-N signal operating at 155.52 Mbps.

OC-12 An OC-N signal operating at 622.08 Mbps.

OC-*N* *See* Optical Carrier-*N*.

Octet Another name for a byte in telecommunications.

Odd parity An error-detection method requiring an odd number of ones in each byte.

OFF The state of an RS-232-C control signal when it is false or low.

Off-hook The status of a phone that has been picked up. Also, the signal sent by the user to the central office when the phone is picked up.

Office code The three-digit prefix that designates the destination central office.

Omnidirectional An antenna that transmits or receives equally in all directions.

ON The state of an RS-232-C control signal when it is asserted, raised, or true.

ONA *See* Open Network Architecture.

1G *See* First generation.

100BASE-T An Ethernet standard for baseband transmission at 100 Mbps over twisted pair wiring.

100VG-AnyLan An emerging IEEE 802.12 local area network standard for 100 Mbps transmission using a demand-priority scheme.

On-hook The status of a phone that has been hung up. Also, the signal sent by the user to the central office when the phone is hung up.

Open Network Architecture (ONA) The post-divestiture FCC requirement that all network services be divided into basic service elements and be made available separately to enhanced service providers.

Open Shortest Path First (OSPF) A protocol used by routers in making routing decisions.

Open Systems Interconnection (OSI) model The International Standards Organization's set of standards that breaks down the task of computer communications into seven independent layers, each with its own tasks. *See* Lower layers, Higher layers.

OpenView A Hewlett-Packard network management product that supports a wide variety of protocols.

Operator The person running the console of a PBX.

Optical Carrier-*N* (OC-*N*) The SONET designation used with fiber optic signals, it supports speeds of 51.84 Mbps and higher.

Options field In IP, the optional area of the header used to extend the protocol beyond its original definition.

Originate/answer modem A type of modem that can place and answer calls.

Originate-only modem A type of modem that can only place calls.

OSI model *See* Open Systems Interconnection model.

OSPF *See* Open Shortest Path First.

Outgoing calls only A term used to describe a packet switching network service that allows DTEs to place calls, but not accept them.

Out-of-band signaling A method of sending signaling bits on a separate channel, rather than sending them interspersed with the data.

Outward WATS trunk A type of PBX trunk that connects to a discounted long-distance service.

Overhead Nondata bits or characters necessary for transmission, error detection, or use by protocols.

Overlay A term used to describe the use of two or more area codes in a single geographic region.

P/F bit The bit in the SDLC control frame that can be used for polling by the Primary station or that can be used to indicate the final frame of transmission by the Secondary station.

Packet A block of data, including addressing, routing, and numbering information.

Packet assembler disassembler (PAD) A device used to connect a packet switching network with equipment that does not perform packet formatting.

Packet Level In packet switching networks, the X.25 level providing for network-level addressing and call connection.

Packet loss The rate at which packets are discarded in a network, it is typically caused by congestion.

Packet switching network (PSN) A network providing a switched service in which data is sent in packets through nodes over various routes and is recombined at its destination in the proper sequence.

Packet-filtering A technique used in firewalls in which packets are screened based on their origin, destination, and type of data.

Packetized A description of data that is divided into packets.

PAD *See* Packet assembler disassembler.

Padding In IP, it is used in conjunction with the options field to ensure that the header length rounds up to a 32-bit increment.

Parallel transmission A method of transmission in which all of the bits in a byte are sent at once on separate wires.

Parallel/serial conversion Changing data from parallel to serial form, and vice versa.

Parallel/serial converter A device that changes data from parallel to serial form, and vice versa.

Parity bit A bit reserved for error detection in the parity checking method.

Parity checking A method of error detection in which a single bit is added by the transmitter and checked by the receiver to determine if errors occurred. *See* Even parity, Mark parity, Odd parity, and Space parity.

Password The most common form of security, it requires the user to enter a secret set of characters to access information or systems.

Payload The 48 bytes of an ATM cell used to carry the user data, it can actually contain up to 4 overhead bytes, resulting in as few as 44 bytes available for user data.

Payload length In IPv6, the number of bytes that follow the header in the packet.

PBX *See* Private branch exchange.

PCM *See* Pulse code modulation.

PCS *See* Personal Communications Service.

PDA *See* Personal digital assistant.

Peer level In the OSI model, the corresponding layers on two communicating host computers (e.g., the Network Layers on each computer).

Period The length of time of a complete cycle of a sine wave.

Peripheral Node In SNA, a single Workstation, or a Cluster Controller with several Workstations.

Personal Communications Service (PCS) A telecommunications service in which calls follow a user from place to place. It can include a mix of wired and wireless telephones.

Personal computer A host computer usually serving only a single user.

Personal digital assistant (PDA) A handheld computing device often used for remote applications, like calendaring, email, and even web browsing.

Personal identification number (PIN) The password used with an automated teller machine.

PGP *See* Pretty Good Privacy.

Phase modulation (PM) The transmission of information by varying the phase of a sine wave.

Phase shift keying (PSK) Another name for phase modulation.

Physical Layer In the OSI model, it is Layer 1, the lowest layer, responsible for the transmission of bits. It is always implemented in hardware. In ATM, it is responsible for the transmission of cells.

Physical Level The lowest level of X.25, it describes the actual interface, which conforms to the ITU(CCITT) V.24/V.28 standard, and it is similar to RS-232-C.

Physical Unit (PU) In SNA, the Network Addressable Unit that manages and monitors a node's resources.

PIN *See* Personal identification number.

Ping A common ICMP message, it requests a reply from another IP device, and it is also known as an echo request.

Plain text Another name for clear text.

Plug-in Typically, a small application, or applet, that downloads to a browser when needed.

PM *See* Phase modulation.

Point of presence (POP) The point at which a long-distance call is handed from the local exchange carrier to the interexchange carrier.

Point-to-Point Protocol (PPP) A Layer 2 protocol used for sending IP packets, or other packets, over a serial link like a telephone line, it provides error detection and allows dynamic address assignment.

Point-to-Point Tunneling Protocol (PPTP) A protocol defined by Microsoft to interconnect remote users securely through the Internet.

Polling The method used by a host computer or front-end processor to ask a terminal if it has data to send.

POP *See* Point of presence.

POP3 *See* Post Office Protocol version 3.

Pop-up advertisements Commercial messages that present themselves in front of an existing web-browser window.

Pop-up blocker Software that prevents pop-up advertisements from being displayed.

Port number In TCP, along with an IP address, it describes an endpoint.

Port-sharing device A device that allows many terminals to share a single front-end port, it is located near the front-end processor. It is often called a concentrator.

Post Office Protocol version 3 (POP3) A protocol for retrieving and sending mail from a mail server.

Postal, telephone, and telegraph (PTT) administration Government agencies in many countries that regulate and often also operate the public network.

PPP *See* Point-to-Point Protocol.

PPTP *See* Point-to-Point Tunneling Protocol.

Preamble The first seven bytes of an Ethernet frame.

Prefix Another name for an office code.

Presence A user's status, indicating if he or she is online and/or available for communications.

Presence server A server that tracks the presence of a set of users and that can report changes as needed.

Presentation Layer Layer 6 of the OSI model, it provides format and code conversion services.

Presubscription The method by which a customer selects a default long-distance carrier.

Pretty Good Privacy (PGP) A very widely used encryption software product, it supports numerous algorithms.

PRI *See* Primary-rate interface.

Primary station In SDLC, the single device or station that communicates with all of the other (secondary) stations.

Primary-rate interface (PRI) The preferred method for attachment to ISDN by PBXs and LANs, it consists of 23 or 30 B-channels for user data and digitized voice and 1 D-channel for signaling.

Print server A shared printing device for local area network users, typically in the form of a personal computer with a high-speed printer, attached to the network.

Priority backoff A backoff method in which each device on a network has a different backoff time, providing those with lower times a higher priority in using the network.

Private branch exchange (PBX) A telecommunications switching system owned by the customer, it acts as an in-house central office with advanced features and capabilities.

Processing unit The intelligent part of a front-end processor, it is actually a special-purpose computer programmed for communications functions.

Protective ground Another name for chassis ground.

Protocol A set of rules precisely defining the methods used to communicate.

Protocol analyzer Another name for a datascope.

Protocol conversion Translating data from one protocol to another.

Protocol converter A device that performs protocol conversion.

Protocol field In IP, the eight-bit field indicating the protocol being carried in the datagram (e.g., TCP).

Proxy servers A common component in a SIP VOIP system, it is used to assist in forwarding call requests to the appropriate location.

PSK Phase shift keying. *See* Phase modulation.

PSN *See* Packet switching network.

PSTN *See* Public switched telephone network.

PTT *See* Postal, telephone, and telegraph administration.

PU *See* Physical Unit.

Public key An asymmetric key published in a directory, it is typically used for encryption, in conjunction with a secret key used for decryption.

Public network The telephone network, also called the direct distance dial network, accessed when using a home telephone.

Public packet switching network A packet switching network owned and operated for customers by service providers.

Public switched telephone network (PSTN) The telephone network operated by various carriers according to agreed upon, published standards.

Public utilities commission (PUC) The regulating body of each state responsible for regulating intrastate phone service.

PUC *See* Public utilities commission.

Pulse code modulation (PCM) A method of digitizing a normal telephone conversation.

Pulse dialing A dialing method, also known as rotary dialing, in which a switch is opened and closed at the end of the local loop at a fixed rate of speed.

Pure time-division multiplexing A time-division multiplexing method in which the transmission speed of the trunk port is at least as great as the sum of the speeds of the branch ports, guaranteeing enough bandwidth to handle the attached devices' maximum transmission.

QoS *See* Quality of Service.

Quadrature amplitude modulation A modulation method used in the ITU(CCITT) V.22 bis standard that combines changes in phase and amplitude to send four bits with each baud.

Quality of Service (QoS) The specific acceptable delay, jitter, and packet loss for a particular type of traffic.

R reference point In ISDN, the point between the TE2 and the TA.

RADSL *See* Rate-Adaptive Digital Subscriber Line.

Raised state The state of an RS-232-C control signal when it is on, asserted, or true.

Random access A contention method allowing devices to transmit whenever they please.

Random backoff A backoff method in which each device picks a random amount of time to wait before retransmitting after a collision.

Rate-Adaptive Digital Subscriber Line (RADSL) A digital access technology that provides a link from the user to the central office over twisted pair wire that is higher speed in one direction than in the other. Its rate varies depending on the transmission line's length and quality.

RBOC *See* Regional Bell Operating Company.

RC *See* Receive Clock.

RC4 The algorithm used in the Wired Equivalent Privacy standard.

RD *See* Received Data.

Real-time Transport Protocol (RTP) A protocol designed to transfer time-sensitive information over a data network.

Receive Clock (RC) The RS-232-C timing signal generated by the DCE to time synchronous data transmission from the DCE to the DTE.

Receive Common One of the RS-423-A signal returns.

Received Data (RD) The RS-232-C data signal received by the DTE from the DCE.

Receiver Not Ready (RNR) In SDLC, the Control Field message indicating a temporary busy condition.

Receiver Ready (RR) In SDLC, the Control Field message indicating that data has been successfully received and that more data can be sent.

Recommended Standard (RS) The designation used by EIA to describe its communications specifications.

Redirect servers A common component in a SIP VOIP system, it is used to assist in forwarding call requests to the appropriate location.

Regional Bell Operating Company (RBOC) Any of seven holding companies, each a collection of local Bell Operating Companies, formed after divestiture to permit the new BOCs to remain efficient and to achieve economies of scale.

Regional Holding Company (RHC) Another name for a Regional Bell Operating Company.

Registrar A common component in a SIP VOIP system, it is where users sign-in and are authenticated.

REJ *See* Reject.

Reject (REJ) In SDLC, the Control Field message indicating that a retransmission of data is necessary.

Reliability The ability of a network to pass data without errors, often measured using a bit or block error rate test.

Remote backup Archiving data to an offsite location.

Remote bridge A type of bridge used to connect networks at two or more locations.

Remote digital loopback test A modem diagnostic technique that can test the phone line itself as well as parts of the modem. It requires two modems, a terminal, a phone line, and a cable.

Remote intelligent controller A device, similar to a line splitter, that can also perform some front-end processor functions.

Remote Network Monitoring (RMON) A LAN management MIB created by the IETF, it is commonly used with SNMP. RMON1 operates on lower layer (MAC) addresses, while RMON2 recognizes higher layer addresses and protocols.

Repeater A device used to keep a digital signal strong and recognizable over long distances.

Request to Send (RTS) The RS-232-C control signal generated by the DTE to ask permission to transmit data.

Resequencing A function performed by destination packet switching nodes to arrange received packets in their proper order before transmitting them to the DTE.

Resolution A measure of image quality, often in lines per inch.

Resource Reservation Protocol (RSVP) A protocol used to reserve bandwidth in an IP network.

Response time Though its definition varies with each application, it often refers to the total amount of time it takes a message to travel from the terminal to the host computer, plus the processing time at the host computer, plus the travel time of the reply.

Reverse charging Another name for collect calls.

RHC Regional Holding Company. *See* Regional Bell Operating Company.

RI *See* Ring Indicator.

Ring Indicator (RI) The RS-232-C control signal generated by the DCE to alert the DTE that a remote device wants to initiate communications.

Ring network A network topology in which all devices are connected in a continuous loop.

Ringback signal A signal provided by the central office to the caller to indicate that the called party's phone is being rung.

Ringing signal A signal provided by the central office to the called party to cause the telephone to ring.

RJ11 A common connector used for twisted pair voice connections.

RJ45 A common connector used for twisted pair data connections.

Rlogin A protocol used with UNIX-based computers to provide remote login capabilities.

RMON *See* Remote Network Monitoring.

RMON1 *See* Remote Network Monitoring.

RMON2 *See* Remote Network Monitoring.

RNR *See* Receiver Not Ready.

Robbed-bit signaling A common T-1 signaling method in which a bit is occasionally stolen from a channel to carry signaling information.

Root name servers The highest-level DNS servers in the Internet, they point to the top-level domain servers.

Rotary dialing Another name for pulse dialing.

Rotary register A device in the central office, used in rotary or pulse dialing, that can detect the opening and closing of a switch at the end of the local loop.

Route optimization Another name for least cost routing.

Router Similar to a bridge, but it includes OSI Layer 3 intelligence.

RR *See* Receiver Ready.

RS *See* Recommended Standard.

RS-232-C One of the most common interface standards for data communications in use today, it is an EIA standard defining exactly how ones and zeroes will be transmitted, including voltage levels needed and other electronic signals necessary for communication.

RS-422-A An EIA standard describing a method of balanced transmission that can be used for RS-449 Category I signals.

RS-423-A An EIA standard describing a method of unbalanced transmission used for RS-449 Category II signals.

RS-449 An EIA standard describing the mechanical and functional characteristics of the DTE/DCE interface and specifying the RS-422-A and RS-423-A standards for transmission.

RSA A public key encryption algorithm widely used in electronic messaging systems, it is named after its inventors, Rivest, Shamir, and Adelman.

RSVP *See* Resource Reservation Protocol.

RTP *See* Real-time Transport Protocol.

RTS *See* Request to Send.

Run length encoding A method of digitally compressing an image to reduce fax transmission time.

S reference point In ISDN, the point between the Network Termination equipment and the TE1 or TA.

S/MIME *See* Secure/Multipurpose Internet Mail Extensions.

SA *See* Source Address.

Sample A snapshot of a signal at a given moment, as used to digitize voice in pulse code modulation.

Satellite An orbiting vehicle often used for communications.

Satellite dish A special antenna used to transmit signals to or receive signals from a satellite.

Satellite transmission The use of an orbiting satellite to repeat signals to all antennas in view of the satellite.

Screen The part of a terminal where received data is displayed.

SCTS *See* Secondary Clear to Send.

SDCD *See* Secondary Data Carrier Detect.

SDH *See* Synchronous Digital Hierarchy.

SDLC *See* Synchronous Data Link Control.

SDSL *See* Single-line Digital Subscriber Line.

Sealed message A type of message that cannot be modified by an unauthorized party.

Search engines A service for indexing or categorizing Internet content.

Second generation (2G) The initial digital cellular standards, it includes USDC, CDMA, TDMA, and GSM.

Secondary Clear to Send (SCTS) The RS-232-C Clear to Send signal for the secondary channel.

Secondary Data Carrier Detect (SDCD) The RS-232-C Data Carrier Detect signal for the secondary channel.

Secondary Received Data (SRD) The RS-232-C Received Data signal for the secondary channel.

Secondary Request to Send (SRTS) The RS-232-C Request to Send signal for the secondary channel.

Secondary station In SDLC, a device or station that communicates with the primary station; there can be several secondary stations.

Secondary Transmitted Data (STD) The RS-232-C Transmitted Data signal for the secondary channel.

Secret key A type of encryption code that is not publicly known.

Secret message A secure message that is encrypted so that it cannot be understood by an unauthorized party.

Secure channel A communications link that is known to be safe from intrusion or eavesdropping.

Secure Sockets Layer (SSL) A protocol that allows common protocols in IP networks, such as HTTP, Telnet, and FTP, to transmit securely using public key encryption techniques.

Secure/Multipurpose Internet Mail Extensions (S/MIME) Extensions to the MIME protocol that provide public key encryption features.

Segment In TCP, data is broken into these, which consist of a TCP header followed by user data. Also, a piece of a LAN, usually that was part of a larger LAN previously. In Ethernet, it typically encompasses a single collision domain.

Segmentation The result of breaking a LAN into smaller pieces.

Segmenting The process of breaking a LAN into smaller pieces.

Selecting A method used by a host computer or front-end processor to ask a terminal if it is ready to receive data.

Selective repeat continuous ARQ A type of automatic repeat request whereby transmission continues until a negative acknowledgment is received, and only the frame with the error is repeated.

Send Common One of the RS-423-A signal returns.

Sequence number In TCP, it is used to track the TCP segments numerically.

Sequenced message A message protected against undetected loss or repetition by numbering.

Serial Line Internet Protocol (SLIP) A Layer 2 protocol used for sending IP packets over a serial line, it offers no error detection and cannot be used with non-IP protocols.

Serial transmission A method of transmission in which the bits in a byte are sent one after the other on the same wire.

Server farm A group of servers often acting as if they were a single server.

Service level The criterion for acceptable network performance.

Session In SNA, a communications path through a network.

Session Initiation Protocol (SIP) The most popular VOIP signaling protocol.

Session Layer Layer 5 of the OSI model, it requests that a logical connection be established or terminated, and it handles logon and password procedures.

Set A type of SNMP message sent from the manager to the agent to change the configuration or settings on a remote device.

SFD *See* Start-of-Frame Delimiter.

SFDM *See* Statistical frequency-division multiplexing.

S-Frame *See* Supervisory Format Frame.

SG *See* Signal Ground.

Shielded twisted pair (STP) A more expensive type of wiring for voice or data for use in noisy environments.

Short-haul modem A modem that transmits data over twisted pair wire over a limited distance on a customer's premises, but not through telephone company central offices.

Signal Ground (SG) The RS-232-C ground that acts as a zero-volt reference for all other signals.

Signal Quality Detect (SQ) The RS-232-C control signal asserted by the DCE when it perceives that transmission is of a high quality and that no errors are occurring.

Signaling In the telephone network, information sent between devices, or between devices and users, to convey status and information, like dialed digits, busy signals, and ringing.

Signaling System 7 (SS7) A standard for network signaling developed in 1984 and already in widespread use in the United States, it plays a key role in ISDN.

Signed message A message that includes proof of the sender's identity.

SIM *See* Subscriber Identity Module.

Simple Mail Transfer Protocol (SMTP) A part of the TCP/IP Protocol Suite, it provides a universal format for exchanging electronic mail.

Simple Network Management Protocol (SNMP) Originally a part of the TCP/IP Protocol Suite, it describes methods for exchanging a common set of network management information. In its second version (SNMPv2), it also includes support for non-IP protocols.

Simplex communications A one-direction communications path.

Sine wave An electronic representation of a pure tone, it is a signal that repeats indefinitely its pattern of peaks of equal height and valleys of equal depth.

Single-line Digital Subscriber Line (SDSL) A digital-access technology that provides a link from the user to the central office over a single twisted pair that is the same speed in both directions, at speeds up to 1.544 Mbps or 2.048 Mbps.

Single-mode fiber A type of fiber optic cable using very thin fiber, ideal for longer distances.

SIP *See* Session Initiation Protocol.

SLIP *See* Serial Line Internet Protocol.

Smart card A credit-card-sized device typically containing a customer's identification and authentication information, among other data.

Smart modem A modem that can accept dialing instructions from the user and dial the call, as well as perform the necessary modulation and demodulation.

Smart terminal A terminal that sends extra information to a host computer beyond what the user types, typically using a protocol containing error checking and addressing information.

SMDS *See* Switched Multimegabit Data Service.

SMTP *See* Simple Mail Transfer Protocol.

SNA *See* Systems Network Architecture.

Sniffer A type of protocol analyzer used to troubleshoot LANs.

SNMP *See* Simple Network Management Protocol.

SNMPv2 *See* Simple Network Management Protocol.

Soft clients Software that provides dialpad, phone book, and other functions to allow a PC to be used as a VOIP endpoint, along with the appropriate microphone, speakers, and headset or handset.

Software encryption A method of programming the encryption algorithm and keys into a host computer or intelligent terminal without the use of separate encryption devices.

SOH In BSC, the character indicating the start of the header.

SolarisNet Manager A Sun Microsystems network management product that supports a wide variety of protocols, it was formerly known as SunNet Manager.

SONET *See* Synchronous Optical Network.

Source Address (SA) Another name for the return address on a data communications network. In IP, it is the field indicating the originator of the IP datagram. In Ethernet, it is the 48-bit field indicating the originator of the Ethernet frame.

Source port In TCP, the port number of the transmitting endpoint.

Source routing One of several methods used by bridges to ensure that there is only one active path between two users.

Source routing transparent One of several methods used by bridges to ensure that there is only one active path between two users.

Space In RS-232-C, sending a zero using an electrical signal between +3 and +15 volts.

Space parity An error-detection method in which the parity bit is always a 0.

Spam Unsolicited commercial email.

Spam-blocking software *See* Antispam software.

Spam-filtering software *See* Antispam software.

Spanning tree protocol One of several methods used by bridges to ensure that there is only one active path between two users.

Spectrum A Cabletron network management product that supports a wide variety of protocols.

Splitter In a DSL system, a device that separates voice and data signals.

Spread spectrum A wireless transmission technology in which voice is broken into pieces and sent on several channels simultaneously.

SPRINT One of many common carriers offering a variety of services.

Spyware Software that tracks a user's actions and reports back to a central site, it is often used to tailor advertisements to a user's tastes.

Spyware detection software Software for identifying and removing spyware.

SQ *See* Signal Quality Detect.

Square wave A signal that alternates between two voltage levels almost instantaneously.

SRD *See* Secondary Received Data.

SRTS *See* Secondary Request to Send.

SS7 *See* Signaling System 7.

SSCP *See* System Services Control Point.

SSL *See* Secure Sockets Layer.

Stamped message A message whose receipt by the correct party is guaranteed.

Standards organization A group or committee that devises specifications or standards for a particular industry or country.

Standby monitor In a token ring network, a station that is ready to take over the monitoring function for the active monitor, if necessary.

Star network A network topology in which each user is connected to a center point and all data is routed through that point.

Starlan Network AT&T's star network for connecting personal computers in an office environment.

Start bit In asynchronous transmission, the bit sent before each character (always a 0).

Start-of-Frame Delimiter (SFD) The eighth byte of an Ethernet frame, it separates the Preamble from the beginning of the frame.

Start–stop transmission Another name for asynchronous transmission.

Star-wired bus network A logical bus network created using wiring in a physical star configuration in conjunction with a hub.

Star-wired ring network A logical ring network created using wiring in a physical star configuration in conjunction with a hub.

Stat mux A device that performs multiplexing using statistical methods like statistical time-division multiplexing.

Station Another name for a device on a LAN, or an end point on a link in the BSC and SDLC protocols.

Station feature A PBX function controlled by and performed for the individual user.

Station line The circuit between a PBX and individual user's phones.

Statistical frequency-division multiplexing (SFDM) A multiplexing method continually changing the allocation of channels to accommodate the demands and needs of the attached devices.

Statistical logging A security method providing a record of which users accessed particular ports and at what times.

Statistical time-division multiplexing (STDM) A multiplexing method continually changing the allocation of time slots to accommodate the demands and needs of the attached devices.

STD *See* Secondary Transmitted Data.

STDM *See* Statistical time-division multiplexing.

STM-1 An STM-N signal operating at 155.52 Mbps.

STM-*N* *See* Synchronous Transport Module-*N*.

Stop bit In asynchronous transmission, the bit or bits sent after each character (always a 1).

Stop-and-wait ARQ A type of automatic repeat request in which transmission halts after each block until an acknowledgment is received.

STP *See* Shielded twisted pair.

Stream A group of IP packets sent sequentially as part of a TCP connection.

STS-N *See* Synchronous Transport Signal-N.

STX In BSC, the character indicating the start of user data.

Subarea In SNA, a Subarea Node and the resources that the node controls.

Subarea Node In SNA, a Host Node or Communications Controller with its attached Workstations.

Submultiplexing A method of dividing an already multiplexed channel into smaller channels.

Subnetting The hierarchical assignment of IP addresses in ranges to simplify and speed the routing process.

Subscriber Identify Module (SIM) A device used by a customer to identify himself or herself to a GSM phone.

SunNet Manager *See* SolarisNet Manager.

Supercomputer An extremely fast host computer dedicated to extensive mathematical calculations.

Supervisory Format Frame (S-Frame) In SDLC, the type of frame used to transfer control information, including acknowledgment of the accurate receipt of data.

Switch A device that routes calls to different locations, such as a PBX or a central office.

Switched Multimegabit Data Service (SMDS) A connectionless service designed to internetwork LANs and offered by many carriers today in North America.

Switched service A type of service requiring a connection to be made to different locations each time, as in the public telephone network or a packet switching network.

Switching hub A device, known as a LAN switch, that creates a true star network for which data is delivered to the appropriate user based only on the destination address.

Switching node In a packet switching network, the device that routes communications.

Symmetric keys An encryption technique using the same key to encrypt and decrypt a message.

SYN In BSC, the sync characters transmitted before the start of actual data.

Sync character In synchronous transmission, the special character sent at the beginning of a block to allow the receiver to adjust to the speed of the transmitting device.

Synchronization In T-1 transmission, the timing function provided by the framing bit.

Synchronous Data Link Control (SDLC) IBM's bit-oriented, full duplex, go-back-N continuous ARQ protocol.

Synchronous Digital Hierarchy (SDH) A CCITT digital transmission standard similar to SONET, it operates at speeds of 155.52 Mbps and higher.

Synchronous Optical Network (SONET) A popular ANSI standard for digital transmission, it operates at speeds of 51.84 Mbps and higher.

Synchronous transmission A transmission method using special characters and clock signals for timing.

Synchronous Transport Module-N (STM-N) The SDH designation used to describe signals, it supports speeds of 155.52 Mbps and higher.

Synchronous Transport Signal-N (STS-N) The electrical equivalent of SONET's Optical Carrier-N signals.

System feature PBX functions performed and controlled for the entire system.

System Services Control Point (SSCP) In SNA, the Network Addressable Unit that monitors and controls a network's resources.

Systems Network Architecture (SNA) IBM's communications architecture that connects a wide variety of devices, it is highly flexible and versatile.

T reference point In ISDN, the point between the NT1 and NT2.

T-1 carrier AT&T's standard for 1.544-Mbps digital transmission over two twisted pairs.

T-1 multiplexer A device that divides the 1.544 Mbps of T-1 bandwidth into 24 separate channels of digitized voice or data.

T-1C A 3.152-Mbps digital transmission standard offering 48 channels.

T-3 A 44.736-Mbps digital transmission standard offering 672 channels.

TA *See* Terminal Adapter.

Tandem office A switch used by the local exchange carrier to route calls between central offices in the same LATA.

Tandem trunk A circuit connecting a central office to a tandem office.

Tap The point at which devices connect to a bus network.

Tariff A complete description of a common carrier's service, including the rate charged for that service.

TASI *See* Time assignment speech interpolation.

TC *See* Transmit Clock.

TCP *See* Transmission Control Protocol.

TCP/IP *See* TCP/IP Protocol Suite.

TCP/IP Protocol Suite A collection of protocols originally designed for use on a network connecting U.S. government agencies with universities performing research, it covers a wide variety of tasks likely to be performed on an open network.

TCT *See* Toll-connecting trunk.

TD *See* Transmitted Data.

TDM *See* Time-division multiplexing.

TDMA *See* Time-Division Multiple Access.

TE *See* Terminal Equipment.

TE1 *See* Terminal Equipment Type 1.

TE2 *See* Terminal Equipment Type 2.

Technical and Office Products (TOP) A user-defined local area network standard developed by Boeing Computer Services, it uses a CSMA/CD bus network.

Telecommunications The exchange of information, usually over a significant distance and using electronic equipment for transmission.

Telecommunications Act of 1996 Legislation designed to increase competition in the industry.

Telenet The original name of a public packet switching network now operated by SPRINT.

Telnet Part of the TCP/IP Protocol Suite, it is a protocol that provides a universal method for accessing a remote host computer through a TCP/IP network.

Temporal Key Interchange Protocol (TKIP) The encryption algorithm used in WPA, it is stronger than RC4 used in WEP.

10BASE-F An Ethernet standard for baseband transmission at 10 Mbps over fiber optic cable.

10BASE-T An Ethernet standard for baseband transmission at 10 Mbps over twisted pair wiring.

Ten-Gigabit Ethernet A version of Ethernet operating at 10 gigabits per second.

Terminal A device permitting users to communicate with a computer, it typically contains a screen and a keyboard. More generally, any device at the end of a communications circuit is sometimes considered a terminal, as in ISDN.

Terminal Adapter (TA) In ISDN, a device connected between the Terminal Equipment Type 2 and the Network Termination equipment.

Terminal Equipment (TE) In ISDN, customer-premises equipment attached to the ISDN network that transmits or receives voice, data, or other information. Examples are digital telephones, host computers, dumb terminals, and smart terminals.

Terminal Equipment Type 1 (TE1) In ISDN, Terminal Equipment that is compatible with the ISDN network.

Terminal Equipment Type 2 (TE2) In ISDN, Terminal Equipment that is not compatible with the ISDN network and that can be connected to the network only through a Terminal Adapter.

Terminal handler Another name for an external PAD.

Terrestrial microwave A medium for transmission of data that uses radio waves over relatively short distances, using dish antennas with a clear line of sight between them.

Thin client User software that is very simple, requiring little processing power.

Third generation (3G) The latest cellular standards, it includes WCDMA, UMTS, and CDMA 2000.

30 B + D The European version of the ISDN primary-rate interface.

3G *See* Third generation.

Throughput A measure of effective network transmission speed, it is the net bandwidth of a network.

Throughput class negotiation A packet switching network service allowing DTEs to negotiate for a certain bandwidth on a virtual circuit.

Tie trunk A telephone circuit connecting two PBXs.

Time assignment speech interpolation (TASI) A method of sharing an intertoll trunk, in which a communications path is allocated a few milliseconds after sound is detected. This method is suitable for voice communications, but it can damage data transmission.

Time division A local area network contention method based on the time-division multiplexing technique.

Time slot The time reserved for a particular channel's communications in time-division multiplexing.

Time to live field In IP, the eight-bit field indicating the number of hops over which the datagram may be routed before it is discarded. It is usually set initially and is decremented with each hop.

Time-Division Multiple Access (TDMA) A transmission technology used in digital cellular telephone systems in which users share time on a transmission channel.

Time-division multiplexing (TDM) A method of allowing lower speed channels to share time on a high-speed communications circuit by allocating separate time slots to each channel.

TKIP *See* Temporal Key Interchange Protocol.

Token A pattern of ones and zeroes with a special meaning in token-passing networks, typically used to control access to the networks.

Token bus A local area network using a bus topology and token passing, as in the IEEE 802.4 standard for Medium Access Control.

Token passing Using a token, typically either a free token or a busy token, to regulate access to a network.

Token ring network A local area network using a ring topology and token passing, as in the IEEE 802.5 standard for Medium Access Control or the IBM Token Ring Network.

Toll call Another name for a long-distance, or inter-LATA, call.

Toll office The switching office of a long-distance carrier.

Toll-connecting trunk (TCT) A telephone circuit between the toll office and the central office.

Toll-free number A service in which the called party agrees to pay the charges for all calls, also known as inward WATS.

TOP *See* Technical and Office Products.

Top-level domain The last part of a URL, for example ".com", it technically refers to a DNS server that contains IP addresses for all resources in the domain.

Topology The form, or physical shape, of a network.

Total length field In IP, the 16-bit field indicating the total length of the datagram in bytes. Its value cannot exceed 65,535 bytes.

Touch-tone dialing Another name for dual tone multifrequency dialing.

Traffic class In IPv6, the field identifying the type of information being carried.

Transfer rate of information bits (TRIB) The ANSI formula for calculating throughput, it is the average rate at which users can expect the network to transport actual information bits to their destination.

Transmission Control Protocol (TCP) Part of the TCP/IP protocol suite, it operates at Layer 4 of the OSI model, the Transport Layer, and it ensures reliable delivery of the user's message.

Transmission Group   In SNA, the communications Links between Subarea Nodes.

Transmission medium   The physical path for carrying information, such as twisted pair wires, coaxial cable, fiber optic cable, terrestrial microwave, and satellite transmission methods.

Transmit Clock (TC)   The RS-232-C timing signal generated by the DCE to time synchronous data transmission from the DTE to the DCE.

Transmitted Data (TD)   The RS-232-C data signal sent by the DTE to the DCE.

Transparent   A term often used to describe pure time-division multiplexing, because its functions are not visible to the user.

Transparent bridge   A type of bridge typically used to connect Ethernet networks.

Transparent data mode   In BSC, a method used to send control characters as data.

Transponder   The device on a satellite that receives signals from uplink stations and transmits them to downlink stations.

Transport Layer   Layer 4 of the OSI model, it is responsible for isolating the function of the lower layers from the higher layers.

Trap   An SNMP message sent by the agent to inform the manager of specific events being monitored at the remote device.

Tree network   A network topology similar to a bus network, but sometimes with many different branches off of the main bus.

Trellis coding   A technique used in conjunction with quadrature amplitude modulation in high-speed modems, usually 4800 bps and above, that relies on a special error-correction process.

TRIB   *See* Transfer rate of information bits.

Tributary station   In BSC, a device or station that communicates with the single Control station.

Triple DES   A form of the Data Encryption Standard used for high-security transactions, the algorithm is actually executed three times to complicate code-breaking efforts.

Trojan horse   Malicious software that hides itself inside another useful program.

True state   The state of an RS-232-C control signal when it is asserted, ON, or raised.

Trunk   A line or circuit connecting two switches.

Trunk port   The high-speed port of a multiplexer, usually attached to the communications circuit.

Tunnel   The encapsulation of data inside a protocol so that it can pass through a network, and the removal of that protocol at the far side of the network.

23 B + D   The North American and Japanese version of the ISDN primary-rate interface.

Twinax   *See* Twinaxial Cable.

Twinaxial cable   A cable similar to coaxial cable, but with two inner conducting wires.

Twisted pair   Typically used in a local loop, it consists of two wires continuously twisted throughout its entire length.

2 B + D The basic-rate interface.

2G *See* Second generation.

2.5G An intermediate generation. Between 2g and 3g cellular standards, it includes GPRS and CDMA 2000.1X.

Two-wire communications Communicating over a single pair of wires; this term is often incorrectly used as a synonym for half duplex transmission; however, both half duplex and full duplex transmission can now occur over two wires.

Tymnet The original name of a public packet-switching network now operated by MCI.

Type of service field In IP, the eight-bit field indicating the type of handling the source is requesting the network to provide for this datagram.

U reference point In ISDN, the point between the NT1 and the rest of the ISDN network.

UADSL *See* Universal Asymmetric Digital Subscriber Line.

UDP *See* Universal Datagram Protocol.

U-Frame *See* Unnumbered Format Frame.

Ultrawideband (UWB) A standard intended for digital audio/video transmission among components, it operates at speeds up to 500 Mbps and at distances up to 10 meters.

UMTS *See* Universal Mobile Telecommunications System.

Unbalanced transmission A method of sending data requiring one wire for data and a common return wire or reference that can be shared with other signals, as in RS-423-A.

UNI *See* User–Network Interface.

Unicast A message sent to one of the users on a network. Sometimes it is sent to everyone, but it is ignored by those it is not addressed to.

Uniform Resource Locator (URL) The names used to identify websites on the Internet, like www.prenticehall.com.

United States Digital Cellular (USDC) A digital cellular standard used throughout the United States, it shares channels with the analog AMPS system and uses TDMA technology.

Universal Asymmetric Digital Subscriber Line (UADSL) An attempt to standardize ADSL deployment across all carriers, it operates at 1.544 Mbps/384 kbps. It is also known as ASDL Lite, DSL Lite, and G.Lite.

Universal Datagram Protocol (UDP) A Layer 4 protocol used to send individual IP packets, or datagrams.

Universal Mobile Telecommunications System (UMTS) Also known as WCDMA, it provides data rates up to 2.4 Mbps.

Universal Serial Bus (USB) A data communications interface designed to connect peripherals to desktop computers, it commonly operates at 12 Mbps.

UNIX A computer operating system commonly used in open networks.

Unnumbered Format Frame (U-Frame) In SDLC, the type of frame used for special functions, including establishing connections and reporting procedural problems, as well as for special cases of data transfer.

Unreliable service As found in IP, packets can be lost, and the protocol does not re-transmit them.

Unshielded twisted pair (UTP) The least expensive type of wiring, it is typically used for voice and data applications in normal office environments.

Uplink The satellite dish transmitting data to the satellite.

Upper layers Another name for the higher layers of the OSI model.

Upper Case The portion of the Baudot character code used for the numbers and punctuation marks.

Uptime The time when a system or network is available.

Urgent pointer In TCP, a mechanism to allow a stream to be interrupted so urgent data can be transmitted.

URL *See* Uniform Resource Locator.

USB *See* Universal Serial Bus.

USB 1.0 The first version of the Universal Serial Bus standard, it operates at speeds up to 1.5 Mbps.

USB 1.1 A version of the Universal Serial Bus standard that operates at speeds up to 12 Mbps.

USB 2.0 A version of the Universal Serial Bus standard that operates at speeds up to 480 Mbps.

USB Hub A device that allows multiple devices to connect to a single USB port.

USB2 *See* USB 2.0.

USDC *See* United States Digital Cellular.

User–Network Interface (UNI) The ATM interface specification describing how to connect customer-premises equipment to a provider network.

UTP *See* Unshielded twisted pair.

UWB *See* Ultrawideband.

V.10 The ITU(CCITT) equivalent of the ANSI RS-423-A standard.

V.11 The ITU(CCITT) equivalent of the ANSI RS-422-A standard.

V.21 The ITU(CCITT) standard for 300-bps modulation, similar to the Bell 103/113 standard popular in the United States.

V.22 The ITU(CCITT) standard for 1200-bps modulation, similar to the Bell 212A standard popular in the United States.

V.22bis The ITU(CCITT) standard for 2400-bps modulation, it is widely used throughout the world.

V.24 The ITU(CCITT) equivalent of the signals in the ANSI RS-232-C standard.

V.28 The ITU(CCITT) equivalent of the voltage levels in the ANSI RS-232-C standard.

V.32 The ITU(CCITT) standard for 4800- and 9600-bps modulation, it is widely used throughout the world.

V.32bis The ITU(CCITT) standard for 14.4-kbps modulation, it is widely used throughout the world.

V.34 The ITU(CCITT) standard for 28.8- and 33.6-kbps modulation, it is widely used throughout the world.

V.35 An ITU standard that combines V.11 balanced transmission of the higher speed signals with unbalanced transmission of the control signals.

V.42 The ITU(CCITT) standard for modem error correction, also known as LAPM.

V.42bis The ITU(CCITT) standard for modem data compression.

V.44 An ITU data compression standard offering ratios of 6 to 1.

V.90 The ITU(CCITT) standard for 56-kbps modulation, it offers 56 kbps in one direction and 33.6 kbps in the other.

V.92 An ITU standard similar to V.90, except that speeds to the central office can reach 48 kbps under ideal conditions, when G.711 transmission is used in both directions.

Variable bit rate A source of data whose speed can change during transmission.

VCI *See* Virtual Channel Identifier.

VDSL *See* Very-high-bit-rate Digital Subscriber Line.

VDT *See* Video display terminal.

Version field In IP, the four-bit field used to indicate the version of IP being used.

Very-high-bit-rate Digital Subscriber Line (VDSL) A digital access technology that provides a link from the user to the central office over twisted pair wire that is higher speed in one direction than in the other. It provides very high speeds, but extremely short distances, so it is often used for a short connection to an existing fiber network.

Video display terminal (VDT) Another name for a terminal.

Video transmission The transmission of moving images, it can be performed using analog or digital techniques.

Virtual Channel Identifier (VCI) The part of the ATM header that designates a particular channel for a single connection.

Virtual circuit A circuit that appears to the user like a permanent connection, it simply ensures that data is appropriately routed, using the network's resources only when data is transmitted.

Virtual Path Identifier (VPI) The part of the ATM header that designates a grouping of channels.

Virtual Private Network (VPN) Creating a tunnel through a public network, typically with secure protocols, to create a safe path for corporate data to travel inside of the publicly shared network.

Virus Software that surreptitiously attaches itself to legitimate software.

Virus hoax False warnings about viruses that often contain damaging instructions or information.

Voice call multiplexing A method of sharing an intertoll trunk in which there is no additional risk of losing voice or data.

Voice grade circuit A standard telecommunications circuit.

Voice Over IP (VOIP) Any transmission of voice signals over an IP network.

VOIP *See* Voice Over IP.

VPI *See* Virtual Path Identifier.

VPN *See* Virtual Private Network.

WACK In BSC, the control character indicating that the device is temporarily busy, but will be ready soon.

WAN *See* Wide area network.

WATS *See* Wide area telecommunications services.

Wave division multiplexing A transmission technique used in fiber optic cables in which different colors of light are used to carry data on separate channels.

WCDMA *See* Wideband Code Division Multiple Access.

WDM *See* Wave division multiplexing.

WEP *See* Wired Equivalent Privacy.

Western Electric AT&T's equipment manufacturing organization.

Wide area network (WAN) A network covering a large geographical area, such as a packet switching network.

Wide area telecommunications services (WATS) A bulk-rate, long-distance service for business users with a high call volume.

Wideband Code Division Multiple Access (WCDMA) Also known as UMTS, it provides data rates up to 2.4 Mbps.

Wi-Fi *See* Wireless Fidelity.

Wi-Fi Protected Access (WPA) An enhancement to Wired Equivalent Privacy, it uses TKIP and EAP.

WiMax One of the available fixed wireless standards. Speeds of several hundred kbps can be achieved depending on distance and terrain.

Window In TCP, the size of the receive buffer of the sender.

Wired Equivalent Privacy (WEP) The first widely deployed security standard for IEEE 802.11 wireless LANs.

Wireless The use of communications equipment without cabling.

Wireless bridges Devices that interconnect standard LANs like a standard bridge, but that use a wireless method, like IEEE 802.11 a/b/g for the physical interconnection.

Wireless fidelity (Wi-Fi) Another name for IEEE 802.11 LAN standards.

Wireless LANs (WLANs) A LAN that does not require cabling.

WLANs *See* Wireless LANs.

Workstation The SNA term for a terminal.

World Wide Web The collection of publicly accessible information stored on servers connected to the Internet, it is usually in HTML format and read with browser software.

Worm Malicious software that reproduces itself repeatedly without human intervention, it can overwhelm a computer or network simply by causing excessive activity or traffic.

WPA *See* Wi-Fi Protected Access.

X.3 The ITU(CCITT) standard for the functions and parameters of an internal PAD.

X.25 The ITU(CCITT) standard for connecting a DTE to a packet switching network.

X.28 The ITU(CCITT) standard for connecting a DTE to an internal PAD in a packet switching network.

X.29 The ITU(CCITT) standard for communications between an internal PAD and the remote host computer.

xDSL A broad title covering the various types of digital access technologies, known as Digital Subscriber Line, that connect the central office with the user using twisted pair wire.

XON/XOFF ASCII control characters that can be used to start and stop a host computer transmission, respectively.

XTC *See* External Transmit Clock.

ZIP A popular file compression format.

Index